THE LAW OF EMPLOYMENT DISCRIMINATION

Sandra F. Sperino
Judge Joseph P. Kinneary Professor
University of Cincinnati College of Law

HORNBOOK SERIES®

WEST ACADEMIC PUBLISHING

444 Cedar Street, Suite 700
St. Paul, MN 55101
1-877-888-1330

Printed in the United States of America

ISBN: 978-1-62810-383-0

To
John and Joe—SFS

Preface

This book explores the four primary federal statutes that prohibit discrimination in employment: Title VII of the Civil Rights Act, the Age Discrimination in Employment Act (ADEA), the Americans with Disabilities Act (ADA), and 42 U.S.C. § 1981.

This is an increasingly complex area of law. Courts have created different ways of evaluating discrimination, depending on what kinds of facts a case presents. The courts have given different labels or names to certain factual scenarios. Judges have then created frameworks to analyze these cases.

Learning employment discrimination law requires learning a new field-specific vocabulary that judges and practitioners use to navigate the complex doctrine. At the outset it is worth noting that very little of this vocabulary is contained in the statutes themselves. Additionally, many of the frameworks do not derive directly from or derive only loosely from the statutory language. This is, in part, due to the fact that the Supreme Court's earliest attempts at interpreting these statutes pre-dated the rise of textualist statutory interpretation methods that happened in the late 1980s.

To break through some of the complexity, the book focuses on the core concepts that students or practitioners would need to understand. When a case is particularly important, the book covers the facts and reasoning of the case in-depth. While the field of discrimination law is complex, the field is endlessly fascinating. This book discusses how the courts have developed the doctrine over time and how the field is responding to new ways of thinking about discrimination.

Many states, cities, and counties also prohibit discrimination through separate statutes or ordinances. This state and local law is an important source of protection, particularly for employees of small employers who often are not covered by federal law. State law also may include different protected classes, may use different administrative procedures, and may provide better remedies. This area of law is beyond the reach of this work; however, many states and localities look to federal law when interpreting their statutes and ordinances.

To make the work more readable, footnotes are limited in number and in length. Often, I ignored the preferred short citation form and included a longer form of citation than required. This will assist readers who are reading only a section or a few sections of a chapter, rather than the entire chapter. Unfortunately, I am also not able to cite to all of the wonderful legal scholarship examining this field. However, I have tried to provide readers with citations to some of the professors working in this area and encourage readers to explore their work.

I am very lucky to work at the University of Cincinnati College of Law, which supported this work through summer research grants. This book benefitted from the contributions of librarian Ron Jones, program coordinator Jennie Edelstein, research assistant Francesca Boland, and the entire team at West Academic. I am especially thankful for the extensive research assistance provided by Alessandro Botta Blondet.

SANDRA F. SPERINO

Summary of Contents

Table of Contents

THE LAW OF EMPLOYMENT DISCRIMINATION

Chapter 1

SCOPE AND COVERAGE OF FEDERAL DISCRIMINATION STATUTES

Analysis

A. INTRODUCTION

§ 1.01 Overview of Title VII, the ADEA, the ADA, and Section 1981

There are four statutes that form the core of federal employment discrimination law: Title VII of the Civil Rights Act of 1964 ("Title VII"),[1] the Age Discrimination in Employment Act ("ADEA"),[2] the Americans with Disabilities Act ("ADA"),[3] and 42 U.S.C.A. § 1981 ("Section 1981").

Congress enacted Title VII in 1964. Title VII prohibits covered entities from discriminating on the basis of race, color, national origin, sex (including pregnancy and related conditions), and religion. Title VII requires employers to accommodate religious practices and beliefs in a limited set of circumstances. Although Title VII does not formally require employers to accommodate pregnancy, it may be intentional discrimination for an employer to refuse to accommodate pregnant women if it accommodates other individuals.[4]

Three years after Title VII, Congress enacted the ADEA. As its name suggests, the ADEA prohibits age discrimination in employment. The ADEA protects individuals aged 40 and older from such discrimination.

Title I of the ADA prohibits discrimination against a qualified individual with a disability. It also requires employers to provide reasonable accommodations to employees. The ADA specifically prohibits employers from discriminating against employees based on their association with an individual with a disability.[5] It also limits employers' ability to use medical examinations and inquiries.[6]

Section 1981 broadly prohibits race discrimination in the making of contracts. This provision applies in the employment context.

All of the statutes also prohibit covered entities from retaliating against individuals who engage in protected activity.[7]

Title VII, the ADEA, and Title I of the ADA deal with discrimination in the employment relationship. Thus, they only govern employment discrimination that happens in certain work relationships, such as between employers and their employees, former employees, and applicants, between unions and their members and potential members, and between employment agencies and their clients. Section 1981 applies to a

---

1 42 U.S.C.A. § 2000e *et seq.*

2 29 U.S.C.A. § 621 *et seq.*

3 42 U.S.C.A. § 12101 *et seq.*

4 Young v. United Parcel Serv., Inc., 135 S. Ct. 1338, 1340 (2015).

5 42 U.S.C.A. § 12112(b)(4).

6 42 U.S.C.A. § 12112(d).

7 42 U.S.C.A. § 2000e–3(a) (Title VII); 29 U.S.C.A. § 623(d) (ADEA); 42 U.S.C.A. § 12203 (ADA). Even though Section 1981 does not explicitly contain an anti-retaliation provision, the Supreme Court interpreted the statute to include one. CBOCS W., Inc. v. Humphries, 553 U.S. 442, 445 (2008).

broader set of relationships. While these statutes offer many protections, they do not prohibit all arbitrary or unfair treatment at the hands of employers, unions, and employment agencies.

§ 1.02 Background and History of Title VII

As its name suggests, Title VII is just one part of the 1964 Civil Rights Act, which covers in separate titles discrimination in voting, public accommodations, education and federally assisted programs. The legislative history of Title VII is complex. Federal civil rights legislation had been proposed in Congress since the 1940s with little success, including a 1963 bill proposed by President John F. Kennedy. The Equal Pay Act, which prohibits employers from paying men and women different wages for the same work, was enacted in 1963. Prior to Title VII, several states had state statutes prohibiting discrimination in employment based on certain protected classes.

Although a full history of the 1964 Act is beyond the purview of this book, an overview is necessary because the history reveals why gleaning helpful information from the legislative history of the original Act is problematic. The bill presented on the House floor was a combination of an administration bill and significant changes added in committee. The presented bill did not originally prohibit sex discrimination. However, with little debate, "sex" was added as a protected class through a floor amendment.

The House bill was read in the Senate, and after debating numerous procedural questions, the Senate voted to take up the bill without referring it to a committee. As Mack Player describes:

> During the next fifty-eight days of floor debate each section of the House-passed bill was explained by bipartisan floor leaders. Interpretative memoranda were prepared and inserted into the Congressional Record. So many floor amendments were offered and accepted that a Senate substitute bill which was offered simply reflected the original House Bill as repeatedly amended. Although considerable sentiment in the Senate favored a "strong" enforcement agency similar to the National Labor Relations Board, that proposal was abandoned. The compromises reflected by the many substantive and cautionary floor amendments, the acceptance of a "weak" enforcement agency, and the intensive behind-the-scenes maneuvering, ultimately resulted in a favorable vote of cloture that ended debate. Once debate closed, the Senate passed the House bill, as amended on the Senate floor.
>
> H.R. 7152, as amended by the Senate, returned directly to the floor of the House without following the usual practice of referring amended bills to a House-Senate Conference Committee. The House accepted the bill without further amendment, and it was signed by President Johnson on July 2, 1964, to be effective one year thereafter.
>
> Because of Title VII's unusual journey through Congress, interpretative guidance cannot be found in the usual sources. The tremendous number of amendments makes the President's message and supporting testimony in committees of limited value. The House reports are useful only where the Senate did not address the issue. Relevant committee reports from the Senate and Conference Committee do not exist. Therefore, the primary source for legislative interpretation of the original 1964 Act, and that source is rich

indeed, is the Senate debate including the detailed explanatory memoranda submitted by the Senate leadership.[8]

Congress amended Title VII in 1972. These amendments gave the EEOC enforcement authority and increased the time periods for filing charges with the EEOC and for filing private suits. Congress reduced the number of employees or union members necessary for private coverage of the Act. It also extended the reach of Title VII to cover public employers and parts of the federal government. Congress expanded the partial exemption for religious organizations and defined "religion" to include religious beliefs and practices.

Congress amended Title VII through the Pregnancy Discrimination Act of 1978. This amendment, among other things, defined "sex" to include pregnancy, childbirth, and related medical conditions.

Congress again amended Title VII in 1991. The 1991 amendments significantly altered the statute's remedies provisions, allowing plaintiffs to recover punitive damages and statutorily defined compensatory damages in certain cases subject to statutory caps. The amendments also allowed jury trials for certain cases. The 1991 amendments codified a disparate impact framework. They also added a definition section clarifying that a plaintiff needs to show a protected trait played a motivating factor in an outcome for disparate treatment claims, and they provided employers a limited affirmative defense to damages in some cases.

The Lilly Ledbetter Fair Pay Act of 2009 amended the period for filing claims for pay discrimination.

§ 1.03 Background and History of the ADEA

During the congressional debates on the Civil Rights Act of 1964, Congress considered adding age to Title VII. Congress decided not to add age as a protected class under Title VII; however, it directed the Secretary of Labor to study the problem of age discrimination in employment and to recommend legislation. That report, The Older American Worker—Age Discrimination in Employment (1965), documented the problem of discrimination against older workers and was used to propose legislation that ultimately became the ADEA. It is often cited by courts related to the purposes and coverage of the ADEA.

The ADEA draws its coverage and substantive provisions directly from Title VII's original language. For the most part, "age" is simply used in place of the Title VII language of "race, color, religion, sex, or national origin." However, since the Secretary of Labor administered the Fair Labor Standards Act, including its Equal Pay Act component, the remedial provisions of the ADEA drew from these sources. ADEA procedures, therefore, combine aspects of both Title VII and the Fair Labor Standards Act. The ADEA's remedies provisions are more similar to the FLSA, than they are to Title VII.

---

[8] Mack A. Player, Employment Discrimination Law, § 5.03 (1988).

When substantive provisions of the ADEA mirror language in Title VII the courts at times give Title VII and the ADEA similar interpretations.[9] However, in some cases, the Supreme Court does not interpret the ADEA and Title VII similarly.[10]

Congress has amended the ADEA several times. Major amendments include the following. In 1974, Congress amended the statute to expand coverage to state and local governments and some federal employees.

Congress extensively amended the ADEA in 1978. The original ADEA only protected workers 40 to 65 years old, thus it did not protect workers who were 66 years old or older. The 1978 Amendments extended that protection to age 70. With a few exceptions, the 1978 amendment also eliminated mandatory retirements. Finally, the 1978 Amendments made certain procedural modifications, including explicitly providing a right to jury trial.[11]

The Older Americans Act of 1984 extended the protections of the ADEA to American workers who work abroad for United States companies and their subsidiaries.[12]

In the fall of 1986 Congress enacted significant amendments to the ADEA. The amendments extended coverage to individuals over the age of 70. Now, the ADEA's general coverage provision apply to people age 40 and over. The amendment did not eliminate 29 U.S.C.A. § 631(c), which permits involuntary retirement of bona fide executives over the age of 65 who have vested retirement benefits over a given dollar amount.

The second major aspect of the amendment was the short-term exemption from the ADEA for certain firefighters and law enforcement officials. The amendments allowed states or political subdivisions to make *hiring* and discharge decisions based on age if such action is: (1) with respect to the employment of a firefighter or law enforcement officer, and the individual has attained the age of hiring or retirement in effect under applicable State or local law on March 3, 1983, and (2) the decision is made pursuant to a bona fide hiring or retirement plan that is not a subterfuge to evade the purposes of the Act. Between 1986 and 1990, Congress amended the ADEA several times.

The Older Worker Benefit Protection Act amendments in 1990 included provisions for calculating fringe benefit reductions for workers and the waiver of rights under the ADEA.

The Civil Rights Act of 1991 attempted to bring ADEA procedures more into conformity with Title VII procedures, although the two are not completely identical. The original Act assigned enforcement to the Secretary of Labor. A 1978 reorganization of the executive department by President Carter transferred enforcement responsibilities to the EEOC.

The 1991 amendments play a major role in how the Supreme Court interprets the ADEA in relationship to Title VII. In 1991, Congress amended both Title VII and the ADEA. The Title VII amendments made it clear that a plaintiff can prevail by showing a protected trait played a motivating factor in a negative action. In 1991, Congress also

---

9 Smith v. City of Jackson, 544 U.S. 228 (2005).

10 *See, e.g.*, Gross v. FBL Fin. Servs., 557 U.S. 167 (2009).

11 *See also* Tax Equity and Fiscal Responsibility Act, 97 Pub. L. 248, § 116, 96 Stat. 324, 353 (1982) and Spending Reduction Act of 1984, Pub. L. No. 98–369, § 2001, 98 Stat. 1036.

12 98 Pub. L. 459, 98 Stat. 1792.

clarified the disparate impact analysis for Title VII claims. When Congress amended the ADEA in 1991, it did not make these same changes to the ADEA. Even though it is unclear why Congress did not amend the ADEA in similar ways, the Supreme Court has held that the non-amendment reflected Congress' desire that the two statutes be read differently.[13]

In 1996, Congress reinstated a provision in the ADEA that allows state and local governments to set mandatory retirement ages for certain public safety officers.

§ 1.04 Background and History of the ADA

The Rehabilitation Act of 1973 is a precursor to the ADA. The Rehabilitation Act prohibits disability discrimination in federal agency programs, in programs that receive federal financial assistance, in federal employment, and in the employment practices of certain federal contractors. Although the Rehabilitation Act still applies to those entities, Congress enacted the ADA in 1990 to expand disability discrimination protections into additional areas, including employment discrimination by private employers.

The courts often look to Title VII cases and sometimes Rehabilitation Act cases to interpret the ADA. It should be noted that the substantive language of the ADA does not exactly mirror the language of Title VII. The ADA prohibits discrimination on the basis of disability and then provides numerous provisions further describing what discrimination entails. This is a distinct contrast to the less-defined language of Title VII as enacted in 1964. Further, the ADA's accommodation obligation is much more robust than the religious accommodation obligation found in Title VII. The ADA incorporates by reference coverage, enforcement procedures, and remedies of Title VII.

In 2008, the Americans with Disabilities Act Amendments Act (ADAAA) extensively amended the ADA. The ADAAA overruled several Supreme Court decisions that narrowly construed the definition of disability under the statute.

§ 1.05 Relationship to State Law

Outside of the federal employer context, the federal discrimination statutes do not preempt state or local laws that provide employees with more protection than federal law. Title VII specifically provides:

> Nothing in this subchapter shall be deemed to exempt or relieve any person from any liability, duty, penalty, or punishment provided by any present or future law of any State or political subdivision of a State, other than any such law which purports to require or permit the doing of any act which would be an unlawful employment practice under this subchapter.[14]

Unless a state law conflicts with Title VII, Title VII does not preempt the state law. Thus, states are free to offer protection against employment discrimination that exceeds what Title VII provides. Courts have held that the ADEA and the ADA do not preempt state law as long as the state law does not conflict with their requirements.[15]

---

[13] Gross v. FBL Fin. Servs., 557 U.S. 167 (2009).

[14] 42 U.S.C.A. § 2000e–7.

[15] 42 U.S.C.A. § 12201(b); Kroske v. U.S. Bank Corp., 432 F.3d 976, 988 (9th Cir. 2005) (citing 29 U.S.C.A. § 633(a)); Danfelt v. Bd. of Cty. Comm'rs, Md., 998 F. Supp. 606, 611 (D. Md. 1998); *see also* Thomas v. Ariel W., No. 14 CV 4459-LTS, 2017 WL 1031277, at *9 (S.D.N.Y. Mar. 15, 2017) (noting that even though

In *California Fed. S. & L. Ass'n v. Guerra*,[16] the Court addressed a state statute that required employers to grant pregnant employees up to four months of unpaid pregnancy leave and reinstatement upon their return. The employer argued that the statute conflicted with Title VII because it required the employer to treat men and women differently. The Court disagreed and held that Title VII did not preempt the statute. The Court noted that the state law provided leave and reinstatement related to the period when a woman faced physical limits due to pregnancy. Thus, the state law was not making a distinction between men and woman, but only giving additional benefits based on pregnancy. The Court noted that this did not conflict with Title VII and that an employer could comply with both the state law and Title VII. If the employer was concerned about differences in disability benefits, it could offer the disability leave and reinstatement to all employees. The Supreme Court noted that Title VII provides a floor, but not a ceiling, on employment discrimination protections. States are allowed to require more protections for employees than that offered by federal law.

§ 1.06 Constitutionality of Title VII, the ADEA, the ADA, and Section 1981

Congress used its powers under Art. I, § 8 ("commerce clause") when it enacted Title VII The statute requires private employers to be engaged in interstate commerce before the Act applies to them. Given Congress' broad power under the commerce clause, Title VII was clearly constitutional.[17]

In *Fitzpatrick v. Bitzer*[18] the Supreme Court held that Congress had the power under § 5 of the Fourteenth Amendment to extend Title VII coverage to state governments. The Court held that the state could not claim immunity under the Eleventh Amendment. The Court noted:

> [W]e think that the Eleventh Amendment, and the principle of state sovereignty which it embodies . . . are necessarily limited by the enforcement provisions of § 5 of the Fourteenth Amendment. In that section Congress is expressly granted authority to enforce "by appropriate legislation" the substantive provisions of the Fourteenth Amendment, which themselves embody significant limitations on state authority. When Congress acts pursuant to § 5, not only is it exercising legislative authority that is plenary within the terms of the constitutional grant, it is exercising that authority under one section of a constitutional amendment whose other sections by their own terms embody limitations on state authority. We think that Congress may, in determining what is "appropriate legislation" for the purpose of enforcing the provisions of the Fourteenth Amendment, provide for private suits against States or state officials which are constitutionally impermissible in other contexts.[19]

ADA does not preempt state law negligence claim, a negligence claim is not presented when the essential claim is that the defendant failed to accommodate a disability).

[16] 479 U.S. 272 (1987).

[17] Heart of Atlanta Motel v. United States, 379 U.S. 241 (1964); Katzenbach v. McClung, 379 U.S. 294 (1964).

[18] 427 U.S. 445 (1976).

[19] 427 U.S. at 456.

Congress also possessed power under the commerce clause to enact the ADEA and ADA, as applied to private employers.[20] While Congress also had the power to regulate the actions of state governments, immunity issues arise under the ADEA and ADA.[21] In *Kimel v. Florida Bd. of Regents*, the Supreme Court held that the ADEA does not abrogate a state government's Eleventh Amendment immunity.[22] The Court reasoned that Congress' power to enact the ADEA arose under the commerce clause and not the Fourteenth Amendment. Thus, the Eleventh Amendment restricts private monetary actions against state government unless the state waives immunity or consents to be sued. The Eleventh Amendment does not prevent the awarding of prospective injunctive relief against state officials sued in their official capacity[23] or recovery of money damages by the federal government.[24] The Eleventh Amendment does not bar private recovery of monetary relief against entities that are not an arm of the state, meaning that suits against local entities can often proceed.[25]

A similar analysis applies to claims brought under Title I of the ADA. In *Board of Trustees of Univ. of Ala. v. Garrett*,[26] the Supreme Court held that ADA Title I claims against states are subject to the restrictions of the Eleventh Amendment. After Congress amended the ADA in 2008, litigants tried to argue that the amendments abrogated states' Eleventh Amendment immunity. As of the writing of this text, those arguments have been unsuccessful.

Eleventh Amendment immunity also applies in the section 1981 context.[27]

B. PEOPLE AND ENTITIES BOUND BY FEDERAL DISCRIMINATION LAW

§ 1.07 General Principles of Coverage

Title VII, the ADEA, and the ADA do not universally protect against all discrimination that happens in the workplace. Instead, the statutes define the kinds of people and entities who are bound by the statutes and thus face consequences for failure to abide by the statutes. A threshold question in an employment discrimination case is whether the defendant is a person or entity that falls within the ambit of federal discrimination law.

As Title VII is the cornerstone federal anti-discrimination statute, each section will first discuss coverage issues under Title VII and will then discuss any major differences that exist under the ADA or the ADEA. For most coverage-related questions, the courts have interpreted Title VII, the ADEA, and the ADA in similar ways. Section 1981 offers much broader protections and coverage for that statute is discussed in a separate section below.

---

20 NLRB v. Jones & Laughlin Steel Corp., 301 U.S. 1 (1937).

21 *See* Edelman v. Jordan, 415 U.S. 651 (1974).

22 528 U.S. 62, 82–83 (2000).

23 Ex parte Young, 209 U.S. 123 (1908).

24 Alden v. Maine, 527 U.S. 706, 757 (1999); *see also* E.E.O.C. v. Commonwealth of Puerto Rico, 451 F. Supp. 2d 296, 302–3 (D.P.R. 2006) (applying *Alden* in discrimination context in case brought by EEOC).

25 Mt. Healthy City School Dist. Bd. of Educ. v. Doyle, 429 U.S. 274 (1977).

26 531 U.S. 356 (2001).

27 *See, e.g.*, Henry v. Fla. Bar, 701 F. App'x 878, 881 (11th Cir. 2017).

Title VII regulates the personnel practices of "employers," "labor organizations," "employment agencies," joint employer-union apprenticeship programs, and certain federal employers.[28] Title VII only governs these statutorily defined entities and does not provide coverage for all people who work.

The ADEA also regulates the actions of "employers," "labor organizations," "employment agencies," and certain federal employers.[29]

The ADA prohibits covered entities from taking certain actions. The ADA defines a covered entity to be an "employer," "labor organization," "employment agency," or a "joint-labor management committee."[30] Most federal employees are not covered by the ADA, but are instead covered by the Rehabilitation Act. However, the ADA does apply to certain employees of the federal legislative branch under the Congressional Accountability Act of 1995.[31]

The federal statutes discussed in this book do not provide the only protection against employment discrimination. State and local laws may also prohibit discrimination.

§ 1.08 Overview of "Employer"

Most Title VII, ADEA, or ADA cases are filed against defendants that fall within the definition of "employer." Title VII and the ADA define an employer as a "person engaged in an industry affecting commerce who has fifteen or more employees for each working day in each of twenty or more calendar weeks in the current or preceding calendar year, and any agent of such person."[32] The ADEA contains a similar definition, but requires the employer to employ at least 20 individuals.[33]

Each statute also specifically excludes certain entities from the definition of employer. Title VII excludes Indian tribes and bona fide membership clubs.[34] Although the ADEA does not expressly exclude Indian tribes, courts have held federally recognized Indian tribes are not employers.[35] The ADEA does not specifically exclude private membership clubs from coverage. The ADA also expressly excludes Indian tribes and bona fide private membership clubs from coverage.[36]

Determining coverage for federal employees is a little trickier. Title VII specifically excludes the United States and its wholly owned corporations from the definition of "employer," as well as departments of the District of Columbia subject to competitive service. Although these entities are not defined as "employers," personnel actions by certain federal employers are regulated by Title VII. Title VII applies to employees or applicants for employment in the following instances:

> (except with regard to aliens employed outside the limits of the United States) in military departments as defined in section 102 of Title 5, in executive

[28] 42 U.S.C. § 2000e(a)–(e), (n).

[29] 29 U.S.C. §§ 630(a)–(e), 633(a).

[30] 42 U.S.C.A. § 12111(2).

[31] 2 U.S.C.A. § 1301.

[32] 42 U.S.C.A. § 2000e(b); 42 U.S.C.A. § 12111(5)(A).

[33] 29 U.S.C.A. § 630(b).

[34] 42 U.S.C.A. § 2000e(b).

[35] Williams v. Poarch Band of Creek Indians, 839 F.3d 1312, 1324 (11th Cir. 2016).

[36] 42 U.S.C.A. § 12111(5)(B).

agencies as defined in section 105 of Title 5 (including employees and applicants for employment who are paid from nonappropriated funds), in the United States Postal Service and the Postal Regulatory Commission, in those units of the Government of the District of Columbia having positions in the competitive service, and in those units of the judicial branch of the Federal Government having positions in the competitive service, in the Smithsonian Institution, and in the Government Publishing Office, the Government Accountability Office, and the Library of Congress[.][37]

The ADEA also excludes the United States or a corporation wholly owned by it.[38] However, the ADEA contains a later provision prohibiting discrimination against applicants and employees of the federal government.[39]

The ADA also excludes the United States or a corporation wholly owned by it from the definition of "employer."[40] Unlike Title VII and the ADEA, the ADA does not later add back in coverage for federal employees and applicants for employment. Instead, the Rehabilitation Act is typically the statute that protects those individuals from disability discrimination.

The Congressional Accountability Act of 1995 extends the protections of Title VII, the ADEA, and the ADA to employees of the federal legislative branch and to an enumerated list of other federal employees.[41]

§ 1.09 Persons Affecting Interstate Commerce

Title VII, the ADEA, and the ADA each defines the term employer by reference to two concepts: (1) whether the employer is a "person engaged in an industry affecting commerce," and (2) whether the entity has the requisite number of employees to fall within coverage.[42]

For non-federal employers, the first step in determining coverage is to determine whether the employer is a person engaged in interstate commerce. Title VII and the ADA define "person" in an odd way to include a vast array of entities. "Person" is defined to include individuals, corporations, partnerships, and other legal entities, such as unincorporated organizations, trusts, bankruptcy trustees, labor unions and state and local governmental agencies.[43] The ADEA has a similarly expansive definition.[44]

The "person" must be in an "industry affecting commerce." As Congress has extensive commerce power,[45] the requirement that an employer be in an industry affecting commerce does not typically meaningfully limit the reach of the federal discrimination statutes.

---

[37] 42 U.S.C.A. § 2000e–16.

[38] 29 U.S.C.A. § 630(b).

[39] 29 U.S.C.A. § 631(b).

[40] 42 U.S.C.A. § 12111(5)(B).

[41] 2 U.S.C.A. § 1301.

[42] 42 U.S.C.A. § 2000e(b); 42 U.S.C. § 12111(5)(A). 29 U.S.C. § 630(b).

[43] 42 U.S.C.A. §§ 2000e(a), 12111(7).

[44] 29 U.S.C. § 630(a).

[45] *E.g.*, Wickard v. Filburn, 317 U.S. 111 (1942) (small farmer selling all products locally is affecting commerce and can be regulated by Congress).

§ 1.10 Numerosity Requirements

Title VII and the ADA each exempt small, non-federal employers from liability. Title VII and the ADA apply to non-federal employers that employ 15 or more employees. Generally, the ADEA applies when an employer has 20 or more employees; however, this limit does not apply to states and their subdivisions.[46] The purpose of the numerosity requirements is to protect smaller employers from the burdens of complying with federal law and to protect them from the costs of lawsuits.

Although these smaller employers are not covered by Title VII, the ADEA, or the ADA, state law may prohibit them from discriminating. Additionally, 42 U.S.C. § 1981 does not base its coverage on meeting a certain threshold number of employees.

The statutes require for coverage the threshold number of employees for "*each working day*" for twenty calendar weeks in the current or proceeding calendar year. Who counts as an employee is discussed extensively in § 1.24.

Courts use the payroll method to determine whether a person is an employee. If the person is on the payroll, even if the individual is not being compensated on a particular day, that person is an employee.[47]

Coverage is measured by a calendar year running from January to December. Coverage exists if the employer has the required number of employees for twenty of the fifty-two weeks of the calendar year in which the alleged act of discrimination took place. These twenty weeks may precede the act of discrimination, such that the employer may be liable, even if it did not possess the required number of employees in the time period in which the discrimination occurred.

The employer who does not meet the numerosity requirement in the year in which the discrimination occurred still will be covered if the employer had the requisite number of employees for twenty of the calendar weeks in the calendar year *preceding* the year in which the discrimination occurred.

The statutes do not require that the necessary twenty weeks be maintained for twenty consecutive weeks. It is the *total* number of weeks in the year during which the required number of employees are employed that controls.

§ 1.11 Aggregating Employers

Usually, the employees are counted within the entire legal entity even though they may work in different "establishments" of the entity. Occasionally, the employees of two separate legal entities may be counted for the purpose of determining both coverage and the joint liability of two ostensibly separate entities, even when one of the two entities is not technically the employer. This idea is expressed under two concepts: joint employer and integrated enterprise (also called single enterprise).

An entity that is not the formal employer may be liable if the actual employer and the second entity are so interrelated that they can be considered to be a single employer. Under this single enterprise or integrated enterprise theory "in appropriate circumstances, an employee, who is technically employed on the books of one entity, which is deemed to be part of a larger 'single-employer' entity, may impose liability for

---

46 Mount Lemmon Fire Dist. v. Guido, 139 S. Ct. 22 (2018).

47 Walters v. Metro. Educ. Enters., Inc., 519 U.S. 202, 206 (1997).

certain violations of employment law not only on the nominal employer but also on another entity comprising part of the single integrated employer."[48]

The idea of a single, integrated employer applies to issues of liability and also coverage. For example, if two entities are deemed to be a single, integrated employer, employees from both entities may be counted toward reaching the minimum employee thresholds under the federal discrimination statutes. This integrated employer idea is sometimes used in cases involving parent corporations and their subsidiaries or in frachisee/franchisor contexts, although courts will not always ignore the technical legal divisions inherent in these relationships.

For integrated enterprise liability, many circuits often use a test borrowed from the National Labor Relations Act context and espoused in EEOC Compliance Manual Section 2. This test requires the court to consider "(1) common management; (2) interrelation between operations; (3) centralized control of labor relations; and (4) degree of common ownership/financial control.[49] As the EEOC notes in its Compliance Manual, "All of the factors should be considered in assessing whether separate entities constitute an integrated enterprise, but it is not necessary that all factors be present, nor is the presence of any single factor dispositive. The primary focus should be on centralized control of labor relations."

Entities that are not formally an employer may also be held liable under the joint employer concept. This idea applies when the formal employer and the second entity are not intertwined enough to be considered an integrated enterprise, but where the second entity exercises sufficient control over an individual to be considered her employer. As one court explained, "When a worker is formally employed by one organization, but important aspects of his work are subject to control by another organization, both organizations are employers of the worker. An independent entity with sufficient control over the terms and conditions of the employment of a worker formally employed by another is a joint employer within the scope of [the statutes.]"[50]

When a second entity jointly controls employees of the formal employer, both sets of employees can be counted for statutory coverage purposes. For example, assume that Jones Corporation employs 12 employees and another 5 employees work for Jones Corporation through a temporary agency. If Jones Corporation and the temporary agency are joint employers of the 5 employees, then Jones Corporation has the requisite number of employees to fall within coverage for both Title VII and the ADA.

Circuits differ on the test to use when determining whether two employers are joint employers. Many courts appear to conflate the integrated enterprise concept with the joint employer concept or to speak inartfully by using the term "joint employer" as an umbrella term to refer to all circumstances where two entities might both be liable for discrimination claims. Therefore, it is sometimes difficult to separate the two concepts.

"[T]wo parties can be considered joint employers and therefore both be liable under Title VII if they 'share or co-determine those matters governing the essential terms and

---

[48] Wright v. Mountain View Lawn Care, LLC, No. 7:15-CV-00224, 2016 WL 1060341, at *7 (W.D. Va. Mar. 11, 2016).

[49] Wright v. Mountain View Lawn Care, LLC, No. 7:15-CV-00224, 2016 WL 1060341, at *7 (W.D. Va. Mar. 11, 2016); *but see* Nesbit v. Gears Unlimited, Inc., 347 F.3d 72, 84 (3d Cir. 2003) (rejecting NLRB test in Title VII context).

[50] Dunn v. Pratt Indus. (U.S.A.), Inc., No. 2:12-CV-269-TLS, 2017 WL 1405356, at *2 (N.D. Ind. Apr. 20, 2017).

conditions of [plaintiff's] employment."[51] An extensive review of all different varieties of the joint employer test is not appropriate here; however, the following sentences provide an overview of some of the tests used. Some courts consider "(1) the extent of the [entity's] control and supervision over the employee; (2) the kind of occupation and nature of skill required, including whether skills were acquired on the job; (3) the [entity's] responsibility for the costs of operation; (4) the method and form of payment and benefits; and (5) the length of the job commitment."[52] Other courts have looked at factors, such as "(1) authority to hire and fire employees, promulgate work rules and assignments, and set conditions of employment, including compensation, benefits, and hours; (2) day-to-day supervision of employees, including employee discipline; and (3) control of employee records, including payroll, insurance, taxes, and the like."[53]

Some courts have described other circumstances in which liability may be appropriate. The Seventh Circuit has recognized that aggregate liability may be appropriate "(1) where the traditional conditions exist to 'pierce the corporate veil;' (2) where the enterprise has split itself into separate companies with the express purpose of avoiding liability under Title VII; and (3) where the parent corporation may have directed the discriminatory act."[54]

§ 1.12 Federal Employers

Title VII specifically excludes the United States and its wholly owned corporations from the definition of "employer," as well as departments of the District of Columbia subject to competitive service. Although these entities are not defined as "employers," personnel actions by certain federal employers are regulated by Title VII. Title VII applies to employees or applicants for employment in the following instances:

> (except with regard to aliens employed outside the limits of the United States) in military departments as defined in section 102 of Title 5, in executive agencies as defined in section 105 of Title 5 (including employees and applicants for employment who are paid from nonappropriated funds), in the United States Postal Service and the Postal Regulatory Commission, in those units of the Government of the District of Columbia having positions in the competitive service, and in those units of the judicial branch of the Federal Government having positions in the competitive service, in the Smithsonian Institution, and in the Government Publishing Office, the Government Accountability Office, and the Library of Congress[.][55]

The ADEA also excludes the United States or a corporation wholly owned by it.[56] However, the ADEA contains a later provision prohibiting discrimination against applicants and employees of the federal government.[57]

---

[51] Butler v. Drive Auto. Indus., 793 F.3d 404, 408 (4th Cir. 2015).

[52] Thomas v. Coach Outlet Store, No. 16 C 3950, 2017 WL 386656, at *3 (N.D. Ill. Jan. 27, 2017) (citing Love v. JP Cullen & Sons, Inc., 779 F.3d 697, 702 (7th Cir. 2015)).

[53] Anderson v. Finley Catering Co., 218 F. Supp. 3d 417, 421 (E.D. Pa. Oct. 28, 2016).

[54] Papa v. Katy Industries, Inc., 166 F.3d 937, 940–41 (7th Cir. 1999).

[55] 42 U.S.C.A. § 2000e–16.

[56] 29 U.S.C.A. § 630(b).

[57] 29 U.S.C.A. § 631(b).

The ADA also excludes the United States or a corporation wholly owned by it from the definition of "employer."[58] Unlike Title VII and the ADEA, the ADA does not later add back in coverage for federal employees and applicants for employment. Instead, the Rehabilitation Act is typically the statute that protects those individuals from disability discrimination.

The Congressional Accountability Act of 1995 extends the protections of Title VII, the ADEA, and the ADA to employees of the federal legislative branch and to an enumerated list of other federal employees.[59]

§ 1.13 State and Local Governments

Title VII originally excluded state and local governments from liability; however, this changed with the 1972 amendments. Those amendments specifically defined state and local governments and their agencies as "persons" under the statutes, and these entities were characterized as "industries affecting commerce." Thus, if the state and local governmental unit has fifteen or more employees, it will be an "employer" subject to the same general proscriptions as a private employer. The ADA adopts Title VII's definition of person.[60]

Like Title VII, the ADEA at first covered private employers; however, Congress amended the ADEA in 1974 adding state and local governments. The ADEA specifically defines the term "employer" to include "a State or political subdivision of a State and any agency or instrumentality of a State or a political subdivision of a State, and any interstate agency."[61] States and their political subdivisions may be sued under the ADEA even if they do not have 20 employees.[62]

Constitutional immunity issues are discussed in § 1.06.

§ 1.14 Foreign Employers

Foreign employers doing business in the United States are bound by the federal discrimination statutes regarding employees who work in the United States. Foreign governments acting in their governmental capacity within the United States, such as embassies and consulates, are not governed by the federal discrimination statutes.[63]

Treaties may allow foreign employers to lawfully discriminate, even if the employer would otherwise fall within the coverage of the federal discrimination statutes. Such treaties will have legal priority over domestic statutes.

However, the terms of the treaty must be met for a foreign employer to be exempt. In *Sumitomo Shoji America, Inc. v. Avagliano,*[64] a company incorporated and operating in the United States was a wholly owned subsidiary of a Japanese corporation. The company claimed that it was not bound by Title VII because a treaty allowed "companies of either party . . . to engage within the territories of the other party, accountants, and other technical experts, executive personnel, attorneys, agents and other specialists of

---

58 42 U.S.C.A. § 12111(5)(B).

59 2 U.S.C.A. § 1301.

60 42 U.S.C.A. § 12111(7).

61 29 U.S.C.A. § 630(b).

62 Mount Lemmon Fire Dist. v. Guido, 139 S. Ct. 22 (2018).

63 *See* McCulloch v. Sociedad Nacional de Marineros de Honduras, 372 U.S. 10 (1963).

64 457 U.S. 176 (1982).

their choice." The Supreme Court held that the treaty was inapplicable to the defendant company because the defendant was not a "company of Japan." As the company was incorporated in the United States, it was a "company of the United States," and the treaty did not sanction the alleged preference.[65]

§ 1.15 Bona Fide Membership Clubs

Title VII and the ADA specifically exclude bona fide private membership clubs from coverage. The acts do not define "bona fide membership club," but indicate that the club must be exempt from taxation under the charitable exemption provision of § 501(c) of the Internal Revenue Code. The courts have defined bona fide membership clubs as organizations designed for social or recreational purposes or for the promotion of a common literary, scientific, or political objective. To be a private membership club, the club must have some meaningful conditions of limited membership, and not be simply open to the public. The club must be "bona fide," meaning that it cannot be formed for the purpose of avoiding the requirements of Title VII or the ADA or for some other anti-social reason. Applying this definition, an employer credit union, although "bona fide" and of limited membership, is not a "club,"[66] nor are hospitals or retirement homes.[67] However, a limited membership country club has been held to meet the definition.[68]

§ 1.16 Indian Tribes

Title VII and the ADA specifically exclude Indian tribes from the definition of "employer."[69] Although an Indian tribe is not defined, presumably the exclusion applies to the semi-sovereign entities of indigenous Americans recognized by federal law. The exemption for the tribe is not limited to its treatment of tribe members, but applies to all employment actions, even those involving non-members of the tribe.[70]

The ADEA does not specifically exclude Indian tribes from coverage. Nonetheless, courts have held that Indian tribes may not be sued under the ADEA if the activity in question otherwise falls within the tribe's sovereign immunity protections.[71]

Title VII explicitly allows discrimination in favor of Indians in specific instances. Under 42 U.S.C. § 2000e–2(i), "any business or enterprise on or near an Indian reservation" may have a "publicly announced employment practice . . . under which a preferential treatment is given to any individual because he is an Indian living on or near a reservation."

§ 1.17 Religious Organizations

Under Title VII, certain religious organizations may discriminate based on religion. Title VII provides: "This title shall not apply . . . to a religious corporation, association, educational institution, or society with respect to the employment of individuals of a

---

65 *See also* Wickes v. Olympic Airways, 745 F.2d 363 (6th Cir. 1984).

66 Quijano v. Univ. Fed. Credit Union, 617 F.2d 129 (5th Cir. 1980).

67 Fesel v. Masonic Home of Delaware, 428 F. Supp. 573 (D. Del. 1977).

68 Hudson v. Charlotte Country Club, Inc., 535 F. Supp. 313 (W.D.N.C. 1982); *see also* Bommarito v. Grosse Pointe Yacht Club, No. 05-CV-73359, 2007 WL 925791, at *5 (E.D. Mich. Mar. 26, 2007).

69 42 U.S.C. §§ 2000e(b), 12111(5)(B)(i).

70 Wardle v. Ute Indian Tribe, 623 F.2d 670 (10th Cir. 1980).

71 Williams v. Poarch Band of Creek Indians, 839 F.3d 1312 (11th Cir. 2016).

particular religion to perform work connected with the carrying on by such corporation, association, educational institution, or society of its activity."[72]

Religious organizations with the requisite fifteen employees are defined "employers." The provision allowing them to discriminate because of religion does not permit the covered religious organization to discriminate based on other protected classes.

Under the original 1964 Act religious associations could discriminate on the basis of religion in employing persons of the religion to carry on the *religious activities* of the association. The 1972 amendments omitted the qualifying term "religious." A religious organizations may discriminate on the basis of religion for work connected with carrying on *any* of its activities, even secular activities.[73]

However, Title VII, the ADEA, and the ADA have not been applied to all of a religious organization's employment practices, because in some cases it would be impossible to regulate those practices without infringing either the First Amendment's Free Exercise Clause or its Establishment Clause. The Supreme Court addressed the ministerial exception in *Hosanna-Tabor Evangelical Lutheran Church & Sch. v. E.E.O.C.*[74] In that case, a teacher alleged that a church school discriminated against her and retaliated against her in violation of the ADA. The church school recognized two categories of teacher, lay teachers and called teachers. The Supreme Court ruled that under the specific circumstances of the case, a called teacher was a minister and the religion clauses of the First Amendment exempted the church from liability under the ADA. As the Court noted:

> Requiring a church to accept or retain an unwanted minister, or punishing a church for failing to do so, intrudes upon more than a mere employment decision. Such action interferes with the internal governance of the church, depriving the church of control over the selection of those who will personify its beliefs. By imposing an unwanted minister, the state infringes the Free Exercise Clause, which protects a religious group's right to shape its own faith and mission through its appointments. According the state the power to determine which individuals will minister to the faithful also violates the Establishment Clause, which prohibits government involvement in such ecclesiastical decisions.[75]

In determining whether an individual is a "minister" the *Hosanna-Tabor* Court relied heavily on the facts of the particular case. The Court declined to adopt a "rigid formula" to determine when an employee could be considered to be a minister. Factors that weighed in favor of recognizing a called teacher as a minister included the following: (1) the church held her out as a minister with duties separate from other church members; (2) the church issued her a diploma of vocation; (3) her job title was "Minister of Religion;" (4) the congregation prayed for her ministry; (5) the school evaluated her

[72] 42 U.S.C. § 2000e–1(a) (Section 702). In addition, § 703(e)(2) of the Act provides that it shall not be unlawful for educational institutions to hire and employ employees of a particular religion if such institution is, in whole or substantial part, owned, supported, controlled, or managed by a particular religion, or if the curriculum of the educational institution is directed toward the propagation of a particular religion. The proviso is largely subsumed by the broader exemption found in § 702.

[73] Corp. of Presiding Bishop v. Amos, 483 U.S 327 (1987).

[74] 565 U.S. 171 (2012).

[75] Hosanna-Tabor Evangelical Lutheran Church & Sch. v. E.E.O.C., 565 U.S. 171, 188–89 (2012).

based on her ministerial activities; (5) she was required to have significant religious training, including an endorsement by the church; (6) she was required to pass an oral examination by faculty at a Lutheran college; (7) she was commissioned as a called teacher by a church congregation; (8) the teacher held herself out as a minister; (9) she took tax exemptions that applied to ministers; and (10) her job duties included conveying the church's message. Even though the teacher only performed religious duties about 45 minutes a day and otherwise taught secular subjects, the Court held that the teacher fell within the ministerial exception.

As the Supreme Court specifically declined to adopt a bright-line rule to govern whether a person falls within the ministerial exception, subsequent cases rely heavily on their particular facts.[76]

§ 1.18 American Employees Abroad: Extra-Territorial Application

Title VII provides: "This subchapter shall not apply to an employer with respect to the employment of aliens outside any State."[77] "State" means not only the fifty states of the Union, but is defined to include "the District of Columbia, Puerto Rico, the Virgin Islands, American Samoa, Guam, Wake Island, the Canal Zone, and Outer Continental Shelf lands defined in the Outer Continental Shelf Lands Act."[78]

This exclusion does not allow American companies to discriminate against Americans simply because they will perform their work on foreign soil.[79] By its terms, the exclusion applies to "aliens" employed outside the United States. The ADEA and ADA have similar limits.[80]

Title VII and the ADEA have a similar limitation applicable to federal employers; they exempt them from coverage with regard to the employment of aliens abroad but do not limit the rights of American citizens employed by the United States government for service abroad.[81]

The Congressional Accountability Act of 1995, which extends the protections of Title VII, the ADEA, and the ADA to certain employees of the federal legislative branch and to an enumerated list of other federal employees covers "any" employee that falls within its definitions.[82] The definition section of that Act does not specifically exclude aliens working outside the United States from coverage.

§ 1.19 Individual Liability

Although the Supreme Court has never addressed the issue, most federal courts hold that individual supervisors or managers are not employers under Title VII, the

---

[76] *See, e.g.*, Conlon v. InterVarsity Christian Fellowship, 777 F.3d 829 (6th Cir. 2015); Cannata v. Catholic Diocese of Austin, 700 F.3d 169, 170 (5th Cir. 2012).

[77] 42 U.S.C.A. § 2000e–1(a).

[78] 42 U.S.C.A. § 2000e(i).

[79] Bryant v. Int'l Sch. Servs., Inc., 502 F. Supp. 472 (D.N.J. 1980), reversed on other grounds 675 F.2d 562 (3d Cir. 1982).

[80] 29 U.S.C.A. § 630(f); 42 U.S.C.A. § 12111(4).

[81] 42 U.S.C.A. § 2000e–16(a); 29 U.S.C.A. § 633a(a).

[82] 2 U.S.C.A. § 1301.

ADEA, or the ADA.[83] Thus, individual supervisors or managers are not proper defendants under these federal discrimination statutes. Courts have reasoned that the statutes' numerosity requirements imply that individual supervisors should not face liability.

This does not mean that all individuals are exempt from liability. For example, the owner of a sole proprietorship with the requisite number of employees may be a proper defendant under the statutes. Section 1981 also allows for individual liability, as do some state discrimination statutes.

Under the federal discrimination statutes, employers are liable for the actions of their agents. In some circumstances, employers may have defenses to liability for the actions of their agents.

§ 1.20 Section 1981

Section 1981 provides: "All persons within the jurisdiction of the United States shall have the same right in every State and Territory to make and enforce contracts . . . as is enjoyed by white citizens." Although Section 1981 prohibits race discrimination in the employment context, it is not limited to just employment. Section 1981 does not contain a minimum-employee threshold, like Title VII, the ADA, and the ADEA. Thus, very small employers face potential liability under Section 1981. Individual liability also exists under Section 1981.

By its terms, Section 1981 does not apply outside the United States. The Eleventh Amendment limits claims under Section 1981.[84] Section 1981 does not apply to discrimination claims against the federal government.[85]

§ 1.21 Labor Organization Coverage

Title VII, the ADEA, and the ADA make it unlawful for a "labor organization" to discriminate against individuals. "Labor organization" itself is defined to include organizations or groups which exist, in whole or in part, to deal with employers concerning grievances, labor disputes, wages, hours, or other terms and conditions of employment.[86]

The "labor organization" also must be "engaged in an industry affecting commerce."[87] Title VII and the ADA set forth the circumstances under which the labor organization is deemed to be "engaged in an industry affecting commerce." First, the union must maintain a hiring hall or have at least 15 members. In addition, it must satisfy at least one of the following: (1) it must be officially certified as a bargaining representative under the National Labor Relations Act or the Railway Labor Act, (2) it must be a lawfully recognized bargaining representative of the employees of an employer, (3) it must be chartered by a labor organization seeking to represent

---

[83] *See, e.g.*, Pouyeh v. UAB Dep't of Ophthalmology, 625 F. App'x 495, 498 (11th Cir. 2015); Williams v. Banning, 72 F.3d 552, 553 (7th Cir. 1995).

[84] Complicated issues also exist about the proper mechanism for suing state actors. *See, e.g.*, Jett v. Dallas Indep. Sch. Dist., 491 U.S. 701, 731 (1989).

[85] *See, e.g.*, Marcus v. Geithner, 813 F. Supp. 2d 11, 19 (D.D.C. 2011).

[86] 42 U.S.C.A. § 2000e(d); 29 U.S.C.A. § 630(d); 42 U.S.C.A. § 12111(7) (noting the definition of "labor organization" under the ADA is the same under Title VII); EEOC v. California Teachers Ass'n, 534 F. Supp. 209 (N.D. Cal.1982).

[87] 42 U.S.C.A. § 2000e(e); 29 U.S.C.A. § 630(e).

employees of an employer, (4) it must have a formalized relationship with a defined "labor organization;" or (5) is "a conference, general committee, joint or system board, or joint council subordinate to a national or international labor organization." A similar definition applies under the ADEA, except the union must maintain a hiring hall or have at least 25 members.

The two key elements for coverage of most unions will be: (1) whether the organization has the requisite number of members, and (2) whether, if not certified, it is chartered by a parent organization and represents "employees" of an "employer."

A union with fifteen or more *employees* will be a defined "employer" subject to Title VII and the ADA provisions regulating employment practices. Unions with 20 or more employees will be a defined employer under the ADEA. However, the mere fact that the union itself is an "employer" subject to Title VII, the ADA, and the ADEA does not itself make the union a "labor organization." The converse is also true. Because the federal discrimination statutes have different substantive provisions that apply to labor organizations than those that apply to employers, it is important to understand in which capacity the union is being sued.

As of the writing of this text, there is a circuit split regarding whether labor organizations that represent federal employees are proper defendants in Title VII cases under the provisions prohibiting discrimination by labor organizations.[88] One argument is that Title VII defines "employer" to exclude the federal government. Since to be a defined "labor organization" the union must either be certified by the NLRB or the Railway Labor Act or represent employees of an "employer," a union representing employees of the federal government cannot be a "labor organization." However, other courts have reasoned that the statute is ambiguous and then deferred to the EEOC's interpretation that unions representing federal employees are covered.

§ 1.22 Employment Agency Coverage

Title VII and the ADA define "employment agency" in expansive terms as "any person regularly undertaking with or without compensation to procure employees for an employer or to procure for employees opportunities to work for an employer."[89] The ADEA has a less expansive definition. It defines an employment agency as "any person regularly undertaking with or without compensation to procure employees for an employer and includes an agent of such a person; but shall not include an agency of the United States."[90]

The statutes tie the definition of employment agency to that of employer. If an agency procures employees for a person or entity that does not qualify as an employer under the statutes, the agency does not meet the statutory definition of "employment agency." For example, if an agency procures employees for private individuals only, its activities would not be covered. A nursing referral service that refers nurses to individual doctors or patients is not covered.[91]

---

[88] Burton v. Am. Fed'n of Gov't Emps. (AFGE) 1988, No. 11-CV-1416 SLT LB, 2012 WL 3580399, at *9 (E.D.N.Y. Aug. 17, 2012) (summarizing circuit split).

[89] 42 U.S.C.A. §§ 2000e(c), 12111(7).

[90] 29 U.S.C.A. § 630(c).

[91] Shrock v. Altru Nurses Registry, 810 F.2d 658 (7th Cir. 1987).

To be an "employment agency" the entity must, to a significant degree, engage in the *profession* of procuring employees for employers or procuring employment opportunities to work for an employer. The statutes do not require the employment agency to be compensated for its work to fall within coverage. A non-profit that allows job listings to be posted on its website, when such listing are just an ancillary part of the organization's undertakings, would not fall within the statutes' coverage.[92] However, the definition of employment agency is broader than just businesses holding themselves out as placement agencies. For example, formalized placement services of educational institutions or professional societies may meet the definition,[93] as well as civil service administrators that regularly provide hiring lists of eligible employees.[94]

State employment services that aid the unemployed in securing private and public employment may be "employment agencies,"[95] as can state or local government personnel boards which administer civil service systems charged with testing and placing applicants for public employment.[96]

A defined "employment agency" will be covered in its own employment relations only if it means the statutory definition of "employer." For example, it will be subject to Title VII in the treatment of its own employees and applicants only if it has fifteen or more employees.[97]

§ 1.23 Apprenticeship and Training Programs

Title VII explicitly makes it unlawful for an employer, a labor organization, or a joint labor-management committee controlling apprenticeships or other training, retraining, and on-the-job training programs to discriminate against individuals in admission to such programs because of race, color, religion, sex, or national origin. Apprenticeship programs are not otherwise defined. The liability of the joint committee for discriminatory operation of a training program will be in addition to the liability of the employer and/or the union. The ADA defines prohibited discrimination as including access to apprenticeship and training programs. Although the ADEA does not contain an explicit provision related to apprenticeship programs, courts have interpreted the statute as applying to them.[98]

---

[92] Stewart v. Am. Ass'n of Physician Specialists, Inc., No. 5:13-CV-01670-ODWDTBX, 2015 WL 7722349, at *5 (C.D. Cal. Nov. 30, 2015).

[93] Watanabe v. Loyola Univ. of Chicago, No. 99 C 4820, 2000 WL 876983, at *5 (N.D. Ill. July 3, 2000); Kaplowitz v. Univ. of Chicago, 387 F. Supp. 42 (N.D. Ill. 1974).

[94] Koger v. Allegheny Intermediate Unit, No. CIV.A. 10–1466, 2012 WL 603565, at *11 (W.D. Pa. Feb. 24, 2012); Scaglione v. Chappaqua Central Sch. Dist., 209 F. Supp. 2d 311, 319 (S.D.N.Y. 2002).

[95] Pegues v. Mississippi State Emp't Serv., 699 F.2d 760 (5th Cir. 1983).

[96] Dumas v. Mt. Vernon, 612 F.2d 974 (5th Cir. 1980); *see also* Scaglione v. Chappaqua Cent. Sch. Dist., 209 F. Supp. 2d 311, 317 (S.D.N.Y. 2002).

[97] Brennan v. Paragon Emp't Agency, Inc., 356 F. Supp. 286 (S.D.N.Y. 1973), affirmed 489 F.2d 752 (2d Cir. 1974).

[98] E.E.O.C. v. Seafarers Int'l Union, 394 F.3d 197, 202 (4th Cir. 2005).

C. PEOPLE PROTECTED BY FEDERAL DISCRIMINATION LAW

§ 1.24 Generally

The federal discrimination statutes do not protect everyone who might face discrimination or retaliation in a work setting. Statutory protection is generally limited to individuals who are current employees, former employees, applicants for employment,[99] or those protected from discrimination by labor organizations or employment agencies. Independent contractors, volunteers, and shareholders are typically not protected under Title VII, the ADEA, and the ADA. Titles are not dispositive, however, and the courts will look at the actual relationship between the plaintiff and the defendant to determine coverage. Section 1981 is not limited to the employment context and so protects a broader class of individuals from discrimination in the workplace.

Whether a person fits within the definition of employee matters in two different contexts in federal discrimination cases. First, employers must have a minimum number of employees to face liability under Title VII, the ADEA, and the ADA. Therefore, the definition of employee is important to knowing who to count for purposes of coverage. Second, many people claim protection under the statutes by virtue of their status as employees.

Title VII, the ADEA, and the ADA all have the same unhelpful definition of "employee." "Employee" is defined as "individual employed by an employer."[100] The Supreme Court has declared that the statutory definition "surely qualifies as a mere 'nominal definition' that is 'completely circular and explains nothing.' "[101] The scope and coverage of the statutes thus is determined by common law concepts of "employee" combined with the federal court's interpretation of those concepts in the specific context of federal discrimination law.

"Employee" necessarily excludes "employers." Therefore, managing partners of a partnership typically are not "employees."[102] Similarly, shareholders and non-working directors of corporations are typically not "employees," even if they receive compensation and benefits similar to that received by workers.[103] However, supervisors, managers, and professionals who meet the common law definition of "employee" will be considered "employees." Courts will look beyond the label assigned to a particular person's job function to determine whether the person is an employee.

In *Clackamas Gastroenterology Assocs. v. Wells*,[104] the Supreme Court considered whether physicians who were shareholder-directors of a medical practice were employees for determining whether the medical practice had the requisite number of employees to face a discrimination claim under the Americans with Disabilities Act. The

---

[99] *But see* Villarreal v. R.J. Reynolds Tobacco Co., 839 F.3d 958 (11th Cir. 2016) (holding that applicants for employment may not proceed under a disparate impact theory under the ADEA).

[100] 42 U.S.C.A. §§ 2000e(f), 12111(4); 29 U.S.C.A. § 630(f).

[101] Clackamas Gastroenterology Assocs., P. C. v. Wells, 538 U.S. 440, 444 (2003).

[102] Burke v. Friedman, 556 F.2d 867 (7th Cir. 1977); *see also Clackamas*, 538 U.S. at 448; Solon v. Kaplan, 398 F.3d 629, 633 (7th Cir. 2005) (holding general partner is not an employee).

[103] Zimmerman v. North Am. Signal Co., 704 F.2d 347 (7th Cir. 1983).

[104] 538 U.S. at 449–51.

ADA's definition of employee is similar to Title VII's definition. The Supreme Court held that in determining whether the shareholder-directors were employees as opposed to owners, the lower courts should consider the following factors:

> Whether the organization can hire or fire the individual or set the rules and regulations of the individual's work;
>
> Whether and, if so, to what extent the organization supervises the individual's work;
>
> Whether the individual reports to someone higher in the organization;
>
> Whether and, if so, to what extent the individual is able to influence the organization;
>
> Whether the parties intended that the individual be an employee, as expressed in written agreements or contracts; and
>
> Whether the individual shares in the profits, losses, and liabilities of the organization.[105]

The Court further indicated that an employer is one "who owns and manages the enterprise. The employer can hire and fire employees, can assign tasks to employees and supervise their performance, and can decide how the profits and losses of the business are to be distributed. The mere fact that a person has a particular title—such as partner, director, or vice president—should not necessarily be used to determine whether he or she is an employee or a proprietor."[106]

However, an individual who is seeking a promotion to a partner may be covered by the statutes, if consideration for the partnership position was one of the terms, conditions or privileges of the plaintiff's employment prior to the partnership decision.[107]

Second, "employees" must be distinguished from persons who serve as independent contractors. Independent contractors are not counted for the purpose of determining coverage and generally are beyond the scope of Title VII, the ADEA, and the ADA. Courts typically use the "right to control" test, the economic realities test, or some hybrid of the two concepts to distinguish employees from independent contractors. The Ninth Circuit has indicated that there is no functional difference between the tests.[108] There is a great deal of variety among the circuits regarding the elements of the appropriate test.[109]

For example, the First Circuit has expounded on the right to control test, holding that the following factors are relevant: "the skills required; the source of the instrumentalities and tools; the location of the work; the duration of the relationship between the parties; whether the hiring party has the right to assign additional projects to the hired party; the extent of the hired party's discretion over when and how long to work; the method of payment; the hired party's role in hiring and paying assistants; whether the work is part of the regular business of the hiring party; whether the hiring

---

105 *Id.*

106 *Id.* at 450.

107 Price Waterhouse v. Hopkins, 490 U.S. 228 (1989); Hishon v. King and Spalding, 467 U.S. 69 (1984).

108 Murray v. Principal Fin. Grp., Inc., 613 F.3d 943, 945 (9th Cir. 2010).

109 California has developed a completely different test for determining employee status. Dynamex Operations W. v. Superior Court, 4 Cal. 5th 903, 416 P.3d 1 (2018), reh'g denied (June 20, 2018).

party is in business; the provision of employee benefits; and the tax treatment of the hired party."[110] No one factor is decisive.

The Seventh Circuit has articulated a hybrid economic realities/right to control test. It considers the following factors "(1) the extent of the employer's control and supervision over the employee; (2) the kind of occupation and nature of skill required, including whether skills were acquired on the job; (3) the employer's responsibility for the costs of operation; (4) the method and form of payment and benefits; and (5) the length of the job commitment.[111]

§ 1.25 Elected Officials and Their Staff

Title VII and the ADEA direct that elected officials, individuals on the personal staff of elected officials, or appointees who hold high policymaking positions cannot be considered "employees." This exemption does not include employees subject to state civil service laws.[112] Even though Title VII and the ADA share many definitions in common, Congress did not exclude elected officials from the definition of employee under the ADA.[113]

The exclusion within Title VII and the ADEA prohibit defined officials from being counted for the purpose of determining whether the entity has a sufficient number of employees to be a defined "employer." In addition, this provision reconfirms that the political election of public officials is not an "employment" decision within the scope of Title VII.

The exclusion of appointed, non-civil service policy-makers from the definition of "employee" does not, on its face, preclude the application of Title VII or the ADEA to these persons. Even though a governmental policy-maker is not an "employee," that person is still an "individual," arguably protected. Nonetheless, the courts have assumed that since the person holding or seeking a policy-making position is not or cannot be an "employee," they are not protected.[114]

The following factors are weighed to determine if the person falls within the personal staff exclusion: (1) powers of the appointing officer, (2) accountability to the elected official, (3) appearance of a close or representative capacity, (4) control by the elected official, (5) organizational level of the employee, and (6) intimacy of the working relationship between the employee and official.[115]

Care should be taken when determining whether discrimination laws are applicable to the staff of politicians because the Government Employees Rights Act allows coverage for some individuals exempted by the language of the federal discrimination statutes.[116]

---

[110] Alberty-Velez v. Corporacion de Puerto Rico Para La Difusion Publica, 361 F.3d 1, 7 (1st Cir. 2004); Brintley v. St. Mary Mercy Hosp., 545 F. App'x 484, 487 (6th Cir. 2013).

[111] Love v. JP Cullen & Sons, Inc., 779 F.3d 697, 702 (7th Cir. 2015).

[112] 42 U.S.C.A. § 2000e(f); 29 U.S.C.A. § 630(f).

[113] 42 U.S.C.A. § 12111(4).

[114] Ramirez v. San Mateo Cty. Dist. Attorney's Office, 639 F.2d 509 (9th Cir. 1981); Carter v. Sedgwick Cty., Kan., 685 F. Supp. 797 (D. Kan. 1988).

[115] Teneyuca v. Bexar Cty., 767 F.2d 148 (5th Cir. 1985); Dintelmann v. Vill. of Freeburg, Illinois, No. 14-CV-855-SMY-DGW, 2015 WL 5176418, at *2 (S.D. Ill. Sept. 3, 2015).

[116] 42 U.S.C.A. § 2000e–16(c).

§ 1.26 Non-Citizens

The federal discrimination statutes apply to foreign nationals employed inside the United States. Persons who do not hold American citizenship are "individuals" entitled to full protection against discrimination.[117] However, undocumented workers may not be entitled to reinstatement or similar remedies should they prevail on a discrimination claim.

Title VII does not prohibit discrimination because of citizenship.[118] However, in some circumstances, proof that an employer discriminated based on citizenship can be evidence of race or national origin discrimination. For example, if an employer employed Canadian nationals but refused to hire Mexican nationals, this might be evidence of national origin discrimination. Likewise, an employer cannot use citizenship as a proxy to engage in intentional discrimination because of a protected trait.

§ 1.27 Military Personnel

Military service in a uniformed service, including the National Guard, is not an employment relationship. Thus, admission into a uniformed military service is not regulated by the federal discrimination statutes, nor are decisions concerning persons in the uniformed services in areas such as assignments, promotions, pay, and discharge.[119]

§ 1.28 Volunteers

A true volunteer is not protected under Title VII, the ADEA, or the ADA. However, courts have often found that volunteers are protected if they receive remuneration for their efforts, even if that remuneration is not a typical paycheck. For example, a court held that a volunteer firefighter was protected because he was entitled to certain benefits, such as disability benefits, survivor benefits, and tuition reimbursement.[120] However, incidental payments will not transform a volunteer relationship into one protected by the statutes. One court found that a person who received reimbursement for some work-related expenses and was admitted for free into an annual luncheon was a volunteer and not covered.[121]

D. REGULATED CONDUCT

§ 1.29 Overview of Prohibited Employer Conduct

As discussed in more detail in subsequent chapters, the courts have interpreted the federal discrimination statutes to prohibit a wide swath of discriminatory behavior. The courts define prohibited conduct using court-created terms of art that are specific to the

---

[117] EEOC v. Arabian Am. Oil Co., 499 U.S. 244, 254 (1991).

[118] Espinoza v. Farah Mfg. Co., 414 U.S. 86 (1973). Alienage discrimination may violate 42 U.S.C.A. § 1981. Manley v. Champlain Stones, Ltd., 741 F. App'x 44, 45 (2d Cir. 2018).

[119] Gordon v. Illinois Army Nat. Guard, 215 F.3d 1329 No. 99–2326, 98–4040, 2000 WL 286091 (7th Cir. 2000); Gonzalez v. Department of the Army, 718 F.2d 926 (9th Cir. 1983); Helm v. California, 722 F.2d 507 (9th Cir. 1983) (exemption applies to National Guard). *See also* Salazar v. Heckler, 787 F.2d 527 (10th Cir. 1986) (exemption applies to commissioned officers of the Public Health Service).

[120] Price v. Grasonville Volunteer Fire Dep't, No. CIV.A. ELH-14-1989, 2014 WL 7409891, at *12 (D. Md. Dec. 30, 2014); *see also* Glatt v. Fox Searchlight Pictures, 811 F.3d 528 (2d Cir. 2016) (FLSA context); Pietras v. Bd. of Fire Comm'rs, 180 F.3d 468 (2d Cir. 1999).

[121] Hall v. Delaware Council on Crime & Justice, 780 F. Supp. 241, 244 (D. Del.), aff'd, 975 F.2d 1549 (3d Cir. 1992).

discrimination context. This section introduces those terms of art, which are explained in greater detail in subsequent chapters.

Most discrimination claims involve claims brought by workers against their employers. Broadly, these discrimination claims typically fall within the following categories: (1) individual disparate treatment, (2) pattern or practice, (3) harassment, (4) disparate impact, (5) failure to accommodate disability or religious beliefs or practices and (6) retaliation.

Individual disparate treatment is the most common claim, in which a worker or a small group of workers alleges that an employer made a specific employment decision because of a protected trait. Pattern or practice cases typically rely on statistical and other evidence to prove that discrimination was the standard operating procedure of an employer, who used a protected trait to make workplace decisions about a larger group of people.

In harassment cases, workers often present evidence that they were subjected to a series of comments or behavior because of a protected class. For example, if a male supervisor repeatedly demeans a female employee because of her sex, this could be sexual harassment under Title VII. A worker may also seek relief if the terms, conditions or privileges of her work are conditioned on the rejection or acceptance of requests for sexual favors.

Under a disparate impact theory, a worker can show that an employer had a policy or practice that disproportionately affected members of a certain protected group. For example, if an employer uses a written test that women disproportionally fail, the test could have a disparate impact on women. The test would be unlawful unless the employer can establish an affirmative defense to liability, which varies depending on the statute.

Title VII requires employers to accommodate religious beliefs and practices, but only at a minimal level. Title VII does not require employers to make religious accommodations if the costs or inconveniences are more than de minimis. In contrast, the ADA requires employers to accommodate people with disabilities unless doing so is an undue hardship. The ADA also prohibits employers from making certain medical requests or inquiries.

All of the statutes also prohibit retaliation. Retaliation occurs when a worker engages in protected activity under the statutes and faces negative consequences as a result. For example, if a worker complains that he was not promoted because of his race and is then fired because of that complaint, this is prohibited retaliation.

Discrimination in regard to relationships other than *employment* are beyond the scope of Title VII, the ADEA, and the employment discrimination portions of the ADA. Section 1981, which is not limited to the employment context, provides a remedy for race discrimination and is not limited to the employment context.

In *Hishon v. King & Spalding*,[122] a female associate in a large law firm alleged that she was denied a promotion to become a partner because of her sex. The Supreme Court held that consideration for partner could be a term or condition of her employment as an

[122] 467 U.S. 69 (1984).

associate and thus covered under Title VII. However, consideration for a common law partnership relationship would not be governed by Title VII in other circumstances.

An employer's interference with a former employee's subsequent employment opportunities is covered.[123] The Supreme Court held that Title VII retaliation can be based on negatives references that an employer provided for a former employee, if those negative evaluations were driven by the former employee's protected activity.[124]

§ 1.30 Unions, Conduct Subject to the Discrimination Statutes

Title VII and the ADEA apply separate rules to restrict the activities of labor organizations in their role as a labor organizations.[125] It is an unlawful employment practice to exclude or expel from union membership any individual because of a protected trait. Under Title VII, a labor organization also cannot "limit, segregate, or classify its membership or applicants for membership, or fail or refuse to refer for employment any individual, in any way which would deprive or tend to deprive any individual of employment opportunities [.]"[126] The ADEA has a similar, but not identical, provision.[127] This provision protects "individuals" from discrimination, not just union members or applicants. Unions cannot cause or attempt to cause an employer to violate the statutes. Nor can they discriminate against a person because of a protected trait in training programs.[128]

Under Title VII and the ADEA, a labor organization also may not retaliate against an individual for engaging in protected activity.[129]

If a labor organization is also an employer under Title VII or the ADEA, the statutory provisions applicable to employers govern its conduct toward its employees, applicants, and former employees.

The ADA defines a labor organization as a covered entity. All of the provisions of the ADA that apply to covered entities also apply to labor organizations in their role as labor organizations. The ADA prohibits any covered entity from discriminating "against a qualified individual on the basis of disability in regard to job application procedures, the hiring, advancement, or discharge of employees, employee compensation, job training, and other terms, conditions, and privileges of employment."[130]

§ 1.31 Employment Agencies, Conduct Subject to the Discrimination Statutes

Title VII and the ADEA prohibit employment agencies from failing or refusing to refer an individual for employment because of a protected trait.[131] They also cannot classify individuals or otherwise discriminate against individuals because of a protected trait. An agency will violate the statutes if it initiates discriminatory referrals or if it

[123] Shehadeh v. Chesapeake & Potomac Tel. Co., 595 F.2d 711 (D.C. Cir. 1978).

[124] Robinson v. Shell Oil Co., 519 U.S. 337 (1997).

[125] 42 U.S.C.A. § 2000e–2(c); 29 U.S.C.A. § 623(c).

[126] 42 U.S.C.A. § 2000e–2(c)(2).

[127] 29 U.S.C.A. § 623(c)(2).

[128] 42 U.S.C.A. § 2000e–2(d).

[129] 42 U.S.C.A. § 2000e–3(a); 29 U.S.C.A. § 623(d).

[130] 42 U.S.C.A. § 12112(a).

[131] 42 U.S.C.A. § 2000e–2(b); 29 U.S.C.A. § 623(b).

honors the discriminatory requests made by employers. The agency cannot maintain segregated files or lists within the agency. Advertisements by an employment agency cannot express unlawful preferences for candidates of certain protected classes, unless doing so would be lawful under the statutes (such as when a protected trait is a BFOQ).[132] An agency that deals exclusively with one race or sex may be in violation of Title VII.[133]

Under Title VII and the ADEA, an employment agency also may not retaliate against an individual for engaging in protected activity.[134]

If an employment agency is also an employer under Title VII or the ADEA, the statutory provisions applicable to employers govern its conduct toward its employees, applicants, and former employees.

The ADA defines an employment agency as a covered entity. All of the provisions of the ADA that apply to covered entities also apply to employment agencies in their role as employment agencies. The ADA prohibits any covered entity from discriminating "against a qualified individual on the basis of disability in regard to job application procedures, the hiring, advancement, or discharge of employees, employee compensation, job training, and other terms, conditions, and privileges of employment."[135]

§ 1.32 Publication

Title VII provides:

> It shall be an unlawful employment practice for an employer, labor organization, employment agency, . . . to print or publish or cause to be printed or published any notice or advertisement relating to employment . . . indicating any preference, limitation, specification, or discrimination, based on race, color, religion, sex, or national origin, except that such a notice or advertisement may indicate a preference, limitation, specification, or discrimination based on religion, sex, or national origin when religion, sex, or national origin is a bona fide occupational qualification for employment.[136]

The ADEA contains a similar, but not identical, limit.[137] The ADA prohibits discrimination in job application procedures.[138] Impermissible advertisements may serve as evidence of discrimination. Newspapers and other media are not held separately liable for publishing such notices, unless the newspaper is acting in its role as a covered entity under the statutes.

§ 1.33 Recordkeeping, Reporting, and Notices

Title VII, the ADEA, and the ADA require employers, labor organizations and employment agencies to maintain records and make reports as the EEOC prescribes by

---

[132] *See* Barnes v. Rourke, 8 FEP Cases 1112, 8 EPD ¶ 9772 (M.D. Tenn.1973).

[133] 29 C.F.R. § 1604.6(a).

[134] 42 U.S.C.A. § 2000e–3(a); 29 U.S.C.A. § 623(d).

[135] 42 U.S.C.A. § 12112(a).

[136] 42 U.S.C.A. § 2000e–3(b).

[137] 29 U.S.C.A. § 623(e).

[138] 42 U.S.C.A. § 12112(a).

regulation.[139] 29 C.F.R. Part 1602 sets forth these record keeping and reporting obligations for Title VII and the ADA. Those regulations provide that larger employers (generally those with 100 or more members or employees, with some exceptions) complete and file standard reporting forms.

In addition, covered entities are required to preserve their compiled records. For example, employers are required to preserve all personnel or employment records, including application forms and records concerned with hiring, promotion, transfer, lay-off, termination, rates of pay, etc. These records must be kept for at least one year, with additional time requirements depending on the type of record. For example, under the ADEA payroll records must be maintained for three years.

All records relevant to the disposition of a charge must be maintained until litigation concerning that charge has been terminated. Unions must similarly preserve their membership and referral records.

Title VII, the ADEA, and the ADA also require employers, labor organizations, and employment agencies to post notices that inform workers of the applicable laws and how to file a complaint for their violation.[140] The ADA requires that these notices be accessible to persons with disabilities.[141]

§ 1.34 The EEOC

The Equal Employment Opportunity Commission (EEOC) is the five-person, presidentially appointed independent agency charged with administering Title VII, the ADEA, and Title I of the ADA. The EEOC does not administer Section 1981.

The EEOC investigates and conciliates possible violations of these statutes. The EEOC typically does not issue final orders determining liability. If the EEOC finds reasonable cause to believe discrimination has occurred, it attempts conciliation. If no reasonable cause is found or if conciliation is unsuccessful, the EEOC typically notifies the charging party of the failure to resolve the dispute and informs the charging party of the right to bring a private judicial action. The EEOC plays a different role in the processing of claims by federal employees and at times acts as an adjudicatory body for those claims.

The EEOC has the power to file a suit in its own name against private entities in the federal district court. The EEOC is empowered to intervene in any suit filed by a private individual, and the EEOC regularly participates as *amicus curiae* in significant appellate cases.

The EEOC has issued a large number of regulations, guidelines, and other material which interpret major segments of the discrimination statutes. Over the years, the courts have varied in the level of deference they provide to EEOC pronouncements, and the level of deference varies by statute and by the method the EEOC chooses to express its judgment.[142]

---

[139] 42 U.S.C.A. § 2000e–8(c); 29 U.S.C.A. § 626(a).

[140] 42 U.S.C.A. §§ 2000e–10(a), 12115; 29 U.S.C.A. § 627.

[141] 42 U.S.C.A. § 12115.

[142] Univ. of Texas Sw. Med. Ctr. v. Nassar, 133 S. Ct. 2517, 2533, 186 L. Ed. 2d 503 (2013) (Supreme Court declined to follow EEOC interpretation); Albemarle Paper Co. v. Moody, 422 U.S. 405 (1975) (Court followed EEOC testing Guidelines). Although beyond the scope of this book, the EEOC also plays a significant role in the procedural process involving federal employees.

Chapter 2

PROTECTED CLASSES

Analysis

§ 2.01 Generally

Title VII prohibits employment discrimination because of race, color, sex (including pregnancy), religion, and national origin. It also requires employers to minimally accommodate religious beliefs and practices. It also requires employers to accommodate pregnancy in some circumstances. Section 1981 prohibits race discrimination. The Age Discrimination in Employment Act (ADEA) prohibits discrimination because of age for individuals who are 40 or over. The Americans with Disabilities Act (ADA) and the Rehabilitation Act prohibit disability discrimination. All of the statutes also prohibit retaliation. Discrimination because of other factors will not violate these federal discrimination statutes.

The employment discrimination statutes require employers to evaluate people as individuals. In *City of Los Angeles v. Manhart*, an employer required women to make larger contributions to retirement than men.[1] The employer justified the increased payments by arguing that women as a class outlived men as a class. The Supreme Court held this was not a valid reason for requiring women to pay more. Even though statistical data supported the employer's reason, the Court noted that the statutes prohibit discrimination against an individual. The Court held that Title VII "precludes treatment of individuals as simply components of a racial, religious, sexual, or national class. If height is required for a job, a tall woman may not be refused employment merely because, on the average, women are too short. Even a true generalization about the class is an insufficient reason for disqualifying an individual to whom the generalization does not apply."[2]

This chapter explores how the statutes and courts define the traits protected under federal employment discrimination law. The definition of "disability" is separately covered in Chapter 8.[3]

§ 2.02 Race

Although the definition of race in the United States has been contested and evolved over time, neither Title VII nor Section 1981 define the term. Judicial discussion defining "race" is surprisingly thin given the central role race discrimination played in the enactment of Title VII. In many cases both the courts and the parties assume that a person can establish a race or a perceived race.[4]

One of the leading Supreme Court cases discussing the term "race" is *Al-Khazraji v. Saint Francis College*.[5] In that case, a professor alleged that he was denied tenure because of his race, religion, and national origin. He brought federal claims under both Title VII and Section 1981. The plaintiff did not timely file his Title VII claim, leaving his Section 1981 claim as the only remaining viable federal claim. Section 1981 provides: "All persons within the jurisdiction of the United States shall have the same right in every State and Territory to make and enforce contracts . . . as is enjoyed by white citizens." The courts have interpreted Section 1981 as creating a cause of action for race

---

[1] City of Los Angeles, Dep't of Water & Power v. Manhart, 435 U.S. 702 (1978).

[2] *Id.* at 708.

[3] Defining concepts such as sex and race is complex and this chapter does not purport to engage in an exhaustive discussion of these topics. Instead, it highlights the major issues that students and practitioners will likely encounter in employment discrimination cases. For additional discussions on race and identity, *see, e.g.*, Lua Kamál Yuille, *Liberating Sexual Harassment Law*, 22 MICH. J. GENDER & L. 345 (2015); Kenji Yoshino, COVERING: THE HIDDEN ASSAULT ON OUR CIVIL RIGHTS (2006); Devon W. Carbado & Mitu Gulati, *Working Identity*, 85 CORNELL L. REV. 1259 (2000); Ian F. Haney López, *The Social Construction of Race: Some Observations on Illusion, Fabrication and Choice*, 29 HARV. C.R.-C.L. L. REV. 1 (1994); Angela Onwuachi-Willig & Mario L. Barnes, *By Any Other Name?: On Being "Regarded As" Black, and Why Title VII Should Apply Even if Lakisha and Jamal Are White*, 2005 WIS. L. REV. 1283, 1324–25 (2005); Kimberlé Crenshaw & Neil Gotanda, CRITICAL RACE THEORY: THE KEY WRITINGS THAT FORMED THE MOVEMENT (The New Press 1996); Kimberlé Crenshaw, *Demarginalizing the Intersection of Race and Sex: A Black Feminist Critique of Antidiscrimination Doctrine, Feminist Theory and Antiracist Politics*, 1989 U. CHI. LEGAL F. 139. For additional discussions on sex, *see, e.g.*, Deborah L. Brake, *On Not "Having It Both Ways" and Still Losing: Reflections on Fifty Years of Pregnancy Litigation Under Title VII*, 95 B.U. L. REV. 995, 996 (2015); Martha Chamallas, Ledbetter, *Gender Equity and Institutional Context*, 70 OHIO ST. L.J. 1037 (2009); Joan C. Williams, *Reconstructive Feminism: Changing the Way We Talk About Gender and Work Thirty Years After the PDA*, 21 YALE J.L. & FEMINISM 79 (2009); Martha Chamallas, INTRODUCTION TO FEMINIST LEGAL THEORY (Aspen).

[4] By discussing how courts define "race," the author is not expressing any agreement with these definitions. It should be noted that the few court decisions that define "race" often do so in a cursory manner, at times using antiquated terms and understandings.

[5] 481 U.S. 604, 608 (1987).

discrimination. Thus, the Court needed to determine whether the professor asserted a viable claim for race discrimination, separate from religion and national origin (which would not be protected under Section 1981).

The employer argued that the professor could not assert a race discrimination claim under Section 1981 because he alleged discrimination because he was Arab. The employer asserted that "Arab" was not a separate race from "Caucasian." As the plaintiff's claim relied on evidence that he was treated differently than white individuals, the employer asserted that the plaintiff had no evidence of race discrimination because Arab individuals are also white.

The Court held that the plaintiff could assert a claim of race discrimination. It noted its prior decision (discussed below), in *McDonald v. Santa Fe Trail Transp. Co.*[6] that the federal discrimination statutes prohibit discrimination against white individuals. The Court then examined the definition of "race," as that term was understood in the mid-19th century when Congress first enacted Section 1981. The Court noted that definitions of race have changed over time. It cited 19th century and modern dictionaries that defined "race" as being "a family, tribe, people, or nation belonging to the same stock."[7] It further noted that defining race along three dimensions (Caucasian, Mongoloid, and Negro) did not occur until the 20th century, well after the passage of Section 1981. The Court continued:

> Encyclopedias of the 19th century also described race in terms of ethnic groups, which is a narrower concept of race than petitioners urge. Encyclopedia Americana in 1858, for example, referred to various races such as Finns, gypsies, Basques, and Hebrews. The 1863 version of the New American Cyclopaedia divided the Arabs into a number of subsidiary races; represented the Hebrews as of the Semitic race, and identified numerous other groups as constituting races, including Swedes, Norwegians, Germans, Greeks, Finns, Italians . . ., Spanish, Mongolians, Russians, and the like. The Ninth edition of the Encyclopedia Britannica also referred to Arabs, Jews, and other ethnic groups such as Germans, Hungarians, and Greeks, as separate races.[8]

The Court also cited legislative history to support its holding that Arab could constitute a different race than Caucasian.

The Court also was skeptical about the idea that three separate, distinct races exist. The Court noted, "Many modern biologists and anthropologists, however, criticize racial classifications as arbitrary and of little use in understanding the variability of human beings. It is said that genetically homogeneous populations do not exist and traits are not discontinuous between populations; therefore, a population can only be described in terms of relative frequencies of various traits."[9] The Court stated that race is likely more a sociopolitical construct than a biological one.

Justice Brennan concurred, noting that there is often little distinction between race and national origin. Justice Brennan noted, "It is true that one's ancestry—the ethnic group from which an individual and his or her ancestors are descended—is not necessarily the same as one's national origin—the country 'where a person was *born*, or,

---

[6] 427 U.S. 273 (1976).

[7] Saint Francis Coll. v. Al-Khazraji, 481 U.S. 604, 611 (1987).

[8] *Saint Francis Coll.*, 481 U.S. at 611–12 (internal citations omitted).

[9] *Saint Francis Coll.*, 481 U.S. at 610 n. 3.

more broadly, the country from which his or her ancestors *came*.' "[10] He continued, "Often, however, the two are identical as a factual matter: one was born in the nation whose primary stock is one's own ethnic group. Moreover, national origin claims have been treated as ancestry or ethnicity claims in some circumstances."[11]

Federal courts have recognized different classifications as constituting race. For example, a plaintiff asserting that he was discriminated against because he was Nigerian could assert national origin, race, and color discrimination claims.[12] Although the term Hispanic "technically . . . denotes an ethnic origin not a race," courts have held that a person may proceed on a race discrimination claim by alleging that he was treated differently because he is Hispanic.[13] The term "Hispanic" often blurs the distinction between ethnic origin and race. Discrimination against indigenous Americans (Eskimos, Native Hawaiians, Samoans, or American Indians) is race discrimination.[14]

Title VII prohibits all discrimination *because of race*, a proscription which goes beyond decisions based on the race of the plaintiff. Thus, it is race discrimination to make distinctions based on the race or color of one's spouse, friends, or social contacts.[15]

There is currently a split in authority regarding whether a plaintiff can prevail under Title VII if the employer took action because of a perceived protected trait.[16]

Title VII's main, operative language provides as follows:

> **(1)** to fail or refuse to hire or to discharge any individual, or otherwise to discriminate against any individual with respect to his compensation, terms, conditions, or privileges of employment, because of such individual's race, color, religion, sex, or national origin; or
>
> **(2)** to limit, segregate, or classify his employees or applicants for employment in any way which would deprive or tend to deprive any individual of employment opportunities or otherwise adversely affect his status as an employee, because of such individual's race, color, religion, sex, or national origin.[17]

Some courts will interpret the "such individual's" language to mean that the employer's action must be because of the person's actual protected trait.[18] Another argument in

---

[10] *Saint Francis Coll.*, 481 U.S. at 614.

[11] *Id.*

[12] *See, e.g.*, Oranika v. City of Chicago, No. 04 C 8113, 2005 WL 2663562, at *2 (N.D. Ill. Oct. 17, 2005).

[13] *See, e.g.*, Torres v. City of Chicago, No. 99 C 6622, 2000 WL 549588, at *2 (N.D. Ill. May 1, 2000); *see also* Manzanares v. Safeway Stores, Inc., 593 F.2d 968, 970 (10th Cir. 1979). For Title VII purposes this distinction is not particularly significant because discrimination against Hispanics and other groups more associated with "nationalities" than "races" would be proscribed "national origin" discrimination. However, as 42 U.S.C.A. § 1981 has been construed to protect race, but not national origin discrimination, such a distinction can be important when that statute is invoked.

[14] *See, e.g.*, Weahkee v. Perry, 587 F.2d 1256, 1263–4 (D.C. Cir. 1978).

[15] Parr v. Woodmen of the World Life Ins. Co., 791 F.2d 888, 892 (11th Cir. 1986); *see also* Loving v. Commonwealth of Virginia, 388 U.S. 1, 12 (1967).

[16] For an excellent discussion of this topic see Jessica A. Clarke, *Protected Class Gatekeeping*, 92 N.Y.U. L. REV. 101, 113 (2017).

[17] 42 U.S.C. § 2000e–2(a)(1)–(2).

[18] *See, e.g.*, Burrage v. FedEx Freight, Inc., No. 4:10CV2755, 2012 WL 1068794, at *5 (N.D. Ohio Mar. 29, 2012); Butler v. Potter, 345 F. Supp. 2d 844, 850 (E.D. Tenn. 2004).

favor of this holding is that the ADA specifically incorporates perceived disability, but Title VII does not contain a similar provision.

However, the weight of modern authority favors allowing a plaintiff to proceed on a perceived protected class claim.[19] These cases tend to rely on the 1991 amendments to Title VII, the purpose of Title VII, and EEOC interpretation of the statute.[20]

In 1991, Congress amended Title VII to clarify than an employer engages in an unlawful employment practice when "the complaining party demonstrates that race, color, religion, sex, or national origin was a motivating factor for any employment practice, even though other factors also motivated the practice."[21] This language does not use the "such individual's" language contained within Title VII's original operative language. Therefore, a plaintiff is not required to establish the discrimination occurred because of her actual protected trait, as long as the discrimination occurred because of a protected trait covered by Title VII.

Likewise, the policy underlying Title VII supports liability based on a perceived protected trait. As one court noted, it seems contrary to the purpose of Title VII to allow an employer to escape liability simply because it was wrong about what protected trait the plaintiff possessed.[22] Such discrimination "is no less injurious to the employee than if the employer guessed correctly regarding the employee's" protected trait.[23]

The ADA specifically prohibits employers from taking action based on a perceived disability.[24] The ADEA remedies are only available to "individuals who are at least 40 years of age."[25] However, this does not mean that the employer must correctly know the employee's actual age. If an employer discriminates against an employee because she is old and she is age 40 and older, this would be sufficient to establish liability under the ADEA.[26]

The language of Section 1981 does not require the plaintiff to establish the discrimination occurred because of the plaintiff's actual race.[27]

§ 2.03 Reverse Discrimination

Title VII and Section 1981 also prohibit reverse discrimination. In *McDonald v. Santa Fe Trail Transp. Co.*,[28] two white employees filed suit for race discrimination under Title VII. They alleged they were terminated for misappropriating cargo from their employer while the employer did not fire a similarly situated black employee. The Supreme Court held that both Title VII and Section 1981 prohibit discrimination against

---

[19] *See, e.g.*, Granger v. New York City Transit Auth., Manhattan, 712 F. App'x 119, 120 (2d Cir. 2018); Gardenhire v. Manville, No. 17–3048, 2018 WL 739379, at *2 (10th Cir. Feb. 7, 2018); Jones v. UPS Ground Freight, 683 F.3d 1283 (11th Cir. 2012), EEOC v. WC & M Enters., Inc., 496 F.3d 393 (5th Cir. 2007); *see also* Arsham v. Mayor & City Council of Baltimore, 85 F. Supp. 3d 841, 849 (D. Md. 2015) (citing district court cases).

[20] Arsham v. Mayor & City Council of Baltimore, 85 F. Supp. 3d 841, 845 (D. Md. 2015).

[21] 42 U.S.C. § 2000e–2(m); *Arsham*, 85 F. Supp. 3d at 847.

[22] *Arsham*, 85 F. Supp. 3d at 845.

[23] *Arsham*, 85 F. Supp. 3d at 846.

[24] 42 U.S.C. § 12102(1)(C).

[25] 29 U.S.C. § 631.

[26] *See, e.g.*, DePriest v. Seaway Food Town, Inc., 543 F. Supp. 1355, 1358 (E.D. Mich. 1982).

[27] 42 U.S.C. § 1981(a).

[28] 427 U.S. 273 (1976).

white individuals. Discrimination against white individuals, especially white males, is often called reverse discrimination.

When interpreting Title VII, the Court noted that the statute's words prohibited discrimination because of an individual's race. It did not limit its protections to certain races. The Court also looked at legislative history suggesting Congress intended to protect white individuals. In *McDonald,* the employer argued that even if Title VII protected white individuals, the plaintiffs should not receive any protection because the employer fired them after they took company property. While the Court noted that theft is a valid, non-discriminatory reason for firing an employee, an employer may not treat black and white employees differently based on the same underlying conduct.

In *McDonald,* the Supreme Court discussed the meaning of "race" under both Title VII and Section 1981. Race is not limited to traditionally defined ethnologic races, but reaches commonly conceived unscientific distinctions based on race-like distinctions.

Section 1981 uses different language than Title VII. It provides: "All persons within the jurisdiction of the United States shall have the same right in every State and Territory to make and enforce contracts . . . as is enjoyed by white citizens." In *McDonald,* the Supreme Court held that the words "all persons" within Section 1981 evinced a congressional intent to include white individuals within its protections, even though the "as is enjoyed by white citizens language" might suggest a contrary result.

§ 2.04 Color

Title VII does not define "color." Color discrimination refers to discrimination that occurs because of the hue of a person's skin color.[29] Color discrimination claims often involve allegations that the lightness or darkness of a person's skin was the basis for negative action. For example, discrimination against individuals with dark skin would be a form of "color" discrimination. Plaintiffs raising color discrimination claims often bring race discrimination claims as well. However, the two are not always coterminous.

§ 2.05 National Origin

Title VII proscribes discrimination because of "national origin." Congress did not define the term in the statute; however, there is legislative history that defines "national origin" to mean, "The country from which you or your forebears came."

It is national origin discrimination to discriminate against a person because of the heritage of one's spouse or children.

Title VII does not prohibit discrimination against people from a particular state or region within the United States unless the employer uses these limits to discriminate against a particular protected class.[30] For example, it would violate Title VII for an employer to not hire people from California if the employer was doing so because it thought Californians would be more racially diverse than candidates from other states.

---

[29] Bryant v. Bell Atl. Maryland, Inc., 288 F.3d 124, 133 n.5 (4th Cir. 2002).

[30] *But see* Feliciano de la Cruz v. El Conquistador Resort & Country Club, 218 F.3d 1, 4 n. 1 (1st Cir. 2000) (citing cases and assuming, without deciding, that a national origin claim would be appropriate based on being from Puerto Rico).

§ 2.06 National Origin and Citizenship

Discrimination against individuals because they are not American citizens is not necessarily national origin discrimination. In *Espinoza v. Farah Mfg. Co.*[31] an employer refused to hire people who were not U.S. citizens. Plaintiff, although legally residing in the United States, was rejected because she was a Mexican national. Plaintiff and the EEOC took the position that discrimination on the basis of lack of citizenship is, inherently, national origin discrimination, because those born in the United States automatically become citizens of the United States while persons born elsewhere must complete demanding requirements for naturalization. Employment based on citizenship therefore involves a consideration of where one was born—clearly a "national origin" distinction.

The Court rejected this argument, holding that citizenship and national origin can be distinct concepts. However, the Court noted that in a different factual context, citizenship discrimination could violate Title VII. For example, if an employer imposed the rule in order to discriminate against a particular race or people of a particular national origin, this would violate Title VII. In *Espinoza,* 97% of defendant's work force were American citizens who were originally from Mexico. Therefore, the plaintiff could not show that the citizenship requirement was a proxy for discrimination based on other protected classes.

Also, if the employer hired non-citizens from certain countries, but refused to hire non-citizens from other countries, this might constitute national origin discrimination. A company could not hire non-citizens from Mexico, while refusing to hire non-citizens from Canada.

Title VII also allows national origin in limited instances where a treaty between the United States and a foreign nation permits companies from those nations to prefer their own nationals. In *Sumitomo Shoji America v. Avagliano*,[32] the treaty permitted "companies of Japan" to engage experts, executive personnel, attorneys, agents and other specialists "of their choice." While the employer was a wholly owned subsidiary of a Japanese corporation, the entity itself was incorporated in the United States. The Court concluded that the treaty had no application to the defendant because it was not a "company of Japan."[33]

§ 2.07 The Immigration Reform and Control Act of 1986

The Immigration Reform and Control Act of 1986 (IRCA) had as one of its principal purposes stemming the tide of undocumented immigration. To accomplish this goal, the Act imposes penalties on employers who hire undocumented individuals. IRCA makes it illegal for an employer to hire undocumented workers and requires employers to verify an employee's status to work legally.[34]

This limit produced a concern that employers would react to the threat of penalties by refusing to hire all non-citizens (which, given the restrictive construction given to Title VII by the Court, would be permissible) and discriminating generally against

---

31 414 U.S. 86 (1973).

32 457 U.S. 176, 189 (1982).

33 *See* Wickes v. Olympic Airways, 745 F.2d 363, 365 & 368 (6th Cir. 1984).

34 8 U.S.C.A. § 1324a.

"foreign looking" individuals. Consequently, IRCA prohibits national origin discrimination in hiring and termination and also prohibits discrimination based on citizenship, but only in certain statutorily defined instances.[35] If an employer asks for verification documents other than those allowed under the statute, such a request is considered to be an unlawful practice.[36]

IRCA provides coverage to all employers of three or more employees, and exempts an entity's discrimination because of national origin discrimination if Title VII covers the entity. Thus, IRCA proscribes national origin discrimination for all employers having between three and fourteen employees.

In prohibiting employers from discriminating because of citizenship in some instances, IRCA extended protections against alienage discrimination well beyond that provided in Title VII.

For example, "intending citizens" are protected against discrimination based on their lack of citizenship. The Act defines "intending citizen" to include aliens lawfully admitted for permanent residence, refugees, asylees, and newly legalized aliens who have filed notice of intent to become United States citizens. Thus, an employer who has a blanket rule denying employment to all who do not possess American citizenship will violate this Act as to all non-citizens who fall into the category of "intending citizen."

Protection of "intending citizens" is subject to a significant caveat:

> [I]t is not an unfair immigration-related employment practice for a person or other entity to prefer to hire, recruit, or refer an individual who is a citizen or national of the United States over another individual who is an alien if the two individuals are equally qualified.[37]

In other words, an employer can prefer American citizens over equally qualified "intending-citizens." This limited preference, however, does not permit an employer to prefer equally qualified non-citizens, using lack of citizenship as a basis for the preference.

The Act permits discrimination because of citizenship status to the extent such discrimination is required by Federal, State, or local law, regulation or executive order; or by virtue of provisions in a government contract between a governmental entity and a private employer. The face of the statute is limited to hiring, referral and discharge, and its language does not extend to cover other terms or conditions of employment.

IRCA established entirely new enforcement mechanisms and procedures within the Department of Justice.[38] To administer and enforce these provisions IRCA creates the Special Counsel within the United States Department of Justice.

An individual aggrieved by any "immigration-related employment practice" must file a charge with the Special Counsel within 180 days of the challenged practice. The Special Counsel is directed to investigate the charge and is given the discretion to file a complaint on behalf of the charging party. The complaint will be filed with and heard before specially designated administrative law judges ("ALJ") who will make findings on

---

[35] 8 U.S.C.A. § 1324(b)(a).

[36] 8 U.S.C.A. § 1324b(a)(6).

[37] 8 U.S.C.A. § 1324b(a)(4).

[38] 8 U.S.C.A. § 1324b(b).

the charge. The decision by the ALJ will be subject to limited review before the appropriate United States Court of Appeals.

If the Special Counsel exercises discretion not to proceed, after waiting 120 days from the filing of the charge, an aggrieved individual is authorized to file a private complaint before the ALJ. The ALJ decision is similarly subject to limited review on petition to the appropriate United States Court of Appeals. In this regard the private action procedures differ from those under Title VII. Title VII provides for a private judicial action before a court, whereas IRCA adopts the processes of an administrative hearing with limited appellate court review.

Remedies authorized by IRCA differ somewhat from Title VII remedies. IRCA provides not only for a hiring order with back pay, but also for "civil penalties," the amount of which varies depending upon whether it is the first offense or a subsequent offense. In addition, the entity can be required to keep records (as required in the employer sanction provisions of the Act) and to retain for three years the names and addresses of all applicants. The Act authorizes an award of attorneys' fees in some circumstances.[39]

§ 2.08 Title VII and Security Clearances

Title VII specifically permits employers to refuse employment if the position or access to the premises requires the individual to have a federal security clearance, and the individual is unable to obtain the necessary clearance.[40] This is true even though security clearances may affect people based on national origin, to the extent that security clearances might be denied based on an individual's relationships to people in certain countries.

However, some courts recognize a Title VII claim if an employer knowingly submits false information about an employee based on a person's protected trait and that false information results in the denial of a security clearance.[41]

§ 2.09 Language Discrimination

Requiring that employees be able to communicate in English is not, on its own, national origin discrimination.[42] However, this does not mean that language-related discrimination never supports a claim under Title VII.

Language discrimination can serve as the basis for disparate treatment, harassment, and disparate impact claims. Evidence that an employer discriminated against an individual based on language may be evidence of discrimination based on traits explicitly covered under Title VII, such as race or national origin.[43] For example, if a supervisor told an employee, "Start speaking English or go back to your own country" and then fired the individual, the supervisor's statement could be evidence of national origin discrimination. Likewise, language-based discrimination may support a

---

39 8 U.S.C.A. § 1324b(h).

40 42 U.S.C.A. § 2000e–2(g).

41 Rattigan v. Holder, 689 F.3d 764, 771 (D.C. Cir. 2012).

42 Frontera v. Sindell, 522 F.2d 1215, 1218 & 1220 (6th Cir. 1975).

43 Panjwani v. Jet Way Sec. & Investigations, LLC, No. 13CIV7186SLTVMS, 2016 WL 3675331, at *13 (E.D.N.Y. Feb. 26, 2016), report and recommendation adopted, No. 13CV7186SLTVMS, 2016 WL 3702969 (E.D.N.Y. July 7, 2016).

harassment claim. A language rule may be discriminatory if it is enacted or enforced to discriminate against a protected class.

Similarly, requiring an employee to pass an English or other language test may subject the employer to disparate impact liability, if the test has a disproportionate impact on certain protected groups and is not justified as being job-related and consistent with business necessity. As with other types of tests, the required level of language knowledge must reflect the level actually required to perform the job or to perform a position at a higher level that most employees obtain after a short time.

Courts tend to scrutinize blanket English-only rules more than they do English-only rules that are limited to work-related conversations or times (i.e., a policy that allows individuals to speak a language other than English during work breaks).[44]

It is national origin discrimination to make distinctions based on the particular accents of employees or applicants or because a worker sounds "foreign." However, it would not be national origin discrimination if an employee was required to communicate in English to perform her job and the worker's accent made it impossible to understand the worker.

The EEOC has taken a stronger stance on language discrimination. The EEOC has indicated that rules that require English to be spoken at all times in the workplace will be presumed to violate Title VII.[45] While the EEOC recognizes that an employer may have legitimate reasons for requiring English to be spoken at certain times, the EEOC maintains that such a rule must be job-related and consistent with business necessity. Additionally, the EEOC requires employers to inform employees about rules related to when English must be spoken. The courts have had a mixed response to the EEOC, with some courts refusing to apply the EEOC guidelines as contrary to the text of Title VII and other courts deferring to the EEOC.[46]

§ 2.10 Sex

Title VII does not define the protected class of "sex." The word has many potential meanings. Understandings of sex, sexual orientation, and sexual identity have radically changed since 1964.

A narrow definition of "sex" prohibits an employer from treating men differently than women. The Supreme Court used this narrow construction in *General Electric Co. v. Gilbert*,[47] which held that pregnancy distinctions were not "sex" distinctions. As discussed below, in 1978, Congress amended Title VII to make it clear that the definition of "sex" includes pregnancy.

When Congress enacted Title VII, it was common for employers to prohibit women from working in certain jobs or to prohibit them from working certain hours, such as the night shift. Some employers had policies requiring women to quit their jobs when they married. These kinds of policies are facial discrimination because of sex, and they violate Title VII.

---

[44] Pacheco v. N.Y. Presbyterian Hosp., 593 F. Supp. 2d 599, 613 (S.D.N.Y. 2009).

[45] 29 C.F.R. § 1606.7.

[46] *See* Reyes v. Pharma Chemie, Inc., 890 F. Supp. 2d 1147, 1163 (D. Neb. 2012) (collecting cases).

[47] 429 U.S. 125, 136 (1976).

In *UAW v. Johnson Controls, Inc.*,[48] the Supreme Court held that it was facially discriminatory for a company to have a policy that excluded fertile or pregnant women from jobs where they would be exposed to lead. Even if the company implemented the policy for what it perceived to be a good reason (the protection of fetuses from lead), the Court held that the policy made a facial distinction between men and women. Even though evidence showed that exposure to lead also affected the reproductive health of men, the policy only applied to women. As the Court noted, the company permitted fertile men to choose whether to risk their reproductive health by taking certain jobs, but did not give that same choice to fertile women.

An employer also violates Title VII when it takes an adverse action against an individual because of sex. For example, if a supervisor refused to promote a woman because he believed that women were not capable of being managers, this would violate Title VII.

Title VII protects not only women from discrimination because they are women, but also protects men against sex discrimination.[49] To be cognizable, the discrimination does not need to be perpetrated by a person of the opposite sex. Men can discriminate against men because of sex. Women can discriminate against women because of sex.[50]

§ 2.11 Sex Stereotyping

In *Price Waterhouse v. Hopkins*, the Supreme Court recognized that an employer violated Title VII by engaging in sex stereotyping.[51] Sex stereotyping occurs when an employer has different expectations for how its employees are expected to behave depending on their sex.

In *Price Waterhouse*, the facts of the case suggested that the employer expected women to act in certain "feminine" ways. In the case, Ann Hopkins was denied partnership in an accounting firm. Of the 662 partners at the firm, 7 were women. In the year the plaintiff was up for partnership, there were 88 proposed partners and Hopkins was the only woman. The Supreme Court noted that when some of the partners evaluated Ms. Hopkins, there "were clear signs" that they "reacted negatively to Hopkins' personality because she was a woman." The evidence in that case showed that some of the male partners stated that Ms. Hopkins was "macho," that she "overcompensated for being a woman," and told her that she needed to take "a course at charm school." One partner noted that Ms. Hopkins "ha[d] matured from a tough-talking somewhat masculine hard-nosed [manager] to an authoritative, formidable, but much more appealing lady [partner] candidate." Another advised her that she needed to "walk more femininely, talk more femininely, dress more femininely, wear make-up, have her hair styled, and wear jewelry." The Supreme Court noted, "An employer who objects to aggressiveness in women but whose positions require this trait places women in an

---

[48] 499 U.S. 187, 198 (1991).

[49] Newport News Shipbuilding & Dry Dock Co. v. EEOC, 462 U.S. 669, 684 (1983). However, employers faced with a conspicuous imbalance of women in traditionally segregated job categories may adopt and apply a reasonable affirmative action plan designed to remedy the imbalance without committing illegal sex discrimination against men. Johnson v. Transportation Agency of Santa Clara County, 480 U.S. 616, 634 (1987).

[50] Oncale v. Sundowner Offshore Servs., Inc., 523 U.S. 75 (1998).

[51] Price Waterhouse v. Hopkins, 490 U.S. 228, 232 (1989) (plurality opinion).

intolerable and impermissible catch 22: out of a job if they behave aggressively and out of a job if they do not. Title VII lifts women out of this bind."[52]

The idea of sex stereotyping has played a large role in some courts holding that Title VII also prohibits discrimination based on sexual orientation or sexual identity. Borrowing from *Price Waterhouse*, the idea is that an employer treats an employee negatively for failure to conform to certain sex stereotypes. For example, an employer might refuse to promote a lesbian because it expects her to act in a more stereotypically feminine way. This idea is discussed in more detail below.

§ 2.12 Sex Plus

It is sex discrimination for an employer to apply different criteria to a subset of men or women. These cases are often called sex plus cases because sex plus another trait cause the differential treatment.

For example, in *UAW v. Johnson Controls, Inc.*,[53] the Court found that an employer violated Title VII when it had a policy that prohibited fertile men, but not fertile women, from certain jobs that risked lead exposure. Even though the policy affected a subset of women, and not all women, it still violated Title VII. Likewise an employer who refuses to hire women with pre-school age children, but hires men with pre-school age children violates Title VII, even though such a policy affects only a subset of women.[54]

It is permissible for an employer to discipline both male and female employees for having extra-marital sexual affairs, but it is forbidden sex discrimination to discipline female employees but not male employees for having such affairs.[55] An employer may inquire about the living arrangements and marriage plans of all applicants, but inquiries about the sex life of only female applicants would be illegal sex discrimination.

§ 2.13 Sexual Activity

The denial of an employment opportunity because of the individual's refusal to have a sexual or dating relationship with a supervisor is discrimination because of sex. Likewise, demanding and receiving sexual favors in exchange for promotions or other tangible employment actions is illegal sex discrimination.[56]

These cases are called "quid pro quo" cases. In these cases the supervisor imposes on the plaintiff the condition of sexual favors as a *quid pro quo* for the supervisor granting employment opportunities, and that condition of sexual favors is not imposed on employees of the opposite sex.[57] The supervisor and the employee do not need to be members of the opposite sex for quid pro quo liability to occur.[58]

---

[52] *Price Waterhouse*, 490 U.S. at 251.

[53] 499 U.S. 187, 198 (1991).

[54] Phillips v. Martin Marietta Corp., 400 U.S. 542 (1971).

[55] Duchon v. Cajon Co., 791 F.2d 43 (6th Cir. 1986); Thorne v. El Segundo, 726 F.2d 459 (9th Cir. 1983).

[56] Valentin-Almeyda v. Municipality Of Aguadilla, 447 F.3d 85, 94 (1st Cir. 2006).

[57] Henson v. Dundee, 682 F.2d 897 (11th Cir. 1982); Katz v. Dole, 709 F.2d 251 (4th Cir. 1983); Craig v. Y & Y Snacks, Inc., 721 F.2d 77 (3d Cir. 1983); Miller v. Bank of Am., 600 F.2d 211 (9th Cir. 1979); Bundy v. Jackson, 641 F.2d 934 (D.C. Cir. 1981).

[58] Oncale v. Sundowner Offshore Servs., Inc., 523 U.S. 75 (1998); Ryczek v. Guest Servs., 877 F.Supp. 754 (D.D.C. 1995); Wright v. Methodist Youth Servs., Inc., 511 F.Supp. 307 (N.D. Ill. 1981); Johnson v. Community Nursing Services, 932 F. Supp. 269 (D. Utah 1996).

It has been suggested that if an employer has a workforce of only one sex or, in the unusual case, if a bisexual employer makes sexual demands on both male and female employees, there would be no violation of Title VII. This is an improperly narrow reading. When an individual is denied employment, a promotion, an assignment, or a training opportunity granted to others, this is discrimination regarding a term or privilege of employment. The only element that must be established is that the discrimination is "because of sex." Proof that the particular treatment of the plaintiff was motivated by sex considerations will establish that element, whether or not the two sexes were treated differently.[59] Thus, even in an all-female workforce, if a particular woman is denied a position because she rejected sexual overtures of her supervisor, then she received this particular treatment *because* she is a woman. Or, if the employer requests sexual favors from all of his employees, each of those employees is subjected to that treatment individually because of their particular sex.

Sexual favors do not need to be requests for actual sex, but can also create liability when the supervisor requests other conduct of a sexual nature, such as wanting to kiss or fondle an employee.[60]

Most courts have held that there is no sex discrimination if a supervisor rewards his paramour by giving him or her employment opportunities to the detriment of other employees.[61] Discrimination against an applicant or current employee because the spouse or relative of that individual refused to have a sexual relationship with the employer states a Title VII claim.[62]

Consensual sexual interaction does not create quid pro quo liability to those involved in the relationship.[63] However, just because conduct is voluntary, does not mean that it is consensual. If a worker agrees to provide sexual favors in exchange for job benefits or because she fears a tangible employment action if she refuses, this is a basis for a quid pro quo claim, even if the sexual favors are not otherwise coerced. Additionally, if a consensual sexual relationship ends, quid pro quo liability may develop if a supervisor continues to demand sexual favors in exchange for favorable treatment or to avoid negative employment actions.

Most quid pro quo cases involve individuals who have the power to take tangible employment actions against the person refusing or acceding to the sexual advances. The courts have typically not allowed quid pro quo cases to proceed when a co-worker is the one demanding sexual favors. These claims typically proceed under the harassment framework. However, a worker may be able to show that her refusal to accede to the sexual demands of a co-worker caused a tangible employment action through a cat's paw theory.[64] For example, if an influential co-worker lied to management after a worker refused his sexual advances and management fired the worker based on the lie, the worker may be able to establish liability.

---

[59] County of Washington v. Gunther, 452 U.S. 161, 170–71, 178–79 (1981); King v. Palmer, 778 F.2d 878 (D.C. Cir. 1985).

[60] McMiller v. Metro, 738 F.3d 185, 189 (8th Cir. 2013).

[61] Becerra v. Dalton, 94 F.3d 145, 149–50 (4th Cir.1996); DeCintio v. Westchester County Medical Center, 807 F.2d 304, 308 (2d Cir. 1986); Ahern v. Omnicare ESC LLC, No. 5:08-CV-291-FL, 2009 WL 2591320, at *5 (E.D.N.C. Aug. 19, 2009).

[62] Simmons v. Lyons, 746 F.2d 265, 270 (5th Cir. 1984).

[63] Souther v. Posen Const., Inc., 523 F. App'x 352, 356 (6th Cir. 2013).

[64] Higgins v. Lufkin Indus., Inc., 633 F. App'x 229, 233 (5th Cir. 2015).

Courts treat threats to take action based on a worker's refusal to submit to requests for sexual favors differently than cases where the threat is carried out. As the Supreme Court has noted: "Cases based on threats which are carried out are referred to often as *quid pro quo* cases, as distinct from bothersome attentions or sexual remarks that are sufficiently severe or pervasive to create a hostile work environment. The terms *quid pro quo* and hostile work environment are helpful, perhaps, in making a rough demarcation between cases in which threats are carried out and those where they are not or are absent altogether[.]"[65]

Employer liability for quid pro quo claims is discussed in the chapter on Harassment.

Title VII does not facially proscribe uniform rules regulating the sexual conduct of employees. If the rule is uniformly applied, was not instituted for the purpose of disadvantaging one protected class, and does not adversely affect a protected class, then the discrimination based on sexual conduct is not "because of sex." The validity of the rule regulating sexual conduct of employees does not depend upon it being relevant to job performance.

Even a rule relating to sexual practices which is uniformly applied must be examined for its adverse impact on one sex. For example, a rule that disciplined individuals for parenting children out of wedlock may have an adverse effect on women. Since it is easier to determine if a woman has a child out of wedlock than it is to determine if a man has, such rules may fall more harshly on women.

§ 2.14 Sexual Orientation and Identity

As of the writing of this book, the courts are divided about whether Title VII prohibits discrimination based only on sexual orientation and gender identity. Until recently, lower courts have held uniformly that discrimination solely on the basis of sexual orientation is not facial "sex" discrimination within the meaning of Title VII.[66] The cases primarily relied on the idea that Congress did not intend the term "sex" to include "sexual orientation."

In an en banc decision the Seventh Circuit held that discrimination against persons because they are gay, lesbian, or bisexual is sex discrimination within the meaning of Title VII.[67] The Supreme Court recently granted a writ of certiorari in three cases that consider whether Title VII prohibits discrimination because of sexual orientation and transgender status.

In *Hively v. Ivy Tech Cmty. Coll. of Indiana*, the Seventh Circuit addressed the case of a worker who alleged that a college refused to hire her as a professor and also cancelled her adjunct teaching contract because she is a lesbian.[68] In holding that Title VII

---

65 Burlington Indus., Inc. v. Ellerth, 524 U.S. 742, 751 (1998).

66 *See, e.g.*, Etsitty v. Utah Transit Auth., 502 F.3d 1215 (10th Cir. 2007); Higgins v. New Balance Athletic Shoe, Inc., 194 F.3d 252, 259 (1st Cir. 1999); Dawson v. Bumble & Bumble, 398 F.3d 211, 217 (2d Cir. 2005); Prowel v. Wise Bus. Forms, Inc., 579 F.3d 285, 290 (3d Cir. 2009); Wrightson v. Pizza Hut of Am., Inc., 99 F.3d 138, 143 (4th Cir. 1996); Blum v. Gulf Oil Corp., 597 F.2d 936, 938 (5th Cir. 1979); Kalich v. AT&T Mobility, LLC, 679 F.3d 464, 471 (6th Cir. 2012); Williamson v. A.G. Edwards & Sons, Inc., 876 F.2d 69, 70 (8th Cir. 1989); Medina v. Income Support Div., 413 F.3d 1131, 1135 (10th Cir. 2005); Fredette v. BVP Mgmt. Assocs., 112 F.3d 1503, 1510 (11th Cir. 1997).

67 Hively v. Ivy Tech Cmty. Coll. of Indiana, 853 F.3d 339, 340 (7th Cir. 2017).

68 Hively v. Ivy Tech Cmty. Coll. of Indiana, 853 F.3d 339, 340 (7th Cir. 2017).

prohibits discrimination based on sexual orientation, the *Hively* court noted the confused analysis that existed related to sexual orientation discrimination. In *Price Waterhouse v. Hopkins*, the Supreme Court held that Title VII prohibited sex stereotyping.[69] In a later case, the Supreme Court held that Title VII prohibited same-sex sexual harassment even though Congress did not contemplate such harassment at the time that it enacted Title VII.[70]

Based on these two cases, some courts have recognized that sexual orientation discrimination cases could proceed if they presented facts showing sexual stereotyping. For example, if an employer refused to promote a lesbian because she did not act in a stereotypically feminine way, this would be sex stereotyping. However, the sex stereotyping idea does not prohibit all sexual orientation discrimination. For example, if the employer refused to promote a lesbian because she is a lesbian and not because of any behavior, this set of facts does not fit neatly within the sex-stereotyping paradigm.[71] However, the *Hively* court accepted the idea that sexual orientation discrimination is a form of sex stereotyping because it is a stereotype that women should be sexually attracted to men. A woman who is sexually attracted to another woman would be breaking this stereotype.

The *Hively* court also noted that failing to recognize sexual orientation discrimination as a form of sex discrimination would be at odds with constitutional cases, especially *Obergefell v. Hodges*[72] (recognizing a constitutional right to same-sex marriage) and *Loving v. Virginia*[73] (discrimination on the basis of the race with whom a person associates is a form of racial discrimination). Cases holding that sexual orientation discrimination is not sex discrimination contradicted a line of Title VII cases in the racial discrimination context that held that it is race discrimination to treat a person negatively because he is married to or has friends of a different race.[74] The *Hively* court recognized that sexual orientation discrimination fits within this same model. The employer is discriminating against an individual because his or her spouse or sexual partner is not of the opposite sex.

The EEOC has recently taken the position that sexual orientation discrimination violates Title VII.[75] Nevertheless, the majority of the courts have found themselves bound by prior decisions; discrimination based solely on one's sexual orientation is not "sex" discrimination within the meaning of Title VII.[76]

As of the writing of this book, there are various opinions about whether gender identity is protected by Title VII, and the cases sometimes depend on the particular

---

[69] Price Waterhouse v. Hopkins, 490 U.S. 228, 250–51 (1989).

[70] Oncale v. Sundowner Offshore Servs., Inc., 523 U.S. 75 (1998).

[71] Kalich v. AT & T Mobility, LLC, 679 F.3d 464 (6th Cir. 2012)

[72] 576 U.S. ___, 135 S.Ct. 2584, 192 L.Ed.2d 609 (2015).

[73] 388 U.S. 1 (1967).

[74] Parr v. Woodmen of the World Life Ins. Co., 791 F.2d 888, 892 (11th Cir. 1986); *see also* Loving v. Commonwealth of Virginia, 388 U.S. 1 (1967).

[75] Baldwin v. Foxx, EEOC Appeal No. 0120133080, 2015 WL 4397641 (July 15, 2015).

[76] The Second Circuit has also held that Title VII covers sexual orientation discrimination. Zarda v. Altitude Express, Inc., 883 F.3d 100, 108 (2d Cir. 2018). The Eleventh Circuit has recently held that Title VII does not prohibit sexual orientation discrimination. Evans v. Ga. Reg'l Hosp., 850 F.3d 1248, 1257 (11th Cir. 2017). Care must be taken in characterizing claims. A court may allow a claim for sex stereotyping to proceed, even if the circuit otherwise does not recognize sexual orientation as a separate protected class.

facts.[77] Some courts have held that gender identity is not a protected class under Title VII and that Congress did not intend for the term "sex" to encompass gender identity.[78] Other courts have held that gender-identity claims can proceed.[79] The Supreme Court recently granted a writ of certiorari in three cases that consider whether Title VII prohibits discrimination because of sexual orientation and transgender status.

Some courts recognize such claims as making facial distinctions because of sex. For example, in one case a transsexual employee contested his employer's policy requiring him to use a gender-neutral bathroom, while other employees used sex-specific restrooms. A federal court recognized that such a policy violated Title VII because it treated the individually differently based both on his anatomical sex (he was not allowed to use the women's bathroom even though he had female genitalia) and his gender identity (he was not allowed to use the male restroom even though he identified as male).[80]

Other courts have recognized that discrimination based on gender-identity involves sex stereotyping as the employer treats the individual differently because of a failure to comply with expectations about how people with a certain biological birth sex are supposed to act or dress.[81]

The EEOC has taken the position that gender-identity discrimination violates Title VII.[82] According to the EEOC, the term "sex" encompasses both the idea of sex (biological differences between men and women) and gender (how one expresses identity). The EEOC has noted:

> When an employer discriminates against someone because the person is transgender, the employer has engaged in disparate treatment "related to the sex of the victim." This is true regardless of whether an employer discriminates against an employee because the individual has expressed his or her gender in a non-stereotypical fashion, because the employer is uncomfortable with the fact that the person has transitioned or is in the process of transitioning from one gender to another, or because the employer simply does not like that the person is identifying as a transgender person. In each of these circumstances, the employer is making a gender-based evaluation, thus violating the Supreme Court's admonition that "an employer may not take gender into account in making an employment decision."[83]

Distinguishing between gay men and lesbians is sex discrimination in that it differentiates men and woman based on their biological sex.[84]

---

[77] Equal Employment Opportunity Comm'n v. R.G. & G.R. Harris Funeral Homes, Inc., 884 F.3d 560, 572 (6th Cir. 2018); Kastler v. Maricopa Cty. Cmty. Coll. Dist., 325 F. App'x 492, 493 (9th Cir. 2009); *see also* Glenn v. Brumby, 663 F.3d 1312, 1316 (11th Cir. 2011).

[78] Etsitty v. Utah Transit Auth., 502 F.3d 1215 (10th Cir. 2007).

[79] Equal Employment Opportunity Comm'n v. R.G. & G.R. Harris Funeral Homes, Inc., 884 F.3d 560, 577 (6th Cir. 2018) (collecting cases); Barnes v. City of Cincinnati, 401 F.3d 729, 733 (6th Cir. 2005).

[80] Roberts v. Clark Cty. Sch. Dist., 215 F. Supp. 3d 1001, 1015 (D. Nev. 2016), reconsideration denied, No. 215CV00388JADPAL, 2016 WL 6986346 (D. Nev. Nov. 28, 2016).

[81] *Barnes*, 401 F.3d at 733.

[82] Macy v. Holder, 2012 WL 1435995, at *1 (Apr. 20, 2012).

[83] *Macy*, 2012 WL 1435995, at *7 (internal citations omitted).

[84] Valdes v. Lumberman. Mut. Cas. Co., 507 F.Supp. 10, 12–13 (S.D. Fla. 1980).

When determining whether sexual orientation or gender identity cases are covered, care must be taken regarding the facts of the case. In some circuits that do not separately recognize these traits as protected sex discrimination, a court may nonetheless allow claims to proceed if the facts suggest the employer engaged in sex stereotyping.

Sexual orientation and gender-identity are not disabilities. The Americans with Disabilities Act (ADA) reflects that view; being homosexual, bisexual, or a transvestite is not an impairment or disability protected by the ADA.[85]

§ 2.15 History of Pregnancy Discrimination

In 1978, Congress amended Title VII to make it clear that the term "sex" included pregnancy. Congressional action followed a series of Supreme Court cases related to pregnancy as a protected class.

In *General Electric Co. v. Gilbert*[86] a private employer had a disability benefit plan that covered non-occupational sickness and disability. The plan excluded pregnancy as a condition that would qualify for benefits. The Supreme Court held that the plan did not violate Title VII.

In doing so, it looked to its earlier decision in *Geduldig v. Aiello*. In that case, the Court had held that it did not violate the Equal Protection Clause for a state to exclude normal pregnancy from the types of disability covered by a state benefit plan that paid workers who were temporarily unable to work due to disabilities not covered by worker's compensation.[87] In *Geduldig*, the Court held that not every classification involving pregnancy is a sex-based classification.

In *Gilbert*, the Court found that the employer's plan and the distinctions within it were not a pretext for invidious discrimination. The Court then examined the plan for any adverse impact on women as a class. Despite the fact that women would not receive a benefit for a condition for which they were required to miss work, the Court held there was no adverse impact on women.

> The "package" going to relevant identifiable groups we are presently concerned with—General Electric's male and female employees—covers exactly the same categories of risk, and is facially nondiscriminatory in the sense that "[t]here is no risk from which men are protected and women are not. Likewise, there is no risk from which women are protected and men are not." As there is no proof that the package is in fact worth more to men than to women, it is impossible to find any gender-based discriminatory effect in this scheme simply because women disabled as a result of pregnancy do not receive benefits; that is to say, gender-based discrimination does not result simply because an employer's disability-benefits plan is less than all inclusive. For all that appears, pregnancy-related disabilities constitute an *additional* risk, unique to women, and the failure to compensate them for this risk does not destroy the presumed parity of the benefits, accruing to men and women alike, which results from the facially evenhanded *inclusion* of risks.

---

[85] 42 U.S.C.A. §§ 12208 and 12211(a).

[86] 429 U.S. 125 (1976).

[87] Geduldig v. Aiello, 417 U.S. 484 (1974).

The following year the Court again addressed a pregnancy distinction in *Nashville Gas Co. v. Satty*.[88] In that case, the employer required pregnant women to take an unpaid leave of absence. For non-pregnancy medical leaves, both men and women retained their seniority when they returned to work. However, women who took a leave of absence because of pregnancy lost their seniority. The employer would not hold a job open for the employee, but would try to place the employee in a temporary or permanent position. Once the female employee obtained a permanent position, she would regain some of her seniority (for things like vacation time and her pension), but she did not regain her seniority related to bidding on future job openings. The Court distinguished *Gilbert* and found that this pregnancy distinction was "because of sex."

> Here, by comparison [to *Gilbert*], petitioner has not merely refused to extend to women a benefit that men cannot and do not receive, but has imposed on women a substantial burden that men need not suffer. The distinction between benefits and burdens is more than one of semantics. We held in *Gilbert* that § 703(a)(1) did not require that greater economic benefits be paid to one sex or the other "because of their different roles in the scheme of existence." But that holding does not allow us to read § 703(a)(2) to permit an employer to burden female employees in such a way as to deprive them of employment opportunities because of their different role.

§ 2.16 Pregnancy Discrimination Act

The outcome in *Gilbert* resulted in the Pregnancy Discrimination Act of 1978. That amendment provides:

> The terms "because of sex" or "on the basis of sex" include, but are not limited to, because of or on the basis of pregnancy, childbirth or related medical conditions; and women affected by pregnancy, childbirth, or related medical conditions shall be treated the same for all employment-related purposes, including receipt of benefits under fringe benefit programs, as other persons not so affected but similar in their ability or inability to work, and nothing in section 703(h) of this title shall be interpreted to permit otherwise. This subsection shall not require an employer to pay for health insurance benefits for abortion, except where the life of the mother would be endangered if the fetus were carried to term, or except where medical complications have arisen from an abortion: *Provided*, That nothing herein shall preclude an employer from providing abortion benefits or otherwise effect bargaining agreements in regard to abortion.[89]

This section defines "sex" to include pregnancy, childbirth and related medical conditions. The first portion makes it illegal to discriminate against a person in hiring, termination, promotions, compensation, and other terms, conditions or privileges of employment because she is pregnant or has delivered a child. It is likewise sex discrimination to take negative action against a woman because of a fear or assumption that she may become pregnant in the future.

---

88 434 U.S. 136, 142 (1977).

89 42 U.S.C.A. § 2000e(k).

Any condition related to pregnancy or childbirth is included within the definition of sex. For example, because lactation is related to childbirth, it is sex discrimination to take an adverse action against a woman because she is lactating.[90]

Aborting a pregnancy is within the broad scope of "pregnancy, childbirth, and related conditions." Thus, rejecting an applicant or firing an employee because she has had an abortion is sex discrimination.[91]

However, Title VII specifically allows different treatment for abortions under health benefit plans. While a plan must cover pregnancy on a parity with other similar medical conditions, it need not provide benefits for elective abortions which result in no medical complications. However, the plan must cover complications arising from any abortion. And the benefit plan must cover, as thoroughly as other medical conditions, any abortion performed because the life of the mother would be endangered if the fetus were carried to term.

The Pregnancy Discrimination Act does not prohibit an employer from providing women benefits based on pregnancy that it does not provide to male employees who do not experience pregnancy. In this regard, the Supreme Court had noted that the Pregnancy Discrimination Act provides a floor under which benefits must not drop, but does not describe the full extent to which employers may accommodate pregnancy.[92] However, as discussed below, an employer may not discriminate against men by giving women benefits unrelated to pregnancy that are not offered to men.

§ 2.17 Pregnancy Accommodation

The question of whether Title VII requires employers to provide accommodations based on pregnancy is a tricky one. On one hand, outside the religious accommodation context, Title VII does not require employers to accommodate employees. However, there are instances where a failure to accommodate pregnancy may create a viable Title VII claim. While Title VII does not generally require employers to accommodate pregnancy, childbirth, or related conditions, it may be sex discrimination for an employer to accommodate other conditions but not pregnancy.

In *Young v. United Parcel Serv., Inc.*,[93] the Supreme Court held that a failure to accommodate pregnancy could constitute pregnancy discrimination in some instances, if the employer accommodated other conditions. In *Young*, the plaintiff worked for United Parcel Service as a part-time driver. Her responsibilities included pickup and delivery of packages. After the plaintiff became pregnant her doctor recommended that she not lift packages heavier than 20 pounds during the first weeks of her pregnancy and not lift more than 10 pounds later in her pregnancy. UPS policy required workers to lift parcels weighing 70 pounds. UPS told the plaintiff she could not work while under the weight restriction. It later rehired the plaintiff after her pregnancy. In *Young*, the plaintiff alleged that UPS' failure to accommodate her pregnancy constituted pregnancy discrimination because UPS accommodated other people with work restrictions, but refused to accommodate pregnant women. Young alleged that UPS accommodated

---

90 EEOC v. Houston Funding II, 717 F.3d 425 (5th Cir. 2013).

91 Doe v. C.A.R.S. Protection Plus, Inc., 527 F.3d 358, 364 (3d Cir. 2008).

92 Cal. Fed. Sav. & Loan Ass'n v. Guerra, 479 U.S. 272, 285 (1987).

93 135 S. Ct. 1338, 1354 (2015),

workers who suffered off-the-job injuries and workers who lost their driver's licenses due to accidents or drunk driving.

Although it is unclear how *Young* will be interpreted in practice, the case stands for the proposition that if an employer accommodates many different kinds of people who need light duty but refuses to provide light duty assignments for pregnant women, this might be intentional pregnancy discrimination.

For a full discussion of the analysis the Supreme Court applied, see § 3.25.

Still, there are numerous cases in which courts have found that an employer is not required to accommodate women under Title VII.[94] For example, if an employer has an attendance policy and it dismisses a woman because she misses work due to morning sickness, the employer would not violate Title VII.[95] As one court noted, "Employers can treat pregnant women as badly as they treat similarly affected but non pregnant employees."[96] Similarly, a court upheld the firing of a probationary employee for violating a policy that limited the number of absences to three days. Notwithstanding that her "excessive" absences were caused by her suffering a miscarriage, the court held: "she was fired because of her absences, not because of her pregnancy. There is no evidence she would have been treated differently if her absences had been due to some reason unrelated to pregnancy."[97]

Other statutes may provide protection. In *Young*, the Supreme Court signaled that the Americans with Disabilities Act might apply in future cases similar to *Young*. Congress amended the ADA in 2008 to make it clear that the definition of disability was broad, contrary to the Supreme Court's prior interpretations of the definition of disability. The Court expressed no opinion about how the ADA might apply in a case with similar facts.[98] While pregnancy itself is not a disability, a pregnant woman may fall within the ADA's protections in several ways. First, the employer might regard the pregnancy as a disability. Second, the employer might have a record of disability related to the pregnancy. In those cases, a woman who faced discrimination because of her pregnancy would also receive protection under the ADA.

Finally, the pregnant woman might experience medical conditions related to pregnancy that qualify as actual disabilities. The EEOC has issued guidance on pregnancy and the ADA.[99] That guidance provides a non-exhaustive list of examples that might qualify: "pregnancy-related anemia, sciatica, carpal tunnel syndrome, gestational diabetes, nausea sufficient to cause severe dehydration, abnormal heart rhythms, swelling, depression, cervical insufficiency as well as post-partum-related impairments." For individuals with actual disabilities, the ADA not only prohibits discrimination but also requires the employer to make reasonable accommodations.

---

94 *See, e.g.*, Stout v. Baxter Healthcare Corp., 282 F.3d 856 (5th Cir. 2002).

95 Troupe v. May Dep't Stores, Co., 20 F.3d 734 (7th Cir. 1994).

96 *Id.* at 738.

97 Stout v. Baxter Healthcare Corp., 282 F.3d 856, 859 (5th Cir. 2002).

98 For more discussion about pregnancy discrimination see Bradley A. Areheart, *Accommodating Pregnancy*, 67 ALA. L. REV. 1125, 1127 (2016); Deborah L. Brake, *On Not "Having It Both Ways" and Still Losing: Reflections on Fifty Years of Pregnancy Litigation Under Title VII*, 95 B.U. L. REV. 995, 996 (2015); Ruth Colker, *Pregnancy, Parenting and Capitalism*, 58 OHIO ST. L.J. 61, 79–81 (1997).

99 EEOC No. 915–003, Enforcement Guidance: Pregnancy Discrimination and Related Issues, 2015 WL 4162723 (June 25, 2015).

The Family and Medical Leave Act is beyond the coverage of this text. However, the FMLA requires covered employers to grant "eligible employees" 12 weeks of unpaid leave for the care of newborn and newly adopted children that is available to both mothers and fathers.

In *Cal. Fed. Sav. & Loan Ass'n v. Guerra*,[100] the Supreme Court considered whether it was sex discrimination to deny a father leave to witness the birth of his child when women received a statutory right for leave to deliver the child. The Supreme Court held that this did not constitute discrimination and that the Pregnancy Discrimination Act merely provided a floor for required conduct and did not prohibit employers or states from providing additional benefits to women based on pregnancy.

It is not sex discrimination to deny a father leave to participate in the *birth* of his child simply because the statutory right to childbirth leave is granted to mothers. However, if an employer provides *childcare* leave to mothers, it is sex discrimination to deny similar *childcare* leave to fathers.[101]

§ 2.18 Pregnancy and the Equal Benefits Clause

Title VII also provides that women affected by pregnancy, childbirth, or related medical conditions must be treated the same for all employment purposes, including receipt of benefits under health care programs, as other persons similar in their ability or inability to work. Title VII does not require the employer to provide health insurance; however, if the employer has a health or disability benefit program, that program must treat pregnancy and childbirth the same as other conditions covered by the plan which similarly affect the ability of employees to work.

If the employer provides a choice of packages to employees, pregnancy within each package must be treated the same as illnesses and similar disabilities covered by that particular package. The employer may not offer as an option a health care package that excludes pregnancy benefits.[102]

If an employee has delivered a child and is physically able to return to work, but requests additional maternity leave, the employer must treat the request in the same way it would treat other non-work-related leave requests.

A few courts have held that benefits plans that exclude fertility do not violate Title VII because infertility impacts both men and women or because infertility is not a condition related to pregnancy.[103] However, a plan that excluded fertility benefits for certain fertility treatments that only women may undergo would violate Title VII.

Women who seek treatment for infertility must be treated the same as men who do so. If an employer terminates a woman for undergoing in vitro fertilization she may have a sex discrimination claim because IVF is available to women only. If an employer discriminates against people who undergo IVF, women would be the only ones affected by such a policy.[104]

---

100 479 U.S. 272, 285 (1987).

101 Shafer v. Bd. of Pub. Educ., 903 F.2d 243, 250 (3d Cir. 1990).

102 EEOC No. 915–003, Enforcement Guidance: Pregnancy Discrimination and Related Issues, 2015 WL 4162723, at*18 (June 25, 2015).

103 Saks v. Franklin Covey Co., 316 F.3d 337, 345 (2d Cir. 2003); Krauel v. Iowa Methodist Med. Ctr., 95 F.3d 674, 680 (8th Cir. 1996).

104 Hall v. Nalco Co. 534 F.3d 644 (7th Cir. 2008).

As of the writing of this text, Congress is considering substantial amendments to the Affordable Care Act (ACA). The ACA explicitly requires contraception and pregnancy benefits.[105] The effects of the ACA are beyond the scope of this text. However, even prior to the ACA, there was a split in authority regarding whether Title VII required employers to offer contraception coverage as part of insurance benefits.[106]

In *Newport News Shipbuilding & Dry Dock Co. v. EEOC,*[107] the employer provided a benefit package that treated the pregnancy of its employees the same as other conditions. However, the employer also provided health care benefits to the dependents of employees. The dependent benefit limited coverage for pregnancy, but the plan did not contain similar limits for other conditions. The Court held that Title VII applied to the dependent benefit coverage.

The Court reasoned that treating the pregnancy of spouses of male employees differently than other similar conditions resulted in sex discrimination against the male employees. "[S]ince the sex of the spouse is always the opposite of the sex of the employee, it follows inexorably that discrimination against the female spouses in the provision of fringe benefits is also discrimination against the male employees." It should be noted that this case was decided prior to Supreme Court recognizing that the Constitution prohibits states from limiting same-sex couple's ability to marry.

§ 2.19 Parenting, Marriage and Relationships

Title VII does not prohibit discrimination based on parental or marital status. Nor does it prohibit employers from having policies prohibiting employees from dating or being married to one another. Such policies, even if they have a disparate impact can typically be justified as job-related and consistent with business necessity.[108]

The problem with these policies is that they are often not uniformly enforced. For example, if an employer has a policy prohibiting premarital sex, but only enforces the policy against women, this violates Title VII.[109]

Nepotism practices that favor the friends or relatives of current employees are not a per se violation of Title VII. However, such a policy can violate Title VII. For example, if the policy is enacted to discriminate against a protected class, it would constitute unlawful discrimination. If the policy results in a disparate impact because of a protected trait, it may be difficult for an employer to establish that such a practice is job-related and consistent with business necessity.[110]

§ 2.20 Religion

Title VII did not originally define the term "religion," and the current version only partially defines it. In 1972, Congress added the following provision to Title VII.

---

105 Burwell v. Hobby Lobby, ___ U.S. ___, 134 S. Ct. 2751 (2014).

106 Erickson v. Bartell Drug Co., 141 F.Supp.2d 1266 (D. Wash. 2001). *Cf.* In re Union Pac. R.R. Employment Practices Litig., 479 F.3d 936 (8th Cir. 2007).

107 462 U.S. 669, 683–84 (1983).

108 EEOC v. Rath Packing Co., 787 F.2d 318, 328 (8th Cir. 1986).

109 Cline v. Catholic Diocese of Toledo, 206 F.3d 651 (6th Cir. 2000).

110 Thomas v. Washington County School Bd., 915 F.2d 922, 925 (4th Cir. 1990); *see also* Roberts v. Gadsden Mem. Hosp., 835 F.2d 793, 797 (11th Cir. 1988).

> The term "religion" includes all aspects of religious observance and practice, as well as belief, unless an employer demonstrates that he is unable to reasonably accommodate to an employee's or prospective employee's religious observance or practice without undue hardship on the conduct of the employer's business.

As discussed earlier, Title VII exempts religious associations from the proscriptions against religious discrimination in hiring.[111]

While Title VII does not completely define religion, the term "religion" necessarily includes the organized and structured faiths, as well as many small, unorthodox, and often unnamed groups or cults.

The EEOC has adopted a broad concept of religion similar to that utilized by the Supreme Court in resolving constitutional issues arising under the First Amendment. A religious belief is a "sincere and meaningful belief which occupies in the life of its possessor a place parallel to that filled by the God."[112] Stated another way, a religious belief is "a genuinely held belief that involves matters of the afterlife, spirituality, or the soul, among other possibilities."[113]

Religion includes:

> moral or ethical beliefs as to what is right and wrong which are sincerely held with the strength of traditional religious views. . . . The fact that no religious group espouses such beliefs or the fact that the religious group to which the individual professes to belong may not accept such belief will not determine whether the belief is a religious belief.[114]

Courts do not typically evaluate whether a religious belief is orthodox or mandated by a particular religious tradition.[115] In another context, a court noted that religion includes "obscure beliefs such as Paganism, Zoroastrianism, Pantheism, Animism, Wicca, Druidism, Satanism, and Santeria. And, casting a backward glance over history, the test assuredly would have included what we now call 'mythology:' Greek religion, Norse religion, and Roman religion."[116]

Religion also includes the absence of religion. For example, a person would be protected if he refused to participate in a prayer service at work because he was an atheist or was agnostic.

Religious beliefs must be more than just a personal preference. It is also important to distinguish religious beliefs from social and political beliefs. Social and political beliefs that are not religious in nature are not generally protected under Title VII.[117] In another

---

[111] Chapter 1, § 1.17.

[112] United States v. Seeger, 380 U.S. 163, 176 (1965); Adeyeye v. Heartland Sweeteners, LLC, 721 F.3d 444, 448 (7th Cir. 2013).

[113] *Adeyeye,* 721 F.3d at 448.

[114] 29 C.F.R. § 1605.1.

[115] *Adeyeye,* 721 F.3d at 452.

[116] United States v. Meyers, 906 F. Supp. 1494, 1503–04 (D. Wyo. 1995), aff'd, 95 F.3d 1475 (10th Cir. 1996).

[117] Distinguishing unprotected social-political beliefs from protected religious convictions can be difficult. Just because a belief is espoused by a social or political organization does not mean that same belief cannot be religious. Peterson v. Wilmur Commc'ns, Inc., 205 F. Supp. 2d 1014, 1023 (E.D. Wis. 2002); see also American Postal Workers Union v. Postmaster General, 781 F.2d 772, 777 (9th Cir. 1986).

context, a court listed the following as social, and not religious: "nihilism, anarchism, pacifism, utopianism, socialism, libertarianism, Marxism, vegetism, and humanism."[118]

New religions and religious practices pose a unique challenge. Courts have been reluctant to declare a system of beliefs non-religious simply because it is new or unconventional. However, a court has rejected the idea that the Church of the Flying Spaghetti Monster is a religion. The court held that this "church" was created as a satire of organized religion and therefore does not meet the test of being a sincerely held belief system.[119]

Religious practices that may require accommodation encompass formal obligations, such as observation of a Sabbath or holy day. Religious activities can fall within Title VII's coverage, even if they are outside of the formal requirements of the religion. Participating in church sponsored sporting events, parties, or picnics may not be considered religious practices requiring accommodation.[120] Such activities are social in nature. Distinguishing between religious activity and social activity on behalf of the religious organization can be difficult.[121] However, even if an employer is not required to accommodate a certain activity, it may not discriminate because of the religious affiliation of the activity. For example, it would violate Title VII for an employer to allow employees to attend a softball game sponsored by a Catholic church, but to discipline employees who attend a similar softball game hosted by a Protestant church, if the difference in treatment is because of religion.

Even if the activity in which the worker engages is religious in nature, the timing of the event may be a personal choice and therefore may be outside the religious accommodation mandates. For example, if a person is required to pick up challah bread before a day of religious obligation, the employee does not need to be given extra time off work to pick up the bread, if the religious belief does not mandate picking up the bread at a certain time. If the employee could pick up the bread on another day or at a time when she did not need to take off work, the employer need not accommodate her request to pick up the bread at a particular time.[122]

Protected religious practices include specific clothing or grooming styles required by one's religion or religious belief.[123]

Religious beliefs or practices must be sincerely held by the individual. Whether a religious belief is sincerely held is "largely a matter of individual credibility."[124] "Credibility issues such as the sincerity of an employee's religious belief are quintessential fact questions. As such, they ordinarily should be reserved for the factfinder at trial, not for the court at summary judgment."[125]

---

118 United States v. Meyers, 906 F. Supp. 1494, 1504 (D. Wyo. 1995), aff'd, 95 F.3d 1475 (10th Cir. 1996).

119 Cavanaugh v. Bartelt, 178 F. Supp. 3d 819 (D. Neb. 2016), aff'd (Sept. 7, 2016).

120 *See, e.g.*, Duran v. Select Med. Corp., No. 08-CV-2328-JPM-TMP, 2010 WL 11493117, at *6 (W.D. Tenn. Mar. 19, 2010); Wessling v. Kroger Co., 554 F.Supp. 548, 552 (E.D. Mich.1982).

121 Davis v. Fort Bend Cty., 765 F.3d 480, 485–86 (5th Cir. 2014).

122 Dachman v. Shalala, 9 F. App'x 186, 192 (4th Cir. 2001).

123 EEOC v. Abercrombie & Fitch Stores, Inc., 135 S. Ct. 2028, 2030 (2015).

124 Davis v. Fort Bend Cty., 765 F.3d 480, 485–86 (5th Cir. 2014).

125 E.E.O.C. v. Union Independiente de la Autoridad de Acueductos y Alcantarillados de Puerto Rico, 279 F.3d 49, 56 (1st Cir. 2002) (internal citations omitted).

§ 2.21 Age

With a few exceptions, the ADEA prohibits age discrimination against individuals aged 40 and older.[126] If an individual under the age of 40 is discriminated against because of her age, there is no federal age discrimination claim. However, some state laws protect younger individuals from employment discrimination because of age.

The ADEA does not define the term "age." In *Dynamics Land Systems v. Cline,*[127] an employer retained retiree health benefits for workers age 50 and older, but eliminated those benefits for workers under the age of 50. Workers within the ADEA's protected class, aged 40 through 49, sued claiming that the employer violated the ADEA by providing them fewer benefits based on an age distinction. The Court held that the company did not violate the ADEA. While noting that the text of the ADEA was not clear, the Court found that the legislative history of the statute suggested that Congress meant to protect workers from being discriminated against because they were older. Here, the company's plan favored older workers.

In *Hazen Paper Co. v. Biggins,*[128] the Supreme Court held that discriminating against an individual because his pension was close to vesting did not constitute age discrimination. In that case, the employer terminated a 62-year old one year before his pension would vest. The pension plan required 10 years of employment before vesting. The Court noted, "Age and years of service are analytically distinct . . . and it is incorrect to say that a decision based on years of service is necessarily age based." The Court noted that it would violate the ADEA for an employer to intend to discriminate against a worker because of age but to cover up that discrimination by claiming that pension-vesting caused the decision. The Supreme Court also noted the outcome of the case might be different in pension plans where vesting was triggered by age, rather than years of service. The Court also indicated that terminating an employee because of pension vesting may violate other federal laws.

Care should be taken when another characteristic correlates with age.[129] For example, higher rates of pay often correlate with age because older workers often have worked for the employer longer and have more experience. Relative rates of pay are analytically distinct from age. However, taking action based on relative rates of pay (such a firing higher paid workers during a reduction in force) could result in liability under the ADEA if the action was motivated by age. For example, if an employer wanted to get rid of most of its older employees, it could not use relative rates of pay as an excuse for age discrimination. If a criteria results in a disparate impact because of age, the employer must establish that the criteria is a reasonable factor other than age.[130] Even though offering a higher wage increase to entry-level workers created a disparate impact based on age, the Supreme Court recognized that an employer's need to attract new workers was a reasonable factor other than age.[131]

---

[126] 29 U.S.C.A. § 631(a).

[127] 540 U.S. 581 (2004).

[128] 507 U.S. 604 (1993).

[129] Allen v. Highlands Hosp. Corp., 545 F.3d 387 (6th Cir. 2008) (laying off workers with the most years of seniority is not necessarily age discrimination).

[130] Smith v. City of Jackson, 544 U.S. 228 (2005).

[131] *Id.*

For the most part, the ADEA prohibits mandatory retirement based on age. However, the statute does allow mandatory retirement in certain instances specifically delineated in the statute. "Bona fide executives" who reach the age of 65 may be subject to mandatory retirements if for the previous two years, they were "employed in an executive or high policy making position, if such employee is entitled to an immediate non-forfeitable annual retirement benefit . . . which equals, in the aggregate, at least $44,000."[132]

State and local governments may have maximum hiring ages and mandatory retirement ages for certain public safety officers pursuant to a "bona fide hiring or retirement plan."[133] A plaintiff may state a discrimination claim under the ADEA if a hiring limit or mandatory retirement age is a subterfuge for violating other provisions of the ADEA. "A plaintiff can establish subterfuge if he or she can demonstrate that a state or local government took advantage of the exemption and imposed a mandatory retirement age for police and firefighting personnel in order to evade a different substantive provision of the statute."[134]

Some federal laws contain mandatory retirement ages. For example, federal law imposes mandatory retirement ages for pilots. The ADEA specifically allows these other mandates to be enforced. However, private employers may not use these laws to justify age discrimination against individuals not covered by such laws or regulations.[135]

The ADEA permits employers to establish that age is a "bona fide occupational qualification."[136] BFOQ is described in more depth in the chapter on Defenses.

The EEOC also has authority to exempt certain practices or policies from coverage. The EEOC has issued regulations exempting federal and state "special employment programs" for the "long-term unemployed, individuals with disabilities, members of minority groups, older workers, or youth."[137]

§ 2.22 Age and Retirement Incentives

The ADEA specifically permits "voluntary early retirement incentive programs" in certain instances.[138] The ADEA also contains specific provisions allowing health care and insurance benefits to older workers in some instances.[139] Both of these topics are complex and beyond the scope of this text.

§ 2.23 Intersectionality

A worker may face discrimination based on more than one protected trait. For example, an employer might treat older women differently or black women differently. These types of claims are often called intersectional claims.[140] In an intersectional discrimination scenario, the worker faces differential treatment based on the combined

---

[132] 29 U.S.C.A. § 631(c)(1).

[133] 29 U.S.C.A. § 623(j)(1), (2).

[134] Minch v. City of Chicago, 363 F.3d 615, 623 (7th Cir. 2004).

[135] Western Air Lines v. Criswell, 472 U.S. 400 (1985).

[136] *Western Air Lines*, 472 U.S. at 414.

[137] 29 C.F.R. § 1625.31.

[138] 29 U.S.C.A. § 623(f)(2)(B)(ii).

[139] 29 U.S.C.A. § 623(i).

[140] *See* Kimberlé Crenshaw, *Demarginalizing the Intersection of Race and Sex: A Black Feminist Critique of Antidiscrimination Doctrine, Feminist Theory and Antiracist Politics*, 1989 U. CHI. LEGAL F. 139, 141.

effect of two or more protected classes. When the protected traits fall within the same statute, there should be no issue with a plaintiff proceeding on such a claim.[141]

Difficulties arise when the intersectionality crosses statutes. For example, if a person alleges that she was treated differently because she was a woman and because she was older, she has alleged discrimination that falls under both Title VII and the ADEA. Given the purposes of the anti-discrimination statutes, plaintiffs should be able to prevail under both statutes. However, over the past decade, the courts have differentiated the proof structures available for claims under Title VII and the ADEA. This differentiation raises difficult questions about how courts should analyze intersectional claims that bridge statutes.

[141] *But see* Bradley Allan Areheart, *Intersectionality and Identity: Revisiting A Wrinkle in Title VII*, 17 GEO. MASON U. CIV. RTS. L.J. 199, 235 (2006).

Chapter 3

INDIVIDUAL DISPARATE TREATMENT

Analysis

A. PROHIBITED CONDUCT GENERALLY

§ 3.01 Title VII and the ADEA Generally

Most employment discrimination cases are brought against employers, and most of the case law in this field relates to employers' obligations under the statutes. Both Title VII and the ADEA define the employers' obligations through two, primary provisions. Under Title VII, it is an unlawful employment practice to do the following:

> (1) to fail or refuse to hire or to discharge any individual, or otherwise to discriminate against any individual with respect to his compensation, terms, conditions, or privileges of employment, because of such individual's race, color, religion, sex, or national origin[.][1]

Title VII also makes it an unlawful employment practice for an employer to do the following:

> (2) to limit, segregate, or classify his employees or applicants for employment in any way which would deprive or tend to deprive any individual of employment opportunities or otherwise adversely affect his status as an employee, because of such individual's race, color, religion, sex, or national origin.[2]

The original text of the Age Discrimination in Employment Act (ADEA) is nearly identical to Title VII, replacing age for the other protected classes.[3]

Unfortunately, Congress did not define many of the key terms in the federal discrimination statutes. Courts have interpreted this statutory language by breaking discrimination into types of discrimination and then creating proof structures that a court will use to determine whether the particular type of discrimination is proven. In the Title VII context, Congress has added additional statutory language to clarify the court-created proof structures.

Courts have created different ways of evaluating discrimination, depending on what kinds of facts a case presents.[4] The courts have given different labels or names to certain factual scenarios. Learning employment discrimination law requires learning a new field-specific vocabulary that judges and practitioners use to navigate the complex

---

1 42 U.S.C.A. § 2000e–2(a)(1).

2 *Id.* at § 2000e–2(a)(2).

3 29 U.S.C.A. § 623(a).

4 For in-depth discussion regarding how the frameworks operate see Sandra F. Sperino & Suja A. Thomas, UNEQUAL: HOW AMERICA'S COURTS UNDERMINE DISCRIMINATION LAW (Oxford 2017).

doctrine. At the outset it is worth noting that very little of this vocabulary is contained in the statutes themselves. Additionally, many of the frameworks do not derive directly from or derive only loosely from the statutory language. This is, in part, due to the fact that the Supreme Court's earliest attempts at interpreting these statutes pre-dated the rise of textualist statutory interpretation methods that happened in the late 1980s.

Individual disparate treatment cases often involve allegations that an employer treated a particular employee or group of employees differently because of a protected trait. Courts often break individual disparate treatment claims into categories depending on the kind of evidence submitted to support the case. These categories include (1) direct evidence, single-motive cases (2) circumstantial evidence, single-motive cases and (3) mixed-motive cases. The courts use a separate framework for evaluating harassment. Claims that an employer intentionally discriminated against a large group of people are sometimes evaluated under the pattern or practice framework.

If a case involves a facially neutral practice that creates a disproportionate impact, the case is evaluated under a disparate impact framework. For religion and disability, the employer may be required to accommodate an employee.[5] Finally, the courts employ separate frameworks for thinking about retaliation.

Title VII and the ADEA as originally enacted shared nearly identical statutory language with regard to the two provisions cited above. For decades, courts largely interpreted the substantive provisions of these statutes in tandem. However, beginning in the mid-2000s, the Supreme Court issued several decisions that interpreted these statutes differently.

§ 3.02 The ADA Generally

The Americans with Disabilities Act (ADA) prohibits discrimination "against a qualified individual on the basis of disability in regard to job application procedures, the hiring, advancement, or discharge of employees, employee compensation, job training, and other terms, conditions, and privileges of employment."[6]

It then further defines discrimination in a separate subsection, containing seven separate definitional sections.[7] Those provisions specifically define discrimination as including the following conduct:

> (1) limiting, segregating, or classifying a job applicant or employee in a way that adversely affects the opportunities or status of such applicant or employee because of the disability of such applicant or employee;
>
> (2) participating in a contractual or other arrangement or relationship that has the effect of subjecting a covered entity's qualified applicant or employee with a disability to the discrimination prohibited by this subchapter (such relationship includes a relationship with an employment or referral agency, labor union, an organization providing fringe benefits to an employee of the covered entity, or an organization providing training and apprenticeship programs);

---

[5] *But see* EEOC v. Abercrombie & Fitch Stores, Inc., 135 S. Ct. 2028, 2030, 192 L. Ed. 2d 35 (2015) (appearing to hold that failure to accommodate religion is a form of disparate treatment).

[6] 42 U.S.C.A. § 12112(a).

[7] *Id.* at § 12112(b).

> (3) utilizing standards, criteria, or methods of administration
>
> (A) that have the effect of discrimination on the basis of disability;
>
> (B) that perpetuates the discrimination of others who are subject to common administrative control;
>
> (4) excluding or otherwise denying equal jobs or benefits to a qualified individual because of the known disability of an individual with whom the qualified individual is known to have a relationship or association;
>
> (5)(A) not making reasonable accommodations to the known physical or mental limitations of an otherwise qualified individual with a disability who is an applicant or employee, unless such covered entity can demonstrate that the accommodation would impose an undue hardship on the operation of the business of such covered entity; or
>
> (B) denying employment opportunities to a job applicant or employee who is an otherwise qualified individual with a disability, if such denial is based on the need of such covered entity to make reasonable accommodation to the physical or mental impairments of the employee or applicant;
>
> (6) using qualification standards, employment tests or other selection criteria that screen out or tend to screen out an individual with a disability or a class of individuals with disabilities unless the standard, test or other selection criteria, as used by the covered entity, is shown to be job-related for the position in question and is consistent with business necessity; and
>
> (7) failing to select and administer tests concerning employment in the most effective manner to ensure that, when such test is administered to a job applicant or employee who has a disability that impairs sensory, manual, or speaking skills, such test results accurately reflect the skills, aptitude, or whatever other factor of such applicant or employee that such test purports to measure, rather than reflecting the impaired sensory, manual, or speaking skills of such employee or applicant (except where such skills are the factors that the test purports to measure).

Despite the differences in the statutory language between Title VII and the ADA, courts have tended to apply Title VII frameworks to ADA cases (outside of the accommodation context). However, given recent Supreme Court cases that distinguish Title VII from the ADEA, care must be taken in applying Title VII analysis in ADA cases.

§ 3.03 Section 1981 Generally

The language of 42 U.S.C.A. § 1981 differs significantly from Title VII, the ADEA, and the ADA. It provides as follows:

> All persons within the jurisdiction of the United States shall have the same right in every State and Territory to make and enforce contracts, to sue, be parties, give evidence, and to the full and equal benefit of all laws and proceedings for the security of persons and property as is enjoyed by white citizens, and shall be subject to like punishment, pains, penalties, taxes, licenses, and exactions of every kind, and to no other.

Section 1981 prohibits race discrimination in employment.

Congress amended Section 1981 to clarify that the statute applies not only to the making of contracts, but to other aspects of the employment relationship. That amendment provides that the term "make and enforce contracts" includes "the making, performance, modification, and termination of contracts, and the enjoyment of all benefits, privileges, terms, and conditions of the contractual relationship."[8]

Courts often borrow frameworks from Title VII to use in Section 1981 cases. There are differences between the statutory regimes. Litigants pursuing a race discrimination claim under Section 1981 cannot proceed under a disparate impact theory. Section 1981 only prohibits race discrimination, unlike Title VII which includes more protected classes. Despite these limits, in many ways Section 1981 is more expansive than Title VII. Litigants do not need to pursue any administrative process prior to filing a claim under Section 1981. Section 1981 provides for individual liability against supervisors, unlike Title VII which places liability on the employer. Section 1981 does not cap available compensatory and punitive damages like Title VII.

§ 3.04 Unfairness

Taken together, Title VII, the ADEA, the ADA, and Section 1981 prohibit discrimination because of race, color, religion, sex (including pregnancy), national origin, age, and disability. The statutes do not otherwise prohibit workplace conduct, even if that conduct is unfair. Instead, in most states, the presumption of at-will employment still applies. Under that concept an employer may make employment decisions based on good reasons, bad reasons, or no reason at all, subject to existing law and applicable contracts.

While the federal discrimination statutes do not generally prohibit unfair workplace conduct, such unfair conduct may be evidence of discrimination, especially when combined with other evidence.

§ 3.05 Disparate Treatment Generally

Courts often use the term "disparate treatment" to describe some of the conduct prohibited under the federal discrimination law. Disparate treatment simply means that a person is treated differently because of a protected trait, such as race or sex. For example, if an employer believes that women are not management material and promotes a man over a more qualified woman, this is disparate treatment. The employer treated the woman worse because of her sex.

The core statutes proscribe discrimination because of a protected class. "A disparate treatment claim cannot succeed unless the employee's protected trait actually played a role in that process and had a determinative influence on the outcome."[9] The courts often describe disparate treatment claims as requiring proof of motive or intent. And, it is true that many workers proceed on such claims by offering evidence that a supervisor or others acted with a bad motive.

However, it is important to remember that the statutes themselves do not require intent or motive and that a bad motive is not necessary to succeed on a claim.[10] Even

---

[8] 42 U.S.C.A. § 1981(b).

[9] Hazen Paper Co. v. Biggins, 507 U.S. 604 (1993).

[10] Stephen M. Rich, *Against Prejudice*, 80 GEO. WASH. L. REV. 1 (2011); *see also* Matthew T. Bodie, Miriam A. Cherry, Marcia L. McCormick, Jintong Tang, *The Law and Policy of People Analytics*, 88 U. Colo. L. Rev. 961, 966 (2017); Pauline T. Kim, *Data-Driven Discrimination at Work*, 58 WM. & MARY L. REV. 857

actions taken to protect a certain group of individuals can be intentional discrimination. For example in *UAW v. Johnson Controls, Inc.*,[11] the Supreme Court held that it was illegal for an employer to bar fertile women from jobs because of concern that their potential children might be exposed to chemicals and suffer birth defects. Even if the employer believed it was acting for a good reason, this is not sufficient to avoid liability for discrimination.

In the cases *Gross v. FBL Fin. Servs., Inc.*[12] and *Univ. of Tex. Sw. Med. Ctr. v. Nassar*,[13] the Supreme Court interpreted the "because of" language to be language of causation. Nonetheless, courts often speak of the discrimination statutes as requiring the plaintiff to establish intent or motive to prove a disparate treatment claim. To date, the courts have not explained with specificity what intent or motive is required and how these concepts intersect with the idea of causation. As one court noted:

> Proof of [illegal motive] is always difficult. Defendants of even minimal sophistication will neither admit animus nor leave a paper trail demonstrating it; and because most employment decisions involve an element of discretion, alternative hypotheses (including that of simple mistake) will always be possible and often plausible. Only the very best workers are completely satisfactory, and they are not likely to be discriminated against—the cost of discrimination is too great. The law tries to protect average and even below average workers against being treated more harshly than would be the case if they were of a different race, sex, religion, or national origin, but it has difficulty in achieving this goal because it is so easy to concoct a plausible reason for not hiring, or firing, or failing to promote or denying a pay raise to a worker who is not superlative.[14]

§ 3.06 Disparate Treatment Frameworks Generally

Courts often subdivide the concept of disparate treatment according to the type of evidence presented. Judges often begin analyzing discrimination cases by determining whether the worker presents direct evidence of discrimination or circumstantial evidence of discrimination.

If the worker presents direct evidence, courts tend to use a fairly simple analysis, inquiring whether the worker shows a negative outcome was caused by a protected trait. Direct evidence, described in more detail below, is evidence that demonstrates discrimination without any required inferences. The best example of direct evidence is a company policy that requires different treatment on the basis of a protected trait. For example, if a company had a policy that stated that women could not be hired as

(2017); Stephanie Bornstein, *Reckless Discrimination*, 105 CAL. L. REV. 1055, 1056 (2017); Katie R. Eyer, *That's Not Discrimination: American Beliefs and the Limits of Anti-Discrimination Law*, 96 MINN. L. REV. 1275 (2012); Melissa Hart, *Subjective Decisionmaking and Unconscious Discrimination*, 56 ALA. L. REV. 741, 745 (2005); Ann C. McGinley, *!Viva La Evolucion!: Recognizing Unconscious Motive in Title VII*, 9 CORNELL J.L. & PUB. POL'Y 415 (2000); Michael Selmi, *Proving Intentional Discrimination: The Reality of Supreme Court Rhetoric*, 86 GEO. L.J. 279 (1997); David Benjamin Oppenheimer, *Negligent Discrimination*, 141 U. PA. L. REV. 899, 900 (1993).

11 499 U.S. 187 (1991); *see also* Goodman v. Lukens Steel Co., 482 U.S. 656 (1987) (holding that union's decision not to process grievances was because of race, even if court assumed that union "leaders were favorably disposed toward minorities").

12 557 U.S. 167 (2009).

13 570 U.S. 338 (2013).

14 Riorian v. Kempiners, 831 F.2d 690 (7th Cir. 1987).

managers, the most qualified person for a manager position was a woman, and the woman was not hired, this would be direct evidence of discrimination.

Direct evidence of discrimination is becoming more rare. If evidence is not direct, courts tend to call it circumstantial evidence. Circumstantial evidence is evidence that requires additional inferences to connect the worker's protected trait with a negative outcome. For example, if a supervisor used sexist language and then later refused to promote a qualified woman, the sexist language suggests (but does not definitely prove) that sex played a role in the promotion decision. It is important to note that the discrimination statutes do not contain any language distinguishing direct from circumstantial evidence. Nor do the Federal Rules of Evidence makes such a distinction. Instead, judges have created these distinctions when interpreting the federal discrimination statutes.

Courts also draw distinctions in disparate treatment cases based on whether the case is a so-called single motive case or a mixed-motive case. In a single motive case, the factfinder is often asked to choose between two competing narratives: the worker's claim that the challenged decision was made because of a protected trait and the employer's claim that the decision was taken because of a non-discriminatory reason.

In contrast, in so-called mixed-motive cases, the factfinder may find that two or more reasons explain an outcome, both a discriminatory reason and a non-discriminatory one. For example, if two people make a hiring decision, one may act for a discriminatory reason and the other might decline to hire an applicant for a non-discriminatory reason. If a factfinder later tries to determine why the employer did not hire the applicant, the true reason may be that both discriminatory and non-discriminatory reasons played a role.

In single-motive cases relying on circumstantial evidence, courts often apply the famous *McDonnell-Douglas* three-part burden-shifting framework to analyze the facts. Outside of the single-motive context, courts often will apply a motivating factor test to Title VII disparate treatment claims. The Supreme Court has rejected the motivating factor test in ADEA cases. It is unclear as of the writing of this book whether the motivating factor test should apply in ADA and Section 1981 cases. These tests are discussed in great detail later in this chapter.

The terms "single motive" and "mixed motive" are not words that the statutes use to define discriminatory conduct. Instead, they are constructs the courts use to describe discrimination law.

B. DIRECT EVIDENCE

§ 3.07 Generally

The discrimination that is easiest to understand is a policy that expressly, on its face, treats classes differently. These policies are now rare. However, at the time Title VII was passed, some employers had policies that limited employment opportunities for workers based on race or sex. At the time the ADEA became law, employers had policies against hiring workers over a certain age or requiring employees to retire at a certain age.[15] These policies are direct evidence of discrimination in that they explicitly link a

[15] W. Air Lines, Inc. v. Criswell, 472 U.S. 400 (1985).

protected trait to a denial of employment opportunity. The courts typically rule in favor of the worker on these types of claims without using a complicated analytical structure.

Other direct evidence cases rely on comments or conduct that tie a negative employment decision to a protected trait. For example, if a supervisor refuses to promote a woman because a job is "too dangerous for a women" or fires a worker because he is "too old to do the job," these remarks would be direct evidence of discrimination.[16] When courts evaluate individual disparate treatment cases with direct evidence, they simply ask whether the direct evidence shows the employer treated the worker differently because of the protected trait.

As the evidence establishes the connection, the worker will typically prevail in a direct evidence case, unless the employer can establish a defense to liability. For example, if a gym only hired women to serve as attendants in a women's locker room, this policy would be direct evidence of discrimination. However, the employer would likely not be liable for discrimination in this context because the employer would have a defense to liability. In a small subset of cases, like in this example, sex can be a bona fide occupational qualification ("BFOQ"), which is allowed under Title VII.

Outside of the context of facially discriminatory policies, courts have had a difficult time defining direct evidence, and definitions regarding what constitutes direct evidence vary. Direct evidence of discrimination can be described as "evidence, that, if believed, proves the existence of a fact in issue without inference or presumption . . . [and] is composed of only the most blatant remarks, whose intent could be nothing other than to discriminate on the basis of some impermissible factor."[17] One court has described direct evidence as that which "essentially requires an admission by the employer," and explained that "such evidence is rare."[18]

Evidence that is not considered to be direct evidence of discrimination is labeled as circumstantial evidence. Circumstantial evidence "allows the trier of fact to *infer* intentional discrimination by the decisionmaker, typically through a longer chain of inferences."[19]

Given the ambiguity inherent in these definitions, courts have been unable when faced with various factual scenarios to consistently determine when evidence rises to the level of direct evidence and when it constitutes circumstantial evidence. The use of powerful racial epithets is often seen as direct evidence of discrimination.[20] However, the use of epithets in other contexts may not be regarded as direct evidence. For example, in one case a plaintiff argued that she had direct evidence of discrimination because she was referred to as a "bitch" in written evaluations.[21] The court disagreed. "Although this pejorative term may support an inference that an employment decision is discriminatory

---

[16] Price Waterhouse v. Hopkins, 490 U.S. 228 (1989).

[17] Rojas v. Fla., 285 F.3d 1339, 1342 n. 2 (11th Cir. 2002) (per curiam).

[18] Argyropoulos v. City of Alton, 539 F.3d 724, 733 (7th Cir. 2008); Vaughn v. Epworth Villa, 537 F.3d 1147, 1154–55 (10th Cir. 2008).

[19] Caskey v. Colgate-Palmolive Co., 535 F.3d 585, 593 (7th Cir. 2008).

[20] *See* Kendall v. Block, 821 F.2d 1142 (5th Cir. 1987) (using racial epithet may be direct evidence of discrimination); Brewer v. Muscle Shoals Bd. of Educ., 790 F.2d 1515 (11th Cir. 1986).

[21] Neuren v. Adduci, Mastriani, Meeks & Schill, 43 F.3d 1507, 1513 (D.C. Cir. 1995).

under different circumstances, . . . in itself, the term is not always conclusive of sex discrimination."[22]

At times, courts consider negative statements made by the decisionmaker and referencing a protected trait to be direct evidence of discrimination.[23] At times, the courts require these statements to be made at or near the time of the allegedly discriminatory action to constitute direct evidence.

§ 3.08 Uniformly Applied Selection Devices Adopted for Proscribed Purposes

Uniformly applied policies or practice can constitute intentional discrimination if the policy or practice is adopted or implemented because of a protected trait. *Albemarle Paper Co. v. Moody*[24] held that a uniformly imposed paper and pencil pre-employment test would violate Title VII if instituted for the purpose of disadvantaging minority applicants. *New York City Transit Auth. v. Beazer*[25] provided that if a rule prohibiting employment of persons on methadone maintenance treatment had been adopted to discourage or disadvantage people based on their race, the rule would have violated Title VII.

It would be unlawful discrimination for an employer to implement educational requirements or tests for the purpose of disadvantaging people based on race.[26] An employer could not adopt a veteran's preference for the purpose of increasing the number of men in its work force.[27] A uniformly applied practice of rejecting all unsolicited "walk-on" applicants will violate federal discrimination law if it is imposed for the purpose of preferring one race over another.[28] An employer that imposed physical requirements for the purpose of disadvantaging women would be engaging in sex discrimination.[29] A rule requiring employees to speak English at work would be illegal if the purpose was to deny or discourage employment of workers of certain races or national origins. A rule stating that the company will only hire U.S citizens would constitute illegal discrimination if it was created to avoid hiring people of certain races or from certain countries.

C. CIRCUMSTANTIAL EVIDENCE, SINGLE MOTIVE

§ 3.09 Circumstantial Evidence

When a worker lacks direct evidence, the courts often characterize the worker's evidence as circumstantial. Circumstantial evidence is evidence that suggests, but does not definitively prove, that a protected trait influenced an outcome.

---

[22] *Id.*

[23] EEOC v. Alton Packaging Corp., 901 F.2d 920 (11th Cir. 1990) (general manager's statement that if it were his company he would not hire blacks is direct evidence of discriminatory animus in failing to promote the plaintiff).

[24] 422 U.S. 405 (1975); *Accord*, Washington v. Davis, 426 U.S. 229 (1976).

[25] 440 U.S. 568 (1979).

[26] Griggs v. Duke Power Co., 401 U.S. 424 (1971).

[27] Personnel Administrator of Mass. v. Feeney, 442 U.S. 256 (1979).

[28] Furnco Construction Corp. v. Waters, 438 U.S. 567 (1978).

[29] Dothard v. Rawlinson, 433 U.S. 321 (1977).

In 1973, the Supreme Court decided *McDonnell Douglas Corp. v. Green*.[30] In that case, the Supreme Court developed the now ubiquitous *McDonnell Douglas* test. This test is the primary test that courts use to analyze single-motive disparate treatment cases based on circumstantial evidence.

For example, if a woman alleges that her supervisor regularly referred to women in a demeaning way and then fired her for no valid reason, the court would likely analyze this case under the *McDonnell Douglas* framework. The woman's case is a disparate treatment case in that she is alleging the supervisor intentionally took her sex into account when firing her. The case is based on circumstantial evidence because her evidence does not prove a direct connection between the comments and the firing. The case is a single-motive case because the facts suggest that only one reason motivated the supervisor.

§ 3.10 *McDonnell Douglas* Overview

McDonnell Douglas Corp. v. Green[31] is one of the most important cases in employment discrimination jurisprudence. It established an analytical framework for evaluating certain kinds of discrimination cases. Courts often use this test in individual disparate treatment cases that rely on circumstantial (as opposed to direct) evidence. The test is used in single motive cases, cases in which the key question is whether to believe the worker's claim (that a protected trait played a role in a negative outcome) versus the employer's explanation (that the negative outcome resulted from a legitimate, non-discriminatory reason).

Before discussing the case, a few observations are helpful. First, the Supreme Court decided this case in 1973, long before a strong form of textualism came to prominence in the late 1980s. This means that the test enunciated by the Supreme Court does not draw significantly from the text of Title VII.

Second, courts have modified the test over the past several decades, adding numerous supporting doctrines to the test. Fully understanding the test means also grappling with other concepts often used by courts alongside *McDonnell Douglas*.

Third, the Supreme Court specifically noted that the test should be modified in cases involving facts different than the ones presented in *McDonnell Douglas*. Although the test is meant to be a fluid one that changes with the facts of particular cases, lower courts do not always apply it in a fluid manner.

Fourth, even though it has been several decades since the court created the test, courts are still confused about aspects of the test and there are many differences among the circuit courts regarding how to articulate the test.

Finally, the Supreme Court has specifically rejected the dichotomy between direct evidence and circumstantial evidence in so-called mixed-motive cases, reasoning that Title VII's language does not provide for such a distinction.[32] Nonetheless, courts continue to distinguish direct and circumstantial evidence when deciding whether it is appropriate to use *McDonnell Douglas*.

---

[30] 411 U.S. 792 (1973).

[31] 411 U.S. 792 (1973).

[32] Desert Palace, Inc. v. Costa, 539 U.S. 90 (2003).

The case that eventually found its way to the Supreme Court was originally bench tried by a district court judge.[33] One aspect of *McDonnell Douglas* that is often overlooked is that the Supreme Court implemented the test at a time when Title VII did not explicitly provide a right to jury trial in individual cases. The Court designed a test to be applied by judges during bench trials and not juries.

Although *McDonnell Douglas* is considered a Title VII discrimination framework, the trial court viewed plaintiff Percy Green's claims as being a discrimination claim under 42 U.S.C. § 1981 and a Title VII retaliation claim.[34] For procedural reasons, the trial court dismissed Mr. Green's Title VII discrimination claim. The trial court conducted its analysis through the lens of Title VII's retaliation provision, arguing that such an analysis would also resolve the section 1981 claim.[35]

The trial court stated that the plaintiff claimed he was not rehired at McDonnell Douglas because of his participation in civil rights activities and because he opposed practices made illegal by Title VII. The employer contended that it did not rehire Mr. Green because he participated in two activities, a stall-in in which people blocked ingress and egress to and from the McDonnell Douglas facility and a lock-in, where people locked employees into part of the facility so they could not leave at the end of a work shift.

After a bench trial, the trial court judge made the following factual findings. The plaintiff had worked at McDonnell Douglas since 1956, and the trial court judge found that the Mr. Green was a qualified mechanic with a satisfactory work record. In 1962, Mr. Green asked about working in another division of the company and was warned against doing so because of the effect it would have on his union seniority and also because work in the second department was expected to decline. The job in the new department was not a unionized position.

In 1963, plaintiff applied for a job in the new department, and he again received warnings about the effect of such a move on his union security and the likelihood that work in the new department would decline. Mr. Green accepted the job in the new department. Mr. Green alleged that he had not been given sufficient training in his new position; however, the trial court judge found that he did not receive training because he had already received training in his prior position.

In August of 1964, McDonnell Douglas laid off Mr. Green.[36] Mr. Green testified that he participated in a number of civil rights activities in the St. Louis area and that the company was aware of these activities at the time it made layoff decisions. The trial court found that Mr. Green's layoff was not due to his civil rights activities. However, it also held that any Section 1981 claim based on the layoff was untimely. Mr. Green could not file a claim based on the layoff under Title VII because Title VII did not become effective until the following year, 1965.

The trial court judge described the layoff in detail in his order. The company originally laid off workers in Mr. Green's department in the spring of 1964, when McDonnell Douglas completed its work on the Gemini simulator. Mr. Green was not part

---

[33] Green v. McDonnell-Douglas Corp., 318 F. Supp. 846, 847 (E.D. Mo. 1970), rev'd sub nom. Green v. McDonnell Douglas Corp., 463 F.2d 337 (8th Cir. 1972).

[34] *Green*, 318 F. Supp. at 847.

[35] *Id.* at 850.

[36] The court dismissed plaintiff's claim that the layoff violated Section 1981 because the court held the plaintiff did not raise the claim within the applicable statute of limitations. *Id.* at 849.

of the original layoff. Prior to the next round of layoffs, the company asked workers to voluntarily take a test to determine eligibility for other jobs in the company. According to the court, Mr. Green refused to take the test.

He also complained to company officials that his layoff was because of his race and civil rights activities. According to the court, plaintiff indicated that he only wanted another job in the company if it did not involve a reduction in job status. The company was not able to find a comparable job, and it laid off the plaintiff along with eight other workers.

After the layoff, Mr. Green engaged in many protest activities, which the trial court described as follows:

> After being laid off, plaintiff initiated protests by writing letters, filing charges, picketing, and various other means to protest his layoff. These various protest activities culminated in a demonstration in October of 1964. Plaintiff and other members of the Congress on Racial Equality organization stalled their cars on the main roads leading to defendant's plant at the time of a shift change. The second demonstration led by plaintiff was at the Roberts Building and resulted in the employees of the defendant being locked in the building at quitting time.[37]

Mr. Green admitted participating in the stall-in. Based on his participation in that event, Mr. Green pleaded guilty to obstructing traffic and paid a fine. It is unclear from the record whether Mr. Green participated in the lock-in, other than not stopping other employees from locking the door.

Mr. Green reapplied for a job at McDonnell Douglas in July of 1965. The company did not rehire Mr. Green. The company claimed the reason it did not rehire Mr. Green was because of his conduct in the stall-in and lock-in.

Without a complicated analysis, the trial court found that the company did not refuse to rehire Mr. Green because of his race or because of legitimate civil rights activities. The court, sitting as factfinder in the case, found that the company refused to rehire Mr. Green because of his participation in the lock-in and stall-in, which the court found were outside the scope of permissible protest. The judge dismissed Mr. Green's complaint with prejudice. Although one might disagree with the factual conclusions of the trial court, the stated analysis was direct and simple. The trial court simply answered the question whether McDonnell Douglas refused to rehire Mr. Green based on his participation in lawful civil rights protests.

The *McDonnell Douglas* case became more complicated when the plaintiff appealed it to the Eighth Circuit Court of Appeals.[38] The appellate court first affirmed the trial court's decision that Mr. Green's section 1981 claim based on his layoff was untimely. The rest of the case was not so straightforward. The three-judge panel produced the panel's opinion, a concurring opinion by Judge Lay and a partial dissent by Judge Johnsen.

The court considered whether Mr. Green stated a claim for retaliation under Title VII based on failure to rehire. The appellate court stated that the record did not demonstrate that Mr. Green participated in the lock-in; therefore, it only considered

---

[37] *Id.* at 848.

[38] Green v. McDonnell Douglas Corp., 463 F.2d 337 (8th Cir. 1972).

whether participating in the stall-in was a sufficient basis for the refusal to rehire.[39] Viewing the response to the stall-in through the lens of Title VII's retaliation provision, the appellate court held that the provision did not protect Mr. Green because the stall-in was not a legal activity. The appellate court affirmed the lower court regarding the core of the case.

The third issue the appellate court considered was whether the trial court properly dismissed Mr. Green's Title VII discrimination claim. Prior to its ruling on the bench trial, the trial court issued a separate order dismissing Mr. Green's Title VII failure to hire discrimination claim. The trial court dismissed this claim because the EEOC only made a reasonable cause finding on the retaliation claim and did not make a finding on the discrimination claim. The appellate court held that the trial court's ruling was erroneous, that Mr. Green had met the prerequisites for filing his discrimination claim, and that the trial court should have considered that claim. The appellate court held that the trial court must consider the discrimination claim, which is separate from a retaliation claim.

Part V of the opinion is where the seeds of what later became the *McDonnell Douglas* test appear.[40] The court opined that subjective judgments by the employer were entitled to less weight than objective ones. The court further opined that once a black applicant showed he was qualified for and was denied a job, this creates a prima facie case of discrimination. The burden then passes to the employer to show a substantial relationship between the reason for the denial and the job requirements. The court concluded, "if McDonnell's refusal to rehire Green rests upon management's personal dislike for Green or personal distaste for his conduct in the civil rights field, Green is entitled to some relief."[41] It did not explain how such dislike would definitely constitute race discrimination.

Judge Lay filed a concurring opinion. He agreed with the rest of the panel regarding the need to retry the Title VII discrimination claim, as the plaintiff had not been given a full opportunity to present his case. However, he noted that if the employer refused to rehire Mr. Green because of his participation in the lock-in and Mr. Green did not participate in the lock-in, this would be evidence of pretext. Judge Lay also questioned the trial court judge's factual finding that McDonnell Douglas based its rehire decision only on unlawful activities, arguing that the evidence showed the company also based its decision, at least in part, on lawful protest activities. In light of this dual motivation, Judge Lay believed it was inappropriate for the company to use a subjective reason to support its decision. Instead, he believed the company should be required to establish that the legal protest activities played no role in the rehire decision.

Senior Circuit Court Judge Johnsen dissented, in part. He agreed with the parts of the decision affirming the dismissal of the section 1981 claim based on the statute of limitations. He also agreed that Title VII's retaliation provision does not protect a person who engages in unlawful protest activities. He also agreed that the trial court erred in ruling that a plaintiff must have a reasonable cause finding by the EEOC before proceeding on his race discrimination claim.

---

[39] Under the later-created *McDonnell Douglas* test if the employer did not believe that Mr. Green participated in the lock-in, but used that as a reason to terminate him, this would be evidence of pretext.

[40] *Green*, 463 F.2d at 344.

[41] *Id.*

However, Judge Johnsen disagreed about Mr. Green's role in the lock-in and would have affirmed the trial court judge's finding that Mr. Green participated in it. Both the trial court and Judge Johnsen believed that Mr. Green's leadership role in the group that effectuated the lock-in, along with his knowledge of and perhaps tacit approval of the lock-in were sufficient participation in it. Judge Johnsen also disagreed with the legal test created by the panel regarding subjective decisionmaking. He also thought that the plaintiff was given ample discovery and opportunity to present his race discrimination claim, despite the trial judge's ruling on the EEOC administrative issue.

After the panel issued its original opinion, it reconsidered it. It then issued a revised opinion, in which it struck Part V of the original opinion and substituted a new Part V. Judge Lay joined in the revised opinion, and reaffirmed his original concurring opinion. Judge Johnsen filed a supplemental dissenting opinion.

The new Part V restated the original opinion's concerns about subjective decisionmaking.[42] Citing to *Griggs v. Duke Power Co.*, the new Part V stated that judicial acceptance of subjective decisions must be limited or else the promises of Title VII would prove illusory.

The new Part V slightly refined the prima facie case by stating that a worker may show discrimination by establishing that he applied for a job for which he was qualified and the employer refused to hire him, but the position remained open. The new Part V also stated that on remand, Mr. Green should have the opportunity to show that the reasons given by the company for its refusal to hire him (the lock-in and the stall-in) were pretexts for discrimination or "otherwise show the presence of racially discriminatory hiring practices by McDonnell which affected its decision."[43] In the old Part V, the discussion of pretext was limited to a footnote. The new Part V more prominently discussed pretext, addressing the concerns outlined in Judge Lay's original concurrence.

The new Part V omitted the court's earlier discussion expressing skepticism that Mr. Green's activities would affect his job performance if the company rehired him, although the court included a footnote indicating that the company's claim that Mr. Green actively participated in the lock-in was not supported.

The new dissent tried to articulate the changes between the old Part V and the new Part V, and the effects these changes would have on remand. However, Judge Johnsen noted that trial court judge would have a difficult time parsing the two Part Vs and understanding what changes the new Part V commanded.

The Supreme Court held oral argument in the *McDonnell Douglas* case on March 28, 1973, and issued its opinion on May 14, 1973. By the time the Supreme Court heard the case, almost nine years had passed since McDonnell Douglas laid off Mr. Green. It had been more than seven years since the company refused to rehire him. Importantly, the Supreme Court decided the case within the first decade of Title VII's passage. McDonnell Douglas was one of the first cases in which the Supreme Court considered any aspect of Title VII.

Justice Lewis Powell delivered the opinion of the unanimous court. Justice Powell, appointed by President Richard Nixon, had served on the Court for a little over a year

---

[42] *Id.* at 353.

[43] *Id.*

at the time the opinion came down. The Court described the case as being about the "proper order and nature of proof" under Title VII.[44]

The Supreme Court found it unnecessary to resolve the factual dispute about whether Mr. Green participated in the lock-in.[45] The Supreme Court also noted that the question of whether the 1964 layoff decision was based on race was not before the Court. Nor did the Court consider whether Title VII's retaliation provision protected employees who engaged in unlawful protests, as Mr. Green did not raise that issue.[46]

The core of the opinion starts with the procedural question of whether Title VII required Mr. Green to obtain a reasonable cause finding from the EEOC before proceeding on his race discrimination claim based on the company's decision not to rehire him. The Court held that a plaintiff is not required to obtain a reasonable cause determination from the EEOC prior to filing a claim in court. It also held that Mr. Green should be allowed a full opportunity to present his race discrimination claim at the trial court level.

The rest of the opinion covered the order and allocation of proof in Title VII discrimination cases. Borrowing from *Griggs v. Duke Power Co.*, the Court asserted that the purpose of Title VII is to stop discriminatory preferences in employment.[47] Title VII is designed "to assure equality of employment opportunities and to eliminate those discriminatory practices and devices which have fostered racially stratified job environments to the disadvantage of minority citizens."[48] The Court continued:

> The broad, overriding interest, shared by employer, employee, and consumer, is efficient and trustworthy workmanship assured through fair and racially neutral employment and personnel decisions. In the implementation of such decisions, it is abundantly clear that Title VII tolerates no racial discrimination, subtle or otherwise.[49]

After this policy discussion, the Court specifically pointed out that the appellate court opinion lacked harmony, noting the separate opinions and that the final result was not clear.[50] What the Supreme Court failed to mention is that the trial court judge did not exhibit the same confusion that existed at the appellate court. Indeed, the trial court judge saw the case as the Supreme Court framed it. There was a factual dispute as to the reason that the company refused to rehire Mr. Green, and the job of the trial court judge in a bench trial was to resolve the factual dispute. The appellate court issued a confusing opinion about how trial courts should consider evidence in Title VII cases; however, it does not appear that the trial court judge was confused. Thus, the *McDonnell Douglas* case at the Supreme Court level starts from a slightly problematic premise. The appellate court was confused, but it is uncertain whether this confusion was endemic or cabined to three judges on one appellate court.

Without any reference to the text of Title VII or to any other source of authority, the Supreme Court articulated the three-part burden-shifting test that is now (in a modified

---

[44] McDonnell Douglas Corp. v. Green, 411 U.S. 792, 793 (1973).

[45] *Id.* at 795 n. 3.

[46] *Id.* at 797 n.6.

[47] *Id.* at 800.

[48] *Id.*

[49] *Id.* at 801.

[50] *Id.*

form) known as the *McDonnell Douglas* test. It is important to point out that the Supreme Court articulated a test that was supposed to be used by trial court judges during bench trials in Title VII discrimination cases. Title VII did not yet provide for jury trials in individual disparate treatment cases. The Court then articulated the three-part burden-shifting test discussed in detail below.

The Court first examined whether Mr. Green met the first step, the prima facie case. The Court held that Mr. Green satisfied the prima face case. He belonged to a racial minority, he applied for a job at McDonnell Douglas for which he was qualified, McDonnell Douglas did not hire him for the job, and the job remained open after McDonnell Douglas made the decision not to hire him. In an important footnote, footnote 13, the Court stated that the exact factors of the prima facie case should change, depending on the underlying facts of the case. One of the problems with the *McDonnell Douglas* test is that the lower courts have not always been attentive to footnote 13 and have failed to appropriately modify the *McDonnell Douglas* test so that it makes sense given the facts of a particular case.

After the prima facie case, the burden shifts to the employer to "articulate some legitimate, nondiscriminatory reason" for its decision.[51] The Court held that the company met its burden by showing that it did not rehire Mr. Green because of his participation in unlawful protests. The Supreme Court explicitly rejected the idea that a court should be skeptical if a company provides a subjective reason for its decision that is not directly related to the ability to perform the job.[52]

The Court then stated that the plaintiff should be afforded the ability to show that the employer's stated reason was pretext. The Court did not clarify whether pretext was the only way to rebut the employer's showing. Nor did it clarify how the evidence presented in the prima facie case would intersect with the pretext inquiry. The Court noted that the plaintiff could show pretext by demonstrating that white employees who engaged in similar conduct as the stall-in were retained or rehired.

The Court further noted that the following factors might be relevant to the pretext inquiry: "facts as to the petitioner's treatment of respondent during his prior term of employment; petitioner's reaction, if any, to respondent's legitimate civil rights activities; and petitioner's general policy and practice with respect to minority employment," including statistics about whether the employer's general practices resulted in a pattern or practice of discrimination.[53] It then noted that Mr. Green should be given a full and fair opportunity to show that the employer's stated reason was a cover-up for race discrimination.

The Court then made an important move that forever impacted the course of all discrimination law. The Court distinguished Mr. Green's case from the *Griggs* case. In *Griggs*, the Court recognized a theory of discrimination called disparate impact, where a facially neutral job requirement disproportionately affects a particular protected class without a sufficient reason for using the job requirement. In *McDonnell Douglas*, the Court affirmed a distinction between cases like Mr. Green's (which came to be known as individual disparate treatment cases) and cases like *Griggs* (known as disparate impact cases). Although the words disparate treatment and disparate impact did not appear in

---

[51] *Id.*

[52] *Id.* at 803.

[53] *Id.* at 804–05.

the original operative language of Title VII, the Court started to separate these two ideas as deriving from different provisions of Title VII and requiring different proof structures.[54]

Although the Supreme Court mentioned the term show or "burden" at three different junctures in the *McDonnell Douglas* test, it did not define what the term meant. In civil procedure, there are three common ways that the term "burden" is used. The term "burden" can refer to a burden of production, meaning the party who must come forward with evidence. The term can also refer to a burden of persuasion, which means the party who must prove the truth of its assertions (in a civil case typically by a preponderance of the evidence). The word "burden" can also refer to burden of proof, which is a confusing term. Sometimes the words "burden of proof" refer only to a burden of persuasion. However, at other times, the term is used to refer to both the burdens of production and persuasion. This ambiguity in the original *McDonnell Douglas* opinion would require the Court to revisit the test in the future.

§ 3.11 The Three-Step *McDonnell Douglas* Model

McDonnell Douglas Corp. v. Green[55] established an analytical model for cases of individual disparate treatment where there is no direct evidence. This is accomplished by a three-step procedure of shifting evidentiary obligations.

In step one, plaintiff establishes a *prima facie* case by presenting evidence from which an inference of illegal discrimination is created. If plaintiff establishes the basic elements of a *prima facie* case along the *McDonnell Douglas* model, this creates a presumption of discrimination "because we presume these acts, if otherwise unexplained, are more likely than not based on the consideration of impermissible factors."[56] Such a showing does not merely *permit* a fact-finder to infer that defendant was illegally motivated. Unless the defendant produces legally adequate evidence to meet and refute the inference drawn from the prima facie case, the fact-finder is *required*, as a matter of law, to render judgment in favor of the plaintiff.[57]

In step two, the defendant must "articulate a legitimate, nondiscriminatory reason" for its treatment of plaintiff. Defendant's burden is to present "reasons" which are "clear and reasonably specific."[58] As explained in greater detail below, in this second step, the defendant only has the burden of production, not persuasion. This is an odd feature of the *McDonnell Douglas* test. At the second stage, the burden of production only shifts.

Once the employer articulates a legitimate, non-discriminatory reason, the burden of production returns to the plaintiff. In step three, the plaintiff must show that the employer's reason is pretext or evidence suggesting that the real reason for the outcome was the plaintiff's protected trait.

---

[54] *See generally* Sandra F. Sperino, *Rethinking Discrimination Law*, 110 MICH. L. REV. 69 (2011).

[55] 411 U.S. 792 (1973).

[56] Furnco Construction Corp. v. Waters, 438 U.S. 567 (1978).

[57] Texas Department of Community Affairs v. Burdine, 450 U.S. 248 (1981). In this regard the inference created by the prima facie showing is not merely a "permissible" inference; the inference is "mandatory."

[58] *Id.*

§ 3.12 The Prima Facie Case

Step one of the *McDonnell Douglas* test requires the plaintiff to establish a prima facie case.[59] In the *McDonnell Douglas* case itself, the Supreme Court articulated the prima facie case as follows: (i) plaintiff belonged to a racial minority, (ii) he applied and was qualified for a job for which the employer was seeking applicants, (iii) despite his qualifications plaintiff was rejected, and (iv) after plaintiff's rejection, the position remained open and the employer continued to seek applicants of plaintiff's qualifications.

In the *McDonnell Douglas* case itself, the plaintiff alleged that the company refused to re-hire him because of his race and because he participated in activities protesting the company's practices. Therefore, the test included factors that centered on this specific factual scenario. For example, the first factor relates to race discrimination and the remaining ones center on whether the company kept the position open and continued to interview other applicants.

The specific factors of the prima facie case must be modified in cases involving other facts.[60] For example, the first factor should be modified to take into account the type of discrimination alleged, and the remaining factors may be modified to reflect the type of negative outcome alleged by the plaintiff. Specific modifications are discussed in greater detail below. The *McDonnell Douglas* model "was never intended to be rigid, mechanized or ritualistic."[61] Ultimately, the inquiry is whether plaintiff was rejected under circumstances which give rise to an inference of unlawful discrimination.

The prima facie case is not meant to be an onerous obstacle. If the plaintiff establishes, the prima facie case, a rebuttable presumption of discrimination arises. If the defendant fails to rebut the presumption, judgment in the plaintiff's favor is technically required. However, in practice this scenario happens very infrequently because it is common for the defendant to offer a legitimate, non-discriminatory reason for its conduct. Absent other evidence of discrimination, the failure of the plaintiff to establish each of the factors in the prima facie case may result in a judgment in favor of the defendant.[62]

§ 3.13 Prima Facie Case, First Factor

While *McDonnell Douglas* spoke in terms of plaintiff being a member of a "racial minority," the *McDonnell Douglas* standard also is applied in cases involving discrimination because of color, national origin, religion, sex, age, and disability. Now, the element is widely restated in terms of plaintiff simply being a member of a "protected class." In most cases, the plaintiff will have no difficulty establishing that she is a member of a protected class, and the defendant often concedes the first element of the prima facie case.

---

[59] At the summary judgment stage, the plaintiff would only need to establish that there is a genuine dispute of material fact as to the elements. Fed.R.Civ.P. 56(a).

[60] McDonnell Douglas Corp. v. Green, 411 U.S. 792, 803 n.13 (1973).

[61] Furnco Construction Corp. v. Waters, 438 U.S. 567 (1978).

[62] It should be noted that if the defendant provides evidence to support its legitimate, non-discriminatory reason, a court is not required to determine whether the plaintiff meets the prima facie case.

Until the 2008 amendments to the ADA, plaintiffs often had difficulty establishing that they were a person with a disability, as defined by the ADA. It is now easier for ADA plaintiffs to prove membership in a protected class.

For a discussion of perceived protected traits, *see* Chapter 2 (§ 2.02).

§ 3.14 Prima Facie Case, Second Factor

In the *McDonnell Douglas* case, the Supreme Court articulated the second step of the prima facie case as follows: "he applied and was qualified for a job for which the employer was seeking applicants." In modern cases, courts often state the second element as requiring that the plaintiff possessed the required qualifications for the desired position (in promotion and hiring cases).[63] In cases involving firings or other negative actions, courts will often require the worker to establish she was qualified for the position held.

The second step is designed to eliminate one of the most common reasons for rejecting an applicant, the lack of the ability to do the job. In *McDonnell Douglas* the plaintiff established this factor by proving that he had previously worked for defendant at the position for which he was applying. The parties conceded that his work performance was satisfactory.

Most courts conclude that a plaintiff is "qualified" if he establishes that he possesses the objective prerequisites for the job established by the employer.[64] For example, if a truck driver position is available, a successful applicant would need to possess the required license to drive a truck. If the plaintiff did not possess such a license, the worker would not be able to prevail using the *McDonnell Douglas* test. The inference to be drawn is that plaintiff was rejected, not because of his protected trait but because he did not possess the established credentials. If the employer has no posted or established qualifications, proof that the applicant had the skill or ability to perform essential job duties will prove that she was "qualified."[65]

It is not appropriate at the second step to analyze whether the plaintiff met the employer's subjective expectations. For example, if an employer sought a marketing director and required applicants to possess charisma, the employer's subjective belief that an applicant did not possess charisma would not be an appropriate inquiry in the prima facie case. However, the employer could articulate this reason in step two of the *McDonnell Douglas* inquiry (that it possessed a legitimate, non-discriminatory reason for acting).

A few courts have held that a *prima facie* showing requires plaintiff to prove qualifications "equal or superior to" those possessed by the person selected to fill the vacancy. This is based upon a rationale that only proof of a comparative, qualitative parity creates an inference that plaintiff was rejected for improper reasons.[66] However, it is not appropriate to place such a burden on the plaintiff in the second step of the prima facie case.[67] This comparative concept of "qualified" tends to distort the *McDonnell*

---

[63] Stucke v. City of Philadelphia, No. 15–2303, 2017 WL 1363874, at *3 (3d Cir. Apr. 12, 2017).

[64] Nicholson v. Hyannis Air Serv., Inc., 580 F.3d 1116, 1123 (9th Cir. 2009); Mitchell v. Baldrige, 759 F.2d 80 (D.C. Cir.1985); Muldrew v. Anheuser-Busch, Inc., 728 F.2d 989 (8th Cir. 1984).

[65] McDonnell Douglas Corp. v. Green, 411 U.S. 792 (1973).

[66] *E.g.*, Gairola v. Virginia Dep't of General Services, 753 F.2d 1281 (4th Cir. 1985).

[67] Johnson v. AutoZone, Inc., 768 F. Supp. 2d 1124, 1143 (N.D. Ala. 2011) (noting that "relative qualifications belong in the rebuttal stage). Some courts make this inquiry in the last stage of the prima facie

Douglas model and places an inappropriate initial burden upon the plaintiff. The relative superiority of two qualified applicants is more properly part of defendant's burden of articulating a legitimate reason for its decision than it is an element of plaintiff's prima facie case.

In some hiring and promotion cases, plaintiff must prove that the employer knew she was seeking employment.[68] While a formal application for a specific vacancy is not required, a general, unfocused inquiry about potential vacancies, or a request for an application form which is never returned to the employer, will not suffice.[69] An application remains viable for a reasonable period of time.

There are many factual scenarios where the plaintiff is not required to establish that she sought the available position. Where "the employer used an informal and subjective hiring process," had a reason to consider the plaintiff for a position, but failed to do so, the plaintiff may still establish the second element of the test.[70] Likewise, in hiring or promotion cases where the discriminatory conduct at issue is the failure to properly advertise open positions to steer decisions to favor certain protected classes and disfavor others, no formal application is required.[71] It would also be inappropriate to require the plaintiff to establish she applied for a position when the employer engaged in conduct to deter her from applying or failed to provide notice that a position was available. A formal application is also not required in cases where the worker reasonably believes that an application would be futile.[72] A formal application may not be required where the plaintiff made reasonable efforts to make his interest in a position known.

In hiring or promotion cases, the plaintiff must prove that a vacancy existed.[73] The vacancy must be of the same type as the job for which the plaintiff applied.

§ 3.15 Prima Facie Case, Third Factor

The *McDonnell Douglas* case involved a plaintiff's claim that his employer refused to rehire him. In that fact scenario, the Supreme Court articulated the third step of the prima facie case to require that "despite his qualifications plaintiff was rejected." As the test applies to cases involving many different factual scenarios, courts often change this third requirement to be more useful in a wider variety of cases. Courts often state the third factor as requiring the plaintiff to show that she was subjected to an "adverse action."[74]

In many cases the third factor is the easiest one for plaintiffs to establish. For example, in a failure to hire or promote case, the plaintiff merely proves that she was

---

case. De la Torre v. Lockheed Martin Corp., No. CIV. 13–127 RBK/AMD, 2014 WL 2931268, at *8 (D.N.J. June 30, 2014).

[68] Carmichael v. Birmingham Saw Works, 738 F.2d 1126 (11th Cir. 1984).

[69] EEOC v. F & D Distributing, Inc., 728 F.2d 1281 (10th Cir. 1984).

[70] Parker v. Chilton Cty. Bd. of Educ., No. 2:12-CV-0650-MEF, 2014 WL 116341, at *7 (M.D. Ala. Jan. 13, 2014).

[71] Volling v. Kurtz Paramedic Servs., Inc., 840 F.3d 378, 383–84 (7th Cir. 2016).

[72] Warshaw v. Concentra Health Servs., 719 F. Supp. 2d 484, 491 (E.D. Pa. 2010).

[73] Phillips v. Joint Legislative Committee, 637 F.2d 1014 (5th Cir. 1981); McLean v. Phillips-Ramsey, Inc., 624 F.2d 70 (9th Cir. 1980).

[74] Ingram v. Pac. Gas & Elec. Co., No. 15–16069, 2017 WL 1735320, at *1 (9th Cir. May 3, 2017). Bejar v. Dep't of Veterans Affairs, No. 16–3218, 2017 WL 1149084, at *1 (10th Cir. Mar. 28, 2017).

rejected or was not offered a position within a reasonable period of time. If plaintiff rejects or does not accept the tender of the job sought, there would be no prima facie case.

Courts routinely hold that the following actions count as an adverse action: failure to hire, termination, failure to promote, and compensation decisions. *Hishon v. King & Spalding*[75] held that awarding law firm partnerships was an adverse action under Title VII. Even though the determination of who should be a partner may not be an employment decision, *eligibility* for promotion to a partner was a "term, condition, or privilege" of employment granted to those hired as associates.

An employee may also prevail if the employee faces a constructive discharge.[76] A constructive discharge occurs when an employee faces discrimination based on a protected trait and a reasonable employee would have resigned under the circumstances. For example, if an employee faces substantial racial harassment and quits due to the harassment, the employee faced a constructive discharge.

Outside of these categories, there is disagreement among the courts about what counts as an adverse action. Some courts have held that negative evaluations, threats of termination, and denying an employee a lateral transfer do not rise to the level of actionable discrimination, even if the employee's protected trait played a negative role in the decision.[77] However, other courts have held that the actions can form the basis of a discrimination claim.[78]

The concept of an "adverse action" as a limit on the reach of the federal discrimination statutes is not an accurate view of the statutes. Title VII, the ADEA, and the ADA all prohibit an employer from limiting the "terms, conditions, or privileges" of employment based on a protected trait. Recent cases focusing on the "adverse action" concept as a limit stray far from this statutory language. In the labor law and arbitration contexts, the words "terms or condition" of employment are construed broadly to reach a wide swath of conduct that occurs in the workplace.

The statutes also prohibit actions that "limit . . . employees . . . in any way which would deprive or tend to deprive any individual of employment opportunities or otherwise adversely affect his status as an employee."[79] To date, the courts have often ignored this provision when determining what constitutes an adverse action. Further, the Supreme Court has stated that the federal discrimination statutes are designed to strike at the entire spectrum of discriminatory conduct.[80]

---

[75] 467 U.S. 69 (1984).

[76] Pennsylvania State Police v. Suders, 542 U.S. 129 (2004).

[77] *See, e.g.*, Alvarado v. Tex. Rangers, 492 F.3d 605, 612 (5th Cir. 2007) (lateral transfers are not actionable); Taylor v. N.Y.C. Dep't of Educ., 11-CV-3582, 2012 WL 5989874, at *7 (E.D.N.Y. Nov. 30, 2012) (being rated as having unsatisfactory performance not sufficient to constitute an adverse action); Myers v. Maryland Auto. Ins. Fund, No. CIV. CCB-09-3391, 2010 WL 3120070, at *1 (D. Md. Aug. 9, 2010) (threatening to fire a worker not actionable).

[78] Collins v. State of Illinois, 830 F.2d 692, 703 (7th Cir. 1987) (finding an adverse action occurred when employer moved employee's office to undesirable location); Czekalski v. Peters, 475 F.3d 360, 364 (D.C. Cir. 2007) (noting that some lateral transfers do constitute adverse actions).

[79] 42 U.S.C.A. § 2000e–2(a)(2); 29 U.S.C.A. § 623(a)(2).

[80] Harris v. Forklift Sys., Inc., 510 U.S. 17, 21 (1993).

Proscribed discrimination is not limited to adversely affecting actual "terms and conditions" of current employment, but includes discrimination that might deny "employment opportunities."[81]

Giving unfavorable references for former employees based on the individual's protected status denies employment opportunities elsewhere, and thus states a claim against the employers providing the harsh references.[82]

Courts tend to view harassment through a separate test, discussed in more detail in a subsequent chapter.

§ 3.16 Prima Facie Case, Fourth Factor

In *McDonnell Douglas*, the Supreme Court held that the fourth factor of the test required the plaintiff to establish that the employer continued to seek applicants. Again, the Court tailored this element to the specific facts of the case before it. If a black worker applies for a job, is qualified for the job, and is rejected, but the employer keeps trying to fill the position, one reason for the rejection might be the worker's race.

Modern courts often broaden the fourth factor to apply it to an expanded range of cases. There is considerable inconsistency among the circuit courts about what the fourth factor entails.

Some circuits require the plaintiff to show "circumstances that give rise to an inference of discrimination."[83] These circumstances can reflect a wide range of evidence, such as racist or sexist comments, differential treatment of workers in different protected classes, or discriminatory treatment of other workers.

It is unclear why the *McDonnell Douglas* test with its shifting burden is necessary in circuits using this broader fourth prong. If a plaintiff has evidence suggesting her race, sex, or other protected trait played a role in a negative outcome, summary judgment is inappropriate and a jury should have the option of finding for the worker.

In many cases a worker will try to create an inference of discrimination by showing that she was treated differently than people outside of her protected class. For example, if a supervisor regularly gives raises to Mormons, but does not give raises to similarly qualified Muslims, the worker's religion might explain the difference in treatment. In these kinds of cases, courts often express the fourth factor in the prima facie case as requiring the worker to establish she was treated differently than similarly situated workers outside of her protected class.

Circuits vary on how similar workers must be for a plaintiff to establish this fourth prong. Some courts require the plaintiff and the comparator co-worker to be nearly identical, meaning that the workers have similar positions, were subjected to decisions made by the same employee, worked in the same locations, and had similar qualifications.[84] In the discipline context, some courts will require that plaintiff's infractions be nearly identical to those of the comparator, including the history of past offenses.

---

[81] Porter v. Shah, 606 F.3d 809 (D.C. Cir. 2010).

[82] Robinson v. Shell Oil Co., 519 U.S. 337 (1997).

[83] Bejar v. Dep't of Veterans Affairs, No. 16–3218, 2017 WL 1149084, at *1 (10th Cir. Mar. 28, 2017).

[84] Alkhawaldeh v. Dow Chem. Co., 851 F.3d 422, 426 (5th Cir. 2017).

However, other courts merely require that the worker and the comparator are similar in all material respects. The workers are not required to be identical, but rather have a reasonably close resemblance.[85]

The requirement of a similarly situated comparator often distracts courts. In some cases, it is not the proper inquiry. For example, if a supervisor fires a woman from a management position and tells her "women are not management material," the woman's case should be able to survive summary judgment even if there is no evidence of a similarly situated man in that position. The supervisor's comments create an inference of discrimination without additional evidence.[86]

In the age discrimination context, some lower courts had held that in comparator cases the plaintiff was required to prove that someone outside the class protected (a person aged 39 or younger) was treated better. The Supreme Court rejected this proposition in *O'Connor v. Consolidated Coin Caterers Corp.*[87] The Court held that a worker can prove the fourth step of the *McDonnell Douglas* test by showing he was treated differently than a substantially younger individual, even if the comparator was over 40 years old. A 56-year-old can establish the fourth prong by showing that a similarly situated 40-year-old received better treatment.

§ 3.17 Reverse Discrimination Cases

Application of the model to white male plaintiffs complaining of "reverse discrimination" presents some interpretative problems. *McDonald v. Santa Fe Trail Transp. Corp.*[88] held that Title VII protects white individuals against race discrimination. However, this holding is in tension with the underlying premise of the *McDonnell Douglas* test, which creates a rebuttable presumption of discrimination if the plaintiff proves the prima facie case.

Consider a scenario in which three equally qualified people applied for a job, a white woman, a white man, and a black man. Under *McDonnell Douglas*, if the white man did not receive the job, he could survive the prima facie case if he applied for the job, was qualified, was rejected, and either of the other two individuals received the job. However, it is difficult to understand how this set of facts creates a presumption of discrimination. At the same time, it seems counterintuitive to refuse to allow the white man access to the *McDonnell Douglas* framework. It would be strange for federal civil rights law to have one set of proof structures for white men and a separate set of proof structures for other litigants.

Some courts process reverse discrimination through the *McDonnell Douglas* framework without modifying it.[89] Other courts have held that the differential treatment of a white male, standing alone, is not enough to create an inference of improper motivation. To create this inference the plaintiff must present "special circumstances"

---

[85] Carris v. First Student, Inc., No. 15–3350, 2017 WL 946741, at *1 (2d Cir. Mar. 8, 2017).

[86] Suzanne B. Goldberg, *Discrimination by Comparison*, 120 YALE L.J. 728 (explaining deficiencies in similarly situated test).

[87] 517 U.S. 308, 313 (1996).

[88] 427 U.S. 273 (1976).

[89] Carey v. Fed. Exp. Corp., 519 F. App'x 772, 776 (3d Cir. 2013).

from which it can be inferred that the white male was a victim of race or sex discrimination.[90]

§ 3.18 Reduction in Force Cases

When an employer goes through a reduction in force, some courts modify the fourth prong of the *McDonnell Douglas* test based on the belief that a likely reason for the plaintiff's termination or demotion is the reduction in force and not the plaintiff's protected class. Some courts will require additional evidence showing that the plaintiff was singled out for discriminatory reasons.[91] Other courts do not require additional evidence in reduction in force cases.[92]

§ 3.19 Rebuttable Presumption of Discrimination

Once a plaintiff establishes the elements of a prima facie case, a rebuttable presumption of discrimination arises. At this point, if the defendant does not respond with appropriate evidence, judgment in the plaintiff's favor is appropriate. However, in practice this rarely happens.

In *Texas Department of Community Affairs v. Burdine*, the Supreme Court indicated that "the burden of establishing a prima facie case of disparate treatment is not onerous."[93] According to the Court, the prima facie case serves the function of "eliminat[ing] the most common nondiscriminatory reasons for the plaintiff's rejection."[94]

§ 3.20 Defendant's Burden: "Legitimate, Nondiscriminatory Reason"

After the prima facie case, the defendant is required to articulate a legitimate, nondiscriminatory reason for its action. At this stage in the *McDonnell Douglas* test, an odd thing happens: the burdens of production and persuasion come apart. The plaintiff retains the burden of persuasion at all times; however, to rebut the presumption of discrimination, the defendant carries the burden of production only to articulate a legitimate, non-discriminatory reason for its action.

Although the burden of production is fairly minimal, the defendant must produce evidence of its reason. As the Supreme Court noted: "Defendant must clearly set forth through the introduction of admissible evidence the reasons for the plaintiff's rejection . . . . An articulation not admitted into evidence will not suffice. Thus, the defendant cannot meet its burden merely through an answer to the complaint or by argument of counsel."[95] Simply denying that that employer acted because of a protected trait or arguing that the employer acted for a good reason is not enough. There must be evidence to support the employer's position.

---

[90] Johnson v. Metro. Gov't of Nashville & Davidson Cty., Tenn., 502 F. App'x 523, 536 (6th Cir. 2012) (plaintiff must present evidence to show that the employer is the unusual employer that discriminates against the majority); Bishopp v. District of Columbia, 788 F.2d 781 (D.C. Cir. 1986); Chaline v. KCOH, Inc., 693 F.2d 477 (5th Cir. 1982).

[91] Slapak v. Tiger Mgmt. Grp., LLC, 594 F. App'x 290, 295 (6th Cir. 2014).

[92] Cruz v. Bristol-Myers Squibb Co., PR, 699 F.3d 563, 571 (1st Cir. 2012).

[93] Texas Department of Community Affairs v. Burdine, 450 U.S. 248, 253 (1981).

[94] *Id.* at 254.

[95] *Id.* at 255 n.9.

Step two does not require the employer to carry the burden of persuasion, which would require the employer to convince the factfinder of the truth of its legitimate, nondiscriminatory reason. Step two does not involve any credibility assessment.[96]

The Court has only broadly defined the parameters of the meaning "legitimate, non-discriminatory."

> [The reason articulated] is sufficient if the defendant's evidence raises a genuine issue of fact as to whether it discriminated against the plaintiff. . . . Placing this burden of production on the defendant [should] . . . frame the factual issue with sufficient clarity so that the plaintiff will have a full and fair opportunity to demonstrate pretext. The sufficiency of the defendant's evidence should be evaluated by the extent to which it fulfills [this] function.[97]

The defendant must offer "more than vague, general averments of good faith so that the plaintiff can understand and try to rebut [the] employer's reasons."[98] A defendant will not meet its obligations it if offers "a content-less and nonspecific statement, such as that a candidate is not 'sufficiently suited' for the position."[99] Many courts, however, have allowed defendants to meet their burden by articulating extremely non-specific, subjective conclusions.[100] Some courts have found that conclusions without supporting detail are not sufficient to meet the defendant's burden.[101]

In *Furnco Construction Corp. v. Waters*[102] the employer had refused to hire the black plaintiffs for bricklayer jobs and articulated as its reason that the plaintiffs were "walk-on" applicants unknown to the supervisor. The Court held that the "walk-on" reason was legitimate and nondiscriminatory. The existence of better, alternative devices with a less discriminatory effect is relevant to suggest that the "walk-on" rule was adopted to achieve a discriminatory result, but does not affect the defendant's showing in the second step.

Reasons may be "legitimate" even if they violate other laws. In *Hazen Paper Co. v. Biggins*, the Supreme Court held that if the employer terminated the plaintiff to avoid paying the plaintiff a pension based on years of service, this was a legitimate, non-discriminatory reason, even if doing so violated other federal law.[103]

§ 3.21 The Final Step

If defendant establishes the existence of a legitimate, non-discriminatory reason, the evidentiary burden of production shifts back to the plaintiff. The burden of persuasion has remained with the plaintiff at all steps of the test.

---

[96] St. Mary's Honor Ctr. v. Hicks, 509 U.S. 502, 509 (1993).

[97] *Burdine*, 450 U.S. at 254–55.

[98] Ramos v. Roche Prod., Inc., 936 F.2d 43, 47 (1st Cir. 1991) (internal citations omitted).

[99] Palacios v. City of Crystal City, No. DR-11-CV-53-AM/VRG, 2013 WL 12177177, at *14 (W.D. Tex. Sept. 30, 2013).

[100] Sabinson v. Trustees of Dartmouth Coll., 542 F.3d 1 (1st Cir. 2008) (acting in a "manner damaging to department" without specifying the "damaging" activity). Loeb v. Best Buy, Co., 537 F.3d 867 (8th Cir. 2008) (lack of "people skills, leadership, and decision-making").

[101] Chapman v. AI Transport, 229 F.3d 1012, 1062 (11th Cir. 2000) (en banc) (Birch C.J., concurring and dissenting in part).

[102] Furnco Construction Corp. v. Waters, 438 U.S. 567 (1978).

[103] 507 U.S. 604 (1993).

In the third step, the plaintiff may present evidence that the defendant's articulated reason was being used as a pretext or present other evidence suggesting the protected trait played a role in the outcome. This final step may be accomplished "either directly by persuading the court that a discriminatory reason more likely motivated the employer or indirectly by showing that the employer's proffered explanation is unworthy of credence."[104] The "ultimate burden of persuading the trier of fact that the defendant intentionally discriminated against the plaintiff remains at all times with the plaintiff."[105] In the third step, the court may consider evidence used to support the prima facie case.

In *St. Mary's Honor Center v. Hicks*, the Court considered whether the factfinder's rejection of the employer's asserted reason for its action mandated a finding for the plaintiff.[106] The Supreme Court held that while the factfinder's rejection of the employer's proffered reason permits the factfinder to infer discrimination, it does not compel such a finding.[107] For example, if the employer offers an untruthful reason for acting, the factfinder may properly reach two conclusions. The factfinder may find for the plaintiff if it believes that the employer is not telling the truth to cover up its true, discriminatory reason for acting. The factfinder may find against the plaintiff if it believes that the employer is not telling the truth, but that the employer still acted for another, non-discriminatory reason.

There is a wide range of evidence that can be presented to support step three. The following are examples of the kinds of evidence the plaintiff might submit. The plaintiff can submit statistical data showing work force imbalances with respect to certain protected classes or can present evidence of a pattern of discrimination. The plaintiff may submit evidence showing bias against the plaintiff or others in the plaintiff's protected class.

Pretext can be established by showing that the articulated reason has not been consistently applied in the past. Plaintiff also can prevail by showing that defendant's reasons are "unworthy of belief." Pretext may be shown if the employer has provided inconsistent reasons for taking the contested action.

A plaintiff may also show pretext by showing that the employer has not treated similarly situated individuals outside plaintiff's protected class in the same way as the plaintiff. For example, if the plaintiff was discharged, and the reason articulated was "fighting," evidence that persons of another race had been involved in similar fights in the past, but had not been similarly disciplined, suggests that discipline was being applied because of race.

At trial, the factfinder must weigh all evidence and determine whether plaintiff has carried the burden of convincing the factfinder that a protected trait caused the negative outcome.[108] Courts often refuse to instruct juries using the three-part burden-shifting framework either because they believe it is too confusing for jurors or because they believe there is no need to use the test after the employer articulates its reason for acting. Thus, the test is most often used at the summary judgment stage.

---

[104] *Burdine*, 450 U.S. at 256.

[105] *Id.* at 253.

[106] St. Mary's Honor Ctr. v. Hicks, 509 U.S. 502, 510–11 (1993).

[107] *Id.*

[108] *See* United States Postal Serv. Bd. of Governors v. Aikens, 460 U.S. 711 (1983).

The key takeaway from the *McDonnell Douglas* case is that the plaintiff may establish discrimination by showing that the employer's reason for a decision was pretextual. From pretext, the factfinder may (but is not required to) infer discrimination. The plaintiff may also use any other evidence to support the claim.

A note of caution with regard to the third step of *McDonnell Douglas*. Some courts view pretext as a narrow inquiry, requiring the plaintiff to establish that the employer's reason is a lie or unworthy of credence. Other courts tend to view pretext as a broader term of art that encompasses any evidence potentially demonstrating discrimination. How courts define pretext is important to whether the plaintiff will prevail. Additionally, if a court defines pretext in the narrow way, it is important to remember that the plaintiff can prevail by either establishing pretext or by presenting other evidence suggesting that the protected trait caused the negative outcome.

§ 3.22 Procedural Issues

The Supreme Court created the three-part burden-shifting framework at a time when all Title VII cases were bench tried. In the modern era, *McDonnell Douglas* is used mostly at the summary judgment stage. Courts have largely ignored the conceptual problems that using the test at the summary judgment stage creates. For example, the defendant often moves for summary judgment and often articulates a legitimate, non-discriminatory reason for its actions. It is unclear what purpose, if any, the prima facie case should serve in such circumstances. Once the defendant articulates a legitimate, non-discriminatory reason for acting, it has eliminated the need to evaluate the prima facie case. Nonetheless, courts often consider the prima facie case in such circumstances.

Over time, courts have increasingly limited the procedural junctures at which they will use the three-part framework. Courts have declared that *McDonnell Douglas* is not required as a pleading standard and that it should not be used to review jury verdicts. In some circuits, it is improper for judges to instruct juries using the three-part framework. Thus, in some circuits, the primary procedural juncture at which courts use *McDonnell Douglas* is the summary judgment stage.

A plaintiff is not required to demonstrate that she meets the elements of *McDonnell Douglas* to properly plead an individual disparate treatment claim. In *Swierkiewicz v. Sorema, N.A.*, the Court held that *McDonnell Douglas* is "an evidentiary standard, not a pleading requirement."[109] The Court further observed that a plaintiff is not required to use the test to prevail on a disparate treatment claim, specifically indicating that plaintiffs with direct evidence would not be required to navigate the three-part test.[110] It also reiterated the flexibility of *McDonnell Douglas*'s prima facie case,[111] noting that until the parties have engaged in discovery, they may not know enough about the facts to determine how to craft a prima facie case that reflects the case's specific factual circumstances.

A majority of circuits also discourage the use of the three-part burden-shifting framework in jury instructions.[112] In 1973, when the Supreme Court decided *McDonnell*

---

[109] Swierkiewicz v. Sorema, 534 U.S. 506, 510 (2002).

[110] *Id.* at 511.

[111] *Id.* at 512.

[112] Weimer v. Honda of Am. Mfg., Inc., 356 Fed. App'x 812, 817–18 (6th Cir. 2009) (noting that "it is generally inappropriate to instruct a jury on the *McDonnell Douglas* analysis as such"); Whittington v. Nordam Grp. Inc., 429 F.3d 986, 998 (10th Cir. 2005); Sanders v. N.Y.C. Human Res. Admin., 361 F.3d 749, 758 (2d

Douglas, Title VII did not provide jury trials.[113] In its early days, when the framework was used at trial in the Title VII context, it was used by trial court judges sitting as finders of fact.[114] In 1991, Congress amended Title VII to provide for jury trials in certain instances.[115] Shortly thereafter, courts and litigants expressed skepticism that the framework could properly be used in jury instructions. Many pattern jury instructions for discrimination claims direct the jury to determine whether an employer took an adverse action because of the plaintiff's protected trait without proceeding through the three-step burden-shifting framework.[116]

The discomfort expressed by the circuits stems from two different criticisms of the test: it is confusing, and its burden-shifting structure does not apply at trial. The Fourth Circuit Court of Appeals has noted that the shifting burdens of production "are beyond the function and expertise of the jury" and are "overly complex."[117] Many courts assert that any discussion of the three-part burden-shifting test in jury instructions would be so confusing that the jury may not be able to render a verdict based on such instructions.[118] Some courts have noted that the "presumptions and burdens inherent in the *McDonnell Douglas* formulation drop out of consideration when the case is submitted to the jury."[119] As one court declared, the "language used in the traditional *McDonnell Douglas* formulation, developed by appellate courts for use by judges, is at best irrelevant, and at worst misleading to a jury."[120]

Cir. 2004); Kanida v. Gulf Coast Med. Pers. LP, 363 F.3d 568, 576 (5th Cir. 2004); Sanghvi v. City of Claremont, 328 F.3d 532, 539–40 (9th Cir. 2003); Watson v. Se. Pa. Transp. Auth., 207 F.3d 207, 221–22 (3d Cir. 2000) (indicating that it is proper "to instruct the jury that it may consider whether the factual predicates necessary to establish the prima facie case have been shown," but noting that it is error to instruct as to the *McDonnell Douglas* burden shifting scheme); Dudley v. Wal-Mart Stores, Inc., 166 F.3d 1317, 1322 (11th Cir. 1999); Ryther v. KARE 11, 108 F.3d 832, 849–50 (8th Cir. 1997) (en banc) (Loken, J., in Part II.A. of the dissent, which a majority of the court joined); Gehring v. Case Corp., 43 F.3d 340, 343 (7th Cir. 1994); Mullen v. Princess Anne Volunteer Fire Co., 853 F.2d 1130, 1137 (4th Cir. 1988) (discussing the likelihood of juror confusion). *But see* Rodriguez-Torres v. Caribbean Forms Mfr., Inc., 399 F.3d 52, 58 (1st Cir. 2005) (finding that the district court instructed the jury to evaluate the evidence by applying the *McDonnell Douglas* burden-shifting framework); Kozlowski v. Hampton School Bd., 77 Fed. App'x 133, 141 (4th Cir. 2003) (discussing use of *McDonnell Douglas* framework in jury instructions); Brown v. Packaging Corp. of Am., 338 F.3d 586, 595 (6th Cir. 2003) (Clay, J., concurring) (approving the use of *McDonnell Douglas* in jury instructions).

While discouraging the use of tests in jury instructions, most circuits do not place an absolute prohibition on using *McDonnell Douglas* in this fashion. For a discussion of various approaches, see Timothy M. Tymkovich, *The Problem with Pretext*, 85 DENV. U. L. REV. 503, 509 (2008). Some circuits that do not generally countenance the use of the framework will find that it is harmless error for such instructions to be given. *See, e.g.*, Sanders, 361 F.3d at 758 (finding it was harmless error for district court to instruct jury as to burden-shifting framework); Vincini v. Am. Bldg. Maint. Co., 41 Fed. App'x 512, 514 (2d Cir. 2002); *Dudley*, 166 F.3d at 1322.

[113] 42 U.S.C.A. § 1981a(c) (2012). Title VII does not provide for jury trials in every instance. *Id.*

[114] *See, e.g.*, Furnco Constr. Corp. v. Waters, 438 U.S. 567, 569 (1978) (noting that case was bench tried and that trial judge had used framework).

[115] West v. Gibson, 527 U.S. 212, 212 (1999) ("In 1991, Congress again amended Title VII in the Compensatory Damages Amendment (CDA), which, among other things, . . . adds that any party in such an action may demand a jury trial, § 1981a(c).").

[116] Federal Civil Jury Instructions of the Seventh Circuit, 3.01 (2009).

[117] Mullen v. Princess Anne Volunteer Fire Co., 853 F.2d 1130, 1137 (4th Cir. 1988).

[118] *See, e.g.*, Sanders v. N.Y.C. Human Res. Admin., 361 F.3d 749, 758 (2d Cir. 2004); Kanida v. Gulf Coast Med. Pers. LP, 363 F.3d 568, 576 (5th Cir. 2004); Sanghvi v. City of Claremont, 328 F.3d 532, 540 (9th Cir. 2003); Dudley v. Wal-Mart Stores, Inc., 166 F.3d 1317, 1322 (11th Cir. 1999).

[119] Whittington v. Nordam Grp. Inc., 429 F.3d 986, 998 (10th Cir. 2005); *Sanders*, 361 F.3d at 758; Gehring v. Case Corp., 43 F.3d 340, 343 (7th Cir. 1994) (indicating that *McDonnell Douglas* is only for use in pretrial proceedings).

[120] Mobasher v. Bronx Cmty. Coll. of N.Y., 269 Fed. App'x 71, 73 (2d Cir. 2008).

In most cases, once the parties have presented their evidence, it no longer makes sense to require the plaintiff to prove the prima facie case, because that prima facie case is designed to force the defendant to articulate its legitimate reason for acting and to raise a rebuttable presumption of discrimination. By the time the jury deliberates, the defendant has already articulated its reason for acting, and the defendant has rebutted any presumption of discrimination created by the prima facie case. Therefore, applying the entire framework at the end of a jury trial only makes sense in those rare instances where the defendant fails to articulate a legitimate, non-discriminatory reason for its actions.

Further, it is unlikely that most members of a jury will understand the subtle distinctions in the test, namely that the second prong is a burden of production only and that this minimal burden is required only to rebut the presumption of discrimination created by the prima facie case. A jury instructed that it is the arbiter of credibility may find it difficult, if not impossible, to relinquish that role when considering the second prong of the *McDonnell Douglas* test.

Not only do district and appellate courts disfavor the *McDonnell Douglas* mechanism for jury decision making, they also limit its post-verdict use. Appellate courts considering a jury's verdict in a discrimination case typically do not use the *McDonnell Douglas* burden-shifting framework in considering whether the jury's verdict is appropriate.[121]

The Supreme Court has agreed with the lower courts with respect to the usefulness of *McDonnell Douglas* in the later stages of litigation. In the 1983 case of *United States Postal Service Board of Governors v. Aikens*, the Court held that using the *McDonnell Douglas* framework to evaluate a case in which a jury verdict exists evades the ultimate question of whether discrimination has been proven.[122] The Court noted:

> [W]hen the defendant fails to persuade the district court to dismiss the action for lack of a *prima facie* case, and responds to the plaintiff's proof by offering evidence of the reason for the plaintiff's rejection, the fact finder must then decide whether the rejection was discriminatory within the meaning of Title VII. At this stage, the *McDonnell-Burdine* presumption drops from the case, and the factual inquiry proceeds to a new level of specificity.[123]

Thus, the Supreme Court has held that the question of whether a plaintiff can make out a prima facie case is irrelevant once the defendant "has done everything that would be required of him if the plaintiff had properly made out a *prima facie* case[.]"[124]

§ 3.23 *McDonnell Douglas* Outside the Title VII Context

The Supreme Court originally decided *McDonnell Douglas* under Title VII of the Civil Rights Act of 1964;[125] however, courts now use it when analyzing claims under the

---

[121] *See, e.g.*, Stover v. Hattiesburg Pub. Sch. Dist., 549 F.3d 985, 993 (5th Cir. 2008) ("When a full trial on the merits has been conducted, as in this case, our focus is on whether the record contains sufficient evidence to support the jury's finding of no race or sex discrimination—not on the plaintiff's prima facie case or the *McDonnell Douglas* framework.").

[122] 460 U.S. 711, 713–14 (1983).

[123] *Id.* at 714–15.

[124] *Id.* at 715.

[125] McDonnell Douglas Corp. v. Green, 411 U.S. 792, 793 (1973).

ADA,[126] the ADEA,[127] and discrimination cases brought pursuant to 42 U.S.C. sections 1983[128] and 1981.[129] Additionally, courts rely on the *McDonnell Douglas* standard to determine whether a plaintiff can establish discrimination under various state anti-discrimination statutes.[130]

Care should be taken when applying *McDonnell Douglas* in the ADEA context. The Supreme Court has used the test in ADEA cases, but has also noted that it has not definitely determined whether use of the test in that context is appropriate.[131]

§ 3.24 Alternatives and Criticism

There is no existing law that compels lower courts to use *McDonnell Douglas* in individual disparate treatment cases that rely on circumstantial evidence. Rather, the test is merely an evidentiary framework that courts may (but are not required to) use when it is helpful for resolving the case. The *McDonnell Douglas* test has been subject to numerous criticisms.

One criticism is that the test is overly complex and distracts courts away from the question of whether a person faced discrimination because of a protected trait. Judge Wood of the Seventh Circuit Court of Appeals, in a concurring opinion joined by Judges Tinder and Hamilton, called attention to "the snarls and knots" that *McDonnell Douglas* inflicts on courts and litigants.[132] She derided the test as "an allemande worthy of the 16th century."[133] Further, she noted that district courts are able to filter other types of cases without reliance on a phalanx of complicated tests.[134] Given the demise of the *McDonnell Douglas* at the trial stage, she urged that the test should likewise be abandoned at the pre-trial stage. Similarly, Judge Tymkovich of the Tenth Circuit has argued that the test is confusing and that it distracts courts away from the ultimate inquiry of whether discrimination occurred.[135] Joining these criticisms, the Eighth Circuit Court of Appeals has opined that the *McDonnell Douglas* test was created without any justification or basis for its complex framework.[136]

As noted earlier, the *McDonnell Douglas* test is not a pleading standard, and it is often inappropriate to use it to instruct juries or on appeal after a jury verdict. Courts primarily use the test at the summary judgment stage. It is unclear how courts could apply one analytical framework to a set of facts at summary judgment, knowing that the factfinder would be instructed using a different framework at trial. Recall that Fed.R.Civ.P. 56 allows a court to grant summary judgment in the employer's favor only

[126] Raytheon Co. v. Hernandez, 540 U.S. 44, 49 (2003).

[127] Reeves v. Sanderson Plumbing Prods., Inc., 530 U.S. 133, 142 (2000) (indicating that the Court assumes, without deciding that it is appropriate to use the framework when analyzing ADEA claims).

[128] *St. Mary's*, 509 U.S. at 506 n.1.

[129] Garcia v. Hartford Police Dep't, 706 F.3d 120, 127 (2d Cir. 2013).

[130] *See, e.g.*, Gamboa v. Am. Airlines, No. 05–13317, 2006 WL 346478, at *1–2 (11th Cir. Feb. 14, 2006) (applying the *McDonnell Douglas* standard to claims asserted under a Florida anti-discrimination statute); Gentry v. Georgia-Pacific Corp., 250 F.3d 646, 650 (8th Cir. 2001) (same under Arkansas law).

[131] Reeves v. Sanderson Plumbing Prods., Inc., 530 U.S. 133, 142 (2000) (indicating that the Court assumes, without deciding that it is appropriate to use the framework when analyzing ADEA claims).

[132] Coleman v. Donahoe, 667 F.3d 835, 863 (2012).

[133] *Id.*

[134] *Id.*

[135] Timothy M. Tymkovich, *The Problem with Pretext*, 85 DENV. U. L. REV. 503, 521–22 (2008).

[136] Griffith v. City of Des Moines, 387 F.3d 733, 740 (8th Cir. 2004) ("Absent from this opinion was any justification or authority for this scheme.").

if no reasonable jury would find in favor of the plaintiff. In cases where a judge uses the *McDonnell Douglas* test at summary judgment when it would not instruct a jury using it, the judge is analyzing the case in a different way than a jury would.

In addition, the Supreme Court held in another context that the federal discrimination statutes do not draw a distinction between direct and circumstantial evidence.[137] After this case, it is unclear why courts continue to rely on this distinction to determine whether to funnel a case through the *McDonnell Douglas* framework. Additionally, Title VII discrimination cases allow a plaintiff to prevail if her protected trait was a motivating factor in a negative outcome. It is uncertain how or whether to integrate *McDonnell Douglas* with this motivating factor standard.[138]

There are alternatives to using *McDonnell Douglas*. As one court noted, "nothing compels the parties to use the *McDonnell Douglas* framework. In the alternative, a plaintiff may simply produce direct or circumstantial evidence demonstrating that a discriminatory reason 'more likely than not motivated' the employer."[139]

As discussed in §§ 3.38 and 3.39, both Title VII and the ADEA have language preventing employers from taking actions that segregate employees based on a protected trait or that limit or tend to limit employment opportunities.[140] Largely due to historical oversight, this provision has rarely been used in individual disparate treatment cases. However, it should provide litigants with an avenue for arguing individual disparate treatment.

Additionally, as discussed in greater detail below, courts recognize other analytical frameworks for cases involving grooming codes or stereotyping. The harassment framework discussed in Chapter 5 provides another basis for making an individual disparate treatment claim.

§ 3.25 *McDonnell Douglas* and Pregnancy Discrimination

In *Young v. United Parcel Serv., Inc.*,[141] the Supreme Court applied the *McDonnell Douglas* test to a pregnancy discrimination case. In that case, the plaintiff claimed that the failure to accommodate her pregnancy was intentional discrimination. The articulated test differs significantly from prior iterations of the test.

In *Young*, the plaintiff worked for United Parcel Service as a part-time driver. Her responsibilities included pickup and delivery of packages. After the plaintiff became pregnant her doctor recommended that she not lift packages heavier than 20 pounds during the first weeks of her pregnancy and no more than 10 pounds later in her pregnancy. UPS' policy required workers to lift parcels weighing 70 pounds. UPS told the plaintiff she could not work while under the weight restriction. It later rehired the

---

[137] Desert Palace, Inc. v. Costa, 539 U.S. 90, 99 (2003).

[138] *See, e.g.*, William R. Corbett, *Fixing Employment Discrimination Law*, 62 SMU L. REV. 81 (2009); Martin J. Katz, *Unifying Disparate Treatment (Really)*, 59 HASTINGS L.J. 643 (2008); Jamie Darin Prenkert, *The Role of Second-Order Uniformity in Disparate Treatment Law:* McDonnell Douglas's *Longevity and the Mixed-Motives Mess*, 45 AM. BUS. L.J. 511, 512–15 (2008) (declaring the continued vitality of the framework, while noting others' calls for its demise); Michael J. Zimmer, *The New Discrimination Law:* Price Waterhouse *Is Dead, Whither* McDonnell Douglas?, 53 EMORY L.J. 1887, 1930 (2004); Michael Evan Gold, *Towards a Unified Theory of the Law of Employment Discrimination*, 22 BERKELEY J. EMP. & LAB. L. 175 (2001).

[139] Reynaga v. Roseburg Forest Prod., 847 F.3d 678, 691 (9th Cir. 2017).

[140] 42 U.S.C.A. § 2000e–2(a)(2).

[141] 135 S. Ct. 1338, 1354 (2015).

plaintiff after her pregnancy. In *Young*, the plaintiff alleged that UPS' failure to accommodate her pregnancy constituted pregnancy discrimination because UPS accommodated other people with work restrictions, but refused to accommodate pregnant women. Young alleged that UPS accommodated workers who suffered off-the-job injuries and workers who lost their driver's licenses due to accidents or drunk driving.

In 1978, Congress amended Title VII through the Pregnancy Discrimination Act. The Pregnancy Discrimination Act makes it clear that Title VII's prohibition on sex discrimination included discrimination based on pregnancy. It also includes a provision requiring employers to treat "women affected by pregnancy . . . the same for all employment-related purposes . . . as other persons not so affected but similar in their ability or inability to work."[142]

The Supreme Court noted that the plaintiff could proceed through a direct evidence model and could also proceed under *McDonnell Douglas*. The Supreme Court then articulated a new *McDonnell Douglas* model that varies in significant ways from previous iterations of the test. The Supreme Court noted that this new test should be limited to the pregnancy discrimination context, although it is unclear why this is the case.

This new test requires the plaintiff to make the following prima facie case: that she belongs to a protected class, sought an accommodation, that the employer did not accommodate her and that the employer accommodated others "similar in their ability or inability to work." The employer must then present a legitimate, non-discriminatory reason for its decision. However, this reason cannot be that it is more expensive or less convenient to add pregnant women to the list of workers who receive accommodation. The plaintiff can then rebut the employer's showing by "providing sufficient evidence that the employer's policies impose a significant burden on pregnant workers" and that the employer's reasons are not sufficiently strong to justify the burden, but rather give rise to an inference of discrimination.

This new test is very different than the traditional three-part, burden-shifting test. First, it appears that lower courts play some role in scrutinizing the employer's legitimate, non-discriminatory reason. For example, let's say an employer has a policy that it only accommodates workers with a disability and workers with on-the-job injuries because other laws require the employer to make these accommodations. It also accommodates workers who are injured at company softball games. This is a facially neutral policy. Yet, the majority opinion seems to require an inquiry into why pregnant women are not also included and whether expense or convenience plays a role. What this inquiry is and how it would happen are left unexplored.

The new test also changes the pretext inquiry in the third step. While the majority focuses on intentional discrimination, its inquiry into burdens and the employer's reasons for acting looks more like the kind of inquiry applied in a disparate impact case. The Court noted that if a worker established that the employer accommodated a large percentage of non-pregnant workers while failing to accommodate a large percentage of pregnant workers, this might be intentional discrimination.

In adopting this analysis, the Court rejected both the plaintiff's and the defendant's proposed interpretations of Title VII. With some caveats, the plaintiff asked the Court

---

[142] 42 U.S.C.A. § 2000e(k).

to apply the actual language of the statute. That language appears to require the employer to treat pregnant women the same as other workers who face a similar inability to work.

However, the Court held that applying a literal version of the statute would not lead to equal treatment of pregnant women, but rather provide them with better treatment than other workers. For example, assume that a company has two types of jobs, hazardous and non-hazardous. The company allows people in hazardous positions work accommodations that it would not grant those in non-hazardous jobs. The Supreme Court noted that if it read the Pregnancy Discrimination Act literally, the company could be held liable if it did not permit a pregnant woman in a non-hazardous job the same accommodations it provided to those who worked in hazardous jobs and could not work. The Court argued that reading Title VII in this literal way would provide pregnant women with more protections than other workers.

The Court also rejected a more defendant-friendly approach that would have denied discrimination protection to pregnant women unless pregnancy was the reason for the refusal to accommodate. Under this interpretation, an employer could grant accommodations for other facially neutral reasons, such as off-the-job injuries. However, its refusal to grant similar accommodations for pregnancy would not be the basis for a pregnancy discrimination claim.

The Supreme Court also signaled that the Americans with Disabilities Act might apply in future cases similar to *Young*. Congress amended the ADA in 2008 to make it clear that the definition of disability was broad, contrary to the Supreme Court's prior interpretations of the definition of disability. The Court expressed no opinion about how the ADA might apply in a case with similar facts.[143]

D. MIXED MOTIVE

§ 3.26 History of Mixed Motive

It is unclear whether the *McDonnell Douglas* works well in cases involving what the courts call mixed motive. At times, the courts have described the test as pitting the employer's reason for acting against the contrary evidence presented by the plaintiff. However, some discrimination cases are more complicated. The employer may have multiple reasons for acting, some discriminatory and some not. Courts labeled these cases "mixed-motive" cases, although that language does not appear within the federal discrimination statutes' operative language. Although this book will continue to refer to some factual scenarios as "mixed-motive" it is important to realize that there is not a separate claim for mixed-motive cases, but rather courts sometimes use different analytical devices for reviewing the facts.

In *Price Waterhouse v. Hopkins*, the Supreme Court considered whether a plaintiff could prevail on a Title VII claim if the evidence established that legitimate and discriminatory reasons both played a role in the employer's refusal to promote her.[144] In the case, Ann Hopkins was denied partnership in an accounting firm. Of the 662

---

[143] For more discussion about pregnancy discrimination see Bradley A. Areheart, *Accommodating Pregnancy*, 67 ALA. L. REV. 1125, 1127 (2016); Deborah L. Brake, *On Not "Having It Both Ways" and Still Losing: Reflections on Fifty Years of Pregnancy Litigation Under Title VII*, 95 B.U. L. REV. 995, 996 (2015); Ruth Colker, *Pregnancy, Parenting and Capitalism*, 58 OHIO ST. L.J. 61, 79–81 (1997).

[144] Price Waterhouse v. Hopkins, 490 U.S. 228, 232 (1989) (plurality opinion).

partners at the firm, 7 were women. In the year the plaintiff was up for partnership, there were 88 proposed partners and Hopkins was the only woman. Hopkins was not fired; rather, she quit after she was passed over for partner twice. She filed suit for sex discrimination.

In *Price Waterhouse*, the decision whether to make Hopkins a partner involved numerous people. Some people supported her candidacy. Some of the people provided neutral reasons for not wanting to make her partner. Others provided discriminatory reasons. The Supreme Court noted that when some of the partners evaluated Hopkins, there "were clear signs" that they "reacted negatively to Hopkins' personality because she was a woman." The evidence in that case showed that some of the male partners stated that Hopkins was "macho," that she "overcompensated for being a woman," and told her that she needed to take "a course at charm school." One partner noted that Hopkins "ha[d] matured from a tough-talking somewhat masculine hard-nosed [manager] to an authoritative, formidable, but much more appealing lady [partner] candidate." Another advised her that she needed to "walk more femininely, talk more femininely, dress more femininely, wear make-up, have her hair styled, and wear jewelry." No one person had final decisionmaking authority, and it is unclear how much the discriminatory evaluations of her performance affected the decision.

After a bench trial, the district court found in favor of the plaintiff, holding that the decision not to promote her to partner was made, in part, based on sex stereotyping. The district court further held that the employer failed to establish by clear and convincing evidence that it would have placed plaintiff's candidacy on hold, even if it had not used the discriminatory considerations. If it had done so, the district court held that the plaintiff would not have been entitled to equitable relief. The appellate court affirmed the ultimate finding of the district court, that Price Waterhouse failed to establish the same-decision defense.

The Supreme Court determined that a so-called mixed-motive fact pattern could proceed under Title VII. It also articulated a framework for considering such claims. Although the main decision is a plurality decision, the broad outlines of the test are joined by a majority of the members of the court. Under the *Price Waterhouse* framework, the plaintiff must establish that a protected trait played a motivating part in an employment decision. This portion of the analysis was joined by a majority of the Court.

If the plaintiff establishes this first step, the plaintiff will prevail unless the defendant can establish an affirmative defense to liability. An employer would be able to completely escape liability for mixed-motive discrimination, if it could prove that the same employment action would have been taken absent the discriminatory motive. Because proving this would be an affirmative defense for the employer, the employer bears both the burden of production and the burden of persuasion. The Court interpreted Title VII as allowing employers to make decisions based on non-discriminatory reasons. The Court reasoned that if the employer would have taken the same decision without consideration of sex, it should not be held liable under Title VII.

If the factfinder believed that Hopkins would have been denied partnership simply because she did not get along with others, without taking her sex into account, the accounting firm would have no liability under Title VII. As a practical matter, it would be difficult for an employer to establish the affirmative defense, given the evidence that many partners appeared to be motivated by sex stereotypes when voting or providing input regarding Hopkins' partnership.

Importantly, a majority of the Court rejected the idea that Title VII requires a plaintiff to establish that a protected trait was the "but for" cause of an employment decision. The plurality reasoned that "to construe the words 'because of' as colloquial shorthand for 'but-for causation,' . . . is to misunderstand them."[145] The plurality held that to prevail on a discrimination claim, the plaintiff must establish that a protected trait is a motivating factor in a decision.[146] In reaching its conclusion, the Court relied heavily on the underlying purpose of Title VII. Reading Title VII's primary operative provision in its entirety, the Court noted: "We take these words to mean that gender must be irrelevant to employment decisions."[147]

The plurality noted that Congress specifically rejected a sole causation standard for Title VII. The plurality recognized an inherent problem with "but for" cause. In essence, "but for" cause requires a strange, hypothetical construct. After an event has taken place, the judicial decisionmaker revisits the event and asks whether if a particular factor was absent the event would happen in the same way. If so, the factor was not a "but for" cause of the outcome.

The plurality recognized that "but for" cause fails in cases that are causally overdetermined. For example, this happens when there are multiple, sufficient causes. These are cases in which two factors are present, but either one individually could have fully caused the outcome. To apply the hypothetical construct of "but for" cause in such instances would mean that neither factor was causally related to the outcome.

The plurality also recognized how multi-person decisionmaking would make it difficult for a plaintiff to establish "but for" cause. The decisionmaking process in *Price Waterhouse* involved at least 32 people, who each submitted an opinion about whether Ms. Hopkins should be promoted to partner. Thirteen partners supported her bid for partnership. Three partners recommended that her candidacy be placed on hold. Eight indicated they did not have an informed opinion about Ms. Hopkins' candidacy, and eight recommended that she be denied partnership. At the end of this internal process, Ms. Hopkins' bid for partner was held in abeyance and she was told she could be reconsidered the following year. The following year, the company refused to reconsider her for partner.

The plurality recognized that some partners raised non-discriminatory concerns about Ms. Hopkins' performance, while other comments appeared to be based on her sex. Given the multi-layered decisionmaking, it would be impossible for the plaintiff to show how each comment and each partner's motivations affected the eventual outcome. The Court indicated that the employee was not required to tease out how all of the comments related to the employment decision affected the outcome. Rather, she established the required causal connection by showing the employer relied on sex-based considerations when making its decision.

The plurality continued by discussing the inherent tension within employment law. While Title VII prohibits discrimination based on protected traits, the employer maintains the ability to make employment decisions on other lawful grounds. The plurality tried to balance the interests of employers and employees. With very little explicit reasoning related to Title VII, the Court declared that the balancing of these interests required the Court to create an affirmative defense to liability. It borrowed the

[145] *Id.*

[146] *Id.* at 244.

[147] *Id.* at 240.

contours of this affirmative defense from First Amendment constitutional law and a decision under the National Labor Relations Act.

If an employee shows that a protected trait played a motivating factor in an employment decision, the employee wins the case unless the employer can establish an affirmative defense. The affirmative defense requires the employer to show that it would have made the same employment decision, even if it had not taken the protected trait into account. If the employer establishes the affirmative defense, it faces no liability under Title VII. The Court noted if an employer allowed a protected trait to infect its decisionmaking process, then the employer should bear the risk that the "influence of legal and illegal motives cannot be separated."[148]

The plurality recognized that the idea of causation has at least two distinct components. The first part is the choice of substantive causal standard, whether that standard is sole cause, "but for" cause, motivating factor, or some other causal standard. The second part involves allocating burdens for establishing cause. *Price Waterhouse* explicitly recognized that there is nothing inherent in the notion of causation that requires the plaintiff to bear the entire causal burden.

The Court also rejected use of the clear and convincing standard, finding that civil cases typically use the preponderance of the evidence standard.

Justice O'Connor's concurrence in *Price Waterhouse* is important for several reasons. First, it is the genesis of the stray remarks doctrine that remains important in employment discrimination law.

Second, Justice O'Connor indicated that the *Price Waterhouse* analytical framework could only be used when a plaintiff possessed direct evidence of discrimination. After *Price Waterhouse*, many lower courts held that a plaintiff had to present direct evidence of discrimination to proceed under this framework. In *Desert Palace, Inc. v. Costa*,[149] the Supreme Court considered this issue. As the plain text of Title VII does not distinguish between direct and circumstantial evidence, the Court held that a plaintiff can proceed under a motivating factor framework by presenting either direct or circumstantial evidence.

§ 3.27 1991 Amendments to Title VII

In 1991, Congress responded to *Price Waterhouse* and other decisions by amending Title VII.[150] One change made by the 1991 amendments was to clarify through statutory language that a plaintiff can prevail on a Title VII claim if she shows a protected trait was a motivating factor in an employment decision. This portion of the amendment codified *Price Waterhouse*'s holding that a plaintiff can establish causation by showing her protected trait played a motivating factor in the outcome.

However, Congress disagreed with a portion of *Price Waterhouse*. In *Price Waterhouse*, the Supreme Court held that a defendant would not face any liability if it established the affirmative defense that it would have made the same decision absent consideration of the protected trait. In the 1991 amendments, Congress made Title VII more plaintiff friendly. Under the amendment, the employer may establish a limited

---

[148] 490 U.S. 228, 250 (1989).

[149] 539 U.S. 90 (2003).

[150] Civil Rights Act of 1991, 42 U.S.C.A. §§ 2000e–2(m), 2000e–5(g)(2)(B) (2012).

defense to damages only if it shows it would have made the same decision absent a protected trait.[151] If the employer establishes the affirmative defense it is still liable for discrimination; however, the court may only grant limited relief to the plaintiff. The court "may grant declaratory relief, injunctive relief [other than for reinstatement, hiring, promotion or payment], and attorney's fees and costs.[152] The court is not otherwise permitted to award damages.

§ 3.28 Motivating Factor in ADEA Discrimination Cases

When Congress amended Title VII in 1991 to explicitly include the motivating factor language and the limited affirmative defense, it did not similarly amend the ADEA. In *Gross v. FBL Fin. Servs., Inc.*,[153] the Court held that to prevail on an ADEA discrimination claim a plaintiff must establish "but for" cause.

Gross is in direct conflict with a majority of the Court in *Price Waterhouse*, which held that a plaintiff proceeding on a discrimination claim under Title VII must establish that a protected trait played a motivating factor in an employment decision.

Gross did not come before the Court as a causation case. The question the Court accepted was whether a worker must present direct evidence of age discrimination to claim the benefit of a motivating factor analysis under the ADEA. The Court did not answer this question. Rather, the Court answered the very different question of whether the ADEA allowed a motivating factor analysis at all.

Given the existence of *Price Waterhouse*, the Court first had to explain why it was not following that decision. In one paragraph, the Court explained that the ADEA is different than Title VII because Congress chose to amend Title VII in 1991 to explicitly include a motivating factor analysis. Congress did not so amend the ADEA. The Court characterized Congress' failure to amend the main provisions of the ADEA as proof that the causation analysis should proceed differently under the two statutes.

The majority then examined the text of the ADEA. Justice Thomas looked up the meaning of the words "because of" in a Webster's dictionary and found these words mean "by reason of" or "on account of." He claimed this is the "ordinary" meaning of the words "because of." He then cited two cases from other contexts and a torts treatise to say that "because of" means "but for" cause. In a quick sentence Justice Thomas then declared that this also means that the plaintiff bears the burden of establishing causation. Justice Thomas reimagined prior ADEA cases as requiring a plaintiff to establish "but for" cause. In Section III of the opinion, Justice Thomas noted that if *Price Waterhouse* came before the current court, it would likely not be decided the same way. He noted that the decision's burden-shifting structure is difficult to apply and should not be extended into the ADEA context.

The analysis in *Gross* is problematic on a number of fronts. *Gross* mischaracterizes the relationship between Title VII, the ADEA, *Price Waterhouse* and the 1991 amendments to Title VII. Title VII has a primary operative provision, which is codified at 42 U.S.C. § 2000e–2(a). It prohibits an employer from taking certain actions "because of" race, color, religion, sex, or national origin. It is the "because of" language in this subsection that the Court interpreted in *Price Waterhouse*. Just three years after it

[151] *Id.*

[152] 42 U.S.C.A. §§ 2000e–2(m), 2000e–5(g)(2)(B).

[153] 557 U.S. 167 (2009).

enacted Title VII, Congress chose to use the exact same "because of" language from Title VII in the ADEA.[154]

In *Price Waterhouse*, the Court interpreted the meaning of those words "because of." A majority of the Court held that those words meant that the plaintiff can prevail on a claim by establishing that a protected trait played a motivating factor in an adverse decision. Congress used the exact same words in the ADEA and these words should have the same meaning as they do under Title VII.

If *Gross* were decided prior to the 1991 amendments to Title VII, it is clear that *Price Waterhouse* would have applied to the ADEA. The question then becomes how the 1991 amendments to Title VII should affect the ADEA causation analysis. In the 1991 amendments, Congress did not choose to amend the main operative provision of Title VII. Rather, it added a new definitional subsection to the statute, reaffirming the *Price Waterhouse* majority that a plaintiff can establish a violation under Title VII by showing a protected trait was a motivating factor in an employment decision.[155]

However, Congress thought the Supreme Court's interpretation of Title VII in *Price Waterhouse* was too conservative. Congress liberalized Title VII through the 1991 motivating factor amendments by making the second part of the *Price Waterhouse* test more employee-friendly. It is highly problematic for the Court in *Gross* to take this history and use it to justify narrowing the reach of the ADEA.

So why did Congress not amend the ADEA in a similar way? There is no record reflecting why this amendment did not occur. In *Gross*, the Supreme Court stated that Congress' failure to amend the ADEA was intentional. It further explained that the intent was to differentiate the ADEA from Title VII. But, this statement is merely a guess by the Court.

There are lots of credible ways to explain Congress' behavior. Given the complex nature of the 1991 amendments to Title VII, it is very possible that Congress forgot about making similar amendments to the ADEA or did not have the time or ability to consider how the amendments would affect the ADEA. It also is possible that Congress intended for the *Price Waterhouse* standard to continue governing ADEA cases. Another option is that Congress wanted the courts to separately evaluate the ADEA.

The causation analysis in *Gross* is also problematic.

The causation analysis has four parts. First, the Court quotes the definition of "because" from various dictionaries. Dictionary definitions of the word "because" provide almost no information about the legal definition of that word. According to *Gross*, the definition of "because of" is "by reason of" or "on account of." There can be many reasons for a particular outcome, and these definitions tell us nothing about how to navigate multiple causes. Non-legal dictionary definitions do not discuss factual or legal cause. Nor do they discuss which party has the burden of proof.

In the second step, the Court makes a huge logical leap in one sentence. The Court noted: "Thus, the ordinary meaning of the ADEA's requirement that an employer took adverse action 'because of' age is that age was the 'reason' that the employer decided to act." The key words in this sentence are "the reason." This sentence is misleading

---

154 29 U.S.C.A. § 623(a).

155 42 U.S.C.A. § 2000e–2(m).

because it makes it sound as if the discrimination statutes require sole causation. It also makes it seem as if employment decisions can have only one reason.

From here, the Court declares that ADEA disparate treatment claims require proof of "but for" cause. To support this decision, the Court cited two cases outside the discrimination context and a torts treatise. Importantly, the Court did not look to *Price Waterhouse*, the Court's last discussion about causation in the discrimination context. In *Price Waterhouse*, the Court had an extensive discussion about why requiring the plaintiff to prove "but for" cause was problematic in employment discrimination cases.

In the final step, the Court reasons that the plaintiff has the burden of establishing causation. As shown in *Price Waterhouse*, plaintiffs do not always have the burden of proving causation.

§ 3.29 Causation in Title VII Retaliation Cases

After *Gross*, it was unclear what causation standard should apply in Title VII retaliation cases. In *Nassar v. University of Texas Southwestern Medical Center*,[156] the Court extended *Gross* to Title VII retaliation cases. It held the plaintiff in these cases must establish that her protected activity was the "but for" cause of a negative employment outcome.[157]

In that case, Dr. Naiel Nassar, who was of Middle Eastern descent, sued his former employer, the University of Texas Southwestern Medical Center, for discrimination and retaliation. Dr. Nassar was both a faculty member at the medical school and a physician at Parkland Memorial Hospital. At trial, he presented the following evidence. One of his supervisors at the medical school had stated, "Middle Easterners are lazy." This same supervisor noted that the medical school has "hired another one" after it hired another doctor of Middle Eastern descent.[158] Additionally, this supervisor excessively scrutinized Dr. Nassar's work and billing practices.[159] The medical center presented evidence to support its position that it had not discriminated or retaliated against Dr. Nassar.

Because of this treatment by the supervisor, Dr. Nassar no longer wanted to work at the medical school. He resigned his teaching position there and arranged to work only as a physician at Parkland Memorial Hospital. When he resigned from the medical school, he sent a letter to several people there stating that he was resigning because of harassment that "stems from . . . religious, racial and cultural bias against Arabs and Muslims."[160] A doctor from the medical school then contacted the hospital where Dr. Nassar had worked and where he had arranged to continue to be employed. The medical school doctor argued that Dr. Nassar's employment at the hospital violated an agreement between the medical school and the hospital that hospital staff should also be members of the medical school faculty. The hospital proceeded to rescind its employment offer to Dr. Nassar. However, contrary to this supposed policy of concurrent

---

156 570 U.S. 338 (2013).

157 *Id.*

158 Nassar v. Univ. of Tex. Sw. Med. Ctr., 674 F.3d 448, 450 (5th Cir. 2012), vacated, 133 S. Ct. 2517 (2013).

159 *Nassar*, 570 U.S. at 344.

160 *Nassar*, 570 U.S. at 344.

appointments, some members of the hospital staff were not faculty members at the medical school.[161]

Dr. Nassar claimed the medical school discriminated against him because of religion and race. He also asserted that the medical school retaliated against him by asking Parkland to rescind his employment offer after he complained about harassment at the medical school. At the trial, after the jury found that the medical school discriminated against Dr. Nassar and retaliated against him, it awarded Dr. Nassar more than $400,000 in back pay for the damages he suffered.[162]

The employer appealed the case, and the appeals' court upheld the jury's finding that the medical school retaliated against Dr. Nassar. The court noted, "Since credibility determinations, the weighing of the evidence, and the drawing of legitimate inferences from the facts are jury functions, not those of a judge, we find no basis to upset the jury's verdict that UTSW retaliated against Nassar because of his complaints of racial discrimination."[163] Thereafter, the medical school appealed the case to the Supreme Court.

In *Nassar*, the Supreme Court decided the meaning of Title VII's retaliation provision. That provision provides, "It shall be an unlawful employment practice for an employer to discriminate against any of his employees . . . because he has opposed any practice made an unlawful employment practice[.]"[164] *Nassar* required the Court to make a choice between three possible interpretations of Title VII, each reflecting a different choice about Title VII's text, Court precedent, and the effects of the 1991 amendments to Title VII on the retaliation provisions.

The Court could apply *Price Waterhouse* to Title VII retaliation claims. Both Title VII's discrimination and its retaliation provision use the word "because." In *Price Waterhouse*, the Supreme Court interpreted this language to require the plaintiff to show her protected trait was a motivating factor. The Court also could apply the 1991 amendments to Title VII's retaliation claim, reasoning as it had in past cases that retaliation is a subset of discrimination and that it was unlikely that Congress intended one standard for discrimination claims and a more onerous standard for retaliation claims under Title VII.

The Court held that plaintiffs in Title VII retaliation cases were required to establish "but for" cause.[165] This choice favors employers because it requires the plaintiff to bear the burden of persuasion related to causation and makes that causal burden a "but for" standard, rather than the less onerous "motivating factor" standard.

The analysis begins by stating that tort claims typically require proof of causation. It then continues by stating that the typical causation standard is "but for" cause. This analysis ignores a long line of tort cases that recognize that requiring the plaintiff to prove "but for" cause is problematic in many instances.[166] For example, in *Price*

[161] 674 F.3d at 451.

[162] *Id.* at 452.

[163] *Id.* at 454 (internal citation omitted). Despite the jury verdict, the appellate court decided that there was insufficient evidence to support the plaintiff's claim of discrimination.

[164] 42 U.S.C.A. § 2000e–3(a).

[165] *Nassar*, 570 U.S. at 346–47.

[166] *See, e.g.*, Summers v. Tice, 199 P.2d 1, 3 (Cal. 1948); Sindell v. Abbott Laboratories, 607 P.2d 924, 928 (1980) (discussing ways that plaintiff could recover despite being unable to establish which defendant caused plaintiff's harm).

Waterhouse, the Supreme Court had a lengthy discussion about the inappropriateness of requiring the plaintiff to establish "but for" cause in cases with multiple, sufficient causes. In such a case, tort law reduces the substantive standard for causation, using a lower motivating factor standard.

Reasoning from *Gross*, the Court then held that the 1991 amendments do not apply to Title VII retaliation claims. The Court expressed the idea that Congress intentionally separated retaliation and discrimination into two provisions and that Congress intended for the two to be separate and governed by separate causation standards.

The Court bolstered its statutory construction with a section of the opinion dedicated to administrability concerns. The Court stated that it chose the more employer-friendly causation standard because to do otherwise would be to "contribute to the filing of frivolous claims, which would siphon resources from efforts by employers, administrative agencies, and courts to combat workplace harassment."[167] Employees who become aware of a pending negative employment action may be tempted to raise unfounded discrimination claims to create a false retaliation claim.[168] The Court gave one final reason for the establishment of a more difficult causation standard. The summary judgment mechanism would not adequately ferret out these claims, even though employers could escape judgment after trial.[169]

§ 3.30 The Future of Motivating Factor

As of the writing of this text, it is unclear what causal standard should apply to claims under Section 1981 and the Americans with Disabilities Act (ADA).

Some pre-*Gross* courts concluded that the roots of the ADA in the Rehabilitation Act of 1973, required plaintiffs to prove that the discrimination they suffered would not have happened had it not been for their physical or mental impairment.[170] Others courts have allowed an ADA plaintiff to establish her disability was a motivating factor in the outcome.[171] After *Gross*, some courts have held that the ADA requires the plaintiff to establish "but for" cause.[172] However, these decisions often do not take into account the 2008 amendments to the ADA. Congress amended the primary operative language of the ADA, prohibiting discrimination "*on the basis of*" a disability.[173] Title VII and the ADEA both use the words "because of," rather than "on the basis of."[174] Other courts have found that plaintiffs do not need to establish "but for" cause to proceed under the ADA. Rather, the ADA incorporates a "motivating factor" standard.[175]

Section 1981 does not use "because of" language and is not modeled on Title VII, the ADEA or the ADA. There are only a handful of cases that have considered the effect, if any, of *Price Waterhouse*, *Gross* and *Nassar* on these claims. Some courts apply a *Price*

---

[167] *Nassar*, 570 U.S. at 340.

[168] *Id.*

[169] *Id.*

[170] Hedrick v. Western Reserve Care Syst., 355 F.3d 444 (6th Cir. 2004).

[171] Parker v. Columbia Picture Indus., 204 F.3d 326 (2d Cir. 2000).

[172] *See, e.g.*, Gentry v. E. W. Partners Club Mgmt. Co., 816 F.3d 228 (4th Cir. 2016); Lewis v. Humboldt Acquisition Corp., 681 F.3d 312 (6th Cir. 2012); Serwatka v. Rockwell Automation, Inc., 591 F.3d 957 (7th Cir. 2010).

[173] 42 U.S.C.A. § 12112(a).

[174] Silk v. Bd. of Trustees, Moraine Valley Cmty. Coll., Dist. No. 524, 795 F.3d 698, 705 (7th Cir. 2015).

[175] *See, e.g.*, Hoffman v. Baylor Health Care Sys., 597 F. App'x 231 (5th Cir. 2015).

Waterhouse analysis.[176] In these cases, once the plaintiff establishes that race was a motivating factor in a decision, the employer can escape liability completely if it proves that it would have made the same decision even absent consideration of race. Some courts have expressed the idea that *Gross* should apply to § 1981 claims, without enshrining this idea in a holding.[177] *Nassar* distinguished Title VII's retaliation provisions from § 1981 given that § 1981 does not contain the same "because of" causation language and does not have the same statutory structure as Title VII.

Whether state law provides for a motivating factor analysis for discrimination and retaliation claims is highly dependent on state-specific issues, including the language of the specific state statute, whether the statute was amended to incorporate changes similar to the 1991 amendments to Title VII, and whether the state tends to follow federal decisions when construing its statute. It is worth noting that many states combine all of the protected traits into one anti-discrimination statute. In these states, it is analytically inconsistent for the state statute to be construed as reflecting the 1991 amendments to Title VII, *Gross* and *Nassar*.

E. OTHER ISSUES

§ 3.31 Cat's Paw

The federal courts use the term "cat's paw" to describe cases with a particular type of fact pattern. In cat's paw cases, the employer alleges that it cannot be held liable for discrimination because a person acting without discriminatory intent actually made the employment decision. For example, if a biased supervisor criticizes an employee's performance in neutral terms and a human resources officer makes a decision to terminate the individual, the employer might argue that there is no discrimination if the human resources did not exhibit any animus, but rather relied on the facially neutral criticism provided by the supervisor. In a cat's paw case, the plaintiff typically argues that the decisionmaker relied on biased information, served as a conduit for the discrimination of others, or merely rubber stamped a discriminatory decision made by another person.

The name "cat's paw" is based on a story in which a monkey wants to get nuts off of a fire. The monkey convinces a cat to obtain the nuts, then steals them, with the result that the monkey obtains the nuts and the cat ends up with a burnt paw. The term "cat's paw" refers to one person being used as the tool of another.[178]

Cat's paw cases present an obvious tension. In a real sense, the plaintiff faced discrimination because of a protected trait. For example, assume that a supervisor has a racial bias. The supervisor reports to the president of the company that a black employee engaged in workplace misconduct when the misconduct did not happen. The president of the company fires the worker based on the supervisor's report. This employee was treated differently because of his race. If the employee was white, the supervisor would not have reported any misconduct and the employee would still have his job. However, from the president's perspective at the time of the decision, there is no known discrimination. The president made the decision without bias, without knowing

[176] *See, e.g.*, Brown v. J. Kaz, Inc., 581 F.3d 175 (3d Cir. 2009); Hardy v. Town of Greenwich, 629 F.Supp.2d 192 (D. Conn. 2009).

[177] *See, e.g.*, Crabb v. Wal-Mart Stores, Inc., 2012 WL 4092427, at *10 (N.D. Miss. Sept. 17, 2012).

[178] Arendale v. City of Memphis, 519 F.3d 587, 604 n. 13 (6th Cir. 2008).

about the bias of the supervisor, and without knowing that the reports about misconduct were false.

The Supreme Court addressed a cat's paw scenario in *Staub v. Proctor Hospital*.[179] The plaintiff Vincent Staub worked for the defendant hospital as an angiography technician. Staub was a member of the United States Army Reserve. He presented evidence that his two immediate supervisors were not happy about his military service. One of them scheduled him for extra shifts without notice and issued corrective discipline notes about his work performance. The vice president of human resources made the decision to terminate Staub based on a corrective action report submitted to her. It was disputed whether the work rule the supervisor claimed Staub violated was even a work rule and also whether Staub actually violated the rule.

A jury found for Staub on his claim of employment discrimination under the Uniformed Services Employment and Reemployment Rights Act (USERRA). USERRA is a federal statute that prohibits discrimination based on military service, such as service in the Army Reserve. The Seventh Circuit reversed, holding that a cat's paw claim would only be successful if the nondecisionmaker exercised such singular influence over the decisionmaker that the decision to terminate was the product of blind reliance.

The Supreme Court held that an employer could be liable if the supervisor intended for the worker to be terminated because of the employee's military status and if the act by the biased supervisor was a proximate cause of the termination. The employer could be liable, even though another person, without the required animus, made the final decision to terminate the employee.

The Court's reasoning is difficult to understand. Justice Scalia began with an assertion that when Congress creates a federal tort that tort is interpreted against the backdrop of the common law. This assertion is problematic on a number of grounds. First, it is unclear that federal discrimination statutes are like any pre-existing common law tort, such that it would be appropriate to import common law concepts from it. Second, there is no general common law that applies to every tort, so the tort law to be applied varies depending on the specific tort chosen. Third, since federal discrimination law is an exception to common law norms of at-will employment, it is unclear why it would be appropriate to re-insert common law analysis.

Justice Scalia continued by discussing common law agency doctrines, but ultimately rejecting them as unhelpful to the case. Instead, he focused on USERRA's language that required that military service be a motivating factor in the outcome. Staub had argued the Court should aggregate together the intent of the two biased supervisors with the action of the ultimate decisionmaker to establish causation. In rejecting this interpretation, Justice Scalia wrote: "When a decision to fire is made with no unlawful animus on the part of the firing agent, but partly on the basis of a report prompted (unbeknownst to that agent) by discrimination, discrimination might perhaps be called a 'factor' or a 'causal factor' in the decision; but it seems to us a considerable stretch to call it 'a motivating factor.' "[180] Justice Scalia did not otherwise explain this sentence and it is unclear why such a scenario would not establish the motivating factor analysis.

---

[179] 562 U.S. 411 (2011); *see also* Rebecca Hanner White & Linda Hamilton Krieger, *Whose Motive Matters?: Discrimination in Multi-Actor Employment Decision Making*, 61 LA. L. REV. 495, 498 (2001).

[180] Staub v. Proctor Hosp., 562 U.S. 411, 418–19 (2011).

The employer argued that it could not be liable unless the ultimate decisionmaker was motivated by the military service. The Court rejected this interpretation.

The Court then indicated that Staub's supervisor intended a consequence (for Staub to be fired) motivated by Staub's military service. Since one person had both the intention for the consequence and the animus or motive, this was sufficient to result in the employer's liability. The Court then indicated that the ultimate decisionmaker's action would not break the causal link between the supervisor's conduct and the termination. The Court indicated that there can be more than one proximate cause of an outcome. The Court also noted that USERRA's purpose would not be served if it allowed employers to shield themselves from liability by isolating ultimate decisionmakers and allowing them to make decisions based on biased recommendations.

Justice Alito concurred in the judgment and advocated a different standard, that the plaintiff is required to show that discrimination motivated the ultimate decision. Justice Alito believed that in instances where high-level supervisors rely on reports from subordinates that the courts could view the employer as having delegated decisionmaking to these lower level individuals.

Although *Staub* was decided under USERRA, the Court referred to Title VII throughout the decision. Lower courts have applied *Staub* in cases under the federal discrimination statutes.

Numerous questions remain after *Staub*. It is unclear how or whether the cat's paw analysis intersects with *McDonnell Douglas*. It is unclear how or whether its reasoning can be applied under the ADEA or in Title VII retaliation cases, where the Supreme Court has held the plaintiff must prove "but for" cause to prevail. It also is unclear if cat's paw analysis can be used when the supervisor intends something less severe than an adverse action. For example, if a biased supervisor submits a false report but only intends for the report to remain in the employee's file, it is unclear whether cat's paw analysis applies if an unbiased decisionmaker later decides to terminate the individual. It also is unclear what actions by the employer would cut off the causal link between the biased actions and the negative employment outcome.

Also, *Staub* did not provide the threshold for when a cat's paw case would be cognizable. Therefore, it is unclear what factual scenarios other than the one outlined in *Staub* would create potential liability for the employer. The Court in *Staub* specifically declined to determine whether liability would exist if a co-worker was biased and the ultimate decision was based on a co-worker's bias.

Care also must be taken in defining what factual scenarios fit within the cat's paw analysis and which do not. As currently defined, cat's paw involves cases where the ultimate decisionmaker was not biased and also did not possess knowledge about the bias of others or the falsity of the misconduct when making a decision. It is unclear what analysis applies when the ultimate decisionmaker knows about the bias of the supervisor or when the ultimate decisionmaker has reason to question the veracity of the information conveyed to her.

§ 3.32 Ancillary Evidentiary Issues

The federal courts will sometimes use other inferences to supplement their analysis of individual disparate treatment claims. These include the same-actor inference, the same protected class inference, the stray remarks doctrine, the honest belief doctrine, and the business judgment rule. Many of these inferences are not found within the text of the federal discrimination statutes, and it is unclear how they intersect with the *McDonnell Douglas* framework and other tests.

The inferences most commonly occur when a court is granting summary judgment on behalf of an employer. A judge will go through his or her analysis and then add on a discussion of the particular inference. The inferences appear to serve as additional reasons to grant summary judgment. However, because the inferences favor employers and often encourage a judge to view evidence in favor of the employer, it is unclear how they are consistent with the summary judgment standard set forth in Fed.R.Civ.P. 56. That standard requires judges to read all evidence and inferences in favor of the non-moving party (typically the employee in an employment discrimination case).

§ 3.33 Same Protected Class and Same Actor Inferences

The same protected class inference presumes that a person who is in the same protected class as the worker would not discriminate against the worker based on the protected trait that they share. For example, the same protected class idea might assume that a person older than 40 years old will not discriminate against other workers over the age of 40.[181]

Similarly, the same actor inference allows a court to assume that if a supervisor made a positive decision in favor of a worker that the same supervisor's later negative action against that same worker cannot be discriminatory.[182] For example, if a supervisor hired an older worker and then a few years later fires the worker, the court will assume that the supervisor did not take age into account when firing the worker. As one court reasoned, "From the standpoint of the putative discriminator, [i]t hardly makes sense to hire workers from a group one dislikes (thereby incurring the psychological costs of associating with them), only to fire them once they are on the job."[183]

Some courts will use the same actor inference where there is a short period of time between the positive decision and the later negative decision; however, courts have applied the doctrine when the time between the positive decision and the negative decision was seven years.[184] Courts in every federal circuit use the same actor inference.[185]

However, many judges and scholars have criticized these inferences.[186] As discussed earlier, it is not clear how these inferences comport with Fed.R.Civ.P. 56, which directs

---

[181] Brown v. CSC Logic, Inc., 82 F.3d 651, 658 (5th Cir. 1996) (internal citations omitted). There is a long line of cases applying the same protected class inference. *See, e.g.*, Elrod v. Sears, Roebuck and Co., 939 F.2d 1466, 1471 (11th Cir. 1991); Cartee v. Wilbur Smith Associates, Inc., No. C/A 3:08–4132, 2010 WL 5059643, at *5 (D.S.C. Oct. 6, 2010); Demesme v. Montgomery Cnty. Gov't, 63 F.Supp.2d 678, 683 (D. Md. 1999); Amirmokri v. Balt. Gas & Elec. Co., 60 F.3d 1126, 1128 (4th Cir. 1995). However, courts also reject the same protected class inference. Kadas v. MCI Systemhouse Corp., 255 F.3d 359, 361 (7th Cir. 2001).

[182] Blair v. Shulkin, No. 15–55748, 2017 WL 1149514, at *1 (9th Cir. Mar. 28, 2017); Brown v. CSC Logic, Inc., 82 F.3d 651, 658 (5th Cir. 1996).

[183] *Brown*, 82 F.3d at 658 (internal citations omitted); *see also* DeJarnette v. Corning Inc., 133 F.3d 293, 298 (4th Cir. 1998) (internal citations omitted).

[184] Proud v. Stone, 945 F.2d 796, 796–97 (4th Cir. 1991); Natasha T. Martin, *Immunity for Hire: How the Same-Actor Doctrine Sustains Discrimination in the Contemporary Workplace*, 40 CONN. L. REV. 1117, 1135 (2008); *but see* Carlton v. Mystic Transp., Inc., 202 F.3d 129, 132 (2d Cir. 2000) (criticizing use of the doctrine when there is a long intervening period between the positive decision and the negative one).

[185] Martin, *supra* note 184, at 1128.

[186] Castaneda v. Partida, 430 U.S. 482 (1977).

judges at summary judgment to view all inferences and evidence in the light most favorable to the non-moving party. In discrimination cases, the non-moving party is typically the employee, and both of these inferences favor the employer. Additionally, it is not clear whether the inferences hold true in many cases. For example, it does not make sense that a 40 year old would be unlikely to discriminate against a 65 year old, just because they both fall within the ADEA's protected class. Further, a man might discriminate against another man because of his sex if he thought the other man did not live up to certain traditional notions of masculinity.

The same actor inference suffers from similar problems. For example, if a man hires a woman one year and refuses to promote her the next year, it is not clear why a court would presume no discrimination occurred. It is also possible that the man believes women should only be hired for certain kinds of jobs and not promoted to jobs with more responsibility.

§ 3.34 Stray Remarks Doctrine

The stray remarks doctrine is a court-created doctrine that allows courts to declare that certain discriminatory remarks are not relevant to an underlying claim of discrimination. An example is helpful. Imagine that a worker brings an age discrimination case. To support his case, he presents evidence that a former co-worker (who no longer works for the employer) made a racist remark ten years ago. It is unlikely that a court will allow this evidence to support the worker's claim because it is probably not relevant. The comment is made by a non-decisionmaker about a different protected class and at a time far removed from the allegations made by the plaintiff. In discrimination parlance, this comment would be a stray remark.

To the extent that courts use the stray remarks doctrine to exclude evidence such as this, the doctrine is uncontroversial. It merely mimics the restrictions already found within Fed.R.Evid. 401 and 403, which allows a judge to exclude evidence that is not relevant or whose probative value is outweighed by the likely prejudice it will cause.

However, the federal courts have used the stray remarks doctrine in ways that are more controversial. For example, in a race discrimination case, a worker presented evidence that his supervisor referred to African-Americans as "lazy," "worthless," and "just here to get paid."[187] The judge refused to consider these comments as supporting a race discrimination claim and reasoned that they were stray remarks, not probative of race discrimination. In an age discrimination case, a court similarly rejected a claim where the worker presented evidence his supervisor told him "you are too damn old for this kind of work" two weeks before he was fired.[188] Judges commonly invoke the stray remarks doctrine to exclude evidence presented by workers, allowing the court to grant summary judgment or other motions in favor of the employer.[189]

The stray remarks doctrine is not contained within the text of any of the main federal discrimination statutes. Instead, the stray remarks doctrine is a special evidentiary rule that courts created and apply in discrimination cases. Through this

---

[187] Chappell v. The Bilco Co., No. 3:09CV00016 JLH, 2011 WL 9037, at *9 (E.D. Ark. Jan. 3, 2011), aff'd sub nom., 675 F.3d 1110 (8th Cir. 2012) (granting summary judgment).

[188] O'Connor v. Consol. Coin Caterers Corp., 56 F.3d 542, 551 (4th Cir. 1995) (Butzner, J., dissenting), rev'd, 517 U.S. 308 (1996).

[189] For more examples of the stray remarks doctrine, see Kerri Lynn Stone, *Taking in Strays: A Critique of the Stray Comment Doctrine in Employment Discrimination Law*, 77 MO. L. REV. 149 (2012).

doctrine, judges can refuse to consider discriminatory comments or actions in the workplace if the court deems the comments too remote in time from the contested decision, not made in the context of the challenged employment practice, not made by a decisionmaker, or too ambiguous to show discriminatory bias.[190]

The stray remarks doctrine first appeared in a concurring opinion by Justice Sandra Day O'Connor in the 1989 case of *Price Waterhouse v. Hopkins*.[191] In that case, Justice O'Connor noted:

> Thus, stray remarks in the workplace, while perhaps probative of sexual harassment, cannot justify requiring the employer to prove that its hiring or promotion decisions were based on legitimate criteria. Nor can statements by nondecisionmakers, or statements by decisionmakers unrelated to the decisional process itself, suffice to satisfy the plaintiff's burden in this regard. . . .[192]

Importantly, Justice O'Connor's discussion of stray remarks did not rely on or even purport to draw from Title VII's statutory language, its legislative history, or its purpose. Nor was Justice O'Connor claiming that the stray remarks were not relevant in intentional discrimination cases. Rather, she was making a narrow claim related to the specific issue raised in *Price Waterhouse* about whether a plaintiff could proceed under a mixed-motive framework without what she called "direct evidence" of discrimination.

While her remarks were part of a concurring opinion and are not controlling law, courts have expanded on her idea. As Professor Kerri Lynn Stone has noted, after *Price Waterhouse*, "the so-called stray comments doctrine . . . had a groundswell of usage, building in popularity year after year."[193]

Courts do not uniformly apply the stray remarks doctrine and some judges have criticized it.[194] Strangely, the Supreme Court has decided numerous cases where it at least implicitly has rejected the stray remarks doctrine, yet the doctrine has continued vitality in the lower courts. For example, in *Ash v. Tyson Foods, Inc.*,[195] the lower courts nullified a jury's verdict in favor of two men who claimed the employer refused to promote them because of their race. The men presented evidence that the plant manager, who made the promotion decision, referred to them as "boy."[196] Although a jury found race discrimination, the trial court judge ruling on post-trial motions noted that the supervisor's use of the word "boy" was not racial in nature.[197] Likewise, the appellate court also found that the use of the word "boy" was not evidence of discrimination.[198] The Supreme Court reversed the appellate court's decision regarding the use of the word

---

190 Mosberger v. CPG Nutrients, Civ. No. 01–100, 2002 WL 31477292, at *8 (W.D. Pa. Sept. 6, 2002) ("Discriminatory stray remarks are generally considered in one of three categories—those made (1) by a non-decisionmaker; (2) by a decisionmaker but unrelated to the decision process; or (3) by a decisionmaker but temporally remote from the adverse employment decision.") (internal quotations and citations omitted); *see also generally* Stone, *supra* note 189.

191 490 U.S. 228 (1989).

192 *Id.* at 277 (O'Connor, J., concurring) (internal citations omitted).

193 Stone, *supra* note 189, at 170.

194 Holmes v. Marriott Corp., 831 F. Supp. 691, 704 (S.D. Iowa 1993).

195 Ash v. Tyson Foods, Inc., 546 U.S. 454, 455–56 (2006).

196 Ash v. Tyson Foods, Inc., No. CIV.A. 96-RRA-3257-M, 2004 WL 5138005, at *1, 6 (N.D. Ala. Mar. 26, 2004), aff'd in part, rev'd in part, 129 F. App'x 529 (11th Cir. 2005), vacated, 546 U.S. 454 (2006).

197 *Id.* at *6.

198 Ash v. Tyson Foods, Inc., 129 F. App'x 529, 533 (11th Cir. 2005), vacated, 546 U.S. 454 (2006).

"boy," noting that the meaning of the term depended on the context in which it was used.[199]

The Supreme Court also discussed stray remarks in *Reeves v. Sanderson Plumbing Products, Inc.* In that case, Roger Reeves alleged that his employer fired him because of his age.[200] At the time he was fired, Mr. Reeves had worked for Sanderson Plumbing Products, Inc. for 40 years and was 57 years old.[201] To support his discrimination claim, at trial, Mr. Reeves presented evidence that a supervisor who was involved in the termination told Mr. Reeves several months before his dismissal that he was so old that he "must have come over on the Mayflower" and that he was "too damn old to do the job."[202]

The jury found in his favor, also finding that the employer's conduct was willful. Reviewing the jury's decision, the appellate court disregarded the age-related comments as stray remarks and rejected the verdict. It noted, "Despite the potentially damning nature of [the] age-related comments, it is clear that these comments were not made in the direct context of Reeves's termination."[203] The Supreme Court corrected the court of appeals' mistake and found that the jury's verdict should stand.[204] The Supreme Court reasoned that when a supervisor says that someone is so old that they must have come across on the Mayflower, and that a worker is too old to do his job, the jury is entitled to infer that age played a role in the worker's termination. Despite both of these Supreme Court cases, the lower courts still continue to use the stray remarks doctrine to exclude evidence in employment discrimination cases.

The inference that courts make in applying the stray remarks doctrine is at odds with the inference they use in same actor context. In stray remarks cases, courts are often inferring that if a decisionmaker made a comment at Time A that the comment does not reflect animus at a later time, Time B. For example, if 10 years ago a supervisor made a racist comment, a court might use the stray remarks doctrine to exclude the evidence, reasoning that the stray remark is not relevant to a race discrimination case 10 years later. However, in the same-actor context, the court is inferring that a person's state of mind remains consistent across time. A person who makes a non-discriminatory decision to hire a person at Time A keeps that non-discriminatory state of mind at a later time, Time B.

§ 3.35 Honest Belief

Under the honest belief doctrine, a court will find that if an employer took a negative action against an employee based on wrong information, there is no discrimination if the employer honestly believed the wrong information at the time it made the decision.[205] For example, if an employer fires a worker for three unexcused absences, the employer will not be held liable for discrimination if it later turns out that the worker did not have

---

199 546 U.S. at 456.

200 Reeves v. Sanderson Plumbing Prods., Inc., 530 U.S. 133, 137 (2000).

201 *Id.*

202 Reeves v. Sanderson Plumbing Prods., Inc., 197 F.3d 688, 691 (5th Cir. 1999), rev'd, 530 U.S. 133 (2000).

203 *Id.* at 693.

204 530 U.S. at 151.

205 There is not one uniform understanding of the honest belief rule. Different appellate courts describe the test in different ways.

three unexcused absences. Even though the employer was wrong, courts reason, the reason for the termination was not the worker's protected trait.

Like the stray remarks doctrine, the underlying intuition of the honest belief doctrine is correct in a limited subset of cases. If the employer truly made its decision under a faulty set of facts and there is no other evidence suggesting discrimination, then it would be appropriate for a judge to find in favor of the employer. No special employment discrimination doctrine is needed to reach this outcome. In such a case, the worker has simply failed to present any evidence that a protected trait played a negative role in an employment outcome. Like the stray remarks doctrine, though, courts often use the honest belief doctrine in cases where the facts are not straightforward.

Unfortunately, some judges apply the honest belief doctrine in cases where the worker has evidence showing that at the time it made its decision, the employer did not believe the reason it later asserted in court.[206] Courts also allow employers to claim they honestly believed they fired an employee for violating company policy even when they do not regularly enforce the policy or when there is evidence that the policy does not even exist.[207] One worker's case was dismissed on summary judgment where a federal appellate judge called the employer's factual investigation "so poor and one-sided as to be 'unworthy of credence.' "[208] Courts have also used the "honest belief" rule to dismiss cases when there was evidence that the supervisor who complained about an employee's performance made racist remarks[209] and where others involved in the decision may have known about the supervisor's bias.[210]

Some judges also will support a supervisor's reasons for acting, even if the supervisor is not able to explain why he made a decision.[211] As one court noted in criticizing the "honest belief" rule, the rule allows employers to "provide an honest reason for firing the employee, even if that reason had no factual support."[212] Courts have even dismissed cases under the "honest belief" rule when employers change the reasons for their actions.[213]

Many honest belief cases seem to contradict Supreme Court precedent.[214] In *McDonnell Douglas v. Green*, the Supreme Court held that a worker may prove discrimination by showing that the reason provided by the employer for its decision is not true, but rather is a pretext for discrimination.[215] In many honest belief cases, the employer gives one reason for its decision, and the worker has evidence that the reason is not true. Nonetheless, many courts choose to believe that the employer had an honest

---

[206] Hamilton v. Boise Cascade Exp., 280 F. App'x 729, 729 (10th Cir. 2008).

[207] *See, e.g.*, Hale v. Mercy Health Partners, No. 14–3522, 2015 WL 1637896, at *10 (6th Cir. Apr. 14, 2015) (White, J., concurring in part and dissenting in part); Wilson v. Cleveland Clinic Found., 579 F. App'x 392, 408 (6th Cir. 2014) (Cole, C.J., dissenting in part).

[208] Seeger v. Cincinnati Bell Tel. Co., 681 F.3d 274, 290 (6th Cir. 2012) (Tarnow, J., dissenting) (discussing honest belief doctrine in context of the Family and Medical Leave Act, which is similar analysis to that used in discrimination cases); *see also* Kariotis v. Navistar Int'l Transp. Corp., 131 F.3d 672, 677 (7th Cir. 1997) (describing employer investigation as "careless").

[209] Clack v. Rock-Tenn Co., 304 F. App'x 399, 403 n.2 (6th Cir. 2008).

[210] *Id.* at 405.

[211] Walton v. McDonnell Douglas Corp., 167 F.3d 423, 426 (8th Cir. 1999).

[212] Smith v. Chrysler Corp., 155 F.3d 799, 806 (6th Cir. 1998).

[213] Bhama v. Mercy Mem'l Hosp. Corp., 416 F. App'x 542, 557 (6th Cir. 2011) (White, J., dissenting).

[214] St. Mary's Honor Ctr. v. Hicks, 509 U.S. 502, 511 (1993).

[215] McDonnell Douglas Corp. v. Green, 411 U.S. 792 (1973).

belief, rather than finding that the employer's reason might be a pretext for discrimination. Although some judges find the rule problematic and some refuse to use it,[216] the honest belief doctrine is still widely used.

§ 3.36 Business Judgment

The federal discrimination statutes do not prohibit employers from making bad decisions or force them to make good ones. Instead, in the disparate treatment context, the discrimination statutes only prohibit discriminatory conduct. Courts have expressed this idea by stating that they must respect the business judgment of employers. Alternatively, in summary judgment orders and other similar contexts, federal judges will often repeat the mantra that they do not sit as super-personnel departments.[217] In its weak form, there is no problem with this idea. The federal discrimination statutes are not a fairness code, and they do not require employers to be nice or to treat employees well. Instead, the statutes prohibit conduct taken because of a protected trait.

However, care must be taken when using this idea. Unfair treatment absent discrimination does not violate federal discrimination law. However, unfair treatment may be evidence of discrimination.

§ 3.37 Grooming Codes

Title VII prohibits an employer from treating men differently than women. Applying this prohibition strictly, grooming codes that differentiate between men and women would violate Title VII.

The courts have largely rejected this view. In general, courts appear reluctant to declare that sex-based grooming codes violate Title VII.

Courts tend not to apply the typical analytical frameworks to grooming code cases alleging sex discrimination. Instead, many cases explore whether the grooming code imposed on one class only would place a significant burden on the class on which it was imposed that is different from that imposed on other individuals outside the class. For example in *Jespersen v. Harrah's Operating Co.*,[218] the Ninth Circuit considered a challenge to an employer's grooming policy that required women to wear make-up and to tease, curl, or style their hair. A standard analysis under Title VII would hold that facial distinctions of this kind are not allowed. Instead, the court's analysis focused on whether the grooming policy was more onerous for women than it was for men and whether women had a significantly greater burden. The plaintiff did not introduce evidence about the expense or time of purchasing and applying make-up, and the court held that the plaintiff did not establish that the policy burdened women more than men. Under this same analysis, some courts will allow employers to have grooming codes that permit women to have long hair but require men to cut their hair.[219]

However, some courts have rejected this reasoning. The Sixth Circuit has noted that "After *Price Waterhouse*, an employer who discriminates against women because, for

---

[216] *See, e.g.*, Dailey v. Accubuilt, Inc., 944 F. Supp. 2d 571, 580 (N.D. Ohio 2013); Obike v. Applied EPI, Inc., No. CIV.02–1653 (JRT/FLN), 2004 WL 741657, at *5 (D. Minn. Mar. 24, 2004) (discussing reluctance of some courts to use doctrine).

[217] Charles A. Sullivan, *Circling Back to the Obvious: The Convergence of Traditional and Reverse Discrimination in Title VII Proof*, 46 WM. & MARY L. REV. 1031, 1115–16 (2004).

[218] 444 F.3d 1104, 1107 (9th Cir. 2006).

[219] Viscecchia v. Alrose Allegria LLC, 117 F. Supp. 3d 243, 252 (E.D.N.Y. 2015).

instance, they do not wear dresses or makeup, is engaging in sex discrimination because the discrimination would not occur but for the victim's sex. It follows that employers who discriminate against men because they *do* wear dresses and makeup, or otherwise act femininely, are also engaging in sex discrimination, because the discrimination would not occur but for the victim's sex."[220]

Courts also will recognize clothing requirements as discriminatory if the required clothing subjects a person to sexual harassment. For example, if a policy required a woman to wear a skimpy outfit, while allowing men to wear more substantial clothing, a female worker could challenge this as discriminatory.[221] Requiring both males and females to wear "business attire" would not be discriminatory. However, if women were required to wear identical, precise uniforms prescribed by the employer, while men are permitted to wear business attire of their choice, this would be discriminatory in that it tends to place women in an inferior, humiliating position.[222]

If an employer requires employees to maintain a certain weight or build, it cannot impose more stringent requirements on one sex. For example, it would violate Title VII to require men to be of a medium or slim build, but to require women to be slim.[223]

A uniformly applied grooming standard can create liability if it is imposed to disadvantage a particular class. Courts have upheld grooming codes that require men and women to dress in the same way (i.e., requiring all employees to wear pants, rather than skirts or dresses).[224]

Differences in grooming codes based on other protected traits violate federal discrimination law as courts are less likely to believe that differences imposed based on race, national origin, color, religion, age, or disability serve any legitimate goal. Difficulties arise when an employer's policy does not contain facial distinctions, but rather the employer has a uniformly applied policy that disallows certain hairstyles or clothing more associated with a particular race or national origin.[225] Courts have held that it is lawful under Title VII to uniformly apply a hairstyle policy that bans the wearing of cornrows.[226] Such outcomes are facing scrutiny because employers may be making decisions about what counts as a "professional" hairstyle based on racial norms.

However, the employer would face liability if it did not evenly enforce its hairstyle policy or if it adopted it to discriminate because of race. It would also likely face liability if it banned employees from wearing hair in a natural hairstyle.[227]

---

[220] Smith v. City of Salem, Ohio, 378 F.3d 566, 574 (6th Cir. 2004); *see also* Hayden ex rel. A.H. v. Greensburg Cmty. Sch. Corp., 743 F.3d 569, 571 (7th Cir. 2014) (rejecting different hair lengths for members of basketball team based on sex under a constitutional analysis).

[221] EEOC v. Sage Realty Corp., 507 F.Supp. 599 (S.D.N.Y.1981).

[222] Carroll v. Talman Federal Sav. & Loan Ass'n of Chicago, 604 F.2d 1028 (7th Cir. 1979).

[223] Compare Jarrell v. Eastern Air Lines, Inc., 430 F.Supp. 884 (E.D. Va.1977), affirmed per curiam, 577 F.2d 869 (4th Cir. 1978) (higher maximum weight for men is non-discriminatory) with Laffey v. Northwest Airlines, Inc., 567 F.2d 429 (D.C. Cir. 1976) (preference for trimness in female flight attendants is discriminatory). *See also* Gerdom v. Continental Airlines, Inc., 692 F.2d 602 (9th Cir. 1982).

[224] Hayden ex rel. A.H. v. Greensburg Cmty. Sch. Corp., 743 F.3d 569, 571 (7th Cir. 2014).

[225] D. Wendy Greene, *Title VII: What's Hair (and Other Race-Based Characteristics) Got to Do with It?*, 79 U. COLO. L. REV. 1355 (2008).

[226] Rogers v. Am. Airlines, Inc., 527 F. Supp. 229, 231 (S.D.N.Y. 1981).

[227] *Id.*

Employers may be required to accommodate an employee's religious beliefs and practices related to grooming and dress. The employer's obligation is discussed in Chapter 7.

§ 3.38 Segregation and Perpetuation of Past Discrimination

Title VII also contains language making it unlawful for an employer to do the following:

> (2) to limit, segregate, or classify his employees or applicants for employment in any way which would deprive or tend to deprive any individual of employment opportunities or otherwise adversely affect his status as an employee, because of such individual's race, color, religion, sex, or national origin.[228]

The ADEA contains similar language.[229] The ADA defines discrimination to prohibit segregation based on disability.[230]

Employers cannot assign employees to work in one division, section, room, or shift based on a protected trait.[231] An employer may not segregate the working environment or company sponsored social events.[232]

§ 3.39 Limit or Classify

Title VII contains language making it unlawful for an employer to do the following:

> (2) to limit, segregate, or classify his employees or applicants for employment in any way which would deprive or tend to deprive any individual of employment opportunities or otherwise adversely affect his status as an employee, because of such individual's race, color, religion, sex, or national origin.[233]

The ADEA contains similar language.[234] The courts have largely treated this provision as related to disparate impact claims and have not fully explored how it would apply to disparate treatment claims. There is nothing in the statutory language that limits this provision to disparate impact.[235]

§ 3.40 Stereotyping

One way to show discrimination "because of" a protected trait is to demonstrate the plaintiff was subjected to stereotyping based on that protected trait. In *Price Waterhouse v. Hopkins*, the Supreme Court recognized that sex stereotyping constituted discrimination under Title VII.[236] In the case, Ann Hopkins was denied partnership in

---

228 42 U.S.C.A. § 2000e–2(a) (2006).

229 29 U.S.C.A. § 623(a).

230 42 U.S.C.A. § 12112(b)(1).

231 *But see* United States Equal Employment Opportunity Comm'n v. AutoZone, Inc., No. 15–3201, 2017 WL 2644332, at *1 (7th Cir. June 20, 2017) (holding that segregation only illegal if it deprives or tends to deprive a person of job benefits or opportunities).

232 Firefighters Institute for Racial Equality v. St. Louis, 549 F.2d 506 (8th Cir. 1977).

233 42 U.S.C.A. § 2000e–2(a) (2006).

234 29 U.S.C.A. § 623(a).

235 Sandra F. Sperino, *Justice Kennedy's Big New Idea*, 96 B.U. L. REV. 1789, 1789 (2016).

236 Price Waterhouse v. Hopkins, 490 U.S. 228, 232 (1989) (plurality opinion).

an accounting firm. Of the 662 partners at the firm, 7 were women. In the year the plaintiff was up for partnership, there were 88 proposed partners and Hopkins was the only woman. Hopkins was not fired; rather, she quit after she was passed over for partner twice. She filed suit for sex discrimination.

In *Price Waterhouse*, the evidence showed that sex stereotyping played a role in some of the partners' evaluations of Hopkins. The Supreme Court noted that when some of the partners evaluated Hopkins, there "were clear signs" that they "reacted negatively to Hopkins' personality because she was a woman." The evidence in that case showed that some of the male partners stated that Hopkins was "macho," that she "overcompensated for being a woman," and told her that she needed to take "a course at charm school." One partner noted that Hopkins "ha[d] matured from a tough-talking somewhat masculine hard-nosed [manager] to an authoritative, formidable, but much more appealing lady [partner] candidate." Another advised her that she needed to "walk more femininely, talk more femininely, dress more femininely, wear make-up, have her hair styled, and wear jewelry."

In *Price Waterhouse*, the Court noted that the company could not place Hopkins in a Catch-22, requiring her to exhibit non-aggressive behavior to fit a more feminine stereotype, but then rewarding male employees who exhibited aggressiveness.[237] The Court also noted that Hopkins was able to tie the comments based on sexual stereotyping to the decision to deny her a partner position because the comments were part of the decisionmaking process and there was no attempt by the company to disavow or blunt the effect of such comments.

Stereotyping can be based on all of the protected traits covered by federal discrimination law.[238] Stereotyping can occur in many different contexts.[239] For example, an employer may have a certain stereotype of people in a certain protected class and then punish employees who do not fit within that stereotype. Or an employer might have positive stereotypes about certain groups and then make decisions disfavoring other groups, based on an assumption that other groups do not possess the positive trait. For example, if an employer assumes that Chinese people work harder than others and only hires people from China, this would be evidence to support a discrimination claim.

Sex stereotyping arguments have played a role in courts recognizing claims for sexual orientation or gender identity discrimination under Title VII.[240] The Seventh Circuit has noted that sexual orientation discrimination relies on a stereotype about one's appropriate sexual partners, that men should be sexually attracted to women and that women should be attracted to men.

§ 3.41 Unconscious Bias and Structural Discrimination

As you consider the available frameworks, you should consider whether the statutes address or should address unconscious bias or structural discrimination. Scholars have argued that workplace culture and unconscious bias result in discrimination.[241] As

[237] *Price Waterhouse*, 490 U.S. at 251.

[238] *See, e.g.*, Thomas v. Eastman Kodak Co., 183 F.3d 38, 58 (1st Cir. 1999).

[239] *Id.* at 61.

[240] Hively v. Ivy Tech Comm. College, 853 F.3d 339, 342 (7th Cir. 2017).

[241] For discussions of structural discrimination and identity performance as a source of discrimination, *see, e.g.*, Samuel R. Bagenstos, *The Structural Turn and the Limits of Antidiscrimination Law*, 94 CAL. L. REV. 1 (2006); Tristin K. Green, *Work Culture and Discrimination*, 93 CAL. L. REV. 623, 625 (2005); Devon W.

Professor Tristin Green writes: "Race, sex, and other protected group characteristics will continue to factor into employment decisions, but the decisions are more likely to be driven by unconscious biases and stereotypes operating within a facilitating organizational context than by conscious animus operating in isolation."[242] Unconscious biases reinforce inequality: these are the "hidden, reflexive preferences that shape most people's worldviews, and that can profoundly affect how welcoming and open a workplace is to different people and ideas."[243] A supervisor may believe he acts in a neutral way, but he is unconsciously affected by societal stereotypes about race, sex, or age.[244]

While some unconscious bias or structural discrimination may be captured by the disparate impact framework, courts have not explicitly and fully considered how and whether these concepts fit within disparate treatment jurisprudence.

Carbado & Mitu Gulati, *Working Identity*, 85 CORNELL L. REV. 1259, 1262 (2000) (discussing how work structure pressures employees to behave in certain ways to perform a work identity).

[242] Tristin K. Green, *A Structural Approach As Antidiscrimination Mandate: Locating Employer Wrong*, 60 VAND. L. REV. 849, 850 (2007).

[243] The following articles are helpful for understanding unconscious or implicit bias. Samuel R. Bagenstos, *Implicit Bias, "Science," and Antidiscrimination Law*, 1 HARV. L. & POL'Y REV. 477 (2007); R. Richard Banks, Jennifer L. Eberhardt & Lee Ross, *Discrimination and Implicit Bias in a Racially Unequal Society*, 94. CAL. L. REV. 1169 (2006); Anthony G. Greenwald & Linda Hamilton Krieger, *Implicit Bias: Scientific Foundations*, 94 CAL. L. REV. 945 (2006); Olatunde C.A. Johnson, *Disparity Rules*, 107 COLUM. L. REV. 374 (2007); Christine Jolls & Cass R. Sunstein, *The Law of Implicit Bias*, 94. CAL. L. REV. 969 (2006); Jerry Kang, *Trojan Horses of Race*, 118 HARV. L. REV. 1489, 1510 (2005); Jerry Kang & Mahzarin R. Banaji, *Fair Measures: A Behavioral Realist Revision of "Affirmative Action,"* 94 CAL. L. REV. 1063 (2006); Linda Hamilton Krieger & Susan T. Fiske, *Behavioral Realism in Employment Discrimination Law: Implicit Bias and Disparate Treatment*, 94 CAL. L. REV. 997 (2006); Charles R. Lawrence III, *The Id, the Ego, and Equal Protection: Reckoning with Unconscious Racism*, 39 STAN. L. REV. 317 (1987).

[244] *See generally* MAHZARIN R. BANAJI & ANTHONY G. GREENWALD, BLINDSPOT: HIDDEN BIASES OF GOOD PEOPLE (2013).

Chapter 4

PATTERN OR PRACTICE

Analysis

§ 4.01 Generally

The last chapter explored individual disparate treatment. In those cases, the plaintiff is trying to establish that an employer took actions against an individual or a small group of individuals because of a protected trait. Another model of proving discrimination is called pattern or practice. Pattern or practice cases are typically brought by the government or in a class action. In such cases, the plaintiffs are trying to establish that the employer has engaged in a pattern or practice of discrimination against an entire group of people based on a protected trait. Once the plaintiff is successful in doing this, the proof of the treatment toward the group establishes a presumption that each person in the group subject to the challenged employment actions was negatively affected. A "pattern or practice case is not a separate and free-standing cause of action . . . , but is really merely another method by which disparate treatment can be shown."[1]

§ 4.02 The *Teamsters'* Model

Int'l Br'hd of Teamsters v. United States[2] established that statistical patterns could be used to prove a pattern or practice of discrimination and outlined the model by which such proof would proceed. In that case, the government sued an employer arguing that it discriminated against African-American and Hispanic truck drivers in hiring, assignments, and promotions. In particular, the government alleged that white drivers were hired and assigned to long-haul driving assignments, which were more lucrative. African-American and Hispanic drivers were rarely hired, and when they were, they were almost always assigned to less lucrative local routes. The government brought this suit pursuant to 42 U.S.C.A. § 2000e–6(a), a provision which provides the government with the ability to seek relief for a pattern or practice of discrimination.

The government's theory of the case was that the company engaged in a pattern or practice of discriminatory actions. The Supreme Court held that the government could

1 United States v. City of N.Y., 717 F.3d 72, 83 (2d Cir. 2013).

2 431 U.S. 324 (1977).

proceed by establishing by a preponderance of the evidence that "racial discrimination was the company's standard operating procedure the regular rather than the unusual practice."[3] The Court noted that to prove this, the government had to do more than show that there were isolated or sporadic instances of discrimination. It further held that the government met this burden.

The government presented statistical data from the employer's workforce. There were 6,4721 employees at the time the government filed the complaint, but only 5% were black and 4% were Hispanic. In the more desirable, line-driver jobs, 0.4% were black and 0.3% were Hispanic. All of the African-American line drivers were hired after the litigation started. In some cities, the employer hired no or almost no black drivers even though a significant portion of the adult working population in those cities was African-American. The government also presented a number of individual examples of qualified individuals who applied for vacancies and were rejected in favor of white applicants.

The employer argued that Title VII explicitly prohibited courts from finding a violation based on a comparison of the racial composition of the employer's workforce to the racial composition of the relevant geographical area. Title VII provides:

> Nothing contained in this subchapter shall be interpreted to require any employer . . . to grant preferential treatment to any individual or to any group because of the race . . . or national origin of such individual or group on account of an imbalance which may exist with respect to the total number or percentage of persons of any race . . . or national origin employed by any employer . . . in comparison with the total number or percentage of persons of such race . . . or national origin in any community, State, section or other area, or in the available work force in any community, State, section or other area.[4]

The Court rejected the employer's interpretation, finding that this provision did not prevent the government from using statistics to support its case. The Court noted that statistics play an important role in proving discrimination.[5] The government did not seek to hold the employer liable merely for a slight imbalance in the employer's work force compared to the areas from which it hired. Rather, the government used the statistical evidence of a large disparity, along with testimony from individuals, to show that the employer explicitly took race into account when hiring and assigning routes.

The Court noted that it had "repeatedly approved the use of statistical proof, where it reached proportions comparable to those in this case, to establish a prima facie case of racial discrimination in jury selection cases." It continued: "Statistics are equally competent in proving employment discrimination. We caution only that statistics are not irrefutable; they come in infinite variety and, like any other kind of evidence, they may be rebutted. In short, their usefulness depends on all of the surrounding facts and circumstances."

The Court also rejected the employer's argument that the plaintiff's evidence should be excluded or minimized because the statistics were general population statistics rather than more refined data which would have showed the racial make-up of the potential work force that possessed the health, qualifications, or proximity to the work place to

[3] *Teamsters*, 431 U.S. at 336.

[4] 42 U.S.C.A. § 2000e–2(j).

[5] For an in-depth discussion of statistics, see Ramona L. Paetzold & Steve L. Willborn, THE STATISTICS OF DISCRIMINATION: USING STATISTICAL EVIDENCE IN DISCRIMINATION CASES.

seek or be considered for employment. "These attacks go only to the accuracy of the comparison . . . . [F]ine tuning of the statistics could not have obscured the glaring absence of minority line drivers . . . . [T]he company's inability to rebut the inference of discrimination came not from a misuse of statistics but from the inexorable zero."[6]

Plaintiff's evidence established that defendant had engaged in a "pattern or practice" of discriminatory hiring. From this, "there are reasonable grounds to infer that individual hiring decisions were made in pursuit of the discriminatory policy."

Pattern or practice cases are typically divided into a liability phase and a remedies phase. The defendant can prevail on the liability phase of a pattern or practice case by rebutting the case made by the plaintiff. If the defendant is successful in doing this, the case ends with no remedies to the plaintiffs. If the defendant is not successful, the case proceeds to the remedies phase.

In a pattern or practice case, the plaintiff does not prove that the company discriminated against each particular individual, as the plaintiff would in an individual disparate treatment case. Rather, the proof of a pattern or practice supports an inference that any employment decision made during the period in which the discriminatory policy was in force, was made in pursuit of that policy. Once the plaintiff proves this, prospective relief (such as an injunction prohibiting future discrimination) is appropriate.

The plaintiff may also secure remedies for individuals aggrieved by the pattern or practice. The plaintiff does this by showing that the individual was within the class against whom the defendant had discriminated and had either applied for a position with defendant or, if he did not apply, that he was deterred from applying because of the employer's discriminatory practices.

In *Teamsters*, the employer argued that individuals who had not applied for jobs should not be permitted to obtain individual relief. However, the Court noted that some individuals might not have applied for jobs because to do so would be futile, given the company's past hiring practices. Disallowing relief in these circumstances would prevent individuals who faced discrimination from obtaining relief. The Court noted that it may be difficult for a plaintiff to prove that he would have applied absent the employer's discriminatory practices.

After the plaintiff meets its burden, the burden then shifts to the employer. "The burden . . . rests on the employer to demonstrate that the individual applicant was denied an employment opportunity for lawful reasons." The burden is more than simply articulating a reason that might have served as a lawful basis for rejecting the applicant. The employer must persuade the trial court it rejected each applicant based on a lawful reason.[7]

The Court noted the difficult decisions the lower courts would need to make to effectuate the appropriate remedy in this case. The trial court should try to place the minority employees in the same position they would have been in had they not faced discrimination, while also balancing the interests of white employees who benefitted from, but who were not responsible for, the company's past discrimination.

---

[6] *Teamsters*, 431 U.S. at 342 n.23.

[7] *See, e.g.*, Hohider v. United Parcel Serv., Inc., 574 F.3d 169, 179 (3d Cir. 2009); Dillon v. Coles, 746 F.2d 998, 1004 (3d Cir. 1984).

In *Teamsters*, the government also sued the union, arguing that the seniority system perpetuated discrimination. The Court held that for acts of discrimination after the effective date of Title VII, individuals who faced discrimination could receive retroactive seniority, placing them in the same seniority position they would have held had they been hired.

However, for discrimination that pre-dated Title VII's effective date, the Court held that Title VII's bona fide seniority system provision (42 U.S.C.A. § 2000e-2(h)) prevented courts from awarding retroactive seniority for that period. Although the seniority provision would lock-in past discrimination, the Court indicated the seniority provision was designed to make it clear that routine use of a bona fide seniority system would remain lawful, even if individuals discriminated against prior to Title VII would perpetually have less seniority than white employees hired during the same period.

Courts have applied pattern or practice analysis to cases brought under the ADEA, the ADA, and Section 1981. Separate issues related to pattern or practice claims under the ADA are considered later in this chapter

§ 4.03 Defining and Refining Statistical Proof: *Hazelwood*

The Supreme Court again considered the pattern or practice framework in *Hazelwood School District v. United States*.[8] The government alleged that the school district discriminated against black applicants for teaching positions.

The school district used a somewhat unstructured and multi-tiered hiring procedure. Applicants submitted materials to a central personnel office. The personnel office then selected three to ten applicants to sit for an interview when there was a teaching vacancy. The personnel office did not screen the applicants, other than determining that the applicants would possess the required teaching license by the time they started a job.

Individuals at the school with a teaching vacancy interviewed the candidates. The hiring criteria were unstructured, and principals at the schools were generally instructed to hire the most competent teacher. In deciding who was the most competent, the principal could use traits such as poise, personality, and the ability to deal with people. The principal almost always had discretion about which individual to hire, and the principal's decision was rarely challenged or overturned.

In the early 1960s, the school district needed to recruit teachers. It recruited at predominantly white universities, and not at the two predominantly black four-year universities in the state of Missouri. The school district did not hire its first black teacher until 1969. The school district gradually increased the number of black teachers it hired from 1970 through 1973.

The particular geography of the case is important to analyzing the evidence presented. The school district was located in St. Louis County and much of the case related to whether the government could make the required showing of a pattern or practice. The city of St. Louis and St. Louis County are separate legal entities, and the city of St. Louis is not contained within St. Louis County. Thus, there was a question of what work force the government could use to make its case: the work force of St. Louis

---

[8] 433 U.S. 299 (1977).

County, of the city of St. Louis, or of the entire St. Louis area (including both the city and the county).

In the years immediately preceding the litigation, 1.8% and 1.4% of Hazelwood's teachers were black. 5.7% of the certified teachers residing in St. Louis County were black. The percentage of black teachers in the St. Louis metropolitan area, which included both the city and the separate county, was 15.4%. In addition, the government presented evidence of the school district's history of discrimination, the relatively unstructured hiring procedure, and evidence from dozens of unsuccessful black applicants.

The district court found against the government, finding that no pattern or practice of discrimination existed. The district court did not find the individual accounts of discrimination to be probative. The district court also relied on an erroneous statistical comparison. It compared the percentage of black students in the school district with the percentage of black teachers in the school district. As there were relatively few black students in the district, the district court held that there was not a statistical imbalance between the number of students and teachers by race.

The appellate court reversed the district court and held that the government had established a pattern or practice. It noted that the district court's statistical analysis was flawed. It also reasoned that the government established a prima facie case of discrimination by comparing the percentage of black teachers employed in the school district with the number of black teachers in the St. Louis metropolitan area.

Relying on *Teamsters* the Supreme Court examined the evidence relied on by the appellate court. The Court discussed the necessity of providing refined data, rather than general work force data, when the position was one that required certain educational and other credentials. The Court noted, "When special qualifications are required to fill particular jobs, comparisons to the general population may have little probative value." In *Teamsters*, general work force data could be used, but this evidence would have been inadequate in *Hazelwood*. "The skill there involved [in *Teamsters*]—the ability to drive a truck—is one that many persons possess or can readily acquire." In contrast, general work force statistics cannot be used in cases involving teachers because most adults do not possess the education and licensing credentials required to be a teacher.

The Court also discussed several potential problems with the way the appellate court reviewed the evidence. First, the appellate court considered data that reflected the school district's hiring prior to the date Title VII became applicable to public employers. The Supreme Court chided the appellate court for ignoring the school district's evidence of post-Act hiring, where the school district submitted evidence regarding the percentage of black teachers hired each year.

The appellate court also failed to consider the district's evidence comparing the number of black teachers who applied for jobs in Hazelwood with the number of black teachers who were hired by the school district (applicant flow data). Instead, the appellate court had relied on the percentage of black teachers working in the Hazelwood school district.

The Court next addressed the proper geographic area. Whether a court chose St. Louis County, the city of St. Louis, or the entire St. Louis metropolitan area would make a difference in the disparity. The city of St Louis engaged in efforts to recruit minority teachers and had a goal that 50 percent of its teachers would be black. This fact might distort the number of area teachers wanting to work in Hazelwood. Without deciding, the Court noted that a more appropriate area upon which to base a work force comparison *might* be St. Louis County, excluding the city data. The percentage of black teachers in St. Louis County was 5.7 percent, a much lower number than the 15.4 percent combined city and county number.

If the court looked at the recent hiring data in Hazelwood and compared it to the number of black teachers in the St. Louis County work force, it would be comparing Hazelwood's hiring of 3.7% of black teachers with the percentage of black teachers in the county, 5.7%. This disparity was much less than the numbers used by the appellate court. The Supreme Court did not decide which statistics should be used by the lower court. Instead, the Court simply noted that the lower courts had not considered all of the relevant evidence related to the statistics and remanded the case for further consideration.

In reaching this conclusion, the Court relied upon "standard deviation analysis." The Court noted that if the difference between the expected number and the observed number is greater than two or three standard deviations, the hypothesis that teachers were hired without regard to race would be suspect. Using this statistical methodology the Court calculated that since the difference between the observed result (3.7%) and the expected result (5.7%) was less than two standard deviations, chance could not be eliminated as a hypothesis. The Court noted, however, that if the trial court accepted St. Louis City and County with its 15.4% black teachers as the more appropriate geographical comparator, then by applying standard deviation analysis, chance would be eliminated as a plausible explanation for the difference.

In summary, *Hazelwood* is important for several reasons. First, the Court approved the use of the "standard deviation analysis" and held that any difference between the expected number and the observed number that exceeded two or three standard deviations could support a hypothesis that chance is not responsible for the deviation. This statistical deviation could support the government's pattern or practice claim.

Second, *Hazelwood* emphasized that if a court is going to use work force statistics, those statistics must be refined in cases where the job requires special education or other credentials. For teachers, the work force data must relate to those individuals who have the required educational and licensing credentials to be a teacher.

Third, if a party is going to rely on work force statistics, those statistics must reflect the area from which the defendant reasonably can be expected to draw its work force. In some cases, the Standard Metropolitan Statistical Area (SMSA),[9] established by the Department of Commerce, will be appropriate.[10] If an employer can be expected to draw significant numbers of applicants from outside the SMSA, a broader comparative population base might be used. However, a smaller area may be appropriate in some circumstances.[11] For example, if a statistical area is very large, a worker living on one side of the area may not be able or willing to commute to a job on the opposite side of the area.

---

[9] This was the term at the time of *Hazelwood.* The term has changed over time, as has the office creating the data. Newer terms include Metropolitan Statistical Area or Primary Metropolitan Statistical Area. Matthews v. Waukesha Cty., 759 F.3d 821, 830 (7th Cir. 2014).

[10] *See, e.g.*, Matthews v. Waukesha Cty., 759 F.3d 821, 830 (7th Cir. 2014).

[11] *See, e.g.*, E.E.O.C. v. Olson's Dairy Queens, Inc., 989 F.2d 165 (5th Cir. 1993).

Fourth, the Court recognized that "applicant flow" data might be relevant in a pattern or practice case. In *Hazelwood*, applicant flow data compared the percentage of minority applicants hired to the percentage of white applicants hired.

§ 4.04 Methodology

In the first step of a pattern or practice case, the plaintiff uses statistics and other evidence to establish that the employer has a pattern or practice of discriminating against a particular class.

The Supreme Court has explained that statistics are relevant in pattern or practice cases.

> Statistics showing racial or ethnic imbalance are probative in a case such as this one only because such imbalance is often a telltale sign of purposeful discrimination; absent explanation, it is ordinarily to be expected that nondiscriminatory hiring practices will, in time, result in a work force more or less representative of the racial and ethnic composition of the population in the community from which employees are hired.[12]

In *Teamsters*, the Court did not require the data to be significantly refined. First, the position in question was one that many people in the work force could perform or could perform with a minimal level of training. Second, *Teamsters* was a case of what the Court called the "inexorable zero," in which almost no employees of certain races worked in certain positions. This was especially suspect because the employer hired from some cities whose work force had a high percentage of minority workers.

In *Hazelwood*, by contrast, if the plaintiff wanted to rely on work force data, the plaintiff was required to provide data for individuals qualified to be teachers, rather than general work force statistics. The Supreme Court noted that several comparisons might be appropriate. A court might consider the difference between the employer's work force and the work force of the appropriate geographic area from which the employer is expected to draw applicants. A court might also compare the employees hired in a particular year or years with the available work force in the appropriate geographic area.

The court might also consider applicant flow data, comparing the teachers who applied for available positions and those who obtained them. Applicant flow data may be skewed. If potential applicants know that the employer traditionally does not hire people in their protected class, they may believe applying is futile, thus changing applicant pool. An employer's recruiting practices may also change the applicant flow. For example, like in *Hazelwood*, the applicant pool would be affected if the employer chose to recruit from predominantly white universities. Or, if the employer made special efforts to recruit from historically black colleges and universities, the applicant pool might contain more minority applicants than expected. In *Hazelwood*, the city of St. Louis' recruitment plan for black teachers may have limited the number of black teachers applying to work in the county.

Although not at issue in *Teamsters* or *Hazelwood*, pattern or practice plaintiffs must also ensure that their statistical evidence is significant, in that it relies on a large enough sample size. Courts have not reached a consensus on a minimum sample size for a reliable inference.

---

[12] Int'l Bhd. of Teamsters v. United States, 431 U.S. 324 (1977).

§ 4.05 Rebutting the Statistics: Defendant's Burden

In the liability phase of a pattern or practice case, the plaintiff presents statistical and other evidence to establish that the employer has a pattern or practice of discriminating against a protected class.[13] During this phase, the employer tries to rebut the plaintiff's evidence. The defendant may do this by showing that the plaintiff's evidence is incorrect or insignificant. In many cases, the defendant will argue that the plaintiff's statistics are inappropriate because the plaintiff did not properly refine the work force data or the plaintiff presented work force data from the wrong statistical area.

The defendant may also argue that the statistical comparison the plaintiff is trying to make is inapt or that a different kind of statistical comparison is more appropriate. For example, in *Hazelwood*, the defendant argued that it was improper for the government to rely on the percentage of black teachers employed by the school district because that data included hiring prior to the effective date of Title VII. The defendant argued that it would be more appropriate to look at applicant flow data or to compare the percentage of black teachers hired in recent years with the work force in the correct geographic area. The defendant also argued that facts particular to the St. Louis area (the city's recruitment plan for black teachers) impacted the relevant statistics.

In most modern pattern or practice cases, the defendant presents its own statistical evidence. The defendant may also rebut the non-statistical evidence presented by the plaintiff.

§ 4.06 Remedies

Given the difficulty of establishing a pattern or practice of discrimination, the main benefit in proceeding under the framework occurs at the remedy stage. During the liability stage, the plaintiff is not required to prove that the pattern or practice affected each individual for whom a remedy is sought. Rather, once the plaintiff establishes the pattern or practice, the presumption is that every individual within the protected class subjected to that practice faced discrimination. Once the plaintiff establishes the required pattern or practice and the defendant fails to properly challenge the plaintiff's evidence, the case enters the remedies phase.

In *Teamsters*, the Supreme Court held that a finding of a pattern or practice justifies prospective relief, without any additional evidence. For example, a court might enter an injunction prohibiting the employer from engaging in the discriminatory practice in the future.

If the plaintiff also seeks individual relief, additional proceedings are typically necessary to determine the appropriateness of individual remedies. During the remedies phase, the presumption that the employer discriminated still remains. The plaintiff does not need to prove that each individual for whom relief is sought faced discrimination. Instead, it is assumed that any individual within the protected class who was subjected to the unlawful practice is entitled to a remedy.[14]

The employer can stop an individual from receiving a remedy by establishing that a particular plaintiff was rejected or would have been rejected for a legitimate, non-

---

[13] United States v. City of New York, 717 F.3d 72, 102 (2d Cir. 2013).

[14] Equal Employment Opportunity Comm'n v. Bass Pro Outdoor World, L.L.C., 826 F.3d 791, 797 (5th Cir. 2016).

discriminatory reason. For example, if a person applied for a position to be a truck driver, but did not have a driver's license, the employer could put forward evidence that no remedy should be given to this particular plaintiff.

Those subjected to a pattern or practice may receive the same remedies as individuals who proceed under an individual disparate treatment theory. Thus, the victims should receive a remedy that makes them whole and places them (as close as possible) to the situation they would have been in if no discrimination had occurred.[15] This includes retroactive seniority.[16] A court may not be able to fully grant a make-whole remedy to the victims of discrimination because the court must also take into account the interests of current workers. For example, a court could not order that the employer fire current workers and hire workers affected by the pattern or practice in their place.

Workers cannot receive seniority for any discrimination that occurred prior to the effective date of the particular federal employment discrimination statute. As more time passes from the effective dates of the federal discrimination statutes, this becomes less of an issue; however, it was an issue in some early pattern or practice cases. The Supreme Court has emphasized that Title VII's remedies are designed both to encourage employers from discriminating in the first place and to make victims of discrimination whole.

Individuals who did not apply for a position may still be entitled to a remedy, if they first demonstrate that they would have applied for the position if defendant had not maintained its discriminatory pattern or practice. As the Supreme Court noted in *Teamsters* responding to the defendants' arguments that non-applicants should not be eligible for a remedy:

> Victims of gross and pervasive discrimination could be denied relief precisely because the unlawful practices had been so successful as totally to deter job applications from members of minority groups. A per se prohibition of relief to nonapplicants could thus put beyond the reach of equity the most invidious effects of employment discrimination—those that extend to the very hope of self-realization. Such a per se limitation on the equitable powers granted to courts by Title VII would be manifestly inconsistent with the "historic purpose of equity to secure complete justice" and with the duty of courts in Title VII cases to render a decree which will so far as possible eliminate the discriminatory effects of the past.[17]

§ 4.07 Government and Non-Government Suits

In *Teamsters*, the government filed suit. Title VII has a specific provision allowing the government to file suit when there is a pattern or practice of discrimination.[18] When the government proceeds under this provision, it is not required to meet the class action prerequisites of Fed.R.Civ.P. 23. Private class actions, using Fed.R.Civ.P. 23, can proceed using the same analytical structure described earlier.

---

[15] Franks v. Bowman Transp. Co., 424 U.S. 747, 764 (1976).

[16] Int'l Bhd. of Teamsters v. United States, 431 U.S. 324, 347 (1977).

[17] *Teamsters*, 431 U.S at 367 (internal citations omitted).

[18] 42 U.S.C.A. § 2000e–6.

In *Wal-Mart Stores, Inc. v. Dukes*,[19] the plaintiffs alleged that Wal-Mart gave discretion to managers to make pay and promotion decisions and that this created a disparate impact on women. It argued that continued use of these subjective practices after knowing about their impact constituted a pattern or practice of discrimination. The Court denied class certification under Rule 23, holding that the plaintiffs were not able to allege common questions of law or fact as required by Rule 23. The discretionary decision-making did not form a pattern or practice because different managers may have made decisions for various reasons, some discriminatory and some not. The Court also noted that the anecdotal evidence submitted by the plaintiffs also did not support a common pattern or practice because the anecdotal evidence related to only 125 employees compared to a proposed class of over a million people. The anecdotal evidence did not support an inference of a pattern or practice across the entire company.

Whether "pattern or practice" analysis can be used in individual, non-class suits is less clear.[20] The term "pattern or practice" derives from 42 U.S.C.A. § 2000e–6, which specifically allows the government to file suit when there is a pattern or practice of discrimination. Courts also allow litigants to use the framework created in *Teamsters* in class actions suits brought under 42 U.S.C.A. § 2000e–2(a)(1). The pattern or practice framework is just another way of proving that discrimination happened because of a protected trait.

However, some recent courts have held that a private plaintiff cannot proceed on a pattern or practice framework unless she is representing a class of plaintiffs.[21] These courts appear to be worried that the plaintiff will somehow prove that there is a general practice or policy of discrimination against a group of people to which the plaintiff belongs, but that the pattern or practice will not establish that the individual plaintiff faced discrimination. The courts express concern that applying the pattern or practice concept in individual cases will improperly place on the defendant the burden of disproving that the practice or policy applied to the plaintiff, when individual treatment frameworks require the plaintiff to bear the burden of proof to show that the employer discriminated against plaintiff. Further, the courts are unsure about how pattern or practice would intersect with other expressed tests for considering individual disparate treatment cases, such as *McDonnell Douglas*.

These cases underappreciate several facets of pattern or practice doctrine. First, it is very difficult for a plaintiff to establish that an employer had a policy or practice of discriminating against an entire group of people. The pattern or practice framework is typically harder to prove than individual disparate treatment. Second, when a plaintiff proves the pattern or practice, the Supreme Court has stated that this creates a presumption that all individuals within the protected class were affected by the practice. Therefore, it would be a rare case where plaintiff would present evidence that a

---

[19] 564 U.S. 338 (2011).

[20] *See, e.g.*, Parisi v. Goldman, Sachs & Co., 710 F.3d 483, 488 (2d Cir. 2013); Semsroth v. City of Wichita, 304 F. App'x 707, 716 (10th Cir. 2008); Bacon v. Honda of Am. Mfg., Inc., 370 F.3d 565, 575 (6th Cir. 2004) ("We therefore hold that the pattern-or-practice method of proving discrimination is not available to individual plaintiffs."); Chin v. Port Auth. of New York & New Jersey, 685 F.3d 135, 149 (2d Cir. 2012); Davis v. Califano, 613 F.2d 957 (D.C. Cir. 1979).

[21] *See, e.g.*, Daniels v. United Parcel Serv., Inc., 701 F.3d 620, 632 (10th Cir. 2012); Chin v. Port Auth., 685 F.3d 135, 147 (2d Cir. 2012). *But see* Davis v. Califano, 613 F.2d 957, 961–62 (D.C. Cir. 1979); Karp v. CIGNA Healthcare, Inc., 882 F. Supp. 2d 199, 213 (D. Mass. 2012).

defendant had a pattern or practice of treating a group in a certain way and that an individual plaintiff within that group was not impacted by that practice.

Finally, and most importantly, it may be unnecessary to decide whether plaintiff can proceed on a separate theory of pattern or practice. It is appropriate for a plaintiff to raise evidence of a pattern or practice to support her individual disparate treatment claim.[22] For most individual cases, there is little practical difference between allowing the plaintiff to proceed on a separate theory of pattern or practice or allowing the plaintiff to use evidence of a pattern or practice in support of her individual discrimination theory.

§ 4.08 ADA and Pattern or Practice

The ADA explicitly allows the government to bring pattern or practice cases.[23] Lower courts have also indicated that pattern or practice cases can proceed under the ADA as a general principle.[24] While courts recognize that pattern or practice claims may proceed under the ADA, the specific requirements of the ADA may require courts to modify the analysis or refuse to certify a class, depending on the particular facts alleged.

Under the ADA, an employer is not required to treat people the same regardless of disability, but instead, may take into account whether the individual is qualified to perform the requirements of the job with or without a reasonable accommodation. Thus, if an individual had a disability that rendered him unable to work, the employer could refuse to hire the individual because of that disability. Likewise, if the individual could only perform the job if the employer accommodated the person in ways that would exceed the requirements of the ADA, the employer could also refuse to hire the individual. ADA analysis therefore sometimes requires an individual inquiry into a particular person's disability, the particular job in question, and whether an accommodation would be reasonable in a particular circumstance. These individualized inquiries may hinder class certification of a pattern or practice claim under the ADA.[25] However, not all pattern or practice ADA claims would necessarily require such an individualized showing.

---

[22] Artis v. Yellen, 309 F.R.D. 69, 74 (D.D.C. 2015), aff'd, No. 15–5260, 2015 WL 10583057 (D.C. Cir. Dec. 21, 2015); Chin v. Port Auth. of N.Y. & N.J., 685 F.3d 135, 150 (2d Cir. 2012).

[23] 42 U.S.C.A. § 12117(a) (incorporating by reference 42 U.S.C.A. § 2000e–6).

[24] Monaco v. City of Jacksonville, 51 F. Supp. 3d 1251, 1261 (M.D. Fla. 2014), aff'd, 671 F. App'x 737 (11th Cir. 2016).

[25] Hohider v. United Parcel Serv., Inc., 574 F.3d 169, 172 (3d Cir. 2009).

Chapter 5

HARASSMENT

Analysis

§ 5.01 Generally

The federal discrimination laws prohibit harassment because of a protected trait. A plaintiff may establish harassment based on any of the traits protected under the federal discrimination laws. Generally, courts follow the same framework for analyzing harassment claims under Title VII, the ADEA, the ADA and Section 1981. Most harassment cases involve allegations that a plaintiff faced demeaning or differential speech or conduct because of a protected trait. For example, a plaintiff might claim that a supervisor regularly made fun of her disability, which might constitute disability harassment under the ADA.

In *Meritor Savings Bank, FSB v. Vinson*[1] the Supreme Court discussed sexual harassment. Sexual harassment occurs in a number of different ways. When the employer conditions employment opportunities upon entering into a sexual or social relationship, this is sexual harassment. Sexual harassment can also be based on negative comments and conduct that is undertaken because of sex. Sexual harassment can consist of conduct and behavior that is sexual in nature. However, the comments and conduct are not required to be sexual in nature.[2] For example, if a supervisor regularly demeans a female employee because of her sex, this can constitute sexual harassment.

---

1 477 U.S. 57 (1986).

2 Vicki Schultz, *Reconceptualizing Sexual Harassment*, 107 YALE L.J. 1683 (1993); Vicki Schultz, *Reconceptualizing Sexual Harassment, Again*, 128 YALE L.J.F. 22, 24 (2018) (discussing how the #MeToo movement also often focuses on sexualized harassment); *see also* Laura T. Kessler, *Employment Discrimination and the Domino Effect*, 44 FLA. ST. U. L. REV. 1041, 1066 (2017); Tristin K. Green, *Was Sexual Harassment Law a Mistake? The Stories We Tell*, 128 YALE L.J.F. 152 (2018), https://www.yalelawjournal.org/forum/was-sexual-harassment-law-mistake.

§ 5.02 Quid Pro Quo

The denial of an employment opportunity because of the individual's refusal to have a sexual or social relationship with a supervisor is discrimination because of sex. Likewise, demanding and receiving sexual favors in exchange for promotions or other tangible employment actions is illegal sex discrimination.[3] Although most courts do not delineate separate elements for quid pro quo cases, some courts tend to look at three factors: (1) whether there was a request for a sexual favor or improper relationship; (2) whether there was a grant or denial of a tangible employment benefit; and (3) whether there was a causal connection between the worker's response to the request and the grant or denial of the employment benefit.[4] "A tangible employment action constitutes a significant change in employment status, such as hiring, firing, failing to promote, reassignment with significantly different responsibilities, or a decision causing a significant change in benefits."[5]

Sexual favors do not need to be requests for actual sex, but can also create liability when the supervisor requests other conduct of a sexual nature, such as wanting to kiss or fondle an employee.[6]

When a female employee is promoted over a male employee because she is having a sexual affair with the supervisor, this should constitute sex discrimination against the rejected male employee. However, most courts have held that there is no sex discrimination if a supervisor rewards his paramour by giving him or her employment opportunities to the detriment of other employees.[7] Discrimination against an applicant or current employee because the spouse or relative of that individual refused to have a sexual relationship with the employer states a Title VII claim.[8]

Consensual sexual interaction does not create quid pro quo liability to those involved in the relationship.[9] However, just because conduct is voluntary, does not mean that it is consensual. If a worker agrees to provide sexual favors in exchange for job benefits or because she fears a tangible employment action if she refuses, this is a basis for a quid pro quo claim, even if the sexual favors are not otherwise coerced. Additionally, if a consensual sexual relationship ends, quid pro quo liability may develop if a supervisor continues to demand sexual favors in exchange for favorable treatment or to avoid negative employment actions.

Most quid pro quo cases involve individuals who have the power to take employment actions against the person refusing or acceding to the sexual advances. The courts have typically not allowed quid pro quo cases to proceed when a co-worker is the one demanding sexual favors. These claims typically proceed under the harassment framework. However, a worker may be able to show that her refusal to accede to the sexual demands of a co-worker caused a tangible employment action through a cat's paw

---

[3] Valentin-Almeyda v. Municipality of Aguadilla, 447 F.3d 85, 94 (1st Cir. 2006).

[4] Alaniz v. Zamora-Quezada, 591 F.3d 761, 772 (5th Cir. 2009).

[5] *Alaniz*, 591 F.3d at 772. Some courts use less strict language such as tangible job detriment, suggesting that the action does not need to meet the high standard of a tangible employment action.

[6] McMiller v. Metro, 738 F.3d 185, 189 (8th Cir. 2013).

[7] Becerra v. Dalton, 94 F.3d 145, 149–50 (4th Cir. 1996); DeCintio v. Westchester Cty. Med. Ctr., 807 F.2d 304 (2d Cir. 1986); Ahern v. Omnicare ESC LLC, No. 5:08-CV-291-FL, 2009 WL 2591320, at *5 (E.D.N.C. Aug. 19, 2009).

[8] *See* Simmons v. Lyons, 746 F.2d 265 (5th Cir. 1984).

[9] Souther v. Posen Const., Inc., 523 F. App'x 352, 356 (6th Cir. 2013).

theory.[10] For example, if an influential co-worker lied to management after a worker refused his sexual advances and management fired the worker based on the lie, the worker may be able to establish liability.

Courts treat threats to take action based on a worker's refusal to submit to requests for sexual favors differently than cases where the threat is carried out. As the Supreme Court has noted: "Cases based on threats which are carried out are referred to often as *quid pro quo* cases, as distinct from bothersome attentions or sexual remarks that are sufficiently severe or pervasive to create a hostile work environment. The terms *quid pro quo* and hostile work environment are helpful, perhaps, in making a rough demarcation between cases in which threats are carried out and those where they are not or are absent altogether[.]"[11]

Employer liability for quid pro quo claims is discussed in § 5.10 below.

§ 5.03 Hostile Working Environment, Generally

Most harassment cases reflect a second kind of harassment called hostile working environment. A hostile working environment can encompass words or conduct that negatively affect the terms and condition of employment. For example, when an employer singles out an employee for particularly rough treatment in the form of hazing, practical jokes, or insulting epithets because of the employee's protected trait, this will violate federal discrimination law. Unusually close supervision, criticism, or reprimands can constitute harassment when they occur because of a protected trait. Repeated sexual inquiries, requests for sexual activity, or unauthorized touching will be improper sex discrimination even if no economic consequences flow from the conduct.[12]

Even when an individual is not the direct object of the harassment, an employer will be violate federal discrimination law if it creates or allows a pervasive atmosphere hostile to members of a protected class. Thus, repeated racist, sexist, or similar jokes, the presence of demeaning graffiti, repeatedly using racial or sexists slurs or belittling comments is discrimination in "terms and conditions of employment." Isolated, non-severe incidents, however, will not violate the statutes. Insults, jokes, comments, and the like must be repeated with sufficient regularity that they constitute a part of the regular working environment.[13]

Although a discriminatory work environment most often involves treating one class differently than another, differential treatment is not necessary. If all of the workers in an all-black work force were subjected to abuse because of their race, such treatment would adversely affect their status as employees in violation of federal discrimination law.

---

[10] Higgins v. Lufkin Indus., Inc., 633 F. App'x 229, 233 (5th Cir. 2015).

[11] Burlington Indus., Inc. v. Ellerth, 524 U.S. 742, 751 (1998).

[12] Meritor Savings Bank v. Vinson, 477 U.S. 57 (1986); EEOC v. Murphy Motor Freight Lines, Inc., 488 F.Supp. 381 (D. Minn. 1980).

[13] Even some sexualized conduct will not meet the requirement. *See* Joanna L. Grossman, *The First Bite Is Free: Employer Liability for Sexual Harassment*, 61 U. PITT. L. REV. 671 (2000).

§ 5.04 Hostile Working Environment, Framework

The Supreme Court developed the basic framework for evaluating hostile environment claims in *Meritor Savings Bank, FSB v. Vinson*[14] and *Harris v. Forklift Sys., Inc.*[15]

In *Meritor*, the Court considered whether a plaintiff could state a claim for a sexual harassment. It noted that the text of Title VII did not limit claims to hiring, promotion, or termination, but rather applied to all "terms, conditions, or privileges" of employment. Relying on the statutory text and EEOC Guidelines, the Court held that Title VII prohibited "[u]nwelcome sexual advances, requests for sexual favors, and other verbal or physical conduct of a sexual nature." Such sexual misconduct constitutes prohibited sexual harassment, even if it is not directly linked to the grant or denial of an economic *quid pro quo,* where "such conduct has the purpose or effect of unreasonably interfering with an individual's work performance or creating an intimidating, hostile, or offensive working environment."[16] The Court also indicated that Title VII provided employees the opportunity to work in environments that are free of discriminatory ridicule, intimidation, and insults.

Quoting a lower court opinion, the Supreme Court noted:

> Sexual harassment which creates a hostile or offensive environment for members of one sex is every bit the arbitrary barrier to sexual equality at the workplace that racial harassment is to racial equality. Surely, a requirement that a man or woman run a gauntlet of sexual abuse in return for the privilege of being allowed to work and make a living can be as demeaning and disconcerting as the harshest of racial epithets.[17]

The Supreme Court indicated that not all conduct would rise to the level of an actionable hostile environment. Rather "it must be sufficiently severe or pervasive to alter the conditions of [the victim's] employment and create an abusive working environment."[18]

Even though *Meritor* was a sexual harassment case, the Supreme Court recognized that claims of racial harassment were also cognizable. Lower courts have recognized harassment claims for all of the protected classes under federal discrimination law.

In *Harris*, a female employee presented evidence that her supervisor made both demeaning and sexual comments to and about female employees, including the plaintiff. The Supreme Court considered how serious conduct or speech needed to be to constitute an actionable hostile environment claim. The Supreme Court noted: "The phrase 'terms, conditions, or privileges of employment' evinces a congressional intent 'to strike at the entire spectrum of disparate treatment of men and women' in employment," which includes requiring people to work in a discriminatorily hostile or abusive environment.[19]

It rejected a standard that would require a person to show she suffered severe psychological trauma. Rather, the Court indicated:

---

[14] 477 U.S. 57 (1986).

[15] 510 U.S. 17 (1993).

[16] *Meritor,* 477 U.S. at 65.

[17] *Meritor,* 477 U.S. at 67.

[18] *Meritor,* 477 U.S. at 67.

[19] Harris v. Forklift Sys., Inc., 510 U.S. 17, 21 (1993).

> Title VII comes into play before the harassing conduct leads to a nervous breakdown. A discriminatorily abusive work environment, even one that does not seriously affect employees' psychological well-being, can and often will detract from employees' job performance, discourage employees from remaining on the job, or keep them from advancing in their careers. Moreover, even without regard to these tangible effects, the very fact that the discriminatory conduct was so severe or pervasive that it created a work environment abusive to employees because of their race, gender, religion, or national origin offends Title VII's broad rule of workplace equality.[20]

In *Harris*, the Supreme Court held that conduct that is severe or pervasive enough to create an objectively hostile or abusive work environment is cognizable. In determining whether an environment is hostile, the Court indicated that it must look at all of the circumstances.

> These may include the frequency of the discriminatory conduct; its severity; whether it is physically threatening or humiliating, or a mere offensive utterance; and whether it unreasonably interferes with an employee's work performance. The effect on the employee's psychological well-being is, of course, relevant to determining whether the plaintiff actually found the environment abusive. But while psychological harm, like any other relevant factor, may be taken into account, no single factor is required.[21]

In addition to looking at whether the environment is objectively hostile, the Supreme Court also held that the worker must subjectively perceive the environment to be hostile.

From the contours provided in *Meritor* and *Harris*, lower courts have fashioned a multiple part framework to evaluate hostile environment cases. Although the elements vary slightly in some circuits, to prove a hostile work environment claim, an employee must establish (1) the employee belongs to a protected class; (2) the employee was subject to unwelcome harassment; (3) the harassment was based on a protected trait; and (4) the harassment affected a term, condition, or privilege of employment.[22] To affect a term, condition, or privilege of employment, the harassment "must be sufficiently severe or pervasive to alter the conditions of [the victim's] employment and create an abusive working environment."[23] In addition, the worker must show that there is a basis for holding the employer liable for the harassment.

§ 5.05 Employee Belongs to a Protected Class

The first factor in the harassment framework is that the plaintiff belongs to a protected class. This is not typically difficult to establish and very few cases discuss this element. Instead, there is more focus on whether the plaintiff can establish that the harassment occurred because of a protected trait.

If a plaintiff claims she faced harassment because of personal animosity unrelated to a protected trait, she does not have a viable harassment claim. Individuals can state a claim for harassment based on a perceived protected trait. For example, if a

---

20 *Harris*, 510 U.S. at 22.

21 *Harris*, 510 U.S. at 23.

22 Aryain v. Wal-Mart Stores Tex. LP, 534 F.3d 473 (5th Cir. 2008).

23 Meritor Savings Bank, FSB v. Vinson, 477 U.S. 57 (1986).

harassment occurs because an individual believes his co-worker is a practicing Muslim, the plaintiff can proceed even if he is not a practicing Muslim.

Harassment because of sexual orientation, transgender status, or gender conformity may raise issues related to protected class. As of the writing of this book, the federal courts are still struggling with whether the federal discrimination statutes prohibit this conduct. The Supreme Court has granted a writ of certiorari in three cases to determine whether Title VII prohibits discrimination because of sexual orientation and transgender status. Issues related to protected classes are discussed in detail in Chapter 2.

§ 5.06 Unwelcome Conduct or Speech

In *Meritor*, the Supreme Court held that harassment must be unwelcome.[24] A worker who welcomes and engages in sexual conduct or crude conduct may not be able to establish this factor. The Supreme Court held that evidence of whether plaintiff welcomed the conduct could be relevant to her case and declined to issue a per se rule excluding such evidence. Harassment is unwelcome if "the employee did not solicit or incite it . . . and the employee regarded the conduct as undesirable or offensive."[25]

Just because conduct is voluntary does not mean it is welcome. In *Meritor*, the Court noted "[T]he fact that sex-related conduct was 'voluntary,' in the sense that the complainant was not forced to participate against her will, is not a defense to a sexual harassment suit brought under Title VII."[26] Instead, "the correct inquiry is whether [plaintiff] by her conduct indicated that the alleged sexual advances were unwelcome, not whether her actual participation in sexual intercourse was voluntary."[27]

Even if the plaintiff and the alleged harasser once had a consensual sexual relationship, this does not mean that subsequent conduct is welcome.[28] Rather, there will often be a factual question about whether continued sexual conduct or speech was unwelcome. A worker does not waive a harassment claim by engaging in crude or vulgar speech or behavior;[29] however, such speech or conduct may make it harder for the plaintiff to establish that harassment is unwelcome. Courts have held that a plaintiff could not prove this element when she engaged in similar behavior to the behavior she was alleging in her harassment suit.[30] Often plaintiffs can show unwelcomeness in these situations by establishing that the conduct or speech of the harasser was different in kind or degree from the conduct in which the plaintiff engaged or that the plaintiff felt compelled to engage in the speech or conduct. Plaintiffs can show that their speech or conduct outside of work is not relevant to whether harassment at the workplace is unwelcome, especially when the speech or conduct does not relate to the alleged harasser.[31]

---

24 *Meritor*, 477 U.S. at 68.

25 Henson v. City of Dundee, 682 F.2d 897 (9th Cir. 1982).

26 *Meritor*, 477 U.S. at 68.

27 *Id.*

28 Crutcher-Sanchez v. Cty. of Dakota, 687 F.3d 979, 985 (8th Cir. 2012).

29 E.E.O.C. v. Fairbrook Med. Clinic, P.A., 609 F.3d 320, 329 (4th Cir. 2010).

30 Scusa v. Nestle U.S.A. Co., 181 F.3d 958, 966 (8th Cir. 1999).

31 E.E.O.C. v. Wal-Mart Stores, Inc., 198 F.3d 257 (10th Cir. 1999); Winsor v. Hinckley Dodge, Inc., 79 F.3d 996, 1001 (10th Cir. 1996) (quoting Katz v. Dole, 709 F.2d 251, 254 n. 3 (4th Cir.1983)); *see also* Burns v. McGregor Elec. Indus., Inc., 989 F.2d 959, 963 (8th Cir. 1993).

§ 5.07 Harassment Because of Protected Trait

The federal discrimination statutes do not prohibit generalized harassment in the workplace. Rather, their scope is limited to harassment that is taken because of a protected trait. If the evidence shows that harassment resulted from personal animosity unrelated to a protected trait, this is not remediable harassment under the federal discrimination statutes, no matter how reprehensible the conduct.

Confusion occasionally arises from the name "sexual harassment." Harassment of a sexual nature presents a claim under Title VII; however, the harassment does not need to be sexual in nature to constitute sexual harassment. If a supervisor regularly makes demeaning comments of a non-sexual nature to a female employee because of her sex, this is sexual harassment. Some courts have "found that there is a distinction between personal animosity arising from a failed, [consensual] relationship, which is not actionable sexual harassment, and animosity based on a person's gender," which would be.[32] However, such cases often involve questions of fact that must be left to the factfinder.

As discussed in greater detail below, same-sex sexual harassment can be a viable claim if the harassment is "because of" sex. For example, it would be sexual harassment for a man to make unwanted sexual advances to another man.

§ 5.08 Harassment Affected the Terms, Conditions, or Privileges of Employment

In *Meritor Savings Bank, FSB v. Vinson*[33] the Court considered whether sexual harassment had to affect the plaintiff economically to state a claim. The Court rejected this argument holding: "Title VII is not limited to 'economic' or 'tangible' discrimination. The phrase 'terms, conditions, or privileges of employment' evinces a congressional intent 'to strike at the entire spectrum of disparate treatment of men and women' in employment." The Court recognized, however, that "not all workplace conduct that may be described as 'harassment' will affect a 'term, condition or privilege of employment' within the meaning of Title VII."

To affect a term, condition, or privilege of employment, the harassment "must be sufficiently severe or pervasive to alter the conditions of [the victim's] employment and create an abusive working environment."[34] This element has both a subjective and an objective component. The particular plaintiff must perceive the harassment as severe or pervasive. In addition a reasonable person in the plaintiff's position must also perceive the conduct as such.

In *Harris*, the Supreme Court held that in determining whether an environment is hostile, the Court indicated that it must look at all of the circumstances.

> These may include the frequency of the discriminatory conduct; its severity; whether it is physically threatening or humiliating, or a mere offensive utterance; and whether it unreasonably interferes with an employee's work performance. The effect on the employee's psychological well-being is, of course, relevant to determining whether the plaintiff actually found the environment

---

[32] Kohutka v. Town of Hempstead, 994 F. Supp. 2d 305, 328 (E.D.N.Y. 2014) (collecting cases).

[33] *Meritor*, 477 U.S. at 64.

[34] *Meritor*, 477 U.S. at 67.

> abusive. But while psychological harm, like any other relevant factor, may be taken into account, no single factor is required.[35]

The Supreme Court has repeatedly reiterated that the federal discrimination statutes are not a "general civility code."[36] However, the Court has also stated that the federal discrimination statutes strike at the entire spectrum of discriminatory conduct. These statements are hard to reconcile, and there is little consistency in federal court rulings about what is serious enough to constitute harassment and what is not.

Conduct must either be severe or pervasive. If one severe action occurs this alone may be sufficient to establish harassment. For example, if a supervisor rapes an employee one time, this would be severe enough to constitute harassment.[37] Conduct that is physical or physically threatening is more likely to be harassment than words alone. However, the federal courts have been inconsistent about whether conduct that might otherwise constitute assault, battery, or sexual assault necessarily rise to the level of being severe or pervasive.[38] At times, courts grant summary judgment to employers even if the plaintiff presents evidence that a co-worker or supervisor touched her breasts or butt or kissed her. These courts find the conduct not to be severe or pervasive enough to be harassment. Other courts will find harassment possible under these circumstances.[39]

Many cases of harassment involve offensive speech or conduct that occurs over a period of time. Whether such activity amounts to harassment is judged by the totality of the circumstances. In looking at whether activity is severe or pervasive, judges will often look at the seriousness of the incidents, how many times they occurred, and the time period over which they occurred. At times, the person engaging in the conduct appears to be important, with conduct by a supervisor deemed to be more serious than conduct by co-workers. The context in which the activity takes place is also important. The Supreme Court has noted that a pat on the butt between a football coach and a player during a game should not be viewed the same as a supervisor doing the same thing in an office environment.

Courts are inconsistent regarding whether the use of epithets is enough to create a hostile environment. In one case, a federal trial court judge found a claim that the worker's supervisor twice called her "porch monkey" was not harassment and dismissed the case.[40] Although the judge did "not question that the term is highly offensive to African Africans," the judge found the isolated comments were not severe or pervasive. The Fourth Circuit affirmed the lower court. While the three-judge panel noted that the use of term "porch monkey" was "racially derogatory and highly offensive," it could not

---

[35] *Harris*, 510 U.S. at 23.

[36] Faragher v. City of Boca Raton, 524 U.S. 775, 788 (1998).

[37] Ferris v. Delta Air Lines, Inc., 277 F.3d 128, 136 (2d Cir. 2001).

[38] *See, e.g.*, Hockman v. Westward Commc'ns, 407 F.3d 317, 328 (5th Cir. 2004); Matherne v. Ruba Mgmt., No. CIV.A. 12–2461, 2014 WL 2938100, at *6 (E.D. La. June 27, 2014) (characterizing the holding of Landers v. CHLN, Inc., Civ. A. No. 07–75, 2009 WL 803777 (E.D. Ky. Mar. 25, 2009), which concluded that plaintiff's evidence of multiple comments about plaintiff's breasts, requests to lick whipped cream and wine off of her, inappropriate touching while hugging plaintiff, requests to go out, rubbing plaintiff's shoulders, arms and rear end and inappropriate text messages were not sufficiently severe or pervasive under Kentucky state law, using similar standard as federal law).

[39] *See, e.g.*, Redd v. N.Y. State Div. of Parole, 678 F.3d 166 (2d Cir. 2012).

[40] Boyer-Liberto v. Fontainebleau Corp., No. CIV. JKB-12-212, 2013 WL 1413031, at *3 (D. Md. Apr. 4, 2013), aff'd, 752 F.3d 350 (4th Cir. 2014), vacated on reh'g en banc, 786 F.3d 264 (4th Cir. 2015). The supervisor denied making the comments.

constitute harassment because there were only two instances of the comment being made. The worker then asked the Fourth Circuit to hear her case en banc, which is a review by the full appellate court, rather than the normal three-judge panel that typically hears appeals.[41] The full Fourth Circuit "en banc" court reversed both of the prior decisions. It held that a reasonable jury could find that the worker was subjected to racial harassment. The court noted that "no single act can more quickly alter the conditions of employment and create an abusive working environment than the use of an unambiguously racial epithet."[42]

Whether the conduct or harassment is directed at the plaintiff also makes a difference in judging its severity. In *Clark Cty. Sch. Dist. v. Breeden*,[43] a woman, her male supervisor, and a male employee were considering job applicants. The psychological report for one of the applicants revealed that the applicant had once said to a co-worker, "I hear making love to you is like making love to the Grand Canyon." The supervisor read the comment aloud and stated, "I don't know what that means." The other employee told the supervisor that he would explain it later. Both men chuckled. The female employee reported the interaction as offensive and then later filed suit for retaliation. The Supreme Court held that the plaintiff could not state a retaliation claim because no reasonable person would believe the underlying conduct constituted sexual harassment. The Court noted:

> No reasonable person could have believed that the single incident recounted above violated Title VII's standard. The ordinary terms and conditions of respondent's job required her to review the sexually explicit statement in the course of screening job applicants. Her co-workers who participated in the hiring process were subject to the same requirement, and indeed, in the District Court respondent "conceded that it did not bother or upset her" to read the statement in the file. App. to Pet. for Cert. 15 (District Court opinion). Her supervisor's comment, made at a meeting to review the application, that he did not know what the statement meant; her co-worker's responding comment; and the chuckling of both are at worst an "isolated inciden[t]" that cannot remotely be considered "extremely serious," as our cases require.[44]

The unique facts of *Breeden* should have limited applicability in other contexts. However, the case does suggest that one comment, which is not directed to or about the plaintiff, is unlikely to rise to the level of cognizable harassment. Just because a comment alone does not establish a claim, does not mean that such a comment would not be admissible evidence to support a plaintiff's claim that other speech or conduct created a hostile working environment. Such evidence may provide information about the environment that existed.

It is worth noting that the case law has become increasingly detached from the statutory language and also from the underlying purpose of harassment law stated in *Meritor*.

---

[41] Boyer-Liberto v. Fontainebleau Corp., 752 F.3d 350, 357 (4th Cir. 2014), vacated on reh'g en banc, 786 F.3d 264 (4th Cir. 2015).

[42] Boyer-Liberto v. Fontainebleau Corp., 786 F.3d 264 (4th Cir. 2015).

[43] 532 U.S. 268, 269 (2001).

[44] *Breeden*, 532 U.S. at 271.

§ 5.09 Same-Sex Sexual Harassment

The federal discrimination statutes do not prohibit all harassment, just harassment that is because of a protected trait. In *Oncale v. Sundowner Offshore Servs., Inc.*, the plaintiff alleged that male employees harassed him.[45] The Supreme Court held that Title VII prohibits same-sex sexual harassment. The Court indicated that allowing same-sex harassment claims would not transform Title VII into a general civility code. Rather, the plaintiff in same-sex harassment cases would still need to establish that the harassment occurred "because of sex." The Court indicated several ways the plaintiff might be able to establish this.

> Courts and juries have found the inference of discrimination easy to draw in most male-female sexual harassment situations, because the challenged conduct typically involves explicit or implicit proposals of sexual activity; it is reasonable to assume those proposals would not have been made to someone of the same sex. The same chain of inference would be available to a plaintiff alleging same-sex harassment, if there were credible evidence that the harasser was homosexual. But harassing conduct need not be motivated by sexual desire to support an inference of discrimination on the basis of sex. A trier of fact might reasonably find such discrimination, for example, if a female victim is harassed in such sex-specific and derogatory terms by another woman as to make it clear that the harasser is motivated by general hostility to the presence of women in the workplace. A same-sex harassment plaintiff may also, of course, offer direct comparative evidence about how the alleged harasser treated members of both sexes in a mixed-sex workplace.[46]

The Supreme Court recognized that Congress was not likely thinking about the problem of same-sex harassment when it enacted Title VII. However, the Supreme Court held that this was not controlling. Rather, the text of Title VII prohibits discrimination because of sex and does not limit its protections to one protected sex or to opposite-sex harassment. The Court also recognized that men can harass men and women can harass women.

§ 5.10 Employer Liability, History

In *Meritor*, the Supreme Court refused to decide when an employer would be liable for a hostile work environment. Rather the Court vaguely suggested that agency principles would apply and that the employer would not be liable for all harassment committed by its employees.[47] The Court also unhelpfully noted that common law agency principles might not be fully transferable to the Title VII context.

The Supreme Court decided the question left open in *Meritor* in two subsequent cases issued on the same day: *Faragher v. City of Boca Raton*[48] and *Burlington Industries, Inc. v. Ellerth*.[49] These cases created a complicated framework for evaluating employer liability. Even though the cases were decided on the same day, they provide differing rationales for the enunciated test.

---

[45] Oncale v. Sundowner Offshore Servs., Inc., 523 U.S. 75, 78 (1998).

[46] *Oncale*, 523 U.S. at 80–81 (1998).

[47] Meritor Savings Bank v. Vinson, 477 U.S. 57, 71 (1986).

[48] 524 U.S. 775 (1998).

[49] 524 U.S. 742 (1998).

In *Faragher*, a lifeguard alleged that two of her supervisors created a hostile working environment by making lewd remarks, subjecting female lifeguards to offensive touching, and making derogatory remarks about women. The lifeguard never formally complained to the city of Boca Raton about the treatment, although she did mention her concerns to another employee who had some supervisory responsibilities. After a bench trial, the district court judge held that the lifeguard faced a hostile work environment and that the city was liable for it because the two harassers were agents of the city and because another individual with some supervisory duties knew about the conduct. The Eleventh Circuit Court of Appeals reversed, finding that the city was not liable for the harassment because the harassers were not acting within the scope of their employment, the city did not have actual or constructive knowledge of the harassment, and the city did not aid the harassers in committing their harassment.

In *Faragher*, the Court noted that *Meritor* provided rough contours for determining employer liability. First, *Meritor* indicated that employers would not be absolved of liability based on the existence of a company complaint procedure or in cases where the employer did not possess actual knowledge of the harassment. Second, *Meritor* indicated that employers would not be automatically liable for a supervisor's sexual harassment. Although these statements in *Meritor* were arguably dicta, the *Faragher* Court built upon these foundational principles and claimed to be bound by stare decisis.

The Court then looked to common-law agency principles to fill in the gap, although it should be noted that both the reasoning and the outcome of the case do not strictly mimic agency law. The Court first looked at agency law related to an employer's liability for its agents. The general principle is that an employer is liable for employee actions within the course and scope of their employment, but is not generally liable for intentional torts outside of the course and scope. Lower courts had held that because sexual harassment is often motivated by individual desire and is often prohibited by employer policies, a harassing employee is typically not acting within the scope of employment. However, the Court noted that agency law was not clear cut and that, in some cases, courts held employers liable for the intentional torts committed by employees even though the conduct was outside the scope of employment. The Court lamented the unhelpfulness of the scope of employment test and noted that outcomes in cases were often driven by policy considerations.

The Court noted: "The proper analysis here, then, calls not for a mechanical application of indefinite and malleable factors set forth in the Restatement, see, *e.g.*, §§ 219, 228, 229, but rather an inquiry into the reasons that would support a conclusion that harassing behavior ought to be held within the scope of a supervisor's employment, and the reasons for the opposite view."[50] The Court then considered whether employers should be liable for a supervisor's harassment because the costs of the supervisor's actions should properly be borne by the employer, rather than the victim of the harassment. The Court rejected applying a blanket rule of liability, noting that there was no reason to assume that Congress intended to reject common law distinctions about the scope of employment. The Court also noted that the majority of lower courts had held co-worker harassment to be outside the scope of an employee's duties and based employer liability on its own negligence.

---

[50] Faragher v. City of Boca Raton, 524 U.S. 775, 797 (1998).

The Court then considered whether employers should be automatically liable for a supervisor's harassment because the employer aides the supervisor by placing him or her in a position of authority. The *Faragher* Court reasoned that it made sense to hold employer's automatically liable for some conduct of supervisors based on this aiding and abetting rationale. The Court noted:

> The agency relationship affords contact with an employee subjected to a supervisor's sexual harassment, and the victim may well be reluctant to accept the risks of blowing the whistle on a superior. When a person with supervisory authority discriminates in the terms and conditions of subordinates' employment, his actions necessarily draw upon his superior position over the people who report to him, or those under them, whereas an employee generally cannot check a supervisor's abusive conduct the same way that she might deal with abuse from a co-worker. When a fellow employee harasses, the victim can walk away or tell the offender where to go, but it may be difficult to offer such responses to a supervisor, whose "power to supervise—[which may be] to hire and fire, and to set work schedules and pay rates-does not disappear . . . when he chooses to harass through insults and offensive gestures rather than directly with threats of firing or promises of promotion." Estrich, *Sex at Work*, 43 STAN. L. REV. 813, 854 (1991). Recognition of employer liability when discriminatory misuse of supervisory authority alters the terms and conditions of a victim's employment is underscored by the fact that the employer has a greater opportunity to guard against misconduct by supervisors than by common workers; employers have greater opportunity and incentive to screen them, train them, and monitor their performance.[51]

The Court then brought *Meritor* back into the analysis, claiming that it prohibited the Court from holding an employer automatically liable for supervisory harassment.

The Court held that an employer would be automatically liable for a supervisor's harassment when it culminated in a tangible employment action, but that an employer would have an affirmative defense to liability when the harassment did not result in a tangible employment action. This concept is explored in detail in the following section.

In crafting this analysis, the Court noted that the purpose of Title VII is not just to remedy discrimination, but to prevent it in the first place. Therefore, the Court thought it made sense to incentivize employers to create complaint and investigation procedures and to incentivize employees to complain about harassment. The Court also indicated that general principles of law required plaintiffs to mitigate damages. Incentivizing employees to complain about harassment so that employers could stop it and prevent future occurrences fit within this mitigation idea. Earlier in the opinion, the Supreme Court recognized that lower courts had consistently held employers to be liable for a harasser's actions that resulted in a tangible employment action.

On the same day it issued *Faragher*, the Supreme Court issued *Burlington Indus., Inc. v. Ellerth*.[52] Although the cases agreed on the same framework for determining employer liability, there is a stark contrast in the reasoning of the cases. In *Ellerth*, a female employee alleged that she quit her job after a mid-level manager at the company

[51] *Faragher*, 524 U.S. at 803.

[52] 524 U.S. 742, 746 (1998).

made lewd comments toward her and suggested that her life at the company would be easier if she "loosened up" and wore shorter skirts.

The Court noted that the facts of the case (although yet unproven because of the case's procedural posture) would allow a factfinder to conclude that the mid-level supervisor threatened to retaliate against the plaintiff if she denied some sexual liberties. The Court first distinguished this set of facts from a quid pro quo case because in the latter case the threats are carried out or the employee accedes to the requests. In contrast, in this case, the plaintiff alleged an unfilled threat. The Court indicated that there would be automatic employer liability in a quid pro quo case.

The *Ellerth* Court stated that Congress instructed the courts to interpret Title VII according to agency law. However, the Court noted it was not bound by cases of state agency law, rather it would look to general principles of agency law. It also cited *Meritor*'s admonition that common law principles are not entirely transferable to Title VII.

The Court started its analysis with master-servant agency principles from the Restatement (Second) of Agency, noting that while employers were not traditionally liable for the intentional torts of their employees, agency principles now recognized that employers were liable for those torts when they were actuated in part to serve the employer's purpose. It then stated that sexual harassment is not conduct within the scope of employment.

The *Ellerth* Court then noted other circumstances in which *Restatement* agency principles would make the employer liable for the acts of its workers.

> (2) A master is not subject to liability for the torts of his servants acting outside the scope of their employment, unless:
>
> (a) the master intended the conduct or the consequences, or
>
> (b) the master was negligent or reckless, or
>
> (c) the conduct violated a non-delegable duty of the master, or
>
> (d) the servant purported to act or to speak on behalf of the principal and there was reliance upon apparent authority, or he was aided in accomplishing the tort by the existence of the agency relation.[53]

The Court noted that section (a) dealt with an employer's direct liability (when the employer itself engaged in the conduct) or situations in which an alter ego of the employer acted. It then indicated that subsections (a) and (c) did not apply to the *Ellerth* case. It also noted that the employer is liable if it is negligent, in that it knew or should have known about the conduct but failed to stop it.

The Court then indicated that the plaintiff in *Ellerth* advocated for a standard of employer liability beyond the standard of negligence. Unlike the *Faragher* decision which found the agency analysis only minimally helpful, the *Ellerth* Court focused on Restatement § 219(2)(d). The Court stated that apparent authority was not relevant to this case, and focused on whether the supervisor was aided in accomplishing the harassment by existence of the agency relationship. The Court then indicated that supervisors were aided in accomplishing harassment when the supervisor takes a

---

[53] *Ellerth*, 524 U.S. at 758.

tangible employment action. It also noted that co-workers were not empowered to take such actions.

Outside of the tangible employment context, the Court stated that it is less obvious whether the supervisor is aided by the employer.

> On the one hand, a supervisor's power and authority invests his or her harassing conduct with a particular threatening character, and in this sense, a supervisor always is aided by the agency relation. See *Meritor,* 477 U.S., at 77, 106 S.Ct., at 2410–2411 (Marshall, J., concurring in judgment) ("[I]t is precisely because the supervisor is understood to be clothed with the employer's authority that he is able to impose unwelcome sexual conduct on subordinates"). On the other hand, there are acts of harassment a supervisor might commit which might be the same acts a coemployee would commit, and there may be some circumstances where the supervisor's status makes little difference.[54]

To resolve this tension, the Court reasoned that the test it articulated was designed to "accommodate the agency principles of vicarious liability for harm caused by misuse of supervisory authority, as well as Title VII's equally basic policies of encouraging forethought by employers and saving action by objecting employees."[55] The *Ellerth* Court then adopted the same framework for employer liability enunciated in *Faragher* and discussed in detail in the following section. Notably, the *Ellerth* Court left open the possibility that there may be additional reasons to hold employers liable for harassment beyond the test it enunciated.

Although the *Faragher/Ellerth* affirmative defense developed in the context of sexual harassment, courts have used it for other protected classes under Title VII, the ADEA, the ADA, and section 1981.[56]

§ 5.11 Employer Liability, Framework

When determining whether an employer is liable for a hostile environment, courts first determine the relationship between the plaintiff and the harasser. The test to be applied varies depending on whether the harasser is (1) an alter ego of the employer; (2) a co-worker or third party; or (3) a supervisor. The following discussion assumes that the plaintiff has already established the other substantive elements of a harassment claim.

If the harasser is an alter ego of the employer, the employer is automatically liable for the hostile environment.[57] Alter egos are individuals who are "indisputably within that class of an employer organization's officials who may be treated as the organization's proxy."[58] The Supreme Court has described this scenario as one "where the agent's high rank in the company makes him or her the employer's alter ego."[59]

---

[54] *Ellerth,* 524 U.S. at 763.

[55] *Ellerth,* 524 U.S. at 764.

[56] Vance v. Ball State Univ., 570 U.S. 421, 429 (2013); Stapp v. Curry Cty. Bd. of Cty. Commissioners, 672 F. App'x 841, 847 (10th Cir. 2016); Spriggs v. Diamond Auto Glass, 242 F.3d 179, 186 n.9 (4th Cir. 2001) (collecting cases).

[57] Townsend v. Benjamin Enterprises, Inc., 679 F.3d 41, 53 (2d Cir. 2012).

[58] Townsend v. Benjamin Enterprises, Inc., 679 F.3d 41, 53 (2d Cir. 2012); Helm v. Kansas, 656 F.3d 1277, 1286 (10th Cir. 2011) (noting that a state court judge is not an alter ego of the state).

[59] *Ellerth,* 524 U.S. at 758.

If the harasser is a co-worker, the employer is only liable for harassment if the employer knew or should have known about the harassment and failed to take prompt remedial action.[60] The plaintiff is required to prove this factor as part of the plaintiff's case. If a plaintiff fails to prove this, the employer will not be held liable for a co-worker's harassment, even if the evidence establishes that the worker faced egregious harassment.

"Generally, a response is adequate if it is reasonably calculated to end the harassment. Appropriate steps "may include promptly initiating an investigation. Even separating the harasser and victim immediately may not be enough without further action on the employer's part."[61] The courts have not provided a definitive test for determining when the employer's response is appropriate. Instead, they have noted that "[f]actors in assessing the reasonableness of remedial measures *may include* the amount of time that elapsed between the notice and remedial action, the options available to the employer, . . . and whether or not the measures ended the harassment."[62]

The employer is held to the same negligence standard if the harasser is a third party (such as a frequent customer)[63] or if the harasser is unknown, such as when an employee is subjected to anonymous threats.[64]

A different set of rules apply when the harasser is the plaintiff's supervisor. Under the framework set forth in *Faragher* and *Ellerth*, the employer will automatically be liable if the supervisor's harassment culminated in a "tangible employment action" against the worker. The concept of "tangible employment action" is a term of art created by the Supreme Court in the specific context of employer liability in hostile work environment cases. It includes actions such as termination, failure to promote, or demotion. The concept of a "tangible employment action" is discussed more fully in the following section. Under the reasoning in *Faragher* and *Ellerth*, the employer is automatically liable for harassment in these instances because the employer aided the supervisor. The concept of a tangible employment action is discussed in greater detail below.

If a supervisor is the harasser and does not take a tangible employment action, the employer is liable for the harassment unless it proves an affirmative defense. In these cases, if a worker proves the elements of harassment, the employer is automatically liable for the harassment if it cannot prove the affirmative defense. However, if the employer establishes the affirmative defense, it escapes liability completely, even if the worker faced egregious harassment.

The affirmative defense has two parts. The employer can avoid liability by showing "(1) that it exercised reasonable care to prevent and promptly correct any harassing behavior and (2) that the plaintiff unreasonably failed to take advantage of any preventive or corrective opportunities that were provided."[65]

---

[60] *See, e.g.*, Pullen v. Caddo Par. Sch. Bd., 830 F.3d 205, 213 (5th Cir. 2016).

[61] Smith v. Rock-Tenn Servs., Inc., 813 F.3d 298, 311 (6th Cir. 2016) (internal citations omitted).

[62] Nichols v. Tri-Nat'l Logistics, Inc., 809 F.3d 981, 988 (8th Cir. 2016), reh'g denied (Feb. 11, 2016).

[63] Pryor v. United Air Lines, Inc., 791 F.3d 488, 498 (4th Cir. 2015); Freeman v. Dal-Tile Corp., 750 F.3d 413, 423 (4th Cir. 2014).

[64] Pryor v. United Air Lines, Inc., 791 F.3d 488, 498 (4th Cir. 2015).

[65] *Ellerth*, 524 U.S. at 765.

In *Faragher*, the city was not able to prove the affirmative defense because the city had failed to distribute its harassment policy to the lifeguards and because it did not oversee the conduct of supervisors. Additionally, the city's policy did not allow a worker to bypass a harassing supervisor in making complaints.[66] Given the size of the city, the Court noted that a complaint procedure could not be effective unless there was a "formal policy against harassment, with a sensible complaint procedure." The Court indicated that a smaller employer might be able to have an informal policy.

The lower courts have fleshed out the two prongs of the test. While there is no definitive way of establishing the first prong, there are some general contours. "An employer can satisfy this element by maintaining an effective anti-harassment policy that informs employees how to report allegations of harassment and conducting prompt investigations pursuant to this policy."[67] Typically, employers should have a policy that expressly forbids harassment.[68] The harassment policy should be disseminated to employees, although courts may allow an employer to prevail if the policy has been discussed and employees are aware of the policy and the complaint procedure. The employer must typically monitor compliance, which may involve steps like harassment training or having an EEO office to monitor compliance.

There must be a reasonable complaint procedure. A complaint procedure is not reasonable if the only avenue to pursue a complaint is to a supervisor and the supervisor is the harasser. Once the employee invokes the complaint procedure, the employer should promptly investigate the complaint.[69] As one court noted:

> By opening a sexual harassment investigation, the employer puts all employees on notice that it takes such allegations seriously and will not tolerate harassment in the workplace. An investigation is a warning, not by words but by action. We have held, however, that the "fact of investigation alone" is not enough[.] An investigation that is rigged to reach a pre-determined conclusion or otherwise conducted in bad faith will not satisfy the employer's remedial obligation.[70]

The remedial steps taken by the employer should be "reasonably calculated to end the harassment."[71]

The employer can meet the second prong by showing that the employee unreasonably failed to invoke the employer's complaint procedure in a timely manner. Reasonableness is a question of fact. Courts have held that an employer can be liable for supervisor harassment without an employee complaint, if the plaintiff reasonably believed her complaint would not be taken seriously or if she faced retaliation. Even if a worker complains, the employer might be able to establish the affirmative defense, if the worker unreasonably refuses to participate in a subsequent investigation of the complaint.

---

[66] Faragher v. City of Boca Raton, 524 U.S. 775, 808–09 (1998).

[67] Brokenborough v. D.C., No. 13-CV-1757 (TSC), 2017 WL 663524, at *6 (D.D.C. Feb. 17, 2017).

[68] *Cf.* Hall v. Bodine Elec. Co., 276 F.3d 345 (7th Cir. 2002).

[69] Swenson v. Potter, 271 F.3d 1184, 1193 (9th Cir. 2001); Sotoj v. Nashville Aquarium, Inc., No. 3:14-CV-00754, 2016 WL 3568591, at *9 (M.D. Tenn. July 1, 2016).

[70] *Swenson*, 271 F.3d at 1193.

[71] Kramer v. Wasatch Cty. Sheriff's Office, 743 F.3d 726, 747 (10th Cir. 2014).

The two prongs of the *Faragher/Ellerth* affirmative defense are joined by an "and," which means the employer must establish both portions. However, courts have routinely allowed employers to prevail where an employee complains and the employer takes reasonably prompt measures to respond to the harassment.[72] Both *Faragher* and *Ellerth* were cases of pervasive harassment. It is unclear what result should follow with a single case of severe harassment. For example, in one case a worker alleged that a supervisor entered her hotel room without her permission, partially undressed her, and fondled her.[73] The employee screamed when she found the man in her bed, and the police came. The employer subsequently terminated the supervisor. In a case such as this one, the employer will not be able to establish the *Faragher/Ellerth* defense, even if it took all reasonable steps prior to and after the incident. Some courts believe that the underlying policy of the *Faragher/Ellerth* defense should allow the employer to escape liability because it took all reasonable steps. However, other courts have noted that the Supreme Court enunciated the test, and the lower courts should not disregard the fact that the employer must establish both prongs.[74]

§ 5.12 Tangible Employment Action

An employer cannot invoke the *Faragher/Ellerth* affirmative defense if the supervisor takes a tangible employment action. A tangible employment action is "a significant change in employment status, such as hiring, firing, failing to promote, reassignment with significantly different responsibilities, or a decision causing a significant change in benefits."[75] As the Court noted in *Ellerth*, "Tangible employment actions are the means by which the supervisor brings the official power of the enterprise to bear on subordinates."[76]

The term "tangible employment action" does not appear in the text of the employment discrimination statutes. Rather, it is a court-created term of art applicable in the *Faragher/Ellerth* context. Tangible employment action is not coterminous with the term "adverse action," which is used to determine the required level of seriousness of actions in the discrimination and retaliation contexts. As discussed in Chapters 3 and 10, the term "adverse action" also does not appear in the text of the statutes. The courts have created separate definitions for this term in the discrimination and retaliation context.

A constructive discharge occurs when a reasonable person would have resigned under the circumstances. For example, if sexual harassment is so bad that a reasonable person would resign and the employee does resign, the courts treat this situation as a discharge for purposes of discrimination remedies.

In *Pennsylvania State Police v. Suders*,[77] the Supreme Court addressed the question of whether a constructive discharge is a tangible employment action for purposes of determining whether an employer may invoke the *Faragher/Ellerth* affirmative defense.

---

72 Van Alstyne v. Ackerley Grp., Inc., 8 F. App'x 147, 153 (2d Cir. 2001).

73 U.S. E.E.O.C. v. Asia Pac. Hotels, Inc., No. 10–00002, 2011 WL 3841601, at *1 (D. N. Mar. I. Aug. 26, 2011).

74 Alalade v. AWS Assistance Corp., 796 F. Supp. 2d 936, 941 (N.D. Ind. 2011) (summarizing arguments).

75 *Ellerth*, 524 U.S., at 761.

76 *Ellerth*, 524 U.S. 742, 762.

77 542 U.S. 129, 134 (2004).

In that case, a police communications officer presented evidence that her supervisors subjected her to a "continuous barrage" of sexual harassment. Although the plaintiff alerted the employer about the issue, she never submitted a formal complaint about it.

On multiple occasions, the plaintiff had taken a test required for work and been told that she had failed the test. The plaintiff presented evidence that she later found the tests in the women's locker room. She believed that they had never been graded and that reports she failed the test were false. She removed the tests from the locker room. Her supervisors then arrested her for theft. The plaintiff then quit her job. After she resigned, the department did not pursue the theft charges.

The trial court granted summary judgment for the employer, finding that the employer could not be held liable for the conduct. The Third Circuit reversed, finding that a constructive discharge caused by a supervisor's conduct resulted in employer liability.

After a lengthy discussion about constructive discharge in the remedies context, the Court addressed how this concept intersected with *Faragher/Ellerth*. The Court reasoned that while an actual termination was always a tangible employment action effectuated through official employer action, a constructive discharge did not necessarily reflect official action. Constructive discharge may occur in many different ways. For example, it can happen through unofficial conduct by a supervisor, through the actions of co-workers or by official actions.

The employer will be automatically liable for a supervisor's harassment in a constructive discharge case "if the plaintiff quits in reasonable response to an employer-sanctioned adverse action officially changing her employment status or situation, for example, a humiliating demotion, extreme cut in pay, or transfer to a position in which she would face unbearable working conditions."[78] If there is no such official action in a case where the plaintiff reasonably quits in response to a supervisor's harassment, the employer may escape liability by establishing the *Faragher/Ellerth* affirmative defense.

§ 5.13 Definition of Supervisor

Whether the harasser is a supervisor is a key question in determining employer liability for the harassment. Recall that the framework for determining employer liability is court-created and is not found within the text of the statute itself. After *Faragher* and *Ellerth*, lower courts struggled with determining when an individual qualified as a supervisor.

The Supreme Court answered this question in *Vance v. Ball State University*.[79] A supervisor is a person empowered by the employer to take tangible employment actions against the individual, *i.e.*, to effect a "significant change in employment status, such as hiring, firing, failing to promote, reassignment with significantly different responsibilities, or a decision causing a significant change in benefits." To reach this outcome, the Supreme Court was not able to rely on the definition of the term "supervisor," because, as the Court noted, the word often has different meanings both in colloquial and legal usages. Instead, the Court reasoned that *Faragher* and *Ellerth* contemplated a sharp division between who was a supervisor and who was not, given that the test enunciated in those opinions relied heavily on the distinction. The Court

---

[78] *Suders*, 542 U.S. at 134.

[79] Vance v. Ball State Univ., 133 S. Ct. 2434, 2443, 186 L. Ed. 2d 565 (2013).

rejected the EEOC's proposed standard, which the Court stated would lead to uncertainty in practice.

The Supreme Court noted that its holding does not mean that plaintiffs would not be protected against harassment if the harasser was an individual with authority over the worker, but not someone who possessed the ability to make tangible employment actions. The Court noted that individuals in these circumstances could still prevail by showing that the employer was negligent, in that it knew or should have known about the harassment and failed to respond appropriately.

In dicta, the Court noted that employers might try to insulate themselves against automatic liability by vesting the authority to make tangible employment actions to only a narrow band of employees. The Supreme Court anticipated that employers might still face automatic liability for harassment in those instances. It noted that in such situations the small group of individuals able to make tangible employment actions would need to rely on the recommendations of other workers to make decisions. "Under those circumstances, the employer may be held to have effectively delegated the power to take tangible employment actions to the employees on whose recommendations it relies."[80]

Both the majority and the dissent recognized that the modern workplace is not always organized along strict hierarchal lines of authority. The majority recognized that people often work in teams, where various members of the team are considered to be the team leader depending on the particular task. The dissent indicated that *Faragher* and *Ellerth* drew distinctions between those individuals who had the power to wield official authority over the plaintiff and those that did not. It argued that the majority did not properly consider that many individuals can control the day-to-day working environment for workers and be reasonably viewed as supervisors, even if those individuals do not formally possess the ability to take tangible employment actions. The dissent also noted that given ambiguities in what counts as a tangible employment action the majority rule also is not clear cut.

---

[80] *Vance*, 133 S. Ct. at 2452.

Chapter 6

DISPARATE IMPACT

Analysis

§ 6.01 Disparate Impact Generally

Under both Title VII and the ADEA, it is unlawful for an employer to "limit, segregate, or classify" individuals in a way "which would deprive or tend to deprive any individual of employment opportunities or otherwise adversely affect his status as an employee" because of the employees' protected trait.[1] The courts have interpreted this language as allowing a disparate impact theory of discrimination.[2]

Disparate impact is a type of discrimination that courts often define in contrast to disparate treatment. In a disparate treatment case, the plaintiff is usually trying to prove that a worker's protected trait motivated a negative outcome. Although the federal discrimination statutes do not use the words motive or intent in their main language, courts tend to characterize disparate treatment claims as focused on these concepts.

---

1 42 U.S.C.A. § 2000e–2(a)(2); 29 U.S.C.A. § 623(a)(2).

2 The original language of the statutes does not contain the term "disparate impact" and 42 U.S.C.A. § 2000e–2(a)(2) and 29 U.S.C.A. § 623(a)(2) are not limited to disparate impact.

Thus, if a supervisor tells a woman that he is not going to promote her because he does not think women are management material, this would be an example of disparate treatment.

In contrast, disparate impact does not focus on motive or intent. In a disparate impact case, workers typically challenge a policy or procedure that is facially neutral.[3] A facially neutral policy or procedure can be illegal discrimination in certain circumstances. If the facially neutral policy has a disproportionate effect on a protected group, it is discriminatory unless the employer can show that it has an appropriate reason for using the practice or policy. The level of justification required for the practice or policy varies depending on whether the case is brought under Title VII or the ADEA.

The quintessential example of a policy that creates a disparate impact is a height or weight requirement. For example, assume a fire department has a policy that all firefighter applicants must be at least five feet and 11 inches tall and must weigh at least 200 pounds. This policy would mean that many women would not be eligible for firefighter jobs. It is unlikely that the fire department has an adequate reason for the height and weight requirement, and therefore, it would constitute unlawful disparate impact. If the fire department needed to test the strength of its applicants, it could devise an appropriate test for strength, rather than improperly relying on an inaccurate proxy like height or weight.

The ADA contains similar language to Title VII and the ADEA, but also contains additional provisions that apply to policies and procedures.[4] The ADA specifically prohibits employers from using "standards, criteria, or methods of administration . . . that have the effect of discrimination on the basis of disability."[5] It also makes it unlawful for an employer to use "qualification standards, employment tests or other selection criteria that screen out or tend to screen out an individual with a disability" unless the test is job-related and consistent with business necessity.[6] Additionally, the ADA requires employers to select and administer tests in a way that ensures the test measures the skills or aptitudes desired for the job, rather than reflecting an impairment.[7] Although the Supreme Court has considered multiple cases involving disparate impact under Title VII and the ADEA, it has not yet taken up the question of disparate impact under the ADA. Many lower courts assume that a disparate impact case under the ADA works similarly to a Title VII disparate impact case.

Many disparate impact cases proceed as government suits or class actions. A plaintiff can pursue disparate impact and disparate treatment theories in the same lawsuit.

A plaintiff may not pursue a disparate impact theory under Section 1981.[8]

---

3 The Supreme Court has held that policies that are intentionally discriminatory can also be challenged under (a)(2). Nashville Gas Co. v. Satty, 434 U.S. 136, 142 (1977); *see also* Adams v. City of Indianapolis, 742 F.3d 720, 731 (7th Cir. 2014) (noting that disparate impact can be used to challenge all policies, not just facially neutral ones).

4 42 U.S.C.A. § 12112(b)(1).

5 42 U.S.C.A. § 12112(b)(3).

6 42 U.S.C.A. § 12112(b)(6).

7 42 U.S.C.A. § 12112(b)(7).

8 General Bldg. Contractors Ass'n, Inc. v. Pennsylvania, 458 U.S. 375 (1982).

§ 6.02 The *Griggs* Model

Facially neutral rules, policies, or practices may be discriminatory if they disproportionately impact a protected class and the employer is not able to justify the reason it continues to use the challenged rule, policy or practice.

The Supreme Court set forth the basic idea of disparate impact in a 1971 case, *Griggs v. Duke Power Co.*[9] In *Griggs*, the employer had a history of segregating employees based on race prior to Title VII's effective date. This pre-Title VII segregation was not at issue in *Griggs*. Instead the Court assumed that the employer no longer intended to discriminate against black employees and applicants based on their race.

The Court scrutinized two qualification requirements the employer used: a high school diploma and a passing score on aptitude tests. The Court of Appeals held that since the employer implemented the requirements in good faith, they did not constitute discrimination because of race.

The Supreme Court reversed, holding:

> The Act proscribes not only overt discrimination but also practices that are fair in form but discriminatory in operation. The touchstone is business necessity. If an employment practice which operates to exclude Negroes cannot be shown to be related to job performance the practice is prohibited. . . . Good intent or the absence of discriminatory intent, does not redeem employment procedures or testing mechanisms that operate as "built-in headwinds" for minority groups and are unrelated to measuring job capability. . . . Congress directed the thrust of the Act to the consequences of employment practices, not simply motivation.[10]

The Court found that these selection devices had an adverse impact on black employees as a class. The employer claimed that it instituted the educational tests and graduation requirements to improve the overall quality of the workforce. The Court held the employer had failed to show how the devices "related to job performance" or "to measuring job capability." The examinations and high school diploma requirements did not meet this requirement for several reasons. The requirements were implemented without much forethought. Rather, the company just hypothesized that the requirements would improve the workforce. Additionally, employees who did not have a high school education or who did not pass the required tests continued to work successfully within the company. Finally, there was no evidence that the general aptitude tests tested for traits or skills related to the specific jobs in question. Consequently, use of these criteria was discrimination "because of race."

While *Griggs* recognized the disparate impact theory and set forth the underlying rationale for it, it did not set forth a specific analytical framework for analyzing such claims. Rather, the Court sketched out the broad underlying theory and rationale of disparate impact and provided a rudimentary framework for analyzing cases. The Court held that disparate impact required: (1) proof that the practice has an adverse impact on a protected class, and (2) absence of proof that the practice is a "business necessity." On

---

[9] Griggs v. Duke Power Co., 401 U.S. 424 (1971).

[10] *Griggs*, 401 U.S. at 431.

the theoretical side, *Griggs* recognized a model of discrimination concerned with the results of policies, rather than on the motivation of certain people.

§ 6.03 Subsequent Title VII Cases

Often in discrimination law, the seminal case in a particular area lays out the broad contours and ideas underlying a concept, and later cases clarify the requirements. While *Griggs* recognized disparate impact, it did not provide a fully functional account of how courts should consider such cases. Understanding *Griggs* became more complicated in 1973, when the Supreme Court decided *McDonnell Douglas v. Green*, which established a framework for analyzing individual disparate treatment cases based on circumstantial evidence.[11] It became unclear how and whether the *Griggs* and *McDonnell Douglas* tests were similar.

Additionally, the composition of the Supreme Court changed over time, leading to shifts in both the methodology judges used in interpreting the statutes and how liberally the judges chose to interpret them. Recall that the text of the statutes is written with very broad language, but the courts have tended to diverge significantly from the specific language in interpreting the statutes.

One such shift in discrimination law is seen in a couple of disparate impact cases. During the late 1980s, the Supreme Court decided two important disparate impact cases that modified the disparate impact analysis: *Watson v. Fort Worth Bank & Trust*[12] and *Wards Cove Packing Co. v. Atonio*.[13]

In *Watson*, the plaintiff challenged a bank's subjective promotion practices. In a portion of the opinion joined by the majority, the Court held that a plaintiff may challenge subjective practices using disparate impact theory. Prior to *Watson*, Supreme Court cases had focused on "objective" requirements, such as pen-and-paper tests and education credentials.

A plurality of the Court was concerned about the pressures employers would face in cases involving disparate impact based on subjective practices. To alleviate this concern, the plurality indicated that to prove a disparate impact the plaintiff must identify "the specific employment practice that is challenged" and must establish statistical evidence of a kind and degree sufficient to show that the protected trait caused the disparity.[14]

The plurality also appeared to decrease the burden on the employer in the second step. The plurality noted that once the plaintiff meets its burden, the burden of proof then shifts to the defendant to show that "its employment practices are based on legitimate business reasons."[15] It also noted that the employer's burden was one of production only.

It also appeared to place additional limits on the plaintiff's ability to prevail under the third step in the analysis. In that third step, the Court had held in another case that the plaintiff could prevail by establishing that other tests or selection devices, without a similarly undesirable racial effect, would also serve the employer's legitimate interest in

---

11 McDonnell Douglas Corp. v. Green, 411 U.S. 792 (1973).

12 487 U.S. 977 (1988).

13 490 U.S. 642 (1989).

14 487 U.S. at 994 (portion of the opinion joined by a plurality).

15 *Id.* at 998.

"efficient and trustworthy workmanship."[16] In *Watson*, the plurality noted that the costs and burdens of alternative devices would be relevant in determining whether the plaintiff met her burden. Thus, while *Watson* arguably expanded the reach of disparate impact by applying it to subjective practices, portions of the opinion also made it more difficult for plaintiffs to establish disparate impact.

This trend continued in *Wards Cove*, in which the Supreme Court specifically addressed the analytical framework for disparate impact cases under Title VII. The plaintiffs in *Wards Cove* were individuals who worked in Alaskan salmon canneries. Each summer during the salmon run, the canneries opened to process the fresh salmon. The cannery jobs were general skill positions in which workers canned salmon on the cannery line. The noncannery jobs consisted of a variety of jobs, including machinists, engineers, quality control personnel, cooks, carpenters, store-keepers, bookkeepers, and other support personnel.

Individuals employed in the cannery jobs were predominantly Filipinos and Alaskan natives, while the individuals in the noncannery jobs were mostly white. The cannery workers alleged that several of the cannery's hiring and promotion practices, such as nepotism, a rehire preference, a lack of objective hiring criteria, separate hiring channels, and a practice of not promoting from within, created a racially imbalanced work force. The plaintiffs brought disparate treatment and disparate impact claims based on race under Title VII.

The Court provided a three-part framework for proving disparate impact cases under Title VII. First, the plaintiff is required to establish a prima facie case of disparate impact by demonstrating that a specific practice of the defendant has a "significantly disparate impact" on a protected group. Although the specific practice requirement was not emphasized in this case, it gains greater importance in future cases and should be noted.

The Supreme Court held that the district court made several mistakes in analyzing the facts of the case. The district court looked at the number of white workers in the cannery jobs compared with the number of workers in the noncannery jobs. A gross disparity existed, so the district court found that discrimination existed. This analysis was incorrect because the district court used the wrong pools of people for comparison. There was no evidence regarding the applicant or potential job pool for each set of jobs. Since the cannery jobs were relatively unskilled positions, it could not be assumed that the applicant pool for those jobs was going to have the same composition as the applicant pool for a wide-range of jobs, including doctors, electricians, and engineers.

The Court indicated that Title VII does not seek to hold employers liable for imbalances that exist in the workforce. The Court expressed a concern that such a holding would essentially require hiring by quota. The Court indicated that the appropriate comparison would be between the workers who held the noncannery jobs and either the pool of individuals with the required skills for the noncannery jobs in the marketplace or the qualified individuals who applied for those positions.

Although the Court remanded the case for reconsideration of the first prong, the Court further articulated how disparate impact claims should be analyzed. In the second step of the framework, the burden shifts to the defendant to articulate a legitimate

16 Albemarle Paper Co. v. Moody, 422 U.S. 405, 425 (1975).

business justification for the practice. The Court held that this was a burden of production; however, Congress would later alter the burden to require the defendant to carry the burdens of production and persuasion.

Note that the Court tried to make the disparate impact test operate in a similar way to the way the *McDonnell-Douglas* test operates. However, unlike *McDonnell Douglas*, the articulated reason under disparate impact analysis has to be supported by a business justification. The defendant must set forth reasons why the challenged practice "serves, in a significant way, the legitimate employment goals of the employer." The employer is not required to show that the practice is absolutely essential to its business—only that there is some good business reason for it. The Court emphasized that the burden of persuasion in a disparate impact case always remains with the plaintiff.

In the third step of the analysis, the plaintiff could still prevail by convincing the court that the employer's justification for its business practice did not serve the legitimate goals of the employer. Or, the plaintiff can persuade the factfinder that "other tests or selection devices, without a similarly undesirable [ ] effect, would also serve the employer's legitimate . . . interest[s]." The Court reasoned that if other non-discriminatory selection devices existed, it was reasonable to believe that the employer had chosen the selection device as a pretext for discrimination. The Court noted that the method proposed by the plaintiff must be similar in costs and burdens to the employer and be similarly effective.

Justice Blackmun's dissent questioned whether the Court should have enunciated a new disparate impact proof structure and whether its view of appropriate evidence was correct. The dissent noted that the requirement of "practice by practice" statistical proof of causation will make it difficult for plaintiffs to establish disparate impact. The dissent also noted that the defendant's racial stratification and segregation resembled a plantation. In a separate dissent, Justice Stevens lamented that the Court appears to ignore the evidence of a racially stratified workforce.

Portions of *Watson* and *Wards Cove* remain good law; however, portions of their disparate impact analysis have undergone modifications as a result of amendments in the 1991 Civil Rights Act, discussed in the next section.

§ 6.04 1991 Amendments to Title VII

In the Civil Rights Act of 1991, Congress, among other things, codified a structure for disparate impact claims under Title VII that differed in some respects from the structure enunciated by the Supreme Court in *Wards Cove*. Congress did not amend the ADEA or ADA relating to disparate impact claims, when it made these changes to Title VII.

The amended statutory language, which is codified at 42 U.S.C. § 2000e–2(k), reads as follows:

> (1)(A) An unlawful employment practice based on disparate impact is established under this subchapter only if—
>
> (i) a complaining party demonstrates that a respondent uses a particular employment practice that causes a disparate impact on the basis of race, color, religion, sex, or national origin and the respondent fails to demonstrate that the challenged practice is job related for the position in question and consistent with business necessity; or

(ii) the complaining party makes the demonstration described in subparagraph (C) with respect to an alternative employment practice and the respondent refuses to adopt such alternative employment practice.

(B)(i) With respect to demonstrating that a particular employment practice causes a disparate impact as described in subparagraph (A)(i), the complaining party shall demonstrate that each particular challenged employment practice causes a disparate impact, except that if the complaining party can demonstrate to the court that the elements of a respondent's decisionmaking process are not capable of separation for analysis, the decisionmaking process may be analyzed as one employment practice.

(ii) If the respondent demonstrates that a specific employment practice does not cause the disparate impact, the respondent shall not be required to demonstrate that such practice is required by business necessity.

(C) The demonstration referred to by subparagraph (A)(ii) shall be in accordance with the law as it existed on June 4, 1989, with respect to the concept of "alternative employment practice".

(2) A demonstration that an employment practice is required by business necessity may not be used as a defense against a claim of intentional discrimination under this subchapter.

(3) Notwithstanding any other provision of this subchapter, a rule barring the employment of an individual who currently and knowingly uses or possesses a controlled substance, as defined in schedules I and II of section 102(6) of the Controlled Substances Act (21 U.S.C. § 802(6)), other than the use or possession of a drug taken under the supervision of a licensed health care professional, or any other use or possession authorized by the Controlled Substances Act [21 U.S.C. § 801 *et seq.*] or any other provision of Federal law, shall be considered an unlawful employment practice under this subchapter only if such rule is adopted or applied with an intent to discriminate because of race, color, religion, sex, or national origin.

The 1991 Act defined the term "demonstrates" to mean "meets the burdens of production and persuasion."[17]

After the 1991 amendments, Title VII disparate impact cases follow a three-part structure. In step one, the plaintiff must establish that the challenged practice causes a disproportionate impact on a protected class. The plaintiff must show the disparate impact for a specific practice. However, if the plaintiff can show that the defendant's decisionmaking process cannot be broken down into specific practices, the plaintiff can challenge the overall decisionmaking process. The employer can challenge the plaintiff's evidence.

If the plaintiff fails to establish the disparate effect, the case ends with a judgment for the defendant. If the plaintiff successfully establishes the disparate effect, the case continues to step two.

In step two, the employer has the burdens of production and persuasion. Thus, Congress explicitly rejected using the *McDonnell Douglas* model's burden of articulation

[17] 42 U.S.C.A. § 2000e(m).

in disparate impact cases. To prevail on the second step, the employer must demonstrate "that the challenged practice is job related for the position in question and consistent with business necessity."

If the defendant fails to make this showing, the plaintiff is entitled to judgment. If the defendant makes the required showing, then the plaintiff can still win the case if she can prove that an alternative employment practice exists that will not result in the same disparate impact and the employer refuses to adopt it. Congress did not further define this third step, but rather stated that it was merely adopting the case law that existed as of June 4, 1989 (the day before the Court decided *Wards Cove*).

§ 6.05 Disparate Impact and the ADEA

Prior to 1993, all of the circuits that had considered the question of whether a disparate impact theory existed under the ADEA determined that it existed or at least assumed, without deciding, that it was viable. In 1993, the Supreme Court issued a decision in an ADEA disparate treatment case that resulted in significant changes in ADEA disparate impact jurisprudence. In *Hazen Paper Co. v. Biggins*,[18] an employee claimed that he was terminated at the age of 62, a few weeks short of the years of service he needed for his pension to vest, so that the employer could avoid making pension payments. *Hazen Paper* was a disparate treatment case.

Nonetheless, the *Hazen Paper* case came to have repercussions on ADEA disparate impact cases based on the concurrence written by Justice Kennedy and joined by Chief Justice Rehnquist and Justice Thomas.

In the brief concurring opinion, Justice Kennedy emphasized that the *Hazen Paper* decision related only to disparate treatment claims—and not to disparate impact claims. He further reiterated that "nothing in the Court's opinion should be read as incorporating in the ADEA context the so-called 'disparate impact' theory of Title VII of the Civil Rights Act of 1964. As the Court acknowledges, we have not yet addressed the question whether such a claim is cognizable under the ADEA, and there are substantial arguments that it is improper to carry over disparate impact analysis from Title VII to the ADEA."[19] After *Hazen Paper*, a circuit split began to develop, with several circuit courts holding that a disparate impact claim was not cognizable under the ADEA.

In *Smith v. City of Jackson* the Court explicitly recognized disparate impact claims under the ADEA.[20] In that case, the petitioners were a group of police officers and police dispatchers who worked for the City of Jackson, Mississippi. The petitioners were challenging a new pay plan adopted by the city, which granted raises to all police officers. One of the purposes of the new pay plan was to increase the starting salaries of police officers to bring them up to the regional average. To accomplish this goal, the pay plan gave different levels of raises to employees depending on their years of service with the city. Individuals who had fewer than five years of tenure received proportionately greater raises than those with more seniority.

---

18 Hazen Paper Co. v. Biggins, 507 U.S. 604 (1993).

19 *Id.* at 618 (Kennedy, J., concurring).

20 Smith v. City of Jackson, Miss., 544 U.S. 228 (2005).

The officers with more seniority did not receive less money than the officers with less seniority. They actually received more in pure dollar amount, but less proportional to their base salary.

The Court held that the ADEA does recognize a disparate impact theory. It considered the broad language of the ADEA, which prohibits an employer from depriving an individual of employment opportunities because of that person's age. The Court also noted that the idea that a disparate impact theory existed was pretty consistent among the circuit courts until *Hazen Paper*, and the Court indicated that the *Hazen Paper* decision was not intended to give any signals about the viability of a disparate impact claim.

The Court noted that if Congress had wanted to explicitly bar disparate impact claims, it could have done so. In footnote 11, the Court pointed out that in the Equal Pay Act, which is part of the Fair Labor Standards Act (FLSA), there are no disparate impact claims. Congress could have used similar language in the ADEA, but did not do so.

The Court indicated that while a disparate impact theory is recognized under the ADEA, courts should analyze these cases differently than they would under Title VII. A particular statutory provision in the ADEA was important, the so-called RFOA (reasonable factor other than age) provision. The statutory text provides: "It shall not be unlawful for an employer, employment agency, or labor organization—(1) to take any action otherwise prohibited under subsections (a) . . . where the differentiation is based on reasonable factors other than age."[21]

The Court interpreted this provision as recognizing that many selection devices are going to correlate with age, but their use would not constitute age discrimination. Prior to passing the ADEA, Congress asked Secretary of Labor Willard Wirtz to report back to Congress about whether age discrimination existed in the American workplace. The Wirtz Report identified several areas in which an employer might possess a legitimate business reason for distinguishing among employees that might be correlated with age. Contrast this with Title VII, where the protected traits are not usually assumed to have any direct correlation with legitimate business reasons.

Because of the RFOA provision and the Wirtz Report, the Court indicated that disparate impact cases under the ADEA work differently than they do in the Title VII context. When Congress amended Title VII in 1991 to codify the disparate impact framework, it did not amend the ADEA.

Despite the recognition of a disparate impact claim, the plaintiffs lost the case. The first problem that the Court identified with their case is that the plaintiffs failed to identify a specific practice that resulted in disparate impact. The Court noted that "petitioners have done little more than point out that the pay plan at issue is relatively less generous to older workers than to younger workers. They have not identified any specific test, requirement, or practice within the pay plan that has an adverse impact on older workers."[22] Given the simple plan at issue in the case, it is unclear how plaintiffs could have made a more specific showing.

The plaintiffs' case also failed because the pay plan was implemented for a reasonable factor other than age. The Court noted: "It is, accordingly, in cases involving

---

[21] 29 U.S.C.A. § 623(f)(1).

[22] 544 U.S. at 241.

disparate impact claims that the RFOA provision plays its principal role by precluding liability if the adverse impact was attributable to a nonage factor that was 'reasonable.' "[23] The ADEA does not require a showing that a practice or policy is job-related and consistent with business necessity. The Court held that although seniority and rank correlate with age, this correlation does not constitute age discrimination.

Under Title VII, alternate, non-discriminatory methods of determining pay would be relevant, but the Court indicated this inquiry is not relevant in the ADEA context. As long as the decision is based on a reasonable factor other than age, the employer does not need to explore other alternatives.

Justice O'Connor's concurring opinion described four separate areas in which age may correlate with the person's ability to perform a job: (1) "physical ability generally declines with age;" (2) mental capacity also may decline with age; (3) "advances in technology and increasing access to formal education often leave older workers at a competitive disadvantage vis-á-vis younger workers;" and (4) "employment benefits, such as salary, vacation time, and so forth, increase as an employee gains experience and seniority."[24] The concurrence essentially instructs employers regarding how to defend against disparate impact cases under the ADEA.

Although the *City of Jackson* case recognized disparate impact claims were cognizable under the ADEA, it was unclear how courts should analyze these claims. In *Meacham v. Knolls Atomic Power Laboratory*,[25] the Court discussed whether the *Wards Cove* framework would apply in ADEA cases.

The Court explained:

> Although *City of Jackson* contains the statement that "*Wards Cove*'s pre-1991 interpretation of Title VII's identical language remains applicable to the ADEA," *City of Jackson* made only two specific references to aspects of the *Wards Cove* interpretation of Title VII that might have "remain[ed] applicable" in ADEA cases. One was to the existence of disparate-impact liability, which *City of Jackson* explained was narrower in ADEA cases than under Title VII. The other was to a plaintiff-employee's burden of identifying which particular practices allegedly cause an observed disparate impact, which is the employee's burden under both the ADEA and the pre-1991 Title VII.[26]

Unlike Title VII cases, ADEA disparate impact cases follow a two-step inquiry. Once the plaintiff proves the existence of the disproportionate effect, the defendant bears the burden of establishing that the practice or policy is based on a reasonable factor other than age. In other words, the reasonable factor other than age inquiry is an affirmative defense, on which the employer bears the burdens of production and persuasion. In ADEA cases, the defendant is not required to establish that its practice or policy is job-related and consistent with business necessity.

---

[23] *Id.* at 239.

[24] *Id.* at 259 (O'Connor, J., concurring).

[25] 554 U.S. 84 (2008).

[26] *Meacham*, 554 U.S. at 98.

§ 6.06 Adverse Impact

The first step in a disparate impact analysis requires the plaintiff to establish that the challenged practice or policy has a disproportionate impact on a protected class. The plaintiff carries the initial burden of proving that a particular device or system adversely affects employment opportunities of a defined protected class when compared to the effect that device has upon the opportunities of other classes. If plaintiff establishes this adverse impact, the plaintiff will win the case, unless the defendant can establish a proper reason for the practice or policy. In Title VII and many ADA cases, the employer is required to establish that the policy or practice is job-related and consistent with business necessity. In ADEA cases, the employer must show that the policy or practice is a reasonable factor other than age.

The plaintiff must prove the disproportionate impact with evidence.[27] There are two common statistical methods by which plaintiffs prove adverse impact: "applicant pool" and "applicant flow." "Flow" data examines the employer's own hiring or promotion experience. "Pool" data examines the percentage of persons in a potential applicant pool that would be affected by the particular device being challenged.

§ 6.07 Applicant Pool

Proving impact through an applicant pool comparison requires plaintiffs to identify the most appropriate pool of potential applicants. Two criteria are typically important to identifying the proper pool. These include identifying the geographical area from which the employer is likely to receive applicants and the type of skills or credentials needed in a particular job.

For example, assume a case challenges an employer's practice of giving priority in hiring to teachers with teaching experience in rural schools and argues that this practice disproportionately excludes African-American workers. If the plaintiff wants to prove her case through pool data, the plaintiff must identify the appropriate geographical area from which the employer would draw applicants. The plaintiff also would be required to submit evidence related to individuals with the required education and licensing to be teachers within the applicable geographic area by race.

Jobs that require specific skills, education, or licensing will require the plaintiff to produce applicant pool data that is refined to show the percentage of people in the relevant pool who possess those skills or requirements.[28] In contrast, if the contested job requires skills that most adult workers possess and does not require advanced education or licensing, the plaintiff can rely on more general evidence about the available labor pool in the applicable geographic area.

The plaintiff then uses the pool data to show how the challenged policy or practice affects individuals in different protected groups. For example, a plaintiff challenging the rural teaching preference might show that African-American teachers in the geographic area teach at rural schools at a significantly lower rate than white teachers.

---

[27] Caldwell v. Univ. of Houston Sys., 520 F. App'x 289, 295 (5th Cir. 2013); Thomas v. Metroflight, Inc., 814 F.2d 1506, 1511 (10th Cir. 1987); Avant v. South Cent. Bell Tel. Co., 716 F.2d 1083 (5th Cir. 1983); Carpenter v. Bd. of Regents of the Univ. of Wis. Sys., 728 F.2d 911 (7th Cir. 1984); Harper v. Trans World Airlines, Inc., 525 F.2d 409 (8th Cir. 1975).

[28] Hazelwood Sch. Dist. v. United States, 433 U.S. 299 (1977).

Griggs v. Duke Power Co.[29] relied upon applicant pool data. Recall that in *Griggs*, the employer implemented a high school diploma requirement and pen-and-paper aptitude tests to qualify employees for employment into manual labor jobs. The Court looked at the appropriate geographic area, the state of North Carolina. As the jobs required no special skill, the Court compared the percentage of blacks and whites in the state who possessed high school diplomas. While 34% of white males had diplomas, only 12% of black males did. The impact of the aptitude test was established by the introduction of an EEOC study, which indicated that when a *similar* test was given, white test takers had a 58% passage rate while black test takers passed at only a 6% rate.[30] The Court held these disparities were sufficient to meet the first step of the disparate impact inquiry.

Another Supreme Court case, *Dothard v. Rawlinson*,[31] also relied upon applicant pool data. In that case, a woman challenged height and weight requirements imposed for certain prison employees. The plaintiff presented a comparison of national height and weight statistics of men and women to establish the adverse impact on women of a 5′2″ height requirement and a 120-pound weight minimum for state prison guards. The data showed that 40 percent of the females in the United States could not meet these requirements, while fewer than 1% of the male population would be disqualified. This disparity was sufficient to establish the required disparate impact in step one of the analysis.

§ 6.08 Applicant Flow

Another method of proving adverse impact is applicant flow.[32] The plaintiff relies on evidence regarding the qualified applicants who applied for a position to establish the disparate impact. For example, if a plaintiff argues that an employer's process of relying on unstructured job interviews negatively impacts women, the plaintiff would present evidence of the number of qualified women and men who applied for a position and show that the unstructured interviews disqualified a disproportionate number of women.

Applicant flow data may be skewed. As the Supreme Court recognized in *Dothard*, "[O]therwise qualified people might be discouraged from applying because of a self-recognized inability to meet the very standard being challenged as being discriminatory."[33] In *Dothard*, because the employer had an announced policy of only hiring people who met certain height and weight requirements, people who did not meet those requirements might self select out of the applicant pool. The applicant flow data would be unlikely to reflect the number of women interested in the position.

In some cases, applicant flow data may not be used because the contested practice or policy has not impacted a sufficiently large number of people to be statistically significant. "Statistics are not trustworthy when minor numerical variations produce significant percentage fluctuations."[34] For example, in one case, data showed 5 of 17 Hispanic applicants passed an examination for accountants. This was deemed to be an

---

29 Griggs v. Duke Power Co., 401 U.S. 424 (1971).

30 *Id.* at 430 n. 6.

31 433 U.S. 321 (1977).

32 29 C.F.R. § 1607.4.

33 Dothard v. Rawlinson, 433 U.S. 321, 330 (1977).

34 Stout v. Potter, 276 F.3d 1118, 1123 n.2 (9th Cir. 2002); Contreras v. Los Angeles, 656 F.2d 1267, 1273 n.4 (9th Cir. 1981).

inadequate universe from which to establish the adverse impact of the selection device on Hispanic applicants.[35]

§ 6.09 Required Disparity

Although the Supreme Court has extensively developed the theory underlying disparate impact liability, it has not been precise in defining the plaintiff's burden.

In *Griggs*, the Court spoke of job requirements "that operate to disqualify [a protected class] at a substantially higher rate than white applicants" and that "render ineligible a markedly disproportionate number of [people in that protected group.]"[36] In *Albemarle Paper Co. v. Moody*,[37] the Court characterized the plaintiff's *prima facie* case as a showing "that the tests in question select applicants for hire or promotion in a racial pattern significantly different from that of the pool of applicants." In *Dothard*, the Court referred to "facially neutral qualification standards [that] work in fact disproportionately to exclude women from eligibility for employment[.]"[38] It commented on *Griggs* and *Albemarle*: "Those cases make clear that to establish a *prima facie* case of discrimination, a plaintiff need only show that the facially neutral standards in question select applicants for hire in a significantly discriminatory pattern."[39] In *New York Transit Auth. v. Beazer*, the Court characterized the *prima facie* case as "statistical evidence showing that an employment practice has the effect of denying members of one race equal access to employment opportunities."[40]

The Court has never stated with any degree of precision how much difference between selection or disqualification rates for members of a protected class and majority employees is "markedly disproportionate" or "substantially higher" or "significantly different" or "significantly discriminatory." In the 1991 amendments to Title VII, Congress did not precisely define the required disparity, only requiring that the plaintiff establish a disparate impact.[41]

In some cases, such as the facts presented in *Griggs* and *Dothard*, the disparities were so stark that the Court did not need to define the level of disparity required to meet the plaintiff's burden. The EEOC's Uniform Guidelines on Employee Selection Criteria adopt an "80 percent rule of thumb"[42] for assessing disparate impact. Under this approach, if the selection rate for a protected class is lower than 80 percent of the selection rate for majority employees, the selection criterion generally is found to have a disparate impact on the protected class.

The Guidelines recognize that the 80 percent rule will not be accurate in all cases. The Guidelines suggest that a selection rate that is greater than 80 percent of the majority rate may still constitute an adverse impact if the difference is significant in "statistical and practical terms" or if the employer has discouraged members of the protected class from applying. The Guidelines also suggest that a selection rate less than

---

35 656 F.2d at 1272–73.

36 401 U.S. at 426.

37 422 U.S. 405 (1975).

38 *Dothard*, 433 U.S. at 329.

39 *Id.*

40 440 U.S. 568, 584 (1979).

41 42 U.S.C.A. § 2000e–2(k)(1)(A)(i).

42 Watson v. Fort Worth Bank & Trust, 487 U.S. 977, 995 n.3 (1988) (plurality opinion). The Supreme Court did not enunciate a standard for determining when an impact is large enough.

80 percent of the majority rate may not constitute an adverse impact if the difference is not statistically significant, the number of applicants or selections is small,[43] or affirmative action in recruiting or otherwise attracting members of the protected class has resulted in a pool of applicants that is atypical of the normal applicant pool from that group.

Another problem involved in intuitively comparing raw data is deciding whether to compare qualification rates or disqualification rates. The outcome of a case involving an intuitive judgment about disparate impact may depend on which rate the court chooses to examine.

One court described this problem in the following way:

> As an illustration, imagine that a police department demographically similar to the Boston Police Department—with approximately 500 black officers and 1200 white officers—implements a policy leading to the termination of 90 black officers and no white officers. If the "selection rate" is taken to be the rate at which employees survived termination, the four-fifths rule detects no disparate impact: 82% of black employees survived, which is more than four-fifths of 100%, the rate at which white employees survived. Yet the policy in this hypothetical illustration undoubtedly has a very significant and disproportionate effect on black officers.
>
> This illustration highlights several flaws in the four-fifths rule. First, to apply the rule in cases involving the selection of current employees for employment consequences such as termination, courts must resolve the rule's ambiguity regarding whether the "selection rate" is the rate at which employees were selected for termination or the rate at which employees survived termination. This choice can be decisive. In the above example, if a court took the "selection rate" as the rate at which employees were fired, the four-fifths rule would indicate a disparate impact, because the 0% firing rate for white employees is less than four-fifths of the 18% firing rate for black employees. Construing the four-fifths rule in this manner, however, would lead to a different problem: the rule would detect a disparate impact even if just one employee were fired (a 0/1200 firing rate for white employees would be less than four-fifths of a 1/500 firing rate for black employees), a result that seems clearly incorrect.[44]

§ 6.10 Other Common Attacks on Data

In *Griggs* and *Dothard* the Supreme Court did not scrutinize the plaintiff's data. In *Dothard*, the Court noted: "If the employer discerns fallacies . . . he is free to adduce countervailing evidence of his own."

However, in *New York City Transit Authority v. Beazer*[45] the Court scrutinized the statistics. In that case, the plaintiffs challenged defendant's policy of refusing to hire individuals who were on methadone maintenance treatment for addiction. Plaintiffs argued the policy violated Title VII because it had a disproportionate effect on minorities.

---

43 *But see* Howe v. City of Akron, 723 F.3d 651, 656 (6th Cir. 2013) (finding disparate impact despite small number of affected positions).

44 Jones v. City of Boston, 752 F.3d 38, 51–52 (1st Cir. 2014).

45 440 U.S. 568 (1979).

Plaintiffs presented evidence that 81% of all employees referred to the employer's medical director for drug abuse were minorities. The Court indicated this evidence was not relevant to the plaintiffs' suit because it looked at all reports of drug abuse and not specifically at reports that complained about a worker's participation in a methadone maintenance program.

The plaintiffs also presented evidence that 63% of all persons in the city's public methadone programs were minorities, compared to the area population, which was 36.3% minority. The Court found this evidence was problematic for several reasons. First, looking at city-wide data did not provide any information about the number of people within public methadone programs who were qualified for jobs with the employer. Additionally, a number of people within the city's methadone program would not be qualified for jobs with the employer because they abused other drugs or alcohol or because they had jobs with other employers. Given the specific facts of the case, the Court found that the relevant group was individuals who had been in methadone maintenance for over a year. The plaintiffs did not provide statistics for this sub-group. Importantly, the plaintiffs did not present data about the racial composition of people in private methadone maintenance programs, which might show a different racial composition than the public program.

In *Beazer*, the Court noted that "at best" the plaintiffs' statistical showing was weak. It held that even if the plaintiffs could make the required statistical showing that their case failed to establish a violation of Title VII because the employer was able to show that its rule was job-related.

§ 6.11 Bottom-Line Defense Rejected

In *Connecticut v. Teal*[46] the Supreme Court considered whether an employer would be liable for disparate impact if one step in a multi-step process created a disparate outcome, but the final result at the end of the process did not show such a disparity.

In that case, the employer used multiple selection devices for promotion to a supervisory positions. If the applicant failed to pass the first qualifying examination, the employer excluded the applicant from further consideration for the positions. About 80% of white applicants passed this first test. Black applicants passed at a rate of slightly above 54%. Thus, black applicants moved beyond this initial screening at a rate of only 68% of the white percentage rate, well below the 4/5 or 80% relative selection rate which suggests adverse impact.

However, for those who passed the initial test, the employer used other selection devices, including personal interviews. Ultimately, at the end of the process, 22.9% of the black applicants were promoted, and 13.5% of the white applicants were promoted. Thus, while black applicants were initially disqualified at a much higher rate than white applicants, at the "bottom line" of selection rates black applicants were in fact hired at a rate higher than whites. The Court held that a system of elimination that adversely affects one group has an adverse impact on that group even if ultimately individuals in the initially disadvantaged group were selected at a rate similar to other groups.

The Court held that Title VII prohibits discrimination against individuals because of a protected class. If the individuals eliminated from the process were disparately impacted by a practice based on race (and if the employer could not justify this practice),

---

[46] 457 U.S. 440 (1982).

these individuals faced discrimination. This is true, even if other individuals in the class were not impacted by the test. The Court noted, "It is clear that Congress never intended to give an employer license to discriminate against some employees on the basis of race or sex merely because he favorably treats other members of the employees' group."

§ 6.12 The Specific Practice or Policy

Many disparate impact cases fail because the courts require the plaintiff to identify the disparate impact caused by a specific employment practice or policy and the plaintiff fails to do so.

For example, in *Smith v. City of Jackson*,[47] the petitioners challenged a new pay plan adopted by the city, which granted raises to all city employees. The pay plan gave different levels of raises to employees depending on their years of service with the city. Individuals who had fewer than five years of tenure received proportionately greater raises than those with more seniority. The officers with more seniority did not receive less money than the officers with less seniority. They actually received more in pure dollar amount, but less proportional to their base salary.

The Court held that the plaintiffs could not prevail on a disparate impact claim because the plaintiffs failed to identify a specific practice that resulted in disparate impact. The Court noted that "petitioners have done little more than point out that the pay plan at issue is relatively less generous to older workers than to younger workers. They have not identified any specific test, requirement, or practice within the pay plan that has an adverse impact on older workers."[48] Given the simplicity of the implementation phase of the pay plan, it is difficult to comprehend how the plaintiffs could have been more specific regarding their allegations.

The plaintiff typically cannot point to a general disparate impact on workers or point to a generalized policy. Title VII has a provision that allows the plaintiff to combine practices if the plaintiff can show that the defendant's practices are not capable of a separate analysis.[49]

In *Wal-Mart Stores, Inc. v. Dukes*, the Supreme Court recognized that "in appropriate cases, giving discretion to lower-level supervisors" could be a specific practice for purposes of disparate impact liability.[50] Inaction can also be the basis of a disparate impact claim. If managers fail to respond to discriminatory decisions, this inaction can support a disparate impact claim.[51]

§ 6.13 Job-Related and Consistent with Business Necessity

Once the plaintiff establishes the required disparity, the burden shifts to the defendant to justify its practice. In Title VII and most ADA cases, the employer is required to establish that use of the device is "job-related" and consistent with "business necessity."[52] Defendant's motivation is not an element of impact analysis; thus the

---

[47] 544 U.S. 228 (2005).

[48] *Id.* at 241.

[49] 42 U.S.C.A. § 2000e–2(k)(1)(B)(i).

[50] 564 U.S. 338, 355 (2011) (internal citation omitted).

[51] Brown v. Nucor Corp., 785 F.3d 895, 917 (4th Cir. 2015).

[52] 42 U.S.C.A. § 2000e–2(k)(1)(A)(i). *See* section 6.18 *infra*, discussing additional ways to proceed under ADA.

defendant cannot establish its case by showing proper motivation. Nor can the defendant prevail on the second step by claiming it implemented the policy or practice in good faith.

Four years after *Griggs*, the Court issued an opinion that created confusion about how a disparate impact framework would operate. In *Albemarle Paper Co. v. Moody*,[53] the Supreme Court indicated that after the plaintiff established a prima facie case, the employer would then have the burden of proving that its tests are job-related. The Court cited *McDonnell Douglas* in its discussion, but did not clarify what it meant that the employer would have the burden of proving the second step. Did the Court mean that the employer had a burden of production or one of both production and persuasion? After the 1991 amendments to Title VII, it is clear that the defendant carries both the burdens of production and persuasion to prove that the practice or policy is job-related and consistent with business necessity.

In the second step of the Title VII and ADA disparate impact analysis, the defendant must prove both that the challenged practice or procedure is "job related" and "consistent with business necessity." Although these appear to be two separate elements, the courts often speak about them in unison.

Job related means that the practice or procedure must be tied to the job in question. An employer would fail to meet the job-related prong if it used a practice across all jobs within the company without any regard for the functions of particular jobs. For example, it would not be job related for an employer to require all employees to be able to lift 50 pounds, if the ability to lift 50 pounds was not required for all jobs. As the Supreme Court noted in *Griggs*, "any tests used must measure the person for the job and not the person in the abstract."[54]

The EEOC has indicated that an employer can meet the standard of "consistent with business necessity" by showing that a selection procedure is "necessary to the safe and efficient performance of the job. The challenged policy or practice should therefore be associated with the skills needed to perform the job successfully. In contrast to a general measurement of applicants' or employees' skills, the challenged policy or practice must evaluate an individual's skills as related to the particular job in question."[55]

An employer may not give practices or polices "controlling force unless they are demonstrably a reasonable measure of job performance."[56] In *Griggs*, the Supreme Court held that since a high school diploma and the general aptitude tests were not shown to have a "manifest relationship" to the job performance of unskilled or semi-skilled workers, they lacked "business necessity."

In both *Griggs* and *Albemarle Paper Co. v. Moody*,[57] the Supreme Court noted that vague ideas that a particular policy or practice related to successful performance in a job would not be sufficient to meet the defendant's burden. In *Albemarle*, the Court recognized that in some instances an employer might be required to support an objective test by having it professional validated.

---

[53] 422 U.S. 405, 425 (1975).

[54] Griggs v. Duke Power Co., 401 U.S. 424, 436 (1971).

[55] 54 U.S. Equal Emp. Opportunity Com'n, Informal Discussion Letters—Title VII and ADA: Applicant screening and Interviews (July 15, 2008).

[56] *Griggs*, 401 U.S. at 436.

[57] 422 U.S. 405 (1975).

To meet its obligation under the second step, the employer cannot rely on "bare or 'common-sense'-based assertions of business necessity."[58] Instead, this second step requires "some level of empirical proof that challenged hiring criteria accurately predict job performance. [E]mployers cannot rely on rough-cut measures of employment-related qualities; rather they must tailor their criteria to measure those qualities accurately and directly for each applicant."[59]

Although there is no blanket rule about when a practice will be job related and consistent with business necessity, the following types of issues often signal that an employer will not be able to establish the second step in the disparate impact analysis.

- The policy or practice concerns traits or skills that are not related to the job in question;
- It requires traits or skills at a level higher than that required for the job in question or a job that the individual is reasonably likely to possess within a short time;
- The employer adopts it based on assumptions about its validity, with no effort to find out whether such assumptions are correct;
- The test or procedure does not actually reveal whether the candidate has the required traits or skills;
- The test or procedure concerns traits or skills that are a small and/or insignificant part of an individual's job;
- A test has been validated with respect to another job, but the job in question differs in material respects from the job for which the test was validated.

Test validity is discussed in great detail in § 6.17.

§ 6.14 Job-Related and Consistent with Business Necessity, Examples

(1) Workplace Rules

The courts will typically find that rational workplace rules are job related and consistent with business necessity. An employer has an almost absolute right to set shifts, regulate attendance and tardiness, restrict on-the-job use of alcohol or illegal drugs, and prohibit and discipline violent conduct. Employer drug testing for illegal drug use is typically held to job-related and consistent with business necessity.[60]

Generalized physical fitness tests typically do not meet the requirements of being job-related and consistent with business necessity. Rather, the employer should focus on the particular type of physical skill required and the specific level of physical skill needed to perform a particular job function.[61] Even more particularized physical ability tests will not pass muster if they have a disproportionate effect on a protected class and there

---

[58] N.A.A.C.P. v. N. Hudson Reg'l Fire & Rescue, 665 F.3d 464, 477 (3d Cir. 2011).

[59] *Id.*

[60] Jones v. City of Boston, 845 F.3d 28, 32 (1st Cir. 2016).

[61] Ernst v. City of Chicago, 837 F.3d 788, 800 (7th Cir. 2016).

is a mismatch between the tested skills and the skills actually required to perform the job.[62] As one court noted:

> [W]hen women characteristically obtain lower scores on the physical entrance exam than men, and the score differences "are not reflected in differences in a measure of job performance," the entrance exam is unfair. *See* 29 C.F.R. § 1607.14(B)(8)(a). We recognize that, in itself, there is nothing unfair about women characteristically obtaining lower physical-skills scores than men. But the law clearly requires that this difference in score must correlate with a difference in job performance.[63]

Additionally, care should be taken with timed performance tests unless the job actually requires performance of a skill within a particular time frame.[64]

Outside of the disparate impact context, employers must take care to comply with other limits on testing, such as those imposed by the Americans with Disabilities Act. Also, it is important to remember that the ADA may require the employer to provide a reasonable accommodation.

(2) Arrests and Convictions

Rules regulating employee conduct away from the workplace, if proved to adversely affect a protected class, will be more difficult to justify as necessary. The employer would have to show how the private conduct affected the job performance.

A rule that imposes discipline on employees who simply are arrested is most likely to be deemed unnecessary.[65] An arrest does not prove that the underlying conduct occurred, no criminal charges may follow the arrest, and an individual is presumed innocent until proven guilty. In many cases, it will be difficult for the employer to prove the connection between the arrest and the job.[66] However, depending on the seriousness of the charges, suspension following arrest, pending the outcome of the charge, may be a reasonable and necessary response. Additionally, EEOC Guidance suggests than an employer would avoid liability if it investigated the individual circumstances of an arrest and made its decision based on the underlying conduct and not the fact of the arrest.

Using criminal convictions as a basis to exclude individuals from jobs may also result in a disparate impact.[67] Rather than using a blanket no-conviction policy, the EEOC recommends that employers consider "at least the nature of the crime, the time elapsed, and the nature of the job."[68] It also recommends that an employer provide "an opportunity for an individualized assessment for those people identified by the screen, to determine if the policy as applied is job related and consistent with business necessity." The EEOC Guidance notes that while Title VII does not always require

---

[62] *Id.* at 803.

[63] *Id.* at 804.

[64] *Id.*

[65] U.S. Equal Emp. Opportunity Comm'n, Consideration of Arrest and Conviction Records in Employment Decisions Under Title VII of the Civil Rights Act of 1964, 2012 WL 1499883, at *2.

[66] Gregory v. Litton Systems, Inc., 316 F.Supp. 401 (C.D. Cal. 1970).

[67] *See* Douglas El v. Southeastern Pennsylvania Transp. Auth., 479 F.3d 232 (3d Cir. 2007) (ultimately holding that use of conviction was legal); Green v. Missouri Pac. R.R. Co., 523 F.2d 1290 (8th Cir. 1975).

[68] Consideration of Arrest and Conviction Records in Employment Decisions Under Title VII of the Civil Rights Act of 1964, 2012 WL 1499883, at *2.

individualized assessments, "the use of a screen that does not include individualized assessment is more likely to violate Title VII."

EEOC Guidance recommends best practices for employers on policies that exclude individuals from employment based on a criminal record. These best practices encourage an employer to do the following:

- Eliminate blanket decisions based on criminal record;
- Train managers and hiring officials;
- Develop a tailored policy for screening individuals;
- "Identify essential job requirements and the actual circumstances under which the jobs are performed;
- Determine the specific offenses that may demonstrate unfitness for performing such jobs;
- Identify the criminal offenses based on all available evidence;
- Determine the duration of exclusions for criminal conduct based on all available evidence;
- Include an individualized assessment;
- Record the justification for the policy and procedures;
- Note and keep a record of consultations and research considered in crafting the policy and procedures;
- When asking questions about criminal records, limit inquiries to records for which exclusion would be job related for the position in question and consistent with business necessity; [and]
- Keep information about applicants' and employees' criminal records confidential. Only use it for the purpose for which it was intended."[69]

If federal law prohibits an employer from hiring or retaining individuals with certain convictions, an employer complying with such a federal law would have a defense to liability under the discrimination statutes. The federal discrimination statutes preempt state law to the extent that the state law requires an employer to do something that is inconsistent with federal discrimination law. Title VII has a national security exemption that allows an employer to exclude an individual from employment if a job requires a security clearance and the employee or applicant fails to qualify for one.[70]

(3) Other Private Conduct

The employer might have rules that govern employees' conduct outside of work. For example, the at-will employment rule would allow the employer to discipline or fire employees based on social media posts or their membership in a controversial organization. Many of these rules will not result in disparate impact liability, because the plaintiff would not be able to prove the rule has a disproportionate effect on a protected class.

---

[69] Consideration of Arrest and Conviction Records in Employment Decisions Under Title VII of the Civil Rights Act of 1964, 2012 WL 1499883, at *22–23.

[70] 42 U.S.C.A. § 2000e–2(g).

However, other rules may create such an impact. For example if the employer fires employees who have children outside of marriage, the policy may have a disparate impact on women because it is easier for the employer to tell that a woman is having a baby than it is to determine if a man fathered one. In such instances, the employer will be required to establish that the rule is job-related and consistent with business necessity. For many employers, it will be difficult to argue that such a rule relates to the job in question. Constitutional concerns may arise related to public employers.

Title VII has a specific provision that exempts employers from disparate impact liability if they take action against employees or applicants who knowingly use or possess certain controlled substances without the supervision of a physician.[71] However, this does not preclude a separate disparate impact claim based on the impact of drug testing programs. Typically employees lose drug testing disparate impact claims because they fail to establish the disparate impact of such policies or fail to establish an alternative method of screening. If an employer uses a reliable drug screening mechanism for illegal drug use, courts typically hold that such a drug screen is job-related and consistent with business necessity. However, if employers use a test that results in too many false positive results and refuse to adopt less discriminatory alternatives (such as using a second screening device to check results from the first test), a plaintiff may be able to establish that the employer failed to adopt a reasonable alternative.[72]

The ADA prohibits employers from discriminating against recovered addicts and care must be taken in cases involving the prior use of illegal substances.[73] The complexities of legal issues related to drug testing are beyond the scope of this text. However, it should be noted that other federal and state laws often regulate drug testing. In the public employer context, constitutional concerns may arise.

(4) Credit History and Similar Considerations

The Consumer Credit Protection Act provides: "No employer may discharge an employee by reason that his earnings have been subject to garnishment for any one indebtedness."[74] The Bankruptcy Act provides: "No private employer may terminate the employment of, or discriminate with respect to employment against an individual who is or has been a debtor under this title, a debtor or a bankrupt under the Bankruptcy Act, or an individual associated with such debtor or bankrupt [.]"[75] This section also prohibits discrimination based on the person's refusal to pay a discharged or dischargeable debt.

Outside of these limits, employers must still consider the disparate impact of policies related to financial responsibility. In many cases, the adverse impact of such a rule may be difficult to establish. Public records might disclose, however, that a particular group is affected at a significantly higher rate than the balance of the population, or the employer's own experience with the rule might disclose that a

---

[71] 42 U.S.C.A. § 2000e–2(k)(1)(C)(3).

[72] Jones v. City of Boston, 845 F.3d 28, 36 (1st Cir. 2016).

[73] For a case discussing this issue, see Lopez v. Pac. Mar. Ass'n, 657 F.3d 762, 768–69 (9th Cir. 2011) (Pregerson, J., concurring in part and dissenting in part).

[74] 15 U.S.C.A. § 1674(a).

[75] 11 U.S.C.A. § 525(b).

statistically significant difference exists between a number of minority employees and non-minority employees who have been subjected to the rule.[76]

If adverse impact is proved, the burden will be upon the employer to establish that the rule is job-related and consistent with necessity under Title VII or the ADA (or an RFOA under the ADEA). Generally, an employer will not be able to make this showing by arguing that it is inconvenient for the employer to process garnishments or by claiming the employer has a belief that individuals with financial problems are not good workers.[77]

(5) Layoffs Using Systems of Seniority or Merit

Title VII specifically permits the use of bona fide merit and seniority systems provided that the system was not the product of an intention to discriminate.[78] *International Broth. of Teamsters v. United States*[79] held that notwithstanding impact, a routine application of an otherwise bona fide seniority system would not violate Title VII.[80]

Title VII similarly preserves objective systems that quantify and measure the relative merit of employees. Such "systems" can be utilized to determine which employees should be laid off. In order to qualify as a bona fide system, however, the system must exist. It must be a concrete, objective, uniformly applied form of evaluation, adopted in good faith and applied without improper motivation. An *ad hoc*, subjective evaluation of employees, unguarded against supervisory prejudice, does not qualify as a "merit system" and thus is outside the protection of § 2000e–2(h). If such a subjective system results in an adverse impact, it must be justified in terms of its business necessity.

§ 6.15 Reasonable Factor Other than Age

Although a disparate impact case can proceed under the ADEA, the second step in the disparate impact analysis is different than the second step in Title VII cases. After the plaintiff establishes that a practice has a disparate impact based on age, the employer may prevail if it establishes that the practice is a "reasonable factor other than age" (RFOA). RFOA is an affirmative defense, and the employer bears both the burdens of production and persuasion to establish the RFOA.[81]

The RFOA affirmative defense does not require the employer to prove that it picked the most reasonable alternative. As long as the employer chooses a reasonable alternative other than age, it meets its burden, even if lesser discriminatory practices are available.[82]

Courts have held that an RFOA exists, even when the employer's chosen criteria correlates with age. For example, in one case, a court noted that selecting people with

---

[76] Johnson v. Pike Corp. of America, 332 F.Supp. 490 (C.D. Cal. 1971).

[77] Wallace v. Debron Corp., 494 F.2d 674 (8th Cir. 1974); Johnson v. Pike Corp., 332 F.Supp. 490 (C.D. Cal. 1971).

[78] 42 U.S.C.A. § 2000e–2(h).

[79] 431 U.S. 324 (1977).

[80] For a discussion of the seniority system defense, *see* Chapter 11 (§ 11.07).

[81] Meacham v. Knolls Atomic Power Lab., 554 U.S. 84, 92 (2008).

[82] Powell v. Dallas Morning News L.P., 776 F. Supp. 2d 240, 266 (N.D. Tex. 2011).

executive titles or higher salaries for termination during a reduction in force was an RFOA, even if people with executive titles or high salaries tended to be older.[83]

In 2012, the EEOC issued regulations explaining how it construes the reasonable factor other than age defense. Those regulations provide as follows:

> (e)(1) A reasonable factor other than age is a non-age factor that is objectively reasonable when viewed from the position of a prudent employer mindful of its responsibilities under the ADEA under like circumstances. Whether a differentiation is based on reasonable factors other than age must be decided on the basis of all the particular facts and circumstances surrounding each individual situation. To establish the RFOA defense, an employer must show that the employment practice was both reasonably designed to further or achieve a legitimate business purpose and administered in a way that reasonably achieves that purpose in light of the particular facts and circumstances that were known, or should have been known, to the employer.
>
> (2) Considerations that are relevant to whether a practice is based on a reasonable factor other than age include, but are not limited to:
>
> (i) The extent to which the factor is related to the employer's stated business purpose;
>
> (ii) The extent to which the employer defined the factor accurately and applied the factor fairly and accurately, including the extent to which managers and supervisors were given guidance or training about how to apply the factor and avoid discrimination;
>
> (iii) The extent to which the employer limited supervisors' discretion to assess employees subjectively, particularly where the criteria that the supervisors were asked to evaluate are known to be subject to negative age-based stereotypes;
>
> (iv) The extent to which the employer assessed the adverse impact of its employment practice on older workers; and
>
> (v) The degree of the harm to individuals within the protected age group, in terms of both the extent of injury and the numbers of persons adversely affected, and the extent to which the employer took steps to reduce the harm, in light of the burden of undertaking such steps.
>
> (3) No specific consideration or combination of considerations need be present for a differentiation to be based on reasonable factors other than age. Nor does the presence of one of these considerations automatically establish the defense.[84]

The regulation further provides that a differentiation based on the average cost of employing older workers is also unlawful under the ADEA, except as to employee benefit plans.[85] As of the printing of this book, there has been no significant litigation considering how courts will apply the EEOC's regulations.

---

[83] Cerni v. J.P. Morgan Sec. LLC, 208 F. Supp. 3d 533, 543 (S.D.N.Y. 2016).

[84] 29 U.S.C.A. § 1625.7.

[85] 29 U.S.C.A. § 1625.7(f).

§ 6.16 Reasonable Alternatives in Title VII and ADA Cases

Under Title VII and the ADA, a plaintiff has an additional way to prevail on a disparate impact claim. The plaintiff can establish an alternative employment practice exists that will not result in the same disparate impact and the employer refuses to adopt it.[86] Congress did not further define this provision, but rather stated that it was merely adopting the case law that existed as of June 4, 1989 (the day before the Court decided *Wards Cove*). The plaintiff bears the burdens of production and persuasion in proving the alternative employment practice. The Supreme Court has noted that the plaintiff may "show that other tests or selection devices, without a similarly undesirable . . . effect, would also serve the employer's legitimate interest in efficient and trustworthy workmanship."[87]

It is difficult for plaintiffs to prevail by establishing an alternative practice. Lower courts have held that they should consider the administrative and other costs and burdens of alternative selection devices. They also require that such alternative practices "would have improved upon the challenged practice . . . not just that such practices exist in the abstract."[88] One appellate court has held this prong requires the plaintiff at summary judgment to show three elements:

> First, does the record contain evidence that would allow a jury to find that there was an "alternative" method of meeting the Department's legitimate needs?
>
> Second, does the record also allow a jury to find that adopting that alternative method would have had less of a disparate impact? And finally, could a jury find that the Department "refuses to adopt" that alternative method?[89]

Even if plaintiffs can establish that a subjective test has a less discriminatory impact than an "objective" test, some courts may reject subjective tests as a viable alternative if they "open the door to random results and real and perceived scoring bias."[90]

There is not much case law interpreting what it means for an employer to refuse to adopt the alternative practice. Some courts analyze whether the employer had an opportunity to adopt the practice, in that it was available and the employer had the choice to use it.[91] One way for a plaintiff to prove an alternative practice is to prove that the employer successfully used the proposed practice in the past, but later adopted a practice that created a disproportionate impact.[92]

A plaintiff may not prevail on an ADEA disparate impact claim by showing a reasonable, alternative practice. If an employer successfully establishes that the practice is based on a reasonable factor other than age, the employer prevails even if the employer could have used an alternate practice that did not result in the disproportionate

---

[86] 42 U.S.C.A. § 2000e–2(k)(1)(A)(ii) & (C).

[87] Albemarle Paper Co. v. Moody, 422 U.S. 405, 425 (1975) (internal citation omitted).

[88] Lopez v. City of Lawrence, Mass., 823 F.3d 102, 120–21 (1st Cir. 2016).

[89] Jones v. City of Boston, 845 F.3d 28, 34 (1st Cir. 2016).

[90] Johnson v. City of Memphis, 770 F.3d 464, 476 (6th Cir. 2014) (also noting that test security should be considered in evaluating plaintiffs' proposed alternative).

[91] Jones v. City of Boston, 845 F.3d 28, 37 (1st Cir. 2016) (noting ambiguities and unanswered questions).

[92] Muhammad v. N.Y. City Transit Auth., 52 F. Supp. 3d 468, 487 (E.D.N.Y. 2014).

impact.[93] The ADEA allows the employer to choose any reasonable alternative other than age and does not require the employer to use the best practices.

§ 6.17 Title VII Tests and Other Selection Devices

Title VII provides:

> It shall not be an unlawful employment practice . . . for an employer to give and to act upon the results of any professionally developed ability test provided that such test, its administration, or action upon the results is not designed, intended or used to discriminate because of race, color, religion, sex or national origin.[94]

This provision might appear to allow employers to escape liability for discrimination based on their use of tests if they used the test in good faith. The Supreme Court rejected this interpretation in *Griggs v. Duke Power Co.*[95] In that case the Court found that the employer's use of two widely used pen and paper tests (Wonderlic Personnel and Bennett Mechanical Comprehension) had an adverse impact on black applicants. The Court reasoned that if a test had an adverse impact on a protected class and was not proved to be "job related," the test was being "used to discriminate" and thus did not fall within the testing provision. It held:

> Nothing in the Act precludes the use of testing or measuring procedures; obviously they are useful. What Congress has forbidden is giving these devices and mechanisms controlling force unless they are demonstrably a measure of job performance [.] What Congress has commanded is that any tests used must measure the person for the job and not the person in the abstract.[96]

The process of demonstrating the necessary relationship between test and job, or proving that test performance accurately predicts job performance, is known as "validation." The EEOC has developed Guidelines for test validation. Although the courts give considerable deference to the Guidelines, they have not been applied rigidly.[97] One court has indicated that the Guidelines are the "primary yardstick" through which tests are validated.[98] If a test is validated according to the Guidelines, the employer will be able to establish the test is job-related and consistent with business necessity. Although employers are not required to validate all tests, it is more difficult to establish "job related and consistent with business necessity" without validation.

An employer is not required to validate a selection procedure that does not produce a disparate impact; however, the Guidelines encourage employers to use valid tests and selection procedures.[99] The Guidelines described below do not apply to the ADEA or the ADA.[100]

---

93 Fulghum v. Embarq Corp., 785 F.3d 395, 418 (10th Cir. 2015).

94 42 U.S.C.A. § 2000e–2(h).

95 Griggs v. Duke Power Co., 401 U.S. 424, 436 (1971).

96 *Id.* at 436.

97 *See* Washington v. Davis, 426 U.S. 229 (1976); *see, e.g.*, Gulino v. New York State Educ. Dept., 460 F.3d 361, 383–84 (2d Cir. 2006).

98 *See, e.g.*, *Gulino*, 460 F.3d at 384.

99 29 C.F.R. § 1607.1.

100 29 C.F.R. § 1607.2(D).

The Guidelines apply to tests and other selection devices that are used a basis for employment decisions. The regulations provide a non-exclusive list of employment decisions: "hiring, promotion, demotion, membership (for example, in a labor organization), referral, retention, and licensing and certification, to the extent that licensing and certification may be covered by Federal equal employment opportunity law. Other selection decisions, such as selection for training or transfer, may also be considered employment decisions if they lead to any of the decisions listed above."[101] The Guidelines note that a validation study should explore other selection devices that do not result in a disparate impact.[102]

Examples of selection procedures include traditional paper and pencil tests, performance tests, interviews, and physical, educational, and work experience requirements. The Guidelines require employers to keep certain records related to selection devices.[103] The Uniform Guidelines on Employee Selection Procedures recognize that validation is not required for unscored or informal selection devices.[104] Rather, the courts analyze non-test selection devices under a general standard of "business necessity" that is both more flexible and more relaxed than professional, statistical validation.

There are three methods by which a test is "validated." (1) It may have content validity; (2) it may have a statistically proven ability to predict job performance, which is established through a criterion-related validity study; or (3) a test may measure "constructs" (traits) that are vital for successful job performance.

A content validity study consists of "data showing that the content of the selection procedure is representative of important aspects of performance on the job for which the candidates are to be evaluated."[105] A common example of a content-based test would be a typing test given to an individual whose job would require typing. Content-based tests measure the knowledge, skills, or abilities required for a particular job.

Another way to validate a selection device is through criterion-related validity. Here, an employer would use data to show that "the selection procedure is predictive of or significantly correlated with important elements of job performance."[106] For example, the employer might show that those who pass a test at certain level typically perform their jobs well, while those who do not pass the test often do not perform their job adequately.

Construct validity demonstrates "that the procedure measures the degree to which candidates have identifiable characteristics which have been determined to be important in successful performance in the job for which the candidates are to be evaluated."[107] For example, if an employer uses a personality or leadership test, it would provide data showing that the test properly predicts personality or leadership traits needed for the job.

There are common recurring issues that arise with respect to validation.

---

[101] 29 C.F.R. § 1607.2(B).

[102] 29 C.F.R. § 1607.3(B).

[103] 29 C.F.R. § 1607.4(A) & (B).

[104] 29 C.F.R. § 1607.6(B).

[105] 29 C.F.R. § 1607.5(B).

[106] 29 C.F.R. § 1607.5(B).

[107] 29 C.F.R. § 1607.5(B).

To be valid, a selection device typically must be relevant to the specific job for which it is being used as an evaluative tool. The employer in *Albemarle Paper*[108] attempted to use a test to select employees for one job when the test had been validated for another job. Although an employer may validate a test in this way, the employer must show that the same work behaviors or skills are required in both jobs. If the jobs require different skills or performance at different levels, the validation of the test for one job may not be relevant to the second position. Similarly, a study that is valid at one plant, or conducted by another employer, can be used by the defendant only upon proof of the fundamental similarity of the job for which the test was validated and the job for which the test is now being used as a selection device.

Typically, the test must assess employees for the types of skills and the level of performance they will be expected to exhibit on the job. A test which is validated for the top levels of a job progression cannot be used to select employees at the entry level of that progression unless the employer can show that the job to which the correlation exists will be occupied by a majority of the persons hired and that they will reach that higher level job within a reasonable period of time.[109] "However, where job progression is not so nearly automatic, or the time span is such that higher level jobs or employees' potential may be expected to change in significant ways, it should be considered that applicants are being evaluated for a job at or near the entry level."[110] Thus, a test that correlates to the performance of a police captain may not be used to select police lieutenants unless most lieutenants, in the normal progression, will be promoted to captains within a reasonable period of time.

A valid test also requires a proper cut-off score. A test that is otherwise valid may be improper if the cut-off score is set too high. For example, if typists at a particular job are required to type about 40 words a minute, a test that required an applicant to demonstrate proficiency at 100 words a minute would not typically be valid, if it creates a disparate impact. The regulations indicate that cut-off scores "should normally be set so as to be reasonable and consistent with normal expectations of acceptable proficiency within the work force."[111] Additionally, if an employer uses ranked scores on a test to select workers, the employer must demonstrate that higher scores on the selection device relate to job performance.[112]

Under Title VII, an employer may not typically have different cut-off scores for different protected classes.[113] For example, an employer may not make the passing cut-off score on an intelligence test 80% passage for women, but only require men to pass at 75%. However, there is conduct that does not fall within this provision.

The United States Court of Appeals for the Fourth Circuit has held that fitness tests that require the same level of fitness from men and women can have different scores to demonstrate that level of fitness. It noted, "an employer does not contravene Title VII when it utilizes physical fitness standards that distinguish between the sexes on the basis of their physiological differences but impose an equal burden of compliance on both

---

108 Albemarle Paper Co. v. Moody, 422 U.S. 405, 432 (1975).

109 29 C.F.R. § 1607.5(J).

110 *Id.*

111 29 C.F.R. § 1607.5(H).

112 Lopez v. City of Lawrence, Mass., 823 F.3d 102, 117 (1st Cir. 2016).

113 42 U.S.C.A. § 2000e–2(*l*).

men and women, requiring the same level of physical fitness of each."[114] Additionally, the Supreme Court has recognized that an employer may adjust evaluation criteria and cut-off scores prior to a test's administration to make sure the selection device does not create a disparate impact.

§ 6.18 Special Note on the ADA

The ADA contains disparate impact language that is similar to that found in Title VII, but also contains additional provisions that apply to policies and procedures.[115] The ADA specifically prohibits employers from using "standards, criteria, or methods of administration . . . that have the effect of discrimination on the basis of disability."[116] It also makes it unlawful for an employer to use "qualification standards, employment tests or other selection criteria that screen out or tend to screen out an individual with a disability" unless the test is job-related and consistent with business necessity.[117] Additionally, the ADA requires employers to select and administer tests in a way that ensures the test measures the skills or aptitudes desired for the job, rather than reflecting an impairment.[118] The Supreme Court has not considered how these additional provisions might alter ADA disparate impact analysis.

§ 6.19 Other Federal and State Laws

Even if a test does not violate any of the federal discrimination statutes, there are numerous other federal and state rules that apply to testing. For example, the Genetic Information Nondiscrimination Act ("GINA") limits the use of genetic information.[119] The Employee Polygraph Protection Act of 1988 restricts and in some cases forbids the use of lie detector tests.[120] Even when polygraph tests are allowed, EPPA contains restrictions on the types of questions that may be asked. As discussed later in this book, the ADA also prohibits testing in certain circumstances.

§ 6.20 Commonly Contested Selection Devices

While disparate impact analysis applies to employer practices and policies, there are certain kinds of practices and policies that recur in the cases. The use of arrest and convictions, drug tests, and financial inquiries was discussed in § 6.14.

(1) Physical Requirements

In *Dothard v. Rawlinson*,[121] the Supreme Court considered a disparate impact claim based on height and weight restrictions. In that case, certain prison employees were required to weight at least 120 pounds and be at least five feet two inches tall. The Court found that this limit would exclude about more than 40 percent of women from these positions, while excluding about 1 percent of men. The Court held the restrictions created a disparate impact on a protected group. The employer was not able to show that the restrictions were job related and consistent with business necessity. It asserted that the

---

[114] Bauer v. Lynch, 812 F.3d 340, 351 (4th Cir. 2016).

[115] 42 U.S.C.A. § 12112(b)(1).

[116] 42 U.S.C.A. § 12112(b)(3).

[117] 42 U.S.C.A. § 12112(b)(6).

[118] 42 U.S.C.A. § 12112(b)(7).

[119] 42 U.S.C.A. § 2000ff–1.

[120] 29 U.S.C.A. § 2002.

[121] *Dothard*, 433 U.S. at 324.

restrictions were a proxy for the strength needed to perform the job. However, the Supreme Court noted there was no evidence that height and weight correlated with strength. Further, the employer could test for strength directly.

Height and weight requirements often create a disparate impact because of sex, and some may even have such an impact based on race or national origin. There are relatively few jobs where certain height and weight requirements are legitimately required to perform the job; therefore, height and weight restrictions should be used with caution.

When strength, fitness or stamina is required for a job, the employer may test for those traits. However, care must be taken to make sure any testing mechanism tests for the traits needed at the appropriate level. For example, if a job required a person to transport boxes weighing at most 50 pounds, a strength test that measured the ability to pick up boxes weighing 75 pounds would be inappropriate if it created a disparate impact.[122] Any testing must also comply with other sources of law, such as the Americans with Disabilities Act.

Height and weight requirements may also constitute disparate treatment because of a protected trait. For example, if an airline required male flight attendants to be a medium or slim weight or below, but required female flight attendants to be slim, this would be disparate treatment.

(2) Educational Credentials and Tests

In *Griggs v. Duke Power Co.*, the Supreme Court considered a case in which a high school diploma requirement and a passing score on certain aptitude test created a disparate impact based on race.[123] Neither were shown to be job related and consistent with business necessity.

Employers may require certain educational credentials or certain scores on aptitude tests when doing so does not create a disparate impact. If the requirement does create a disparate impact, the employer must be able to show that it is job related and consistent with business necessity (under Title VII or the ADA) or a reasonable factor other than age (under the ADEA).

Courts appear to be more skeptical of education credential requirements for jobs that are not professional jobs or that do not require a significant amount of discretion or risk.[124] One way that employers have tried to lessen disparate impact liability related to educational credentials is to provide multiple ways to meet a requirement. For example, job criteria might include a high school diploma, a GED, or comparable work experience. Employers may require employees to have licenses or certifications required by the government.[125]

Pen and paper tests are often challenged under a disparate impact theory.[126] For common issues related to these tests, see § 6.17 related to test validation. As noted

---

[122] Ernst v. City of Chicago, 837 F.3d 788, 802 (7th Cir. 2016).

[123] *See* Griggs v. Duke Power Co., 401 U.S. 424 (1971).

[124] Davis v. City of Dallas, 777 F.2d 205, 210–11 (5th Cir. 1985).

[125] Osborne v. Travis Cty., 638 Fed.Appx. 290 (5th Cir. 2016) (stating that county could not be liable for disparate impact related to requiring certain attorneys to have license because requirement was imposed by state); *but see* Gulino v. Bd. of Educ. of N.Y., 555 Fed. Appx. 37 (2d Cir. 2014).

[126] Griggs v. Duke Power Co., 401 U.S. 424 (1971); Lopez v. City of Lawrence, Mass., 823 F.3d 102, 107 (1st Cir. 2016).

throughout this chapter, such tests must be valid and relate to the particular job in question. As one court noted in a case involving a pen and paper test given to firefighters:

> [T]here is a difference between memorizing (or absorbing through past experience) fire fighting terminology and being a good fire fighter. If the Boston Red Sox recruited players on the basis of their knowledge of baseball history and vocabulary, the team might acquire authorities like John Kieran but who could not bat, pitch or catch. The test does not examine traits seemingly more relevant to a fire fighter's performance such as agility, stamina, quick thinking under pressure, poise, mechanical aptitude and the ability to work with others. Experts for both sides agreed that verbal memory is not a very important attribute for the job. And unlike the motor vehicle rules covered in a driver's test, it seems unessential whether the candidate absorbs the tested vocabulary before or after acceptance. Nomenclature and similar matters can be mastered during training and on the job. Testing them before acceptance puts a premium on ability to memorize terms that, at the time, contain only abstract meaning.[127]

Paper and pen tests that might be inappropriate for entry-level employees, may be appropriate for supervisory employees.[128]

(3) Word-of-Mouth Hiring, Nepotism and Anti-Nepotism

Insular hiring practices may result in a disparate impact, especially if the employer's work force or certain positions within that work force are comprised largely of people of a particular protected class. For example, if an employer uses word-of-mouth hiring, this hiring practice may create a disparate impact if the employer's work force is largely male. [129] If the plaintiff can establish the disproportionate impact of such a practice,[130] the employer may find it difficult to establish that the practice is justified. Even if the employer can justify the practice, Title VII and the ADA would still allow a plaintiff to prevail by showing the availability of a less discriminatory alternative.

Cronyism, where a person appoints friends to positions may also be challenged under a disparate impact theory.[131] Likewise, some plaintiffs have challenged tap-on-the-shoulder promotion practices, where an employer often does not post or advertise available promotion opportunities and where promotions are often given to individuals identified or recommended by their supervisors.

As one court noted:

> Courts generally agree that, whatever the benefits of nepotism and word-of-mouth hiring, those benefits are outweighed by the goal of providing everyone with equal opportunities for employment. *See, e.g., Robinson v. Lorillard Corp.*, 444 F.2d 791, 798 n. 5 (4th Cir. 1971) (restriction of union membership to relatives of current members); *Barnett v. W.T. Grant Co.*, 518 F.2d 543, 549 (4th Cir.1975) ("Word-of-mouth hiring . . . is discriminatory because of its

---

[127] Boston Chapter, N.A.A.C.P., Inc. v. Beecher, 504 F.2d 1017, 1023 (1st Cir. 1974).

[128] Lopez v. City of Lawrence, Mass., 823 F.3d 102, 116 (1st Cir. 2016).

[129] United States v. Brennan, 650 F.3d 65, 126 (2d Cir. 2011).

[130] Attenborough v. Constr. & Gen. Bldg. Laborers' Local 79, 691 F. Supp. 2d 372, 386 (S.D.N.Y. 2009) (finding that plaintiff did not present proper evidence of disproportionate effect).

[131] Hagan v. City of N.Y., 39 F. Supp. 3d 481, 499 (S.D.N.Y. 2014).

> tendency to perpetuate the all-white composition of a work force."); *Bonilla v. Oakland Scavenger Co.*, 697 F.2d 1297, 1303 (9th Cir. 1982) ("Title VII case law has from the beginning made clear that nepotistic concerns cannot supersede the nation's paramount goal of equal economic opportunity for all."). Nepotism and word-of-mouth hiring constitute badges of discrimination in the context of a predominantly white work force.
>
> Nepotism is not per se violative of Title VII. Given an already integrated work force, nepotism might have no impact on the racial composition of that work force. In such cases, nepotism, word-of-mouth hiring, and similar practices might simply amount to "bad acts" which discriminate against all outsiders without having any disparate impact on racial or religious minorities. "Title VII is not a 'bad acts' statute" and does not proscribe that type of discrimination. *Holder v. City of Raleigh,* 867 F.2d 823, 828 (4th Cir. 1989). However, when the work force is predominantly white, nepotism and similar practices which operate to exclude outsiders may discriminate against minorities as effectively as any intentionally discriminatory policy.[132]

Anti-nepotism rules have been challenged as having a disparate impact. However, it is often difficult for plaintiffs to establish the required disparate impact, given the small number of workers typically affected by such rules.[133]

(4) Grooming

A disparate impact theory can be used to challenge grooming standards, such as requirements relating to hair length, beards, or clothing. Plaintiffs often have a difficult time prevailing in such cases.

Some courts have refused to analyze certain grooming code cases under disparate impact because the policy is not neutral on its face. For example, a policy might explicitly differentiate grooming standards for men and women.[134] As discussed in Chapter 3 (§ 3.37), the analysis in grooming code cases often does not mirror the analysis found in other cases. In the disparate treatment context, courts have often allowed facial distinctions between men and women in grooming codes, even though courts would not allow the same distinctions to be made in other areas. Some courts seems to be skeptical of claims that Title VII intended to impose sex-neutrality in grooming and clothing standards. Plaintiffs may also have difficulty establishing the disparate impact of practices given the small number of employees that may be impacted by certain grooming requirements.[135]

In the cases where the plaintiff is able to establish a disproportionate effect, employers are often able to establish that the grooming standard is job-related and consistent with business necessity. For example, in some cases, grooming codes have been upheld because they are required for safe performance of a job.[136] In public facing

---

[132] Thomas v. Washington Cty. Sch. Bd., 915 F.2d 922, 925 (4th Cir. 1990) (some internal citations omitted).

[133] Austin v. Memphis Light, Gas & Water Div., 129 F.3d 1263 (6th Cir. 1997).

[134] McNeil v. Greyhound Lines, Inc., 983 F.Supp.2d 447, 451 (E.D. Pa. 2013); Eatman v. United Parcel Serv., 194 F.Supp.2d 256, 267 (S.D.N.Y. 2002).

[135] Eatman v. United Parcel Serv., 194 F.Supp.2d 256, 267 (S.D.N.Y. 2002).

[136] Stewart v. City of Houston, No. CIV.A. H-07-4021, 2009 WL 2849728, at *11 (S.D. Tex. Sept. 3, 2009); *but see* Simon v. Harris Cty. Sheriff's Dep't, No. CIVA H-08-2111, 2010 WL 1463459, at *3 (S.D. Tex. Apr. 12,

jobs, the employer may be able to show that a certain "professional" appearance is required for the position.[137] If the employee does not meet the public, and there is no health or safety reason *(e.g.,* need to wear a gas mask) for grooming standards, it may be harder for the employer to establish job-related and consistent with business necessity.[138]

If a neutral rule impacts a person's religious beliefs or practices, the employer may be required to accommodate the religious belief or practice if doing so would not constitute an undue hardship.

(5) Military Service

Title VII provides: "Nothing contained in this title shall be construed to repeal or modify any Federal, State, territorial or local law creating special rights or preference for veterans."[139] Even though veterans' preferences may create a disparate impact based on a protected class, an employer may use them if they are created by federal, state, territorial or local law.

(6) Seniority

Use of seniority to determine promotions may perpetuate past race and sex patterns. However, Title VII specifically permits the use of bona fide merit and seniority systems provided that the system was not the product of an intention to discriminate.[140] *International Broth, of Teamsters v. United States*[141] recognized: "Were it not for . . . the seniority system [the practice] would seem to fall under the *Griggs* [impact] rationale," but concluded: "Title VII would not outlaw such differences in treatment among employees as flowed from a bona fide seniority system. [T]he routine application of a bona fide seniority system would not be unlawful under Title VII."

§ 6.21 The Intersection of Disparate Impact and Disparate Treatment, *Ricci*

If an employer uses a test or selection device that results in a disparate impact, the employer may face disparate treatment liability for disregarding the results of such a test. In *Ricci v. DeStefano*,[142] a group of white and Hispanic firefighters challenged a city's refusal to honor the results of a promotion exam. After giving the promotion exam, the city was concerned that the exam had a disparate impact based on race given few African-American candidates would have been eligible for promotion based on the results of the exam. When the city decided that it would not make promotions based on the test results, a group of white and Hispanic firefighters sued, claiming that the city's decision constituted intentional discrimination on the basis of race.

2010) (questions of fact remained about necessity of blanket policy when it was unclear whether safety rationale applied to all workers).

[137] Care should be taken when employers declare "unprofessional" certain hair or clothing styles worn more predominantly by particular races. D. Wendy Greene, *Splitting Hairs: The Eleventh Circuit's Take on Workplace Bans Against Black Women's Natural Hair in* EEOC v. Catastrophe Management Solutions, 71 U. MIAMI L. REV. 987 (2017).

[138] Stewart v. City of Houston, No. CIV.A. H-07-4021, 2009 WL 2849728, at *11 (S.D. Tex. Sept. 3, 2009).

[139] 42 U.S.C.A. § 2000e–11; *see also* Pers. Adm'r of Massachusetts v. Feeney, 442 U.S. 256 (1979).

[140] 42 U.S.C.A. § 2000e–2(h).

[141] 431 U.S. 324 (1977).

[142] Ricci v. DeStefano, 557 U.S. 557, 566 (2009).

The Supreme Court held that the city's conduct was intentional discrimination that violated Title VII. The Court based its reasoning on the statutory prohibition against test result adjustments[143] indicating:

> If an employer cannot rescore a test based on the candidates' race, then it follows *a fortiori* that it may not take the greater step of discarding the test altogether to achieve a more desirable racial distribution of promotion-eligible candidates . . . .[144]

The Court held that the city could only invalidate the test results if it had a strong basis in evidence to believe that it would be liable for disparate impact if it did not invalidate the test results. Even though the test results met the first step in proving a prima facie case of disparate impact, the Supreme Court held this alone was not a defense to an intentional discrimination claim. The Court found that the city did not have a strong basis in evidence to believe that the test did not satisfy the requirements of being job-related and consistent with business necessity. The Court also found that the city did not have a strong basis in evidence for believing that alternative selection devices existed that would meet the city's needs and that would not result in a disparate impact.

The outcome in *Ricci* is difficult to square with its procedural posture. The Supreme Court determined that summary judgment in the firefighters' favor was appropriate, even though the Court's discussion suggested that many questions of fact existed about whether the test was job-related and consistent with business necessity and whether alternate selection devices existed. The district court had granted summary judgment for the defendants, which was affirmed by the court of appeals. The Supreme Court held that summary judgment in the plaintiffs' favor was warranted. The length of the opinion itself brings into question whether all of the material facts were undisputed, an issue which the dissent also addresses. Justice Ginsburg's dissent provides a very different version of the facts than those presented in the majority opinion.

Ricci covers cases in which the test or selection device has already been used, creating an expectation for those subjected to it. The Court indicated that it would be permissible for an employer to take actions prior to using a test or selection device to make sure that it did not create a disparate impact.

§ 6.22 The Intersection of Disparate Impact and Disparate Treatment, *Wal-Mart*

As of the writing of this book, it is unclear whether an employer's continued use of a selection device constitutes disparate treatment if the employer knows that the selection device results in a disparate impact. In *Wal-Mart Stores, Inc. v. Dukes*,[145] the plaintiffs alleged that the company gave individual supervisors discretion in making pay and promotion decisions. The plaintiffs claimed that this discretion resulted in a disparate impact to women, who were paid less and promoted less often than men. The plaintiffs also claimed that because the company was aware of the effect of this discretion and did not cabin it, that the company was liable for intentional discrimination.

---

[143] 42 U.S.C.A. § 2000e–2(*l*).

[144] 557 U.S. at 584.

[145] Wal-Mart Stores, Inc. v. Dukes, 564 U.S. 338, 344 (2011).

While the majority noted that a disparate impact claim may exist based on discretion given to supervisors that then causes a disparate impact, it did not resolve the larger question of whether knowledge of this effect and the failure to ameliorate it would constitute disparate treatment. Instead, the case focused on whether the plaintiffs could band together in a class action.

Class actions allow named parties to represent the interests of an entire class. They are contrary to normal civil procedure joinder devices, which usually do not allow joinder of so many plaintiffs. The Federal Rules of Civil Procedure provide for class actions because class actions allow large groups of people to band together to vindicate common claims in a more efficient manner than if all of the individuals sued separately. The class action mechanism also makes it easier for plaintiffs to sue on claims that it would be difficult or inefficient to raise in individual cases. The typical example of this is the so-called negative value suit, where each individual has a claim for a small amount of money that only makes sense to litigate in the aggregate.

The context of *Wal-Mart* is important. If certified, the class would have consisted of a million and a half people, and any verdict likely would have been very large. Further, if the named plaintiffs pursued their claims separately there are two practical considerations that would make their individual claims weaker. First, given the amount of research, effort, and expense required to prove the allegations in this suit, it is unlikely to make economic sense for a private plaintiff's lawyer to pursue the individual case with individual damages. Second, even if some, smaller groups of plaintiffs were allowed to band together to sue, a court may not allow them to make nationwide allegations against Wal-Mart or present evidence of nationwide statistics. A court might find such evidence irrelevant to the case by characterizing plaintiffs' claims as local or regional in nature, or a court might find such evidence more prejudicial than probative. Thus, the fact that this case is fashioned as a class action has overwhelming practical importance.

To certify a class under Fed.R.Civ.P. 23, a class representative must meet two separate requirements. First, the class representative must establish all of the requirements of Rule 23(a): numerosity, commonality, typicality, and adequacy of representation. After meeting all the requirements of 23(a), the class must also be certified under at least one of the three options provided by Rule 23(b). There are three important aspects of Rule 23(b). First, Rule 23(b)(1) & (2) classes do not allow class members to opt out of the lawsuit in most circumstances. Thus, if the class is certified under one of these two mechanisms individuals with strong individual cases would be covered by the class resolution, in most circumstances. Second, Rule 23(b)(1) & (2) classes do not require notice to potential class members (unless the court orders it), but certification under Rule 23(b)(3) does require such notice. This notice can be very expensive, especially because many courts require individual, written notice (usually via mail) to the last known address of all potential class members. Finally, the basis for certification under 23(b)(1) & (2) are considered to be less controversial than (b)(3) certifications. It is worth noting that 23(b)(2) has traditionally been viewed as an important mechanism for vindicating civil rights, at least where the relief sought is primarily injunctive or declaratory relief.

Two issues predominated the majority's discussion of the class certification issue. First, the Court considered whether the women's claims evidenced commonality under Rule 23(a). The fact that the majority opinion characterized the argument under Rule 23(a) is important, because the holding on commonality would affect all class actions, no matter which Rule 23(b) certification is sought. The second issue was whether the claims could be certified under Rule 23(b)(2), which requires that "the party opposing the class has acted or refused to act on grounds that apply generally to the class, so that final injunctive relief or corresponding declaratory relief is appropriate respecting the class as a whole."

The district court and the Ninth Circuit Court of Appeals sitting en banc certified the class. The Supreme Court reversed the Ninth Circuit holding that the class cannot be certified because the named plaintiffs cannot establish commonality and because class certification failed under 23(b)(2).

The plaintiffs all alleged injury under the same federal statute. They all alleged sex discrimination for pay and promotion on the same theories. Despite these similarities, the majority held that plaintiffs did not establish commonality. The Court noted: "That common contention, moreover, must be of such a nature that it is capable of classwide resolution—which means that determination of its truth or falsity will resolve an issue that is central to the validity of each one of the claims in one stroke."

The majority then suggested ways that plaintiffs might be able to establish commonality. They could allege a common testing or other evaluative method that created a disparate impact or was a result of intentional discrimination. They also could allege a general policy of discrimination. However, because the managers each exercised their discretion in a different way, this discretion could not be the basis of a common answer.

After holding that the plaintiffs did not establish commonality, the Court also indicated that the case could not be certified under Rule 23(b)(2) because the request for money damages was more than incidental to the requests for declaratory and injunctive relief.

Justice Ginsburg, with whom Justice Breyer, Justice Sotomayor, and Justice Kagan joined, concurred in part and dissented in part. These Justices agreed that certification under Rule 23(b)(2) was improper; however, these Justices would not have precluded certification under Rule 23(b)(3). Justice Ginsburg argued that Wal-Mart's tap on the shoulder promotion process and the discretion given to supervisors to make pay and promotion decisions demonstrated enough factual commonality to bind together the class.

Although many courts assert it is only appropriate to apply disparate impact analysis to facially neutral claims, it is unclear why courts draw this distinction. Some courts have noted that evidence of biased conduct can support a claim of disparate impact. In one case, plaintiffs argued that unchecked discretion given to supervisors resulted in fewer African-American workers being promoted.[146] The court noted that the workers' disparate impact claim could be bolstered by evidence of racial animus because this evidence supports the fact that giving discretion to supervisors would result in a disparate impact.

[146] Brown v. Nucor Corp., 785 F.3d 895, 916 (4th Cir. 2015); *see also* Adams v. City of Indianapolis, 742 F.3d 720, 731 (7th Cir. 2014) (noting that disparate impact can be used to challenge all policies, not just facially neutral ones).

Chapter 7

RELIGIOUS ACCOMMODATION

Analysis

§ 7.01 Generally

Title VII prohibits discrimination because of religion. For example, a plaintiff may sue for harassment, individual disparate treatment, pattern or practice, or disparate impact based on religion. In addition, Title VII requires employers (at least at a minimal level) to accommodate religious beliefs and practices. Title VII provides:

> The term "religion" includes all aspects of religious observance and practice, as well as belief, unless an employer demonstrates that he is unable to reasonably accommodate to an employee's or prospective employee's religious observance or practice without undue hardship on the conduct of the employer's business.[1]

This is the only provision of Title VII that formally requires accommodation.[2] Additional discussions about the definition of "religion" and exemptions from coverage for religious organizations are discussed in Chapter 1 (§ 1.17) and Chapter 2 (§ 2.20). As discussed in Chapter 2, Title VII allows religious organizations to discriminate based on religion and the ministerial exception also allows discrimination based on other protected classes, at least in some instances.

§ 7.02 Religion, Defined

While Title VII does not define religion, the term "religion" includes belief structures that many people would formally recognize as religions, such as Roman Catholic, Protestant, Islam, Hindu, and Jewish. However, the concept is not limited to large, formal belief structures.

The EEOC has adopted a broad concept of religion borrowed from First Amendment jurisprudence. A religious belief is a "sincere and meaningful belief which occupies in

---

[1] 42 U.S.C.A. § 2000e(j).

[2] *But see* Young v. United Parcel Serv., Inc., 135 S. Ct. 1338, 1354 (2015) (holding that failure to accommodate pregnancy can be discrimination in some instances).

the life of its possessor a place parallel to that filled by the God."[3] Stated another way, a religious belief is "a genuinely held belief that involves matters of the afterlife, spirituality, or the soul, among other possibilities."[4]

Religion includes:

> moral or ethical beliefs as to what is right and wrong which are sincerely held with the strength of traditional religious views. . . . The fact that no religious group espouses such beliefs or the fact that the religious group to which the individual professes to belong may not accept such belief will not determine whether the belief is a religious belief.[5]

Courts do not typically evaluate whether a religious belief is orthodox or mandated by a particular religious tradition.[6] In another context, a court noted that religion includes "obscure beliefs such as Paganism, Zoroastrianism, Pantheism, Animism, Wicca, Druidism, Satanism, and Santeria. And, casting a backward glance over history, the test assuredly would have included what we now call 'mythology': Greek religion, Norse religion, and Roman religion."[7]

Religion also includes the absence of religion. For example, a person would be protected if he refused to participate in a prayer service at work because he was an atheist or was agnostic.

Religious beliefs must be more than just a personal preference. It is also important to distinguish religious beliefs from social and political beliefs. Social and political beliefs that are not religious in nature are not generally protected under Title VII.[8] In another context, a court listed the following as social, and not religious: "nihilism, anarchism, pacifism, utopianism, socialism, libertarianism, Marxism, vegetism, and humanism."[9]

New religions and religious practices pose a unique challenge. Courts have been reluctant to declare a system of beliefs non-religious simply because it is new or unconventional. However, a court has rejected the idea that the Church of the Flying Spaghetti Monster is a religion. The court held that this "church" was created as a satire of organized religion and therefore does not meet the test of being a sincerely held belief system.[10]

Religious practices that may require accommodation encompass formal obligations, such as observation of a Sabbath or holy day. Religious activities can fall within Title VII's coverage, even if they are outside of the formal requirements of the religion. Participating in church sponsored sporting events, parties, or picnics may not be

---

[3] *See* United States v. Seeger, 380 U.S. 163 (1965); Adeyeye v. Heartland Sweeteners, LLC, 721 F.3d 444, 448 (7th Cir. 2013).

[4] *Adeyeye*, 721 F.3d at 448.

[5] 29 C.F.R. § 1605.1.

[6] *Adeyeye*, 721 F.3d at 452.

[7] United States v. Meyers, 906 F. Supp. 1494, 1503–04 (D. Wyo. 1995), aff'd, 95 F.3d 1475 (10th Cir. 1996).

[8] Distinguishing unprotected social-political beliefs from protected religious convictions can be difficult. Just because a belief is espoused by a social or political organization does not mean that same belief cannot be religious. Peterson v. Wilmur Commc'ns, Inc., 205 F. Supp. 2d 1014, 1023 (E.D. Wis. 2002); see also American Postal Workers Union v. Postmaster General, 781 F.2d 772, 777 (9th Cir. 1986).

[9] United States v. Meyers, 906 F. Supp. 1494, 1504 (D. Wyo. 1995), aff'd, 95 F.3d 1475 (10th Cir. 1996).

[10] Cavanaugh v. Bartelt, 178 F. Supp. 3d 819 (D. Neb. 2016), aff'd (Sept. 7, 2016).

considered religious practices requiring accommodation.[11] Such activities are social in nature. Distinguishing between religious activity and social activity on behalf of the religious organization can be difficult.[12] However, even if an employer is not required to accommodate a certain activity, it may not discriminate because of the religious affiliation of the activity. For example, it would violate Title VII for an employer to allow employees to attend a softball game sponsored by a Catholic church, but to discipline employees who attend a similar softball game hosted by a Protestant church, if the difference in treatment is because of religion.

Even if the activity in which the worker engages is religious in nature, the timing of the event may be a personal choice and therefore may be outside the religious accommodation mandates. For example, if a person is required to pick up challah bread before a day of religious obligation, the employee does not need to be given extra time off work to pick up the bread, if the religious belief does not mandate picking up the bread at a certain time. If the employee could pick up the bread on another day or at a time when she did not need to take off work, the employer need not accommodate her request to pick up the bread at a particular time.[13]

Protected religious practices include specific clothing or grooming styles required by one's religion or religious belief.[14]

Religious beliefs or practices must be sincerely held by the individual. Whether a religious belief is sincerely held is "largely a matter of individual credibility."[15] "Credibility issues such as the sincerity of an employee's religious belief are quintessential fact questions. As such, they ordinarily should be reserved for the factfinder at trial, not for the court at summary judgment."[16]

§ 7.03 Reasonable Accommodation

Title VII requires employers to provide "reasonable accommodation" for religious beliefs and practices. The employer is not required to provide an accommodation if doing so would cause an undue hardship.

Most reasonable accommodation claims arise after an employer takes a negative action related to a needed accommodation. In examining these reasonable accommodation cases, courts often look at the following: (1) whether the observance or practice conflicts with an employer requirement and is religious; and (2) whether the employer was motivated by the need for religious accommodation in taking an adverse action against the employee. In some instances where the need for the religious accommodation is not known or suspected, the plaintiff may also need to establish that the employer had a reason to know about the need for a religious accommodation.[17] The employer can still prevail by showing that it could not accommodate the employee's religious beliefs without undue hardship or that it did provide a reasonable

[11] *See, e.g.*, Duran v. Select Med. Corp., No. 08-CV-2328-JPM-TMP, 2010 WL 11493117, at *6 (W.D. Tenn. Mar. 19, 2010); Wessling v. Kroger Co., 554 F.Supp. 548, 552 (E.D. Mich.1982).

[12] Davis v. Fort Bend Cty., 765 F.3d 480, 485–86 (5th Cir. 2014).

[13] Dachman v. Shalala, 9 F. App'x 186, 192 (4th Cir. 2001).

[14] EEOC v. Abercrombie & Fitch Stores, Inc., 135 S. Ct. 2028, 2030, 192 L. Ed. 2d 35 (2015).

[15] Davis v. Fort Bend Cty., 765 F.3d 480, 485–86 (5th Cir. 2014).

[16] E.E.O.C. v. Union Independiente de la Autoridad de Acueductos y Alcantarillados de Puerto Rico, 279 F.3d 49, 56 (1st Cir. 2002) (internal citations omitted).

[17] Adeyeye v. Heartland Sweeteners, LLC, 721 F.3d 444, 449 (7th Cir. 2013).

accommodation. An accommodation is reasonable when it eliminates the conflict between the employee's religious belief or practice and the employer's rule.

In *Ansonia Board of Education v. Philbrook*[18] the Supreme Court considered whether Title VII required an employer to provide an employee with his requested religious accommodation, if the request was reasonable. In that case, a high school employed Ronald Philbrook as a teacher. Philbrook belonged to the Worldwide Church of God, which required members not to work on certain holy days. These holy days required Philbrook to miss about six school days each year.

The school board had a collective bargaining agreement that determined teachers' entitlement to leave. The collective bargaining agreement allowed teachers to take three days' annual leave for religious holidays. The school board also allowed teachers to take up to three days of leave for "necessary personal business." However, the collective bargaining agreement provided that the teacher could not use the three days of personal leave to gain extra days off for activities already covered under the collective bargaining agreement. An employee who took three days of leave for religious holidays could not use his personal leave to take additional days off for religious holidays.

Until 1976, Philbrook took three days for religious holidays and then took unpaid leave for his remaining religious holidays. In 1976, instead of taking unpaid leave, he scheduled medical appointments on holy days and also worked on several holy days. Philbrook then asked the school to do one of two things. His preference was for the school to allow him to use personal business leave on holy days. In the alternative, he asked if he could pay the cost of a substitute teacher on some holy days, rather than take unpaid leave. The school rejected both proposals.

The Supreme Court held that Title VII's religious accommodation provision did not require the employer to provide an employee the particular accommodation he requested. As long as the employer provided a reasonable accommodation, the employer met its Title VII obligation. The Court remanded the case for further consideration about whether the employer provided a reasonable accommodation. It opined that generally requiring an employee to take unpaid leave would be a reasonable accommodation. However, the Court noted that this would not be reasonable if the employer only required employees to take unpaid leave when they needed leave for religious reasons.

The Supreme Court provided:

> We find no basis in either the statute or its legislative history for requiring an employer to choose any particular reasonable accommodation. By its very terms the statute directs that any reasonable accommodation by the employer is sufficient to meet its accommodation obligation. . . . Thus, where the employer has already reasonably accommodated the employee's religious needs, the statutory inquiry is at an end. The employer need not further show that each of the employee's alternative accommodations would result in undue hardship. . . . Once the Court of Appeals assumed that the school board had offered to [the employee] a reasonable alternative, it erred by requiring the board to nonetheless demonstrate the hardship of [the employee's] alternatives.

* * *

[18] 479 U.S. 60, 60 (1986).

> We accordingly hold that an employer has met its obligation under § 701(j) when it demonstrates that it has offered a reasonable accommodation to the employee.[19]

If the employer provides a reasonable accommodation, the employer fulfills its obligation under Title VII, even if the employer could have offered additional reasonable accommodations that impacted the worker less.[20]

§ 7.04 Extent of the Employer's Duty to Make Accommodation: *TWA v. Hardison*

Trans World Airlines, Inc. v. Hardison[21] involved an employee whose religious beliefs prohibited him from working from sundown on Friday until sundown on Saturday. The religion also required him to observe certain holy days. TWA fired Larry Hardison when it said it could not accommodate his Sabbath. The Supreme Court considered whether the company could have provided the plaintiff with a reasonable accommodation that did not constitute an undue hardship.

Larry Hardison worked in the Stores Department, which operated 24 hours a day, seven days a week. If an employee took off work in that department, another employee was required to take his place, given the nature of the work. TWA had a collective bargaining agreement that governed Hardison's position. Generally, the agreement used relative seniority within an employment unit to provide employees the ability to select work shifts.

TWA was originally able to accommodate Hardison by allowing him to work the 11 p.m. to 7 a.m. shift; however, Hardison soon asked for and received a transfer to a different building, which had a separate seniority system. While Hardison had enough seniority in the first building to avoid working on his Sabbath, he did not have enough seniority in the new building.

The company agreed to permit the union to explore a work schedule for Hardison that would violate the seniority provisions. While the union may have been willing to allow Hardison to change shifts with a willing employee, it would not require another employee with more seniority to switch shifts with Hardison. The company rejected allowing Hardison to work four days a week. The company stated that his position was essential and that on the weekends he was the only person there to perform it. It could not leave the position empty on the weekend. If it replaced him with a supervisor, other functions would be neglected. If the company hired a replacement employee, it would be required to pay that employee premium wages. Hardison refused to work on his Sabbath, and TWA fired him. Hardison sued both TWA and the union.

The Supreme Court held that the plaintiff has been provided a reasonable accommodation. The company had allowed the plaintiff to observe his holy days by switching shifts with another employee. The employer had also approved of the union finding a voluntary weekend replacement for plaintiff, and had searched for another position within the company for Hardison. The employer could not have switched Hardison's shift unilaterally without violating the collective bargaining agreement.

---

[19] *Id.* at 69.

[20] Ansonia Bd. of Educ. v. Philbrook, 479 U.S. 60, 68 (1986). *But see* 29 C.F.R. § 1605.2(c).

[21] 432 U.S. 63 (1977).

The Court held that TWA was not required to modify the seniority system to accommodate Hardison. The Court first noted the difference between occasional holy days and consistent Sabbath days. With occasional holy days, the employer is often able to accommodate the employee by finding another employee to willingly switch jobs with the individual. Given the infrequent nature of holy days, they present a different issue than Sabbath days do.

For a Sabbath, the employer must find someone to regularly work on the weekend. This is not the preferred shift for most employees. TWA and the union had agreed to schedule shifts through a seniority-based system. The Court noted that 42 U.S.C. § 2000e–2(h) permits employers to honor the terms of a bona fide seniority system. The Court held that TWA was not required to make an exception to the collective bargaining agreement to accommodate Hardison. The Court concluded: "It would be anomalous to conclude that by 'reasonable accommodation' Congress meant that an employer must defy the shift and job preference of some employees, as well as deprive them of their contractual rights, in order to prefer the religious needs of others."

The Court held that the other requested accommodations would constitute an undue hardship because they would require the employer to bear more than a de minimis cost, either in efficiency or money. The Court noted:

> To require TWA to bear more than a *de minimis* cost in order to give [the plaintiff] Saturdays off is an undue hardship. Like abandonment of the seniority system, to require TWA to bear additional costs when no such costs are incurred to give other employees the days off that they want would involve unequal treatment of employees on the basis of their religion. While incurring extra costs to secure a replacement for Hardison might remove the necessity of compelling another employee to work involuntarily . . . in Hardison's place, it would not change the fact that the privilege of having Saturdays off would be allocated according to religious beliefs.

The Court seemed to be concerned about providing too much preference to employees because of their religion, in part because doing so might raise constitutional concerns about the government requiring employers to give religious preferences that are more than de minimis.

Justices Marshall and Brennan dissented, arguing that accommodations by their nature require employers to alter otherwise neutral rules for specific reasons. The dissent also argued that the employer and the union had not tried to find a volunteer to work Hardison's weekend hours. The dissent noted that the employer could have paid another employee to work overtime and then required Hardison to work overtime at regular pay or it could have transferred Hardison back to his old job.

§ 7.05 Religious Accommodation, Examples

(1) Religious Holidays or Observances

A request to observe a religious holiday should be distinguished from requests to observe a Sabbath. Typically, when employees request time off for religious holidays or observances, they only need a few days off each year. An employer can often accommodate such requests without undue hardship.[22] The employer is required to

[22] Adeyeye v. Heartland Sweeteners, LLC, 721 F.3d 444, 456 (7th Cir. 2013).

explore possible schedule adjustments. The employer may fulfill its obligations by facilitating a voluntary switching of shifts between employees. The employer can publicize the employee's need to other employees, or provide the employees with an effective forum, such as a bulletin board or newsletter, for the communication of such information.

The employer may be required to accept employee-arranged schedule changes unless there is a sound reason not to do so, such as if the replacement worker lacks the ability to safely and efficiently perform the job.[23] Situations where there is a capable, willing substitute who does not require additional pay must be distinguished from situations in which the substitute cannot fully perform the employee's job functions, the substitute is compelled to be a substitute, or where additional compensation is required. As discussed below, each of these facts might make an accommodation an undue hardship.[24]

If an employer has a leave policy allowing a worker to take leave for any reason, the employer must allow the worker to take that leave for religious reasons. When the employee does not have paid leave available for the purpose of religious holidays, the employer may provide unpaid leave as an accommodation.[25] Nonetheless, "unpaid leave is not a reasonable accommodation when paid leave is provided for all purposes *except* religious ones."[26]

Courts have denied a plaintiff's claim when the plaintiff proved she was required to make a religious pilgrimage, but that the timing of the pilgrimage was not religiously mandated.[27] In such an instance, the pilgrimage is a religious belief, but the particular timing of the trip is a personal preference.

(2) Sabbath

Many Sabbath accommodations require a permanent readjustment of a working day or days each week. An employee's paid leave time is typically inadequate to cover all of the required days. The employer should still try to see if other qualified employees would trade shifts with the worker seeking an accommodation; however, as a practical matter this may be difficult as many Sabbaths fall on the weekend and other workers typically prefer not to work on the weekend.

Whether a sabbath accommodation is an undue hardship may vary by the employer. For example, if an employee has a Sunday Sabbath, the employer may be able to allow the employee to work on Saturday instead. The employer may be able to transfer the employee to a department where weekend work is not required. *Hardison* held that an employer is not required to hire a part-time employee or require other workers to work overtime. Doing so is more than de minimis.

Some Sabbath accommodations do not require a full day off work. For example, for employees who cannot work after sundown on particular days, a Sabbath accommodation may only require to the employee to leave a few minutes early during the winter. The employer might accommodate the employee by allowing her to arrive

---

[23] Davis v. Fort Bend Cty., 765 F.3d 480, 488 (5th Cir. 2014).

[24] *Davis*, 765 F.3d at 488.

[25] Adeyeye v. Heartland Sweeteners, LLC, 721 F.3d 444, 456 (7th Cir. 2013).

[26] Ansonia Bd. of Educ. v. Philbrook, 479 U.S. 60, 71 (1986).

[27] Tiano v. Dillard Dep't Stores, Inc., 139 F.3d 679, 682 (9th Cir. 1998).

early or to work through lunch. The employer might ask other employees to work the extra time. Spreading work among available workers on a regular basis may also be more than de minimis.[28]

(3) Clothing and Grooming

A fairly common request for accommodation relates to clothing and grooming standards. For example, an employee may ask to wear a particular piece of clothing that she believes is required for her religious practice. Or an employee might request to be able to keep a beard if an employer's rules require employees to be clean shaven.

At times, the employee's request may conflict with safety precautions or requirements. Typically, an employer need not accommodate an employee in such instances. For example, if an employee requests to work in long skirts in an area where the skirt may become tangled in machinery, the employee's request would likely constitute an unreasonable accommodation.[29] Likewise, an employer might not allow an employee to have a beard, if doing so inhibits the effective use of safety masks.[30]

Outside of safety concerns, clothing and grooming requests are often reasonable. Some employers require employees to wear uniforms. Often, the employer can allow employees to modify the uniform to accommodate a religious practice. Police officers, firefighters, and airline employees probably can be required to maintain the essence of the prescribed uniform.[31]

Some public employers may be able to refuse to allow employees to wear religious clothing or insignia when the appearance of religious neutrality is important to the particular job.[32]

(4) Evangelizing or Displays of Religious Materials

Some employees claim that their religious practice requires them to spread the message about their religion or to make religious displays in the workplace. These cases often involve very fact-specific inquiries about the time, place, and manner of the worker's conduct, as well as the employer's rules. It also involves balancing the interests of other employees. For example, if a supervisor proselytizes to her subordinates, the subordinates might bring a claim for religious harassment under Title VII.[33]

The employer must also take care to avoid a disparate treatment claim. If the employer refuses to allow employees of one religion to proselytize, but allows workers of other religions to do so, the employer would be treating employees differently because of their religion. Or, if the employer allows all employees to engage in small talk about all subjects during working hours, it might be religious discrimination to only prohibit conversations about religious topics.

---

[28] *See, e.g.*, Davis v. Fort Bend Cty., 765 F.3d 480, 489 (5th Cir. 2014); George v. Home Depot Inc., 2002 WL 31319124, at *4 (5th Cir. Sept. 27, 2002).

[29] Finnie v. Lee Cty., 907 F.Supp.2d 750, 779–80 (N.D. Miss. 2012).

[30] Bhatia v. Chevron, U.S.A., Inc., 734 F.2d 1382, 1383 (9th Cir. 1984).

[31] Webb v. City of Philadelphia, 562 F.3d 256, 261 (3d Cir. 2009).

[32] Daniels v. City of Arlington, 246 F.3d 500 (5th Cir. 2001) (discussing police officer wearing cross on uniform).

[33] Chalmers v. Tulon Co. of Richmond, 101 F.3d 1012, 1021 (4th Cir. 1996).

Constitutional considerations arise when the employee works for the government. Courts have held that it would be an undue hardship to a government employer to require it to allow public employees to evangelize to the public or to allow employees to display religious materials in places where the public or customers could see them.[34] However, denying all religious speech in the workplace is problematic, and even a government employer may be required to allow periodic religious speech or religious speech that is not heard by the public or customers.[35]

§ 7.06 Notice

The refusal to hire a person because the employee would or might need a reasonable religious accommodation is a disparate treatment claim. In *EEOC v. Abercrombie & Fitch Stores, Inc.*,[36] the Court considered the case of Samantha Elauf, a practicing Muslim, who applied to work at Abercrombie. Elauf wore a headscarf to her interview. The employee who interviewed Elauf was worried that the headscarf would conflict with Abercrombie policy that forbid employees from wearing hats and sought guidance on how to proceed. A manager told the hiring employee that the headscarf would violate the policy, and Elauf did not receive a job.

The employer argued that it could not be liable for discrimination because it did not have actual knowledge of Elauf's need for a religious accommodation. The Supreme Court rejected this argument. It held that the text of Title VII does not require the employer to know about the need for a religious accommodation. If the need for an accommodation is the reason the employer acts, this is enough to establish liability, even if the employer merely suspects (but does not definitely know) that the individual needed a religious accommodation.

The Court also noted that Abercrombie could not defend against the religious discrimination case by showing that its no headwear policy was neutral and not adopted to discriminate. Title VII imposes affirmative obligations for religious accommodation, meaning that, at times, an employer will be required to modify a neutral policy to accommodate an individual's religious belief or practice.

There are cases when an employee is required to provide notice of her need for a religious accommodation. For example, if an employee observes Saturdays as a day of religious obligation, but does not tell the employer, the employer would be able to terminate the employee for failing to show up for work on Saturdays, as long as it did not know or suspect that the employee's absence was due to a need for religious accommodation.

§ 7.07 Accommodation Requests and Retaliation

A request for a religious accommodation is protected activity under Title VII's retaliation provision.[37] A plaintiff may bring a retaliation claim if she requests a religious

[34] Berry v. Dep't of Soc. Servs., 447 F.3d 642, 655 (9th Cir. 2006); Knight v. State, Dep't of Health, No. 3:97CV2114 (DJS), 2000 WL 306447, at *5 (D. Conn. Feb. 22, 2000), aff'd sub nom. Knight v. Connecticut Dep't of Pub. Health, 275 F.3d 156 (2d Cir. 2001).

[35] Brown v. Polk County, Iowa, 61 F.3d 650, 658–59 (8th Cir.1995).

[36] 135 S. Ct. 2028, 2030, 192 L. Ed. 2d 35 (2015).

[37] Geter v. Gov't Publ'g Office, No. CV 13-916 (RC), 2016 WL 3526909, at *12 (D.D.C. June 23, 2016); Lewis v. N.Y. City Transit Auth., 12 F. Supp. 3d 418, 449 (E.D.N.Y. 2014); *but see* Perlman v. Mayor & City Council of Baltimore, No. CV SAG-15-1620, 2016 WL 640772, at *6 (D. Md. Feb. 18, 2016) (noting that while request is not opposition, subsequent action after making request may be).

accommodation and she later faces an adverse employment action because of that request.

§ 7.08 Religious Discrimination by Unions

Unions may not discriminate because of religion.[38] A union may not refuse membership to a person because of religion or engage in discriminatory work referrals based on religion.

Title VII defines religion to include an obligation on *employers* to make reasonable accommodations not constituting an "undue hardship," but is silent as to a union's obligation to make similar accommodation.[39] The courts have construed Title VII to impose an accommodation obligation on unions.[40]

The union's independent duty to accommodate has arisen most frequently in the administration of collective bargaining agreements that require employees to pay dues to the union.[41] The reasonable accommodation is to allow the employee with bona fide religious objections to dues payments to make a charitable contribution in lieu of dues payment. This accommodation places Title VII in line with labor law.

Section 19 of the National Labor Relations Act provides:

> Any employee who is a member of and adheres to established and traditional tenets or teachings of a bona fide religion, body, or sect which has historically held conscientious objections to joining or financially supporting labor organizations shall not be required to join or financially support any labor organization as a condition of employment; except that such employee may be required in a contract between such employees' employer and a labor organization in lieu of periodic dues and initiation fees, to pay sums equal to such dues and initiation fees to a nonreligious, nonlabor organization charitable fund exempt from taxation under section 501(c)(3) of Title 26 [Internal Revenue Code] chosen by such employee from a list of at least three such funds, designated in such contract or if the contract fails to designate such funds, then to any such fund chosen by the employee. If such employee who holds conscientious objections pursuant to this section requests the labor organization to use the grievance-arbitration procedure on the employee's behalf, the labor organization is authorized to charge the employee for the reasonable cost of using such procedure.[42]

Once the court concludes that the employee's religious objection is entitled to accommodation, the standards of § 19 of the National Labor Relations Act have been adopted for use under Title VII. Thus, an employee with bona fide objections to dues payments could not simply refuse to make any form of contribution.[43] Moreover, insisting

---

[38] 42 U.S.C.A. § 2000e–2(c)(1), (2).

[39] 42 U.S.C.A. § 2000e(j).

[40] Reed v. Int'l Union, No. 07–2505, 2009 WL 5943111, at *2 (6th Cir. May 7, 2009); 29 C.F.R. § 1605.2(d)(2).

[41] Reed v. Int'l Union, United Auto., Aerospace & Agric. Implement Workers of Am., 569 F.3d 576, 582 (6th Cir. 2009).

[42] 29 U.S.C.A. § 169.

[43] Yott v. North Am. Rockwell Corp., 602 F.2d 904, 909 (9th Cir. 1979); *see also* Reed v. Int'l Union, United Auto., Aerospace & Agric. Implement Workers of Am., 523 F. Supp. 2d 592, 600 (E.D. Mich. 2007), aff'd

on alternative payment to a religious organization, even on the basis of religious belief, will not suffice. As required by § 19, payment must be to a nonreligious, nonlabor organization. As stated by one court, the employee is not entitled to "more accommodation than those people who are members" of established religions.[44]

§ 7.09 The Religious Freedom Restoration Act (RFRA)

An emerging issue in federal discrimination law is the impact of the Religious Freedom Restoration Act. As discussed in Chapter 1 (§ 1.17), Title VII allows religious organizations to discriminate on the basis of religion.[45] The ministerial exception also provides religious organizations a limited ability to discriminate on the basis of other protected traits as to those individuals who fall within the exception.

The Religious Freedom Restoration Act of 1993 (RFRA), 42 U.S.C. § 2000bb–1 prohibits:

> [The] Government [from] substantially burdening a *person's* exercise of religion even if the burden results from a rule of general applicability [unless the Government] demonstrates that the application of the burden to the *person*—(1) is in furtherance of a compelling governmental interest, and (2) is the least restrictive means of furthering that compelling interest.

RFRA provides a "defense to persons whose religious exercise is substantially burdened by the government."[46] A person whose religious exercise is burdened may assert RFRA as "a claim or defense in a judicial proceeding."[47]

Recently courts have addressed whether RFRA provides employers with a basis for refusing to comply with all or portions of the federal discrimination statutes. In *Equal Employment Opportunity Comm'n v. R.G. & G.R. Harris Funeral Homes, Inc.*,[48] the EEOC filed suit on behalf of a transgender individual who started working at a funeral home presenting as a male employee. After the employee announced that she would be transitioning to a female, the funeral home fired her. It was undisputed that after the employee's transition, she intended to follow the funeral home's dress code for female employees. However, the funeral home fired her, and there was evidence that it was because the employee would be dressed at work as a woman after the transition.

The district court, relying on the Supreme Court's decision in *Burwell v. Hobby Lobby Stores, Inc.*[49] held that the funeral home qualified for protection as a person under RFRA because it was a closely held corporation. The court also determined that the funeral home and its owner had a protectable religious belief under RFRA. The court cited to representations that the business was a Christian business, that the owner was a Christian, and that the owner believed that the Bible teaches that a person's given sex

---

sub nom. Reed v. Int'l Union, United Auto., Aerospace & Agric. Implement Workers of Am., 569 F.3d 576 (6th Cir. 2009).

[44] Stern v. Teamsters Local No. 200, 626 F.Supp. 1043 (E.D. Wis.1986). *See generally*, H.R. Rept. No. 96–496, 96th Cong. 2d Sess.

[45] 42 U.S.C. § 2000e–1.

[46] 42 U.S.C.A. § 2000bb(b)(2).

[47] 42 U.S.C.A. § 2000bb–1(c).

[48] 201 F. Supp. 3d 837, 854 (E.D. Mich. 2016), *reversed by* Equal Employment Opportunity Comm'n v. R.G. & G.R. Harris Funeral Homes, Inc., 884 F.3d 560 (6th Cir. 2018). The Supreme Court granted a writ of certiorari in this case.

[49] 573 U.S. 682 (2014).

is immutable. The district court further found that allowing the employee to appear at work in women's clothes would be a substantial burden on the employer's religion.

Once the plaintiff meets its burden, the government must show that its burden on the employer is in furtherance of a compelling government interest and is the least restrictive method for accomplishing this interest. The trial court assumed without deciding that Title VII furthers a compelling government interest, but then found that the government failed to make its case because it did not prove that allowing the worker to come to work dressed as a woman was the least restrictive method of accomplishing its interest. The court noted that the EEOC did not propose any lesser restrictive option, and the Court suggested that a gender-neutral dress code might resolve the tension without violating the employer's religious beliefs.

The Sixth Circuit reversed.[50] It held that the funeral home could not rely on its beliefs that customers might be uncomfortable seeing a transgender employee in gendered clothing that does not match their birth sex. Biased customer preferences cannot create a substantial burden. The Court also found that the employer was not being required to endorse the employee's transition. The Court continued by finding that the government had a compelling interest in enforcing Title VII and eliminating workplace discrimination and that enforcing Title VII was the least restrictive means of meeting this goal.

Several important questions remain to be resolved. First, courts have not resolved which types of employers would qualify as persons under RFRA. *Hobby Lobby* and the case discussed in this section both dealt with closely held corporations, and it is unclear how or whether RFRA would apply to other corporate entities.

It is clear that prohibiting employment discrimination is a "compelling governmental interest."[51] In most instances, it appears that the least restrictive way of meeting this interest is to prohibit employers from discriminating on the basis of protected traits. In the unique cases where alternatives are available, it is unclear when the government must propose the alternatives and how the negotiation of these alternate practices would work.

Several courts have also held that RFRA can only be invoked when the government is a party to the litigation and it does not provide a defense when a private party is suing a private party.[52]

The use of RFRA by workers to prohibit the government from limiting their religious expression at work is beyond the scope of this text.

---

[50] Equal Employment Opportunity Comm'n v. R.G. & G.R. Harris Funeral Homes, Inc., 884 F.3d 560 (6th Cir. 2018).

[51] Wygant v. Jackson Bd. of Educ., 476 U.S. 267 (1986).

[52] *See* Listecki v. Official Comm. of Unsecured Creditors, 780 F.3d 731 (7th Cir. 2015) Gen. Conference Corp. of Seventh-Day Adventists v. McGill, 617 F.3d 402 (6th Cir. 2010) (same); Sutton v. Providence St. Joseph Med. Ctr., 192 F.3d 826 (9th Cir. 1999); Mathis v. Christian Heating & Air Conditioning, Inc., 158 F. Supp. 3d 317, 325–26 (E.D. Pa. 2016).

Chapter 8

DISABILITY DISCRIMINATION

Analysis

---

§ 8.01 Disability Discrimination Generally

The Americans with Disabilities Act ("ADA") prohibits disability discrimination in employment, public services, and public accommodations provided by both public and private entities. The ADA greatly expanded disability discrimination protections provided at the federal level. Title I of the ADA covers employment discrimination.[1] Its main operative provision states as follows:

> No covered entity shall discriminate against a qualified individual on the basis of disability in regard to job application procedures, the hiring, advancement, or discharge of employees, employee compensation, job training and other terms, conditions, and privileges of employment.[2]

---

1 42 U.S.C.A. §§ 12111–12117.

2 42 U.S.C.A. § 12112(a).

In 2008, President George W. Bush signed a major amendment to the ADA into law. This amendment is called the ADA Amendments Act of 2008 (ADAAA). The ADAAA rejects several Supreme Court cases that interpreted the ADA narrowly.

The Rehabilitation Act of 1973 is a precursor to the ADA. It prohibits disability discrimination by programs receiving federal financial assistance, by certain federal contractors, and against some federal employees.[3] There is significant overlap in how the Rehabilitation Act and the ADA are interpreted, and this chapter focuses mostly on the ADA.

The ADA has a purpose section that is part of the statute. Congress specifically noted that disability discrimination is a "serious and pervasive social problem."[4] This discrimination exhibits itself in a number of ways, including "outright intentional exclusion, the discriminatory effects of architectural, transportation, and communication barriers, overprotective rules and policies, failure to make modifications to existing facilities and practices, exclusionary qualification standards and criteria, segregation, and relegation to lesser services, programs, activities, benefits, jobs, or other opportunities."[5]

Like Title VII and the ADEA, the ADA prohibits discrimination in employment. Generally, the frameworks that apply to Title VII and the ADEA apply to the ADA, as well. However, in recent years, the Supreme Court has differentiated some of the frameworks that apply to Title VII and the ADEA.[6] As discussed later in this chapter, the Supreme Court has not resolved how any of these distinctions apply to the ADA. The ADA also prohibits retaliation.[7]

The ADA is unlike Title VII and the ADA, in that it also includes a robust accommodation requirement.[8] It prohibits the employer from making some medical inquiries.[9] The ADA also prohibits "excluding or otherwise denying equal jobs or benefits to a qualified individual because of the known disability of an individual with whom the qualified individual is known to have a relationship or association."[10]

§ 8.02 ADA Coverage Generally

The anti-discrimination provisions of the ADA require an individual seeking relief under the statute to be a "qualified individual" and for the employer to take a negative action on the basis of disability.[11] Under these provisions, an employer may not discriminate against a qualified individual because of a disability. For example, if a person has diabetes and can perform the essential functions of her job, the employer may not discriminate against her because she has diabetes.

---

3 29 U.S.C.A. § 701 *et seq.*

4 42 U.S.C.A. § 12101(a).

5 42 U.S.C.A. § 12101(a).

6 *See, e.g.*, University of Tex. Sw. Med. Ctr. v. Nassar, 570 U.S. 338 (2013); Gross v. FBL Fin. Servs., Inc., 557 U.S. 167 (2009).

7 42 U.S.C.A. § 12203(a).

8 42 U.S.C.A. § 12112(b)(5)(A).

9 42 U.S.C.A. § 12112(d).

10 42 U.S.C.A. § 12112(b)(4).

11 526 U.S. 795 (1999).

The ADA does more than prohibit discrimination on the basis of disability. It also requires employers to accommodate certain individuals. Under the ADA, an employer commits an unlawful employment practice by:

> not making reasonable accommodations to the known physical or mental limitations of an otherwise qualified individual with a disability who is an applicant or employee, unless such covered entity can demonstrate that the accommodation would impose an undue hardship on the operation of the business of such covered entity.[12]

If a person has cancer and can perform the essential functions of a job with reasonable accommodation, the ADA requires the employer to provide the accommodation and makes it illegal for the employer to discriminate against the person because of her cancer. The employer may refuse to provide an accommodation if doing so would constitute an undue hardship.

For many ADA claims, coverage questions depend on understanding two concepts: "qualified individual" and "disability." Some ADA claims do not require a person to be a qualified individual. For example, a person contesting medical exams or inquiries or a person claiming associational discrimination need not be a qualified individual. A plaintiff does not need to meet the definition of disability to bring a retaliation claim.

Given these limits, the ADA does not provide for "reverse" disability discrimination. It is legal under the ADA for an employer to treat a person with a disability better than it treats other individuals without a disability.

A "qualified individual" is "an individual who, with or without reasonable accommodation, can perform the essential functions of the employment position that such individual holds or desires."[13]

The ADA defines a "disability" as:

> (A) A physical or mental impairment that substantially limits one or more major life activities of such individual;
>
> (B) A record of such an impairment; or
>
> (C) Being regarded as having such an impairment.[14]

A person is only required to meet one of these three definitions of disability. The ADA also contains a list of conditions that are excluded from the definition of disability.[15]

Prior to the ADAAA, the Supreme Court issued several opinions narrowly construing the definition of disability. The ADAAA explicitly rejects the central holdings of two Supreme Court cases:[16] *Sutton v. United Air Lines, Inc.*,[17] and *Toyota Motor Manufacturing, Kentucky, Inc. v. Williams*.[18] The ADAAA specifically indicates that the definition of disability under the Act should be construed broadly in favor of coverage.[19]

---

12 42 U.S.C.A. § 12112(b)(5)(A).

13 42 U.S.C.A. § 12111(8).

14 42 U.S.C.A. § 12102(1)(A)–(C).

15 42 U.S.C.A. § 12211.

16 42 U.S.C.A. § 12101(a)(4)–(8).

17 527 U.S. 471 (1999)

18 534 U.S. 184 (2002).

19 42 U.S.C.A. § 12101(b)(1).

Whether a person is a qualified individual under the ADA is a separate question from whether a person meets the definition of disability under other statutes. In *Cleveland v. Policy Management Systems Corp.*, the Supreme Court considered whether a person who applied for or received Social Security Disability Insurance would be excluded from ADA coverage.[20] Some SSDI coverage depends on proof that the person is disabled and unable to work. In some instances, the Court noted the plaintiff would be required to explain why her SSDI claims and ADA coverage were consistent, since the ADA requires a person to be able to perform the essential functions of a job. The Court reasoned that some SSDI beneficiaries do work and that coverage for others does not take into account the possibility of reasonable accommodation. Thus, SSDI did not consider whether a person would be able to work if the employer provided a reasonable accommodation. Since the ADA requires an employer to provide a reasonable accommodation, the two statutes define disability and the ability to work differently. The Supreme Court held that courts would need to individually consider each case to determine whether an SSDI application or receipt of benefits was consistent with ADA coverage.

The ADA does not preempt any federal or state law that provides equivalent or greater protection.

§ 8.03 Qualified Individual

A "qualified individual" is "an individual who, with or without reasonable accommodation, can perform the essential functions of the employment position that such individual holds or desires."[21] This is an important limit on ADA coverage. The ADA is not a general social insurance statute, and it only requires employers to hire and retain people who can perform essential job functions. For example, if a person's disability is so severe that the person cannot perform the job even with reasonable accommodation, the ADA allows the employer to discriminate against that individual.

The statute defines the term "qualified individual" as follows:

> an individual who, with or without reasonable accommodation, can perform the essential functions of the employment position that such individual holds or desires. For the purposes of this title, consideration shall be given to the employer's judgment as to what functions of a job are essential, and if an employer has prepared a written description before advertising or interviewing applicants for the job, this description shall be considered evidence of the essential functions of the job.[22]

In determining whether a person is a qualified individual, it is first necessary to separate essential functions from non-essential ones. An employer may not discriminate against a qualified individual if the individual is not able to perform non-essential functions of the job. Essential functions include "the fundamental job duties of the employment position the individual with a disability holds or desires," but not "the marginal functions of the position."[23] A function may also be essential "because of the limited number of employees available among whom the performance of that job function

[20] 526 U.S. 795 (1999).

[21] 42 U.S.C.A. § 12111(8).

[22] 42 U.S.C.A. § 12111(8).

[23] Wickware v. Manville, 676 F. App'x 753, 760 (10th Cir. 2017) (citing 29 C.F.R. § 1630.2(n)(1)).

can be distributed" or "[t]he function may be highly specialized so that the incumbent in the position is hired for his or her expertise or ability to perform the particular function."[24]

In determining whether a function is essential, the ADA provides that the court must consider the employer's judgment about what is essential and that written job descriptions used in advertising for an open position or interviewing for it, are considered evidence. Courts often defer to the employer's judgment about which functions are essential; however, this does not mean such judgments are unassailable or conclusive.[25] For example, a court might not defer to an employer if the employer did not require all of the employees in a certain job to perform the functions it claims are essential. However, some circuits have noted that the ADA does not require courts to defer to the employer's judgment, but rather to consider it.[26] ADA regulations provide additional factors to consider in determining whether a job function is essential:

> (1) the amount of time spent on the job performing the function, (2) the consequences of not requiring the incumbent to perform the function, (3) the terms of the collective bargaining agreement, (4) the work experience of past incumbents in the job, and (5) the current work experience of incumbents in similar jobs.[27]

If a function is essential, the person must be able to perform it with or without reasonable accommodation. If a person cannot perform an essential function even with a reasonable accommodation, the individual is not a "qualified individual" under the ADA. For example, assume that a person wants to be hired to be an ID checker at the entrance to a building. The only function required for this job is being able to visually check IDs to make sure the picture on the ID matches the person entering the building. If a visually impaired person applies for the job, cannot perform this function, and there is no reasonable accommodation that would allow him to do so, the ADA would allow the employer to refuse to hire the individual because of his visual impairment.[28]

§ 8.04 Actual Disability, Impairment

A person has an actual disability if she has a "physical or mental impairment that substantially limits one or more major life activities of such individual."[29] This idea involves three separate concepts: (1) a physical or mental impairment that (2) substantially limits (3) one or more major life activities.

The EEOC defines a physical or mental impairment as follows:

> Physical or mental impairment—any physiological disorder, or condition, cosmetic disfigurement, or anatomical loss affecting one or more of the following body systems: neurological, musculoskeletal, special sense organs, respiratory (including speech organs), cardiovascular, reproductive, digestive, genito-urinary, immune, circulatory, hemic, lymphatic, skin, and endocrine; or

---

[24] 29 C.F.R. § 1630.2(n)(2)(ii), (iii).

[25] *See, e.g.*, Wickware v. Manville, 676 F. App'x 753, 761 (10th Cir. 2017).

[26] *See, e.g.*, Rorrer v. City of Stow, 743 F.3d 1025, 1042 (6th Cir. 2014); E.E.O.C. v. Ford Motor Co., 782 F.3d 753, 775 (6th Cir. 2015) (Nelson Moore, C.J., dissenting) (collecting cases).

[27] 29 C.F.R. § 1630.2(n)(3); *see also* Feldman v. Olin Corp., 692 F.3d 748, 755 (7th Cir. 2012).

[28] 29 C.F.R. Pt. 1630, App. § 1630.2(*o*).

[29] 42 U.S.C.A. § 12102(1).

> any mental or psychological disorder, such as an intellectual disability (formerly termed "mental retardation"), organic brain syndrome, emotional or mental illness, and specific learning disabilities.[30]

This list is not exhaustive. The Supreme Court has held that HIV infection,[31] carpal tunnel syndrome,[32] severe myopia,[33] and hypertension[34] are all impairments under the ADA. A plaintiff's case rarely fails based on an inability to establish impairment.

The ADA does not cover as an impairment limits that are not physical or mental in nature. For example, if a person has a poor ability to read, the person will not have an impairment under the ADA, if the poor reading ability was caused by a lack of educational opportunity. However, if the person has dyslexia, the dyslexia would qualify as an impairment under the ADA. The term also does not include physical characteristics, like "eye color, hair color, left-handedness, or height, weight, or muscle tone that are within normal range and are not the result of a physiological disorder."[35] In some instances, obesity can arise from a physical impairment.[36]

While pregnancy itself is not an impairment, conditions that arise in conjunction with pregnancy can be covered under the ADA as an actual disability if they are impairments that substantially limit a major life activity.[37]

§ 8.05 Actual Disability, Substantially Limits

To constitute an actual disability, an impairment must substantially limit a major life activity. In 2008, the ADAAA rejected several Supreme Court cases that narrowly interpreted the "substantially limits" portion of the definition of actual disability.[38]

In *Sutton v. United Air Lines, Inc.*, the Supreme Court held that mitigating measures must be considered in determining whether an impairment substantially limits a major life activity.[39] In that case, two sisters with severe myopia applied to be pilots. Their vision could be corrected with glasses or contact lenses. However, the airline refused to hire them because of their uncorrected vision. The Supreme Court held that the sisters did not have an actual disability under the ADA because with their glasses their vision was not impaired. In *Toyota Motor Manufacturing, Kentucky, Inc. v. Williams*, the Court held that to be limited in the major activity of working, the individual had to be limited in a broad class of jobs, not just the particular job that the plaintiff had or wanted.[40]

---

[30] 29 C.F.R. § 1630.2(h).

[31] Bragdon v. Abbott, 524 U.S. 624 (1998).

[32] Toyota Motor Manufacturing v. Williams, 534 U.S. 184 (2002).

[33] Sutton v. United Air Lines, 527 U.S. 471 (1999).

[34] Murphy v. UPS, 527 U.S. 516 (1999).

[35] Appendix to Part 1630—Interpretive Guidance on Title I of the ADA (interpretive guidance), 29 C.F.R. Pt. 1630, App. § 1630.2(h) (emphasis added).

[36] Morriss v. BNSF Ry. Co., 817 F.3d 1104, 1109 (8th Cir. 2016).

[37] Jeudy v. Attorney Gen., Dep't of Justice, 482 F. App'x 517, 520 (11th Cir. 2012).

[38] 42 U.S.C.A. § 12101(a)(4)–(8).

[39] 527 U.S. 471 (1999).

[40] 534 U.S. 184 (2002).

The ADAAA specifically rejects *Sutton* and *Toyota*.[41] In general, mitigating measures do not impact whether an impairment substantially limits a major activity. The ADA provides as follows:

> (E) (i) The determination of whether an impairment substantially limits a major life activity shall be made without regard to the ameliorative effects of mitigating measures such as—
>
> (I) medication, medical supplies, equipment, or appliances, low-vision devices (which do not include ordinary eyeglasses or contact lenses), prosthetics including limbs and devices, hearing aids and cochlear implants or other implantable hearing devices, mobility devices, or oxygen therapy equipment and supplies;
>
> (II) use of assistive technology;
>
> (III) reasonable accommodations or auxiliary aids or services; or
>
> (IV) learned behavioral or adaptive neurological modifications.[42]

However, the ameliorative effects of "ordinary eyeglasses or contact lenses" are considered in determining whether an impairment substantially limits a major life activity. In other words, a person who has a typical eyeglass prescription cannot establish that she is substantially limited in the life activity of seeing, if the glasses correct her vision to a typical range. EEOC Guidance provides that a person who mitigates the effects of an impairment may show that it would be substantially limiting without the mitigating measures by showing "evidence of limitations that a person experienced prior to using a mitigating measure, evidence concerning the expected course of a particular disorder absent mitigating measures, or readily available and reliable information of other types."[43]

The ADAAA also provides that courts had construed the term "substantially limits" too narrowly. EEOC regulations provide that the term "shall be construed broadly in favor of expansive coverage," and is "not meant to be a demanding standard."[44] It should not require extensive analysis.[45] However, courts must conduct an individual analysis about whether the particular plaintiff is substantially limited.[46] Scientific, medical, or statistical evidence is not required to establish that an impairment substantially limits a major life activity.[47] An impairment only needs to limit one major life activity.

The regulations further explain,"[a]n impairment need not prevent, or significantly or severely restrict, the individual from performing a major life activity."[48] Instead, it need only "substantially limit[ ] the ability of [the] individual to perform a major life activity as compared to most people in the general population."

EEOC regulations provide a list of factors to consider in undertaking this inquiry:

---

41 42 U.S.C.A. § 12101(a)(4)–(8).

42 42 U.S.C.A. § 12102(4)(E).

43 29 C.F.R. Pt. 1630, App. § 1630.2(j)(1)(vi).

44 29 C.F.R. § 1630.2(j)(1)(i).

45 29 C.F.R. § 1630.2(j)(1)(iii).

46 29 C.F.R. § 1630.2(j)(1)(iv).

47 29 C.F.R. § 1630.2(j)(1)(v).

48 29 C.F.R. § 1630.2(j)(1)(ii) (2017).

> Consideration of facts such as condition, manner, or duration may include, among other things, consideration of the difficulty, effort, or time required to perform a major life activity; pain experienced when performing a major life activity; the length of time a major life activity can be performed; and/or the way an impairment affects the operation of a major bodily function. In addition, the non-ameliorative effects of mitigating measures, such as negative side effects of medication or burdens associated with following a particular treatment regimen, may be considered when determining whether an individual's impairment substantially limits a major life activity.[49]

The EEOC further provides that the focus should be on how the major life activity is affected and not the outcome of the worker's efforts.[50] For example, a person with a cognitive impairment can be substantially limited in learning, even if the person is able to obtain high grades. The person may be required to study longer to achieve the same results as a person in the general population.

Impairments that are episodic or in remission can be actual disabilities, if they would limit a major life activity when active. For example, a plaintiff created a dispute of material fact about whether she had an actual disability when she presented evidence that she had hyperthyroidism that periodically flared up. During the flare ups, she suffered "extreme fatigue, reduced cognitive functioning, and bouts of severe dizziness."[51] In another case, a plaintiff could establish that her post-partum depression and separation anxiety constituted an actual disability, even though some of the results (such as panic attacks) occurred episodically.[52] The EEOC Guidelines note:

> Other examples of impairments that may be episodic include, but are not limited to, hypertension, diabetes, asthma, major depressive disorder, bipolar disorder, and schizophrenia. See 2008 House Judiciary Committee Report at 19–20. The fact that the periods during which an episodic impairment is active and substantially limits a major life activity may be brief or occur infrequently is no longer relevant to determining whether the impairment substantially limits a major life activity. For example, a person with post-traumatic stress disorder who experiences intermittent flashbacks to traumatic events is substantially limited in brain function and thinking.[53]

§ 8.06 Actual Disability, Major Life Activity

The impairment must substantially affect a major life activity. The ADAAA broadly defines "major life activities" to include the following:

> (A) In general.
>
> For purposes of paragraph (1), major life activities include, but are not limited to, caring for oneself, performing manual tasks, seeing, hearing, eating, sleeping, walking, standing, lifting, bending, speaking, breathing, learning, reading, concentrating, thinking, communicating, and working.

---

49 29 C.F.R. § 1630.2(j)(4)(ii).

50 29 C.F.R. § 1630.2(j)(4)(iii).

51 Barlia v. MWI Veterinary Supply, Inc., 721 F. App'x 439, 447 (6th Cir. 2018).

52 Hostettler v. Coll. of Wooster, 895 F.3d 844, 854 (6th Cir. 2018).

53 29 C.F.R. Pt. 1630, App. § 1630.2(j)(1)(vii).

(B) Major bodily functions.

For purposes of paragraph (1), a major life activity also includes the operation of a major bodily function, including but not limited to, functions of the immune system, normal cell growth, digestive, bowel, bladder, neurological, brain, respiratory, circulatory, endocrine, and reproductive functions.[54]

§ 8.07 Actual Disability, Cases

An actual disability is present when a plaintiff establishes that an impairment substantially limits a major life activity. Although this requires an individualized assessment of the particular plaintiff, it does not necessarily require a significant amount of individualized evidence in every case.[55] Some impairments will virtually always result in substantial limits on a major life activity.[56] A plaintiff is not required to provide medical evidence to support a claim of actual disability, if the plaintiff can establish the elements of actual disability without it.[57] Although it is impossible to list all of the conditions and limits that might qualify as actual disabilities in specific cases, this section provides recent examples to illustrate the concept.

The Eleventh Circuit has held that a back problem caused by a herniated disc could constitute an actual disability when the plaintiff presented evidence of the medical condition, what the medical condition caused, and the limits on the plaintiff's major life activities.[58] The Seventh Circuit has held that a knee injury is an actual disability when it substantially limited the plaintiff's ability to walk, stand, squat and kneel.[59] Hypothyroidism which limited the plaintiff's endocrine system and caused extreme fatigue, dizziness, and reduced cognitive function was an actual disability when it flared up.[60]

Severe autism or cognitive impairments can constitute an actual disability.[61] Post-partum depression and separation anxiety are actual disabilities when the plaintiff presented evidence that they caused her to suffer repeated panic attacks and caused "difficulty breathing, and limited ability to communicate, focus, and make decisions."[62]

§ 8.08 Record of Disability

In addition to actual disability, the ADA protects individuals who have a "record of" disability. Prior to the ADAAA, many courts had read the "record of" definition so restrictively that few plaintiffs could meet it. Some courts had held, for example, that the record must actually show that the employer believed that the employee was

---

[54] 42 U.S.C.A. § 12102(2).

[55] Lacy v. Cook Cty., Illinois, 897 F.3d 847, 865 n.37 (7th Cir. 2018).

[56] Lacy v. Cook Cty., Illinois, 897 F.3d 847, 865 n.37 (7th Cir. 2018); *see also* 29 U.S.C.A. § 1630.2(j)(3) (providing list of when the inquiry should be simple and straightforward).

[57] Mancini v. City of Providence by & through Lombardi, No. 18–1011, 2018 WL 6074267, at *7 (1st Cir. Nov. 21, 2018) (noting that medical evidence not required when a jury could understand limits of knee injury).

[58] Mazzeo v. Color Resolutions International, LLC, 746 F.3d 1264 (11th Cir. 2014).

[59] Rowlands v. United Parcel Serv.—Fort Wayne, 901 F.3d 792, 800 (7th Cir. 2018).

[60] Barlia v. MWI Veterinary Supply, Inc., 721 F. App'x 439, 446–47 (6th Cir. 2018)

[61] A.L. by & through D.L. v. Walt Disney Parks & Resorts US, Inc., 900 F.3d 1270, 1290 (11th Cir. 2018).

[62] Hostettler v. Coll. of Wooster, 895 F.3d 844, 854 (6th Cir. 2018).

substantially limited in a major life activity. Since few records contained this level of detail or used this kind of language, it was hard for plaintiffs to proceed under this prong.

Under EEOC regulations, a person has a record of disability "if the individual has a history of, or has been misclassified as having, a mental or physical impairment that substantially limits one or more major life activities."[63] The regulations favor giving a broad reading of the term "substantially limits."[64] A plaintiff can prove this definition, even if the record shows a transitory condition or episodic condition, as long as the condition would meet the definition when active.[65] A record of a hospitalization or medical care is not per se evidence of a record of disability.[66] Even after the ADAAA, there are few "record of" cases compared to cases pursued under "actual disability" or "regarded as" definitions.

A qualified individual with a record of disability is entitled to reasonable accommodation.[67]

§ 8.09 Regarded as

A person can fall within ADA coverage if she is regarded as having a disability. For example, if an employee does not have cancer, but the employer fires her because it mistakenly believes she has cancer, she would be regarded as having a disability. Likewise, if the employee had a minor impairment, but the employer wrongfully believed it was substantially limiting, the employee would be regarded as having a disability.

Prior to the ADAAA, there were few cases under the regarded as prong, both because there were fewer cases that fell within these factual scenarios and also because the courts had narrowly interpreted the provision.

Under the ADAAA, an individual is "regarded as having such an impairment" if the individual establishes that "he or she has been subjected to an action prohibited under this Act because of an actual or perceived physical or mental impairment whether or not the impairment limits or is perceived to limit a major life activity."[68] This change greatly expanded this provision and also increased the number of plaintiffs who might try to establish coverage through it. If the employer took an action because of a perceived physical or mental impairment, the employer faces liability under the ADA, even if the condition does not substantially limit a major life activity and even if the employer did not perceive it in that way.[69] For example, a court has held that when a decisionmaker thought a worker suffered a concussion that caused dizziness, the worker met the definition of regarded as because concussions that cause these problems are impairments in neurological functions.[70]

"[F]or a plaintiff alleging disability discrimination to show that the employer regarded him as having an impairment, the plaintiff must show that (1) he has an actual

---

[63] 29 C.F.R. § 1630.2(k)(1).

[64] 29 C.F.R. § 1630.2(k)(2).

[65] 29 U.S.C.A. § 1630.2(j)(1)(ix).

[66] Graham v. Three Vill. Cent. Sch. Dist., No. 11-CV-5182, 2013 WL 5445736, at *17 (E.D.N.Y. Sept. 30, 2013) (citing cases).

[67] 42 U.S.C.A. § 12201(h).

[68] 42 U.S.C.A. § 12102(3).

[69] Adair v. City of Muskogee, 823 F.3d 1297 (10th Cir. 2016).

[70] Baker v. Roman Catholic Archdiocese of San Diego, 725 F. App'x 531, 532 (9th Cir. 2018).

or perceived impairment, (2) that impairment is neither transitory nor minor, and (3) the employer was aware of and therefore perceived the impairment at the time of the alleged discriminatory action."[71]

Given that this prong is less onerous to prove than the actual disability prong, many cases will proceed under the regarded as provision, even when the plaintiff has an actual disability. However, if the plaintiff requires an accommodation, the case must proceed through the actual disability (or record of) prong.[72]

There is another limit on the provision. An employer may discriminate against an individual if it regards an individual as having an impairment that is both transitory and minor in nature. The statute defines transitory as having a duration of six months or less.[73] For example, if the employer perceived a person as having a normal cold, the employer could take negative actions against the employee because of the cold under the ADA. EEOC Guidance indicates that whether a condition is transitory and minor is based on an objective inquiry.

> For example, an employer who terminates an employee whom it believes has bipolar disorder cannot take advantage of this exception by asserting that it believed the employee's impairment was transitory and minor, since bipolar disorder is not objectively transitory and minor. At the same time, an employer that terminated an employee with an objectively "transitory and minor" hand wound, mistakenly believing it to be symptomatic of HIV infection, will nevertheless have "regarded" the employee as an individual with a disability, since the covered entity took a prohibited employment action based on a perceived impairment (HIV infection) that is not "transitory and minor."[74]

§ 8.10 Reasonable Accommodation, Generally

Under the ADA, an employer commits an unlawful employment practice by:

> (5) (A) not making reasonable accommodations to the known physical or mental limitations of an otherwise qualified individual with a disability who is an applicant or employee, unless such covered entity can demonstrate that the accommodation would impose an undue hardship on the operation of the business of such covered entity.[75]

The reasonable accommodation requirement under the ADA is more robust than Title VII's religious accommodation requirement.

"The reasonable accommodation requirement is best understood as a means by which barriers to the equal employment opportunity of an individual with a disability are removed or alleviated."[76] The ADA provides a non-exhaustive list of examples of accommodations that may be reasonable:

---

[71] Adair v. City of Muskogee, 823 F.3d 1297, 1306 (10th Cir. 2016); *see also* Equal Employment Opportunity Comm'n v. BNSF Ry. Co., 902 F.3d 916, 923 (9th Cir. 2018), as amended (Sept. 12, 2018).

[72] 42 U.S.C.A. § 12201(h).

[73] 42 U.S.C.A. § 12102(3).

[74] 29 C.F.R. Pt. 1630, App. § 1630.2(*l*).

[75] 42 U.S.C.A. § 12112(b)(5)(A).

[76] 29 C.F.R. Pt. 1630, App. § 1630.9.

> Reasonable accommodation.—The term "reasonable accommodation" may include—
>
> (A) making existing facilities used by employees readily accessible to and usable by individuals with disabilities; and
>
> (B) job restructuring, part-time or modified work schedules, reassignment to a vacant position, acquisition or modification of equipment or devices, appropriate adjustment or modifications of examinations, training materials or policies, the provision of qualified readers or interpreters, and other similar accommodations for individuals with disabilities.[77]

EEOC regulations provide a list of reasonable accommodations that includes the following:

> (i) Modifications or adjustments to a job application process that enable a qualified applicant with a disability to be considered for the position such qualified applicant desires; or
>
> (ii) Modifications or adjustments to the work environment, or to the manner or circumstances under which the position held or desired is customarily performed, that enable an individual with a disability who is qualified to perform the essential functions of that position; or
>
> (iii) Modifications or adjustments that enable a covered entity's employee with a disability to enjoy equal benefits and privileges of employment as are enjoyed by its other similarly situated employees without disabilities.
>
> (2) Reasonable accommodation may include but is not limited to:
>
> (i) Making existing facilities used by employees readily accessible to and usable by individuals with disabilities; and
>
> (ii) Job restructuring; part-time or modified work schedules; reassignment to a vacant position; acquisition or modifications of equipment or devices; appropriate adjustment or modifications of examinations, training materials, or policies; the provision of qualified readers or interpreters; and other similar accommodations for individuals with disabilities.[78]

The Guidance emphasizes that this list is not exhaustive and provides further examples of accommodations that might be reasonable.

> For example, other accommodations could include permitting the use of accrued paid leave or providing additional unpaid leave for necessary treatment, making employer provided transportation accessible, and providing reserved parking spaces. Providing personal assistants, such as a page turner for an employee with no hands or a travel attendant to act as a sighted guide to assist a blind employee on occasional business trips, may also be a reasonable accommodation.[79]

---

[77] 42 U.S.C.A. § 12111(9).

[78] 29 C.F.R. § 1630.2(*o*).

[79] 29 C.F.R. Pt. 1630, App. § 1630.2(*o*).

An employee may not force an employer to make a specific accommodation, as long as the employer provides a reasonable one.[80] However, if an employee refuses an effective accommodation, the employee may no longer be a qualified individual if she cannot perform the essential functions of the job.

An accommodation must be effective. An employer does not meet its obligation under the ADA by offering an accommodation that does not effectively allow a person to perform the essential functions of the position.

§ 8.11 Undue Hardship

Under the ADA, the employer must provide a reasonable accommodation to a worker unless doing so would cause an undue hardship. The employer's obligation to provide accommodation under the ADA is much more robust than its obligations to provide religious accommodation under Title VII. The employer may choose to provide more accommodation than the ADA requires.

The term "undue hardship" means the following:

> (A) In general.—The term "undue hardship" means an action requiring significant difficulty or expense, when considered in light of the factors set forth in subparagraph (B).
>
> (B) Factors to be considered.—In determining whether an accommodation would impose an undue hardship on a covered entity, factors to be considered include—
>
> (i) the nature and cost of the accommodation needed under this chapter;
>
> (ii) the overall financial resources of the facility or facilities involved in the provision of the reasonable accommodation; the number of persons employed at such facility; the effect on expenses and resources, or the impact otherwise of such accommodation upon the operation of the facility;
>
> (iii) the overall financial resources of the covered entity; the overall size of the business of a covered entity with respect to the number of its employees; the number, type, and location of its facilities; and
>
> (iv) the type of operation or operations of the covered entity, including the composition, structure, and functions of the workforce of such entity; the geographic separateness, administrative, or fiscal relationship of the facility or facilities in question to the covered entity.[81]

This is a fact-specific inquiry. Accommodations that might be an undue hardship for one employer, may not constitute an undue hardship for a different employer. The employer has the burden of establishing undue hardship.

EEOC Guidance gives examples of some ways an employer may be able to demonstrate undue hardship.

> Excessive cost is only one of several possible bases upon which an employer might be able to demonstrate undue hardship. Alternatively, for example, an employer could demonstrate that the provision of a particular accommodation

---

[80] Talley v. Family Dollar Stores of Ohio, Inc., 542 F.3d 1099, 1108 (6th Cir. 2008).

[81] 42 U.S.C.A. § 12111(10).

> would be unduly disruptive to its other employees or to the functioning of its business. The terms of a collective bargaining agreement may be relevant to this determination. By way of illustration, an employer would likely be able to show undue hardship if the employer could show that the requested accommodation of the upward adjustment of the business' thermostat would result in it becoming unduly hot for its other employees, or for its patrons or customers. The employer would thus not have to provide this accommodation. However, if there were an alternate accommodation that would not result in undue hardship, the employer would have to provide that accommodation.[82]

Undue hardship may not be based on the prejudices or discomforts of co-workers or customers related to the person's disability.[83]

§ 8.12 Interaction of Reasonableness, Undue Hardship, and Essential Function

Tricky questions arise when determining whether a request is a request for an accommodation or a request for the employer to eliminate an essential job function. The ADA does not require the employer to eliminate essential job functions.

Consider the following request by an employee. The employee develops cancer and needs to have a surgery to remove a malignant tumor. Prior to the surgery, the cancer causes the employee to be substantially limited in major life activities. The employee asks for two weeks off of work to have the surgery and to recover. Imagine that the employee has no available sick leave and is not entitled to leave under other sources of law, such as the Family Medical Leave Act. Has the employee asked for an accommodation or has the employee asked for the employer to eliminate an essential function of the job, i.e., showing up for work? Much depends on how the court chooses to characterize the request.

In recent years, some courts have required employers to grant relatively short leaves of absences to employees as reasonable accommodations under the ADA, if the requested leave is of a definite duration and will allow the employee to return to work in the immediate future.[84] However, the law in this area is still developing.

A request to work from home or for a flexible work schedule may pose similar issues. In the early days of the ADA, courts routinely dismissed cases involving these types of requests based on the idea that regular attendance at work during specific work hours was an essential function of most jobs. However, as workplaces have changed over time, some courts have held that such accommodations are reasonable and do not constitute an undue hardship. The analysis often depends on the particular circumstances of the job in question.

---

[82] 29 C.F.R. Pt. 1630, App. § 1630.15(d).

[83] Nicole B. Porter, *Reasonable Burdens: Resolving the Conflict Between Disabled Employees and Their Coworkers*, 34 FLA. ST. U. L. REV. 313 (2007).

[84] *See, e.g.*, Delaval v. Ptech Drilling Tubulars, L.L.C., 824 F.3d 476, 481 (5th Cir. 2016); Delgado Echevarria v. AstraZeneca Pharm. LP, 856 F.3d 119, 130 (1st Cir. 2017); EEOC v. Midwest Gaming & Entertainment, LLC, 2018 U.S. Dist. LEXIS 88367, at *8 (E.D. Ill. 2018).

For example, it may not be reasonable for a person to request to work from home when her job requires regular face-to-face contact with customers or patients.[85] However, the same employer may be required to allow an employee in a different job to work from home.

A different question arises in cases where the parties dispute whether a job function is an essential or marginal function. Recall that if a job function is non-essential, the employer may not discriminate against a person with a disability for failure to be able to perform that function. There is an argument that the ADA's language requires the plaintiff to prove she can perform the essential functions of a job, which entails proving which functions are essential.[86] However, some courts have recognized that proving that a job function is essential should fall on the employer, based in part on the idea that the employer has better access to information related to whether job functions are essential or not.[87]

Another question arises at the intersection of the concepts of "reasonable" accommodation and undue hardship. In an ADA accommodation case, the plaintiff is required to establish that the accommodation is reasonable.[88] To avoid liability, the employer is required to establish that the reasonable accommodation is an undue hardship.[89]

In *U.S. Airways v. Barnett*,[90] the Supreme Court considered how these issues intersect. In *Barnett*, an employee with a back injury transferred to a job in the mailroom. Under the company's seniority system, the mailroom position was open to bidding from senior employees. The employee argued that it would be a reasonable accommodation for the employer to allow him to stay in the mailroom position, despite the seniority system. The employer refused and Mr. Barnett lost his job.

The employer argued that because the accommodation would conflict with the seniority system, it was not reasonable. The Court rejected this argument, reasoning that the ADA's accommodation requirement by its very nature would require an employer to modify its work rules if doing so would accommodate the disability and be reasonable. In the accommodation context, the ADA may require an employer to change otherwise neutral rules and to permit a worker with a disability to "violate a rule that others must obey."

Barnett argued that the term "reasonable" only meant that a worker needed to establish the requested accommodation was effective. He argued a conflict with a seniority system would never make the requested accommodation unreasonable, but that the employer could use the conflict to try to establish the requested accommodation was an undue hardship. The Court rejected these arguments. Ordinary definitions of the

---

[85] *See* EEOC v. Ford Motor Co., 782 F.3d 753 (6th Cir. 2015) (*en banc*); Samper v. Providence St. Vincent Med. Ctr., 675 F.3d 1233, 1238–39 (9th Cir. 2012) (neo-natal nurse); EEOC v. Yellow Freight Sys., Inc., 253 F.3d 943, 949 (7th Cir. 2001) (forklift operator).

[86] 42 U.S.C.A. §§ 12112 & 12111(8); Richardson v. Friendly Ice Cream Corp., 594 F.3d 69, 76 (1st Cir. 2010).

[87] Rehrs v. The Iams Co., 486 F.3d 353, 356 (8th Cir. 2007); Hamlin v. Charter Twp. of Flint, 165 F.3d 426, 439 (6th Cir. 1999).

[88] 42 U.S.C.A. § 12112(b)(5)(A).

[89] 42 U.S.C.A. § 12111(10).

[90] 535 U.S. 391 (2002).

word reasonable do not equate it with the word effective. Additionally, the Court found that the EEOC regulations did not conflate these two words.

The Court described the "practical conflict" that arises because the ADA requires a plaintiff to establish a reasonable accommodation, while requiring the employer to establish undue hardship.

> The practical burden of proof dilemma arises, Barnett argues, because the statute imposes the burden of demonstrating an "undue hardship" upon the employer, while the burden of proving "reasonable accommodation" remains with the plaintiff, here the employee. This allocation seems sensible in that an employer can more frequently and easily prove the presence of business hardship than an employee can prove its absence. But suppose that an employee must counter a claim of "seniority rule violation" in order to prove that an "accommodation" request is "reasonable." Would that not force the employee to prove what is in effect an absence, *i.e.*, an absence of hardship, despite the statute's insistence that the employer "demonstrate" hardship's presence?[91]

The Court noted that lower courts have reconciled this dilemma.

> They have held that a plaintiff/employee (to defeat a defendant/employer's motion for summary judgment) need only show that an "accommodation" seems reasonable on its face, *i.e.*, ordinarily or in the run of cases. . . .
>
> Once the plaintiff has made this showing, the defendant/employer then must show special (typically case-specific) circumstances that demonstrate undue hardship in the particular circumstances. . . .[92]

The Court then addressed the specific facts of the case. It noted that generally, the plaintiff's request to assignment to a position in the mailroom would be reasonable. However, the existence of the seniority system changes that reasonableness inquiry. The Court held that it is not reasonable in the ordinary case for the plaintiff's request to trump the seniority system. The Court discussed the importance of collectively bargained seniority systems. Although the system at issue in *Barnett* was not collectively bargained, the Court noted that seniority systems generally provide important employee benefits by creating and enforcing expectations about uniform treatment in advancement and layoffs.

Although a request to change a seniority system would not generally be reasonable, the plaintiff may still show that the requested accommodation is reasonable in the particular case. The Court then provided a non-exhaustive list of examples of when a plaintiff may be able to establish reasonableness: (1) the employer retained the right to unilaterally change the system and does so frequently; or (2) the system already contains numerous exceptions that make an additional change unlikely to matter.

§ 8.13 Notice and Interactive Process

The employer must know about the need for accommodation. In some instances, the need for accommodation is obvious. For example, if an employee uses a wheelchair and

---

[91] *Barnett*, 535 U.S. at 400.

[92] *Barnett*, 535 U.S. at 402.

cannot maneuver her wheelchair into rooms where important work meeting are held, the employer will be put on notice once it realizes the employee cannot access the rooms.

In many instances, notice requires the employee to make the employer aware of the need, typically through a request for an accommodation. However, there are no "magic words" that are required for the notice. The worker is not required to invoke the ADA specifically or to use the word "accommodation." The "employee can simply inform the employer of a need for adjustment [in working conditions] due to a medical condition."[93]

The ADA contemplates that once the employer has notice, that the worker and the employer will engage in an interactive process to determine whether a reasonable accommodation is possible. Engaging in this interactive process is important because it allows the parties to try to reach a good outcome without litigation. If litigation later ensues, participation in the interactive process is evidence that the employer attempted in good faith to make a reasonable accommodation. Establishing such "good faith" is an affirmative defense to the plaintiff's recovery of punitive damages.[94]

The EEOC Guidance provides an outline of how to conduct the interactive process:

> When an individual with a disability has requested a reasonable accommodation to assist in the performance of a job, the employer, using a problem solving approach, should:
>
> (1) Analyze the particular job involved and determine its purpose and essential functions;
>
> (2) Consult with the individual with a disability to ascertain the precise job-related limitations imposed by the individual's disability and how those limitations could be overcome with a reasonable accommodation;
>
> (3) In consultation with the individual to be accommodated, identify potential accommodations and assess the effectiveness each would have in enabling the individual to perform the essential functions of the position; and
>
> (4) Consider the preference of the individual to be accommodated and select and implement the accommodation that is most appropriate for both the employee and the employer.[95]

§ 8.14 Failure to Accommodate Framework

The exact framework for evaluating a failure to accommodate varies by circuit. The frameworks typically require the employee to show (1) that he is qualified individual with a disability; (2) that the employer had notice of his disability; and (3) that the employer failed to make a reasonable accommodation.[96] Even if the employee makes this showing, the employer will not be required to provide an accommodation if it can establish that doing so will constitute an undue hardship.

---

[93] Dunlap v. Liberty Nat. Prod., Inc., No. 3:12-CV-01635-SI, 2015 WL 1778477, at *7 (D. Or. Apr. 20, 2015), aff'd, 878 F.3d 794 (9th Cir. 2017).

[94] *See* 42 U.S.C.A. § 1981a(a)(3).

[95] 29 C.F.R. Pt. 1630, App. § 1630.9.

[96] Hooper v. Proctor Health Care Inc., 804 F.3d 846, 852 (7th Cir. 2015); Stephenson v. Pfizer, Inc., 641 F. App'x 214, 219 (4th Cir. 2016).

§ 8.15 Other Proof Structures

The ADA prohibits discrimination, harassment, and retaliation and often uses frameworks used under Title VII to resolve those cases. The Supreme Court has applied *McDonnell Douglas* to a claim of discrimination under the ADA.[97] Lower courts consistently allow plaintiffs to proceed under *McDonnell Douglas*.[98] Courts will modify the frameworks for the disability context. For example, in some cases, the plaintiff may be required to prove she is a qualified individual or has a disability to establish she falls within the protection of the statute.

Throughout this book, we have discussed how the courts have created different frameworks for cases under Title VII and the ADEA. Where such differences exists, courts will need to determine whether the ADA (1) follows the Title VII model; (2) follows the ADEA proof structure; (3) or whether the ADA requires its own analytical frameworks.

One current issue is whether the ADA allows a plaintiff to prevail by establishing that her disability was a motivating factor in a decision. In two cases, the Supreme Court held that a plaintiff proceeding on an ADEA discrimination claim or a Title VII retaliation claim must prove "but for" cause, rather than the more lenient "motivating factor" standard used for Title VII discrimination claims.[99] Courts are considering which standard to apply in ADA cases.[100] It should be noted that the ADA discrimination provisions do not fully mimic the language of either Title VII or the ADEA, and the ADA uses the words "based on" rather than "because of."[101] The ADA incorporates by reference the Title VII remedies provision, including its reference to 42 U.S.C.A. § 2000e–5(g). However, Congress did not amend the ADA to include the motivating factor language that it added to Title VII.

Another issue is whether a plaintiff pursuing an ADA discrimination or retaliation claim must establish that she faced an adverse employment action as the courts have defined that concept in the Title VII discrimination and retaliation context. On its face, the ADA uses different language than Title VII. The ADA provides:

> No covered entity shall discriminate against a qualified individual on the basis of disability in regard to job application procedures, the hiring, advancement, or discharge of employees, employee compensation, job training and other terms, conditions, and privileges of employment.[102]

In addition, the ADA more specifically defines prohibited discrimination in a seven-part definitional section.[103] A few courts have noted that the adverse actions prohibited under the ADA are not coterminous with those prohibited under Title VII.[104] In one case, the

---

[97] Raytheon Co. v. Hernandez, 540 U.S. 44, 53 (2003).

[98] Marshall v. The Rawlings Co. LLC, 854 F.3d 368, 384 (6th Cir. 2017); Oehmke v. Medtronic, Inc., 844 F.3d 748, 755 (8th Cir. 2016); Caldwell v. KHOU-TV, 850 F.3d 237, 241 (5th Cir. 2017); Williams v. FedEx Corp. Servs., 849 F.3d 889, 896 (10th Cir. 2017); Kilcrease v. Domenico Transportation Co., 828 F.3d 1214, 1220 (10th Cir. 2016).

[99] University of Tex. Sw. Med. Ctr. v. Nassar, 570 U.S. 338 (2013); Gross v. FBL Fin. Servs., Inc., 557 U.S. 167 (2009).

[100] Wesley-Dickson v. Warwick Valley Cent. Sch. Dist., 586 F. App'x 739, 745 n.3 (2d Cir. 2014).

[101] 42 U.S.C.A. § 12112(a).

[102] 42 U.S.C.A. § 12112(a).

[103] 42 U.S.C.A. § 12112(b).

[104] Hoffman v. Caterpillar, Inc., 256 F.3d 568, 576 (7th Cir. 2001).

Seventh Circuit held that an ADA plaintiff could proceed on a claim that her employer failed to provide training to her based on her disability. The court noted that training is specifically listed in the ADA and that the plaintiff was not required to separately prove that the failure to train materially impacted her employment.[105]

Similar issues exist regarding the appropriate structure for disparate impact analysis under the ADA. In prior chapters, this treatise discusses how Title VII and the ADEA use separate analytical frameworks for disparate impact. As of the writing of this book, it is unclear whether the ADA follows either of these structures or whether a separate structure is required. Under the ADA, an employer may defend a disparate impact by showing that the challenged policy or practice is job-related and consistent with business necessity.[106] The ADA would require the court to consider the possibility of reasonable accommodation.[107] In addition, a court would need to consider that the ADA more specifically defines prohibited discrimination in a seven-part definitional section.[108]

§ 8.16 Direct Threat Affirmative Defense

Under the ADA, an employer does not face liability for disability discrimination, if the employee or prospective employee has a condition that would be a direct threat to the worker or others. This is an affirmative defense under the statute. The ADA provides:

> It may be a defense to a charge of discrimination under this Act that an alleged application of qualification standards, tests, or selection criteria that screen out or tend to screen out or otherwise deny a job or benefit to an individual with a disability has been shown to be *job-related and consistent with business necessity*, and such performance cannot be accomplished by *reasonable accommodation*, as required under this title.
>
> The term "qualification standards" may include a requirement that an individual shall not pose a direct threat to the health or safety of other individuals in the workplace.[109]

A direct threat requires a significant risk to the health or safety of others that cannot be eliminated by reasonable accommodation.[110] EEOC regulations clarify that there must be an individualized assessment about the threat. That assessment must be based on "a reasonable medical judgment" using "the most current medical knowledge and/or on the best available objective evidence.[111] Factors to consider regarding whether a person is a direct threat include "(1) the duration of the risk; (2) the nature and severity of the potential harm; (3) the likelihood that the potential harm will occur; and (4) the imminence of the potential harm."[112]

---

[105] *See, e.g.*, Hoffman v. Caterpillar, Inc., 256 F.3d 568, 576 (7th Cir. 2001).

[106] 29 C.F.R. Pt. 1630, App. § 1630.15(b) and (c).

[107] 29 C.F.R. § 1630.15.

[108] 42 U.S.C.A. § 12112(b).

[109] 42 U.S.C.A. § 12113(a) & (b).

[110] 42 U.S.C.A. § 12111(3).

[111] 29 C.F.R. § 1630.2(r).

[112] 29 C.F.R. § 1630.2(r).

In *Chevron v. Echazabal*, the Supreme Court held that a person could constitute a direct threat if the threat were to the employee himself and not other employees.[113] In that case, Mario Echazabal worked as an independent contractor at an oil refinery owned by Chevron. He twice applied for a job to work directly for Chevron. He received conditional offers of employment subject to his passing a company physical. However, he did not receive the jobs after the physical exams showed that Mr. Echazabal had a liver abnormality caused by Hepatitis C. Chevron withdrew the conditional offers of employment and the second time asked the contractor to reassign Mr. Echazabal to another job where he would not be exposed to chemicals within the refinery. The contractor laid him off.

Mr. Echazabal filed suit under the ADA. The Supreme Court considered whether the statutory language of the ADA allowed an employer not to hire an individual who did not pose a direct threat to others. The statutory language of the ADA (quoted above) seems to require that the person pose a direct threat to the health or safety of other individuals. However, the EEOC regulations interpreting the statute stated the "term 'qualification standard' may include a requirement that an individual shall not pose a direct threat to the health or safety of the individual or others in the workplace."[114] The Supreme Court upheld the agency interpretation. It reasoned that the direct threat to others language in the statute was not language that limited the reach of the provision. Rather, the Court said the language was an example of the kind of qualification standard that would be allowed under the statute. The use of the example did not preclude other types of direct threats.

Mr. Echazabal had also argued that Congress specifically rejected the threat to self interpretation. He relied on the fact that the EEOC had interpreted the Rehabilitation Act to include a threat to self limit, even though its statutory language only mentioned threats to other individuals. Mr. Echazabal argued that if Congress meant to include threat to self in the ADA, it should have used the specific language from the regulation and its failure to do so meant that it was specifically rejecting the regulation's language. However, the Supreme Court noted that multiple agencies interpreted the Rehabilitation Act and other agencies did not include threat to self in their regulations. Therefore, it was unclear whether Congress rejected the EEOC interpretation of the Rehabilitation Act when it created the ADA. The Court upheld the reasonableness of the EEOC regulation.

§ 8.17 Drug and Alcohol Use

The ADA specifically provides that a person who is currently engaged in the use of illegal drugs cannot be a "qualified individual with a disability."[115] Illegal use of drugs refers both to the use of unlawful drugs and to the unlawful use of prescription drugs.[116] The EEOC Guidance provides:

> Individuals who are erroneously perceived as engaging in the illegal use of drugs, but are not in fact illegally using drugs are not excluded from the definitions of the terms "disability" and "qualified individual with a disability." Individuals who are no longer illegally using drugs and who have either been

[113] 536 U.S. 73 (2002).

[114] 29 C.F.R. § 1630.15(b)(2) (2001).

[115] 42 U.S.C.A. § 12114(a).

[116] 29 C.F.R. Pt. 1630, App. § 1630.3(a) through (c).

rehabilitated successfully or are in the process of completing a rehabilitation program are, likewise, not excluded from the definitions of those terms.[117]

Alcoholism can be a disability under the ADA; however the ADA provides that an employer may hold:

> an employee who engages in the illegal use of drugs or who is an alcoholic to the same qualification standards for employment or job performance and behavior that such entity holds other employees, even if any unsatisfactory performance or behavior is related to the drug use or alcoholism of such employee.[118]

§ 8.18 Associational Discrimination

The ADA also prohibits "excluding or otherwise denying equal jobs or benefits to a qualified individual because of the known disability of an individual with whom the qualified individual is known to have a relationship or association."[119]

For example, if a company considered hiring a mother with a child with severe disabilities, it could not refuse to hire her based on assumptions it made about her need to take off work to care for the child. The required relationship does not need to be a family relationship.[120]

§ 8.19 Medical Examinations and Inquiries Generally

The ADA limits when and how employers can subject employees and prospective employees to medical exams and disability-related inquiries.

The ADA provides:

> (d) Medical examinations and inquiries.
>
> (1) In general. The prohibition against discrimination as referred to in subsection (a) of this section shall include medical examinations and inquiries.
>
> (2) *Pre-employment.*
>
> (A) Prohibited examination or inquiry. Except as provided in paragraph (3), a covered entity shall not conduct a medical examination or make inquiries of a job applicant as to whether such applicant is an individual with a disability or as to the nature or severity of such disability.
>
> (B) Acceptable inquiry. A covered entity may make pre-employment inquiries into the ability of an applicant to perform job-related functions.
>
> (3) *Employment entrance examination.* A covered entity may require a medical examination after an offer of employment has been made to a job applicant and prior to the commencement of the employment duties of such applicant, and may condition an offer of employment on the results of such examination, if

---

[117] 29 C.F.R. Pt. 1630, App. § 1630.3(a) through (c).

[118] 42 U.S.C.A. § 12114(c)(4).

[119] 42 U.S.C.A. § 12112(b)(4). For an interesting discussion of the required test to prove associational discrimination, see Bukiri v. Lynch, 648 F. App'x 729, 731 n.1 (9th Cir. 2016).

[120] 29 C.F.R. Pt. 1630, App. § 1630.8.

(A) all entering employees are subjected to such an examination regardless of disability;

(B) information obtained regarding the medical condition or history of the applicant is collected and maintained on separate forms and in separate medical files and is treated as a confidential medical record, except that

(i) supervisors and managers may be informed regarding necessary restrictions on the work or duties of the employee and necessary accommodations;

(ii) first aid and safety personnel may be informed, when appropriate, if the disability might require emergency treatment; and

(iii) government officials investigating compliance with this chapter shall be provided relevant information on request; and

(C) the results of such examination are used only in accordance with this subchapter.

(4) *Examination and inquiry.*

(A) Prohibited examinations and inquiries. A covered entity shall not require a medical examination and shall not make inquiries of an employee as to whether such employee is an individual with a disability or as to the nature or severity of the disability, unless such examination or inquiry is shown to be job-related and consistent with business necessity.

(B) Acceptable examinations and inquiries. A covered entity may conduct voluntary medical examinations, including voluntary medical histories, which are part of an employee health program available to employees at that work site. A covered entity may make inquiries into the ability of an employee to perform job-related functions.

(C) Requirement. Information obtained under subparagraph (B) regarding the medical condition or history of any employee are subject to the requirements of subparagraphs (B) and (C) of paragraph (3).[121]

These provisions apply to employees or prospective employees, whether or not they have a disability. A person without a disability may challenge an employer's improper use of a medical exam or inquiry. The statute creates a framework where the employer's ability to subject employees or prospective employees to a medical exam or inquiry differs depending on when it occurs.

An employer is prohibited from making disability-related inquiries and requiring medical exams prior to giving a job offer.[122] An employer may ask a person whether she is able to perform the essential functions of a job with or without accommodation.

When an employer extends a job offer, the employer can make that offer conditional on the person's passing a medical exam. The exam must be given to all applicants within the job category.[123] In theory, an employer is allowed to require a person to submit to an

[121] 42 U.S.C.A. § 12112(d).

[122] 42 U.S.C.A. § 12112(d)(2)(A).

[123] 42 U.S.C.A. § 12112(d)(3).

exam or inquiry that is not job-related at this stage. However, it would be highly problematic for an employer to use that exam or inquiry to reject an individual.

Once employment has started, the employer can require medical examinations and make disability-related inquiries if they are "job-related and consistent with business necessity."[124]

Employers must keep information about medical exams and inquiries confidential and in a separate file from the employee's normal personnel file.[125]

The EEOC has issued guidance on medical examinations and inquiries generally.[126] The EEOC has issued guidance that focuses on medical exams and disability-related inquiries given to employees.[127]

The ADA is not the only federal law that may limit an employer's ability to require exams or make inquiries. For example, the Employee Polygraph Protection Act (EPPA) limits employers' ability to request and use polygraphs.[128] The Genetic Information Non-Discrimination Act of 2008 (GINA)[129] limits employers' ability to request and use genetic information (as defined by the statute).

§ 8.20 Disability-Related Inquiries and Medical Examinations

In the pre-offer and employment contexts, the first issue that must be addressed is whether the employer is requiring a medical exam or making a disability-related inquiry. If the employer is not doing either of these, then the employer's actions are not covered, even if they somehow seem related to the physical or mental condition of the employee.

The EEOC defines a disability-related inquiry as question or series of questions "that is likely to elicit information about a disability."[130] The EEOC Guidance provides a non-exhaustive list of questions that might be disability-related inquiries, including the following:

- asking an employee whether s/he has (or ever had) a disability or how s/he became disabled or inquiring about the nature or severity of an employee's disability;
- asking an employee to provide medical documentation regarding his/her disability;
- asking an employee's co-worker, family member, doctor, or another person about an employee's disability;
- asking about an employee's genetic information;
- asking about an employee's prior workers' compensation history;

---

[124] 42 U.S.C.A. § 12112(d)(4)(A).

[125] *See* 42 U.S.C.A. § 12112(d)(3)(B).

[126] EEOC Enforcement Guidance: Preemployment Disability-Related Questions and Medical Examinations (Oct. 10, 1995).

[127] Enforcement Guidance on Disability-Related Inquiries and Medical Exams of Employees Under the Americans with Disabilities Act.

[128] 29 U.S.C.A. §§ 2001–2009.

[129] 29 U.S.C.A. § 2000ff *et seq.*

[130] Enforcement Guidance on Disability-Related Inquiries and Medical Exams of Employees Under the Americans with Disabilities Act, General Principles § B.1.

- asking an employee whether s/he currently is taking any prescription drugs or medications, whether s/he has taken any such drugs or medications in the past, or monitoring an employee's taking of such drugs or medications; and,
- asking an employee a broad question about his/her impairments that is likely to elicit information about a disability (*e.g.*, What impairments do you have?).[131]

The EEOC Guidance also gives a list of questions that are allowed:

- asking generally about an employee's well being (*e.g.*, How are you?), asking an employee who looks tired or ill if s/he is feeling okay, asking an employee who is sneezing or coughing whether s/he has a cold or allergies, or asking how an employee is doing following the death of a loved one or the end of a marriage/relationship;
- asking an employee about nondisability-related impairments (*e.g.*, How did you break your leg?)
- asking an employee whether s/he can perform job functions;
- asking an employee whether s/he has been drinking;
- asking an employee about his/her current illegal use of drugs;
- asking a pregnant employee how she is feeling or when her baby is due; and,
- asking an employee to provide the name and telephone number of a person to contact in case of a medical emergency.[132]

The EEOC Guidance defines a "medical examination" as a "procedure or test that seeks information about an individual's physical or mental impairments or health."[133] The EEOC provides several factors related to this term:

> (1) whether the test is administered by a health care professional; (2) whether the test is interpreted by a health care professional; (3) whether the test is designed to reveal an impairment or physical or mental health; (4) whether the test is invasive; (5) whether the test measures an employee's performance of a task or measures his/her physiological responses to performing the task; (6) whether the test normally is given in a medical setting; and, (7) whether medical equipment is used.[134]

The EEOC also provides a non-exhaustive list of activities that count as medical exams:

- vision tests conducted and analyzed by an ophthalmologist or optometrist;
- blood, urine, and breath analyses to check for alcohol use;

---

[131] Enforcement Guidance on Disability-Related Inquiries and Medical Exams of Employees Under the Americans with Disabilities Act General Principles § B.1.

[132] Enforcement Guidance on Disability-Related Inquiries and Medical Exams of Employees Under the Americans with Disabilities Act General Principles § B.1.

[133] Enforcement Guidance on Disability-Related Inquiries and Medical Exams of Employees Under the Americans with Disabilities Act General Principles § B.2.

[134] Enforcement Guidance: Preemployment Disability-Related Questions and Medical Examinations Under the Americans with Disabilities Act of 1990, at 14.

- blood, urine, saliva, and hair analyses to detect disease or genetic markers (*e.g.*, for conditions such as sickle cell trait, breast cancer, Huntington's disease);
- blood pressure screening and cholesterol testing;
- nerve conduction tests (*i.e.*, tests that screen for possible nerve damage and susceptibility to injury, such as carpal tunnel syndrome);
- range-of-motion tests that measure muscle strength and motor function;
- pulmonary function tests (*i.e.*, tests that measure the capacity of the lungs to hold air and to move air in and out);
- psychological tests that are designed to identify a mental disorder or impairment; and,
- diagnostic procedures such as x-rays, computerized axial tomography (CAT) scans, and magnetic resonance imaging (MRI).[135]

The EEOC Guidance also provides a list of procedures that generally are not considered to be medical exams under the ADA. These include the following:

- tests to determine the current illegal use of drugs;
- physical agility tests, which measure an employee's ability to perform actual or simulated job tasks, and physical fitness tests, which measure an employee's performance of physical tasks, such as running or lifting, as long as these tests do not include examinations that could be considered medical (*e.g.*, measuring heart rate or blood pressure);
- tests that evaluate an employee's ability to read labels or distinguish objects as part of a demonstration of the ability to perform actual job functions;
- psychological tests that measure personality traits such as honesty, preferences, and habits; and,
- polygraph examinations.[136]

§ 8.21 Employees: Job-Related and Consistent with Business Necessity

When an employer makes a disability-related inquiry or requires a medical exam for employees, that exam must be "job-related and consistent with business necessity." The EEOC has issued guidance that focuses on medical exams and disability-related inquiries during employment.[137]

An inquiry or exam can meet this requirement if the employer "has a reasonable belief, based on objective evidence, that: (1) an employee's ability to perform essential job functions will be impaired by a medical condition; or (2) an employee will pose a direct

[135] Enforcement Guidance on Disability-Related Inquiries and Medical Exams of Employees Under the Americans with Disabilities Act General Principles § B.2.

[136] Enforcement Guidance on Disability-Related Inquiries and Medical Exams of Employees Under the Americans with Disabilities Act General Principles § B.2.

[137] Enforcement Guidance on Disability-Related Inquiries and Medical Exams of Employees Under the Americans with Disabilities Act.

threat due to a medical condition."[138] For example, the employer may ask an employee who takes leave for a medical reason to provide documentation showing that the employee can perform the essential functions of her job.

The EEOC Guidance further provides than an employer can make "[d]isability-related inquiries and medical examinations that follow up on a request for reasonable accommodation when the disability or need for accommodation is not known or obvious also may be job-related and consistent with business necessity."[139] The Guidance cautions that employers cannot ask for documentation in relation to a request for reasonable accommodation that is not related to the request.

Periodic medical examinations and monitoring may meet the job-related and consistent with business necessity requirement under certain circumstances.[140] For example, the EEOC Guidance provides "periodic medical examinations of employees in positions affecting public safety that are narrowly tailored to address specific job-related concerns are permissible."[141] Employers may make inquiries or examinations that are required under federal law.[142]

The Guidance also discusses acceptable inquiries related to Employee Assistance Programs, voluntary wellness programs, and affirmative action plans.[143]

---

[138] Enforcement Guidance on Disability-Related Inquiries and Medical Exams of Employees Under the Americans with Disabilities Act, Job-Related and Consistent with Business Necessity § A.5.

[139] Enforcement Guidance on Disability-Related Inquiries and Medical Exams of Employees Under the Americans with Disabilities Act, Job-Related and Consistent with Business Necessity § A.5.

[140] Enforcement Guidance on Disability-Related Inquiries and Medical Exams of Employees Under the Americans with Disabilities Act, Job-Related and Consistent with Business Necessity § A.5.

[141] Enforcement Guidance on Disability-Related Inquiries and Medical Exams of Employees Under the Americans with Disabilities Act, Periodic Testing and Monitoring § D.18.

[142] Enforcement Guidance on Disability-Related Inquiries and Medical Exams of Employees Under the Americans with Disabilities Act, Other Acceptable Disability-Related Inquiries and Medical Examinations § D.21.

[143] Enforcement Guidance on Disability-Related Inquiries and Medical Exams of Employees Under the Americans with Disabilities Act, Other Acceptable Disability-Related Inquiries and Medical Examinations § D.20, 22, 23.

Chapter 9

AFFIRMATIVE ACTION

Analysis

---

§ 9.01 Affirmative Action Generally[1]

There is not a settled definition of what conduct falls within the concept of affirmative action. The legality of any affirmative action depends on the actions being taken. Affirmative action can simply be proactive outreach to underrepresented groups. For example, an employer may try to recruit minority students by ensuring that its college interviews are held at a variety of college campuses. Employers might also evaluate job requirements to remove artificial barriers to employment. These kinds of activities, sometimes called "soft" affirmative action are typically not open to viable legal challenges.[2]

Stronger forms of affirmative action may implicate federal discrimination law and the Constitution when race, sex, or other protected traits are explicitly used to determine workplace outcomes. However, the Supreme Court has allowed space for limited affirmative action under a narrow set of circumstances. The contours of allowable affirmative action are changing. Additionally, there is some uncertainty about the exact contours of affirmative action in the employment discrimination context because recent Supreme Court cases on affirmative action focus on the education context. It is unclear how these cases apply in the employment context.

Additionally, care must be taken to distinguish affirmative action taken to remedy proven discrimination and affirmative action taken in other contexts. Title VII specifically allows courts to take any affirmative action necessary to remedy proven

---

[1] I would like to thank my research assistant Alessandro Botta Blondet who wrote the first drafts for many of the case summaries provided in this chapter.

[2] 29 C.F.R. § 1608.3(c).

discrimination.[3] However, as discussed below, the courts have placed limits on courts' ability to order affirmative action as a remedy.

Ultimately, affirmative action in its strongest form is still contested because it is one area where ideas about formal equality and substantive equality collide. It is uncontested women and racial minorities historically faced explicit workplace discrimination, often being denied certain jobs or paid less because of sex or the color of their skin. Affirmative action raises important questions about what should be done to remedy this historic discrimination. It also implicitly questions whether the modern workplace is free from historic patterns of discrimination and if not, what should be done in response.

§ 9.02 Reverse Discrimination

Title VII and Section 1981 prohibit reverse discrimination. In *McDonald v. Santa Fe Trail Transp. Co.*,[4] two white employees filed suit for race discrimination under Title VII. They alleged they were terminated for misappropriating cargo from their employer while the employer did not fire a similarly situated black employee. The Supreme Court held that both Title VII and Section 1981 prohibit discrimination against white individuals. Discrimination against white individuals, especially white males, is often called reverse discrimination.

When interpreting Title VII, the Court noted that the statute's words prohibited discrimination because of an individual's race. It did not limit its protections to certain races. The Court also looked at legislative history suggesting Congress intended to protect white individuals. In *McDonald*, the employer argued that even if Title VII protected white individuals, the plaintiffs should not receive any protection because the employer fired them after they took company property. While the Court noted that theft is a valid, non-discriminatory reason for firing an employee, an employer may not treat black and white employees differently based on the same underlying conduct.

Section 1981 uses different language than Title VII. It provides: "All persons within the jurisdiction of the United States shall have the same right in every State and Territory to make and enforce contracts . . . as is enjoyed by white citizens." In *McDonald*, the Supreme Court held that the words "all persons" within section 1981 evinced a congressional intent to include white individuals within its protections, even though the "as is enjoyed by white citizens language" might suggest a contrary result.

§ 9.03 Workforce Imbalance

While Title VII and Section 1981 prohibit reverse discrimination, an employer may face liability under these statutes when members of protected classes are significantly underrepresented. In *Int'l Bhd. of Teamsters v. U.S.*,[5] the Supreme Court recognized that the government could prevail on a pattern or practice claim by relying on statistical evidence that the defendant's workforce contained significantly fewer black and Hispanic truck drivers when compared to the demographics of the cities from which the employer recruited its workforce. In this case, the government supplemented its evidence

---

3 42 U.S.C.A. § 2000e–5(g)(1).

4 427 U.S. 273 (1976).

5 431 U.S. 324 (1977).

with specific examples of racial discrimination against applicants and potential applicants for the positions in question.

In *Teamsters*, the Supreme Court addressed the applicability of 42 U.S.C. § 2000e–2(j), which provides that Title VII shall not be

> interpreted to require * * * [the] grant of preferential treatment to any individual because of . . . race, color, religion, sex, or national origin . . . on account of an imbalance which may exist with respect to the total number or percentage of persons of such race, color, religion, sex, or national origin . . . in the available work force.

In *Teamsters*, the Court interpreted this language as prohibiting liability solely based on workforce imbalance. This provision does not prohibit a plaintiff from using workforce imbalance, along with other evidence, to show that an employer discriminated because of a protected trait.

Employers also face liability under Title VII when employment practices result in a disparate impact.[6] Statistical disparities will be used in such cases to establish that the practice had a disproportionate impact on a protected class.

§ 9.04 Voluntary Affirmative Action Under Title VII: Generally

Some employers voluntarily adopt affirmative action plans. The legality of such plans may be challenged in reverse discrimination cases. For example, a white job applicant might argue that he was impermissibly denied a job because the employer impermissibly used race to favor a candidate of another race.

The Supreme Court addressed the legality of voluntary affirmative action plans in *United Steelworkers v. Weber*.[7] The legal question in this case was whether Congress, in passing and amending Title VII, left employers and unions in the private sector free to take race conscious steps to eliminate manifest racial imbalances in traditionally segregated job categories.[8] The Court held that it did.

In that case, the United Steelworkers of American ("USWA") and Petitioners Kaiser Aluminum & Chemical Corp. ("Kaiser") entered into a collective bargaining agreement covering the terms and conditions of employment at 15 Kaiser plants.[9] The agreement contained an affirmative action plan ("plan") designed to remedy Kaiser's conspicuous racial imbalances, which included a workforce of almost exclusively white craft workers. The company had historically hired people with prior experience, and the unions that could provide the experience discriminated against non-white workers by not allowing them to become union members.

Kaiser's goal for each plant was to match its percentage of black craft workers to the percentage of black workers in the respective local labor forces. To meet its goals, Kaiser set up on-the-job training programs to teach untrained production workers, both black and white, the skills necessary to become craft workers.[10] The plan reserved 50% of the openings in this program for black employees.

---

6 Griggs v. Duke Power Co., 401 U.S. 424 (1971); 42 U.S.C. § 2000e–2(k).

7 443 U.S. 193, 197 (1979).

8 *Id.*

9 *Id.* at 198.

10 *Id.*

Weber arose from Kaiser's Gramercy, Louisiana, plant. At this plant, prior to 1974, only 1.83% of the skilled craft workers were black and the work force in the area was approximately 39% black. The selection of craft trainees was made on the basis of seniority, with the condition that at least 50% of the new trainees were to be black until the percentage of black skilled craft workers approximated the percentage of African-American workers in the local workforce.[11]

During the plan's first year, 13 trainees were selected from Kaiser's local production force; seven were black and six were white. The most senior black trainee had less seniority than several white employees not selected for the training positions. One of those rejected white employees, Brian Weber, sued. Weber argued that the filling of the trainee positions pursuant to the plan had resulted in junior black employees receiving training in preference to more senior white employees, thus discriminating against the unselected white employees in violation of Title VII.[12]

The District Court held that the plan violated Title VII.[13] A divided Fifth Circuit panel affirmed, holding that, "all employment preferences based upon race, including those preferences incidental to bona fide affirmative action plans, violated Title VII . . . ."[14]

The Supreme Court reversed, emphasizing the narrowness of the inquiry.[15] The Court clarified the only question it was answering was whether Title VII forbids private employers and unions from voluntarily agreeing upon bona fide affirmative action plans that accord racial preferences for the purpose of eliminating conspicuous racial imbalances. The Court was not addressing constitutional arguments because private actors undertook the affirmative action plan. The Court held that the plan was voluntary, even though it also indicated in a footnote that the company was likely creating the plan so that it could compete for federal government contracts that required affirmative action.

The Court noted that Weber's argument that Congress intended Title VII to forbid all race-conscious affirmative action plan rests upon a combination of a literal interpretation of the act and the Court's *McDonald v. Santa Fe Trail Transp. Co.*[16] holding.[17] The Court held that this argument is "not without force," but that it overlooked the significant fact that two private parties voluntarily adopted the plan with the purpose of eliminating traditional patterns of racial discrimination.[18]

The Court held that instead of a literal reading, Title VII must be read against the background of its legislative history and the historical context from which the act arose. The Court noted that Congress' primary concern while enacting Title VII, was the "plight of the Negro in our economy."[19] The purpose of Title VII was to eliminate the last vestiges of racial discrimination in employment. Further, based on the House Report

---

[11] *Id.* at 199.

[12] *Id.*

[13] *Id.* at 200.

[14] *Id.*

[15] *Id.*

[16] 427 U.S. 273 (1976) (holding that Title VII forbids discrimination against white workers as well as black workers).

[17] *Weber*, 443 U.S. at 201.

[18] *Id.*

[19] *Id.* at 202.

accompanying the Civil Rights Act, the Court stated that it appeared clear that Congress did not intend wholly to prohibit private and voluntary affirmative action efforts as one way of solving racial injustice.[20] Thus, given this legislative history, the Court could not agree with the proposition that Congress intended to prohibit the private sector from taking effective steps to accomplish Title VII's goals.[21]

The Court also stated that, had Congress meant to prohibit all race-conscious affirmative action, it could have easily stated that Title VII would not require or permit racially preferential integration efforts.[22] Instead, Title VII provides that nothing in the act "shall be interpreted to require any employer . . . to grant preferential treatment . . . to any group because of the race . . . of such . . . group on account of a de facto racial imbalance in the employer's workforce."[23] Title VII does *not* state that "nothing in Title VII shall be interpreted to *permit* voluntary affirmative efforts to correct racial imbalances."[24] Thus, the Court held, the natural inference is that Congress chose not to forbid all voluntary race conscious affirmative action.

Finally, the Court noted that it did not define the limits of what are permissible and impermissible affirmative action plans.[25] It did, however, hold that the Kaiser-USWA plan fell on the permissive side because it did not "unnecessarily trammel" the interests of white employees or prevent their advancement. The plan fell on the permissible side because it did not require the discharge of white workers and their replacement with black workers and did not create an absolute bar to the advancement of white employees. The plan was a temporary measure, and it was not intended to maintain—but to eliminate—a racial imbalance.[26] Further, the plan would end once its goals were met.

The other major voluntary affirmative action in employment case is *Johnson v. Transportation Agency*.[27] In that case, the defendant implemented an affirmative action plan to remedy the underrepresentation of women in its workforce. Pursuant to its affirmative action plan, the employer promoted Diane Joyce, a female employee, to the position of road dispatcher and passed over Paul Johnson, a male employee. The issue in this case is whether the Agency, in promoting Joyce, impermissibly took into account the sex of the applicants in violation of Title VII.[28] The Supreme Court indicated that the parties did not raise any constitutional arguments, and so the Court solely considered the case under Title VII.

In 1978, the Santa Clara Transit District Board of Supervisors adopted an Affirmative Action Plan ("Plan") for the Agency because "mere prohibition of discriminatory practices is not enough to remedy the effects of past practices and to permit attainment of an equitable representation of minorities, women, and handicapped persons."[29] The Agency Plan provided that, in making promotions for positions within a traditionally segregated job in which women have been significantly

---

[20] *Id.* at 203.

[21] *Id.*

[22] *Id.* at 205.

[23] *Id.* at 205–6.

[24] *Id.* at 206.

[25] *Id.* at 208.

[26] *Id.*

[27] 480 U.S. 616, 619 (1987).

[28] *Id.*

[29] *Id.*

underrepresented, the Agency is authorized to consider as one factor the sex of a qualified applicant.[30]

The Agency noted that in its workforce, women were represented in much lower proportions than the county's labor force both as a whole and in five of seven different work categories. The Plan noted that this underrepresentation was due in part to the fact that women had not been traditionally employed in these job categories and that women had not been strongly motivated to seek training or employment due to limited opportunities.[31]

The Plan's intention was to achieve a "statistically measurable yearly improvement in hiring, training, and promotion of minorities and women" throughout all underrepresented job categories.[32] The Agency's long-term goal was to attain a workforce whose composition reflected the proportion of women and minorities in the area's labor force.[33] The Plan also acknowledged some factors that might make it unrealistic to rely on its long-term goal as a progress evaluation tool. These factors included low turnover rates in some classifications, the involvement of heavy labor in some of the jobs, the small number of positions within a job category, the limited number of positions leading to technical and skilled craft positions, and the limited number of qualified women and minorities for some of the positions.[34] As a result, the plan called for short-range goals and an annual adjustment as a more realistic guide.

In 1979, the Agency announced a vacancy for the promotional position of road dispatcher in the Agency's road division.[35] Twelve employees applied for the promotion, including Joyce and petitioner Johnson. Joyce worked for Santa Clara County for almost ten years. For five of those years, she worked as an account clerk. In 1974, she applied for a road dispatcher position but was rejected for lack of road maintenance experience. In 1975, she began working as a road maintenance worker, becoming the first woman to do so. In this capacity, she occasionally worked as a road dispatcher.[36] Johnson began work with Santa Clara County in 1967 as a work yard clerk. Before working with the County, Johnson worked as a supervisor and dispatcher in the private sector. While working with the County, he also occasionally worked as a dispatcher.[37]

Nine of the applicants were deemed qualified for the job, including Joyce and Johnson, and were interviewed by a two-person board. Seven of the applicants scored a 70 or higher, all eligible for selection by the appointing authority. Johnson was tied for second with a score of 75 and Joyce was third with a score of 73. Second interviews were conducted, and Johnson was recommended for promotion.[38] Prior to the second interview, Joyce reached out to the County's Affirmative Action Office out of fear she would not be considered for the job for being a woman. The Affirmative Action Office then contacted Agency's Affirmative Action Coordinator, who recommended to the Director of the Agency that Joyce be promoted. Joyce was ultimately promoted. In

30 *Id.* at 621.

31 *Id.*

32 *Id.*

33 *Id.* at 621–22.

34 *Id.* at 622.

35 *Id.* at 623.

36 *Id.*

37 *Id.*

38 *Id.* at 624.

defending his decision, the Director of the Agency testified that he tried to "look at the whole picture," including the combination of Joyce and Johnson's qualification qualifications, tests scores, expertise, background, and affirmative action matters.[39]

Johnson filed suit, claiming that he was not promoted because of his sex. The district court found that Johnson was more qualified than Joyce and that sex was a determining factor in her selection. The trial relied on the criteria announced in *Weber*[40] to evaluate the plan.[41] The court found the Agency's Plan invalid on the ground that the evidence did not meet *Weber*'s criterion that the Plan be temporary.

The Ninth Circuit Court of Appeals reversed, holding that the lack of an express termination date was not dispositive because the Plan sought attainment—not maintenance—of a workforce mirroring the county's labor force. The Ninth Circuit further held that the Agency's consideration of Joyce's sex was lawful because the Plan had been adopted to remedy a conspicuous disparity in the Agency's workforce.

The Supreme Court affirmed the Ninth Circuit. The Supreme Court first noted that the petitioner bears the burden of establishing the invalidity of the agency's plan.[42] The Court also noted that this case fits within the *McDonnell Douglas v. Green*[43] analytical burden-shifting framework.[44] The Court then stated that the question of the Plan's legality must be guided by *Weber*.[45]

With *Weber* in mind, the first issue the Supreme Court analyzed in *Johnson* was whether the consideration of the sex of the applicants for skilled craft jobs was justified by the underrepresentation of women in such categories.[46] To determine whether an imbalance exists that would justify taking sex into account, the Supreme Court pointed out that where a job requires special training, the proper comparison is with those in the labor force who possess the relevant qualifications and not the general population.[47] The Plan's requirement that the imbalance relate to a "traditionally segregated job category" provided assurance both that sex or race will be taken into account in a manner consistent with Title VII's purpose, and that the interests of employees not benefiting from the Plan will not be unnecessarily infringed.[48]

Regarding the first issue, the Supreme Court held that the Agency's decision to hire Joyce was clearly made pursuant to a permissible Agency Plan that dictated that sex or race be taken into account when remedying women and minority underrepresentation.[49] Initially, the Plan's long-term goal was to attain a workforce that mirrored in its major job classifications the relevant labor pool. The plan, however, pointed out some limitations to its long-term goal and dictated that annual short-term goals would provide a more realistic indication of the degree to which sex should be taken into account in filling particular positions. Thus, from the outset, the Plan sought annual development

---

[39] *Id.* at 625.

[40] United Steelworkers v. Weber, 443 U.S. 193 (1979).

[41] *Johnson*, 480 U.S. at 625.

[42] *Id.* at 627.

[43] 411 U.S. 792 (1973).

[44] *Johnson*, 480 U.S. at 627.

[45] *Id.* at 627–28.

[46] *Id.* at 631.

[47] *Id.*

[48] *Id.* at 632.

[49] *Id.* at 634.

and refinement of the measurements of the underrepresentation in each relevant category.[50] The Court noted that had the Plan simply calculated all sex and racial imbalances and directed that hiring be governed solely by those figures, its validity could be called into question.

This concern, as noted above, was not present in the Agency Plan. The Plan did not allow for such blind hiring. It expressly required that numerous factors be taken into account, including the qualifications of female applicants for particular jobs.[51] Thus, the first *Weber* factor, that the employment decision be made to further an affirmative action plan designed to eliminate workplace imbalance, is fulfilled.[52]

The second issue the Supreme Court analyzed in *Johnson* was whether the Agency Plan unnecessarily trammeled the rights of male employees or created an absolute bar to their advancement.[53] The Court pointed out that the Plan set aside no positions for women and that the Plan expressly stated that its goals were not to be construed as quota requirements.[54] The Court found Joyce's sex was one of many factors that the Director of the Agency took into account in making the employment decision. Further, the Plan required that women compete with all other qualified applicants; no qualified applicants were automatically excluded.[55]

The Court also noted that Johnson did not have absolute entitlement to the road dispatcher position as the Director had the authority to promote any of the seven qualified applicants. Further, Johnson was not terminated. He retained employment with the agency with the same salary and seniority level and remained eligible for other promotions.[56]

Finally, the Court found that the Agency Plan was intended to attain, not maintain, a balanced workforce.[57] The Agency sought to take a gradual approach to eliminating the imbalance in its workforce though realistic guidance on employment decisions and minimal intrusion on the legitimate expectations of the other employees.[58]

The Supreme Court also noted that in evaluating the compliance of an affirmative action plan with Title VII's discrimination prohibitions, courts should be mindful of the Supreme Court's and Congress' consistent emphasis on the value of voluntary efforts to further the objectives of the law. The Agency in this case had taken a voluntary effort with full recognition of the difficulties and the potential for intrusion on male employees and non-minorities.[59] The Agency's Plan dictated, from its inception, that employment decisions may not be justified solely by reference to the workforce imbalance but must be based on a multitude of factors. Thus, the Supreme Court held that the Agency appropriately took into consideration as one factor Joyce's sex in determining that she should be promoted.

---

50 *Id.*

51 *Id.* at 637.

52 *Id.*

53 *Id.* at 638.

54 *Id.*

55 *Id.*

56 *Id.*

57 *Id.* at 639.

58 *Id.*

59 *Id.* at 640–41.

Justice Stevens concurred. He wrote separately to emphasize that the majority's opinion did not establish the permissible outer limits of voluntary programs undertaken by employers to benefit disadvantaged groups.[60]

§ 9.05 Affirmative Action: Consent Decrees

If the affirmative action plan is the product of a compromise or settlement of a possible or pending Title VII suit, and is approved by the trial court as part of a consent decree, the plan will be viewed as a "voluntary" affirmative action plan subject to the standards of *Weber* and *Johnson* rather than the more stringent constitutional and statutory requirements that circumscribe a trial court's power to impose such a plan as a remedy on unwilling litigants.[61]

§ 9.06 Voluntary Affirmative Action Under Title VII: Overarching Principles

The EEOC has issued guidelines related to affirmative action that reflect three aspects of *Weber* and *Johnson*. To be valid, such plans must be (1) based on a reasonable self-analysis, (2) have a reasonable basis, and (3) be a reasonable response to the workplace imbalance.[62]

In *Weber* and *Johnson*, the courts were considering affirmative action plans that gave preferences in hiring, apprenticeship programs, or promotion opportunities to women and people of color. Recall that many forms of "soft" affirmative action do not provide the same type of preferences and are not required to be a plan and fit the criteria of legitimate, affirmative action plans.

McDonald v. Santa Fe Trail Transp. Corp.[63] prohibited *ad hoc* decisions preferring one race over another. In *Johnson*, the Supreme Court held a written plan identifying imbalances, establishing reasonable goals of women and minority employment into specified underrepresented job categories, coupled with a general instruction to decision-makers to consider those goals in making employment and promotion selections, satisfied the *Weber* requirement of a "plan." The plan goals were based on identified underrepresentation in certain categories.

Johnson and *Weber* hold that a workforce imbalance need not be caused by an employer's past discriminatory practices in order for the employer to try to address it through affirmative action. The Supreme Court held: "[A]n employer seeking to justify the adoption of a plan need not point to its own prior discriminatory practices, nor even to evidence of an 'arguable violation' on its part. Rather, it need point only to a 'conspicuous imbalance in traditionally segregated job categories.'"[64] This separates voluntary affirmative action plans from instances where affirmative action is ordered as a remedy. In these latter cases, the plaintiff first establishes the employer's liability for egregious or widespread discrimination before the court orders affirmative action.[65]

---

60 *Id.* at 642.

61 Local 98, Int'l Ass'n of Firefighters v. City of Cleveland, 478 U.S. 501 (1986).

62 29 C.F.R. § 1608.4.

63 427 U.S. 273 (1976).

64 *Johnson*, 480 U.S. at 630 (citing *Weber*).

65 United States v. Paradise, 480 U.S. 149, 149 (1987).

In *Johnson*, the employer developed its plan by determining the percentage of employees in each job category by race and sex. It then compared this information with available information about the percentage of women or minorities in the relevant workforce. If a job does not require specific skills, a general workforce comparison can be used. However, if the job requires special expertise or training, the comparison needs to be made using the portion of the workforce with the required skills. In *Weber*, the Court recognized that an employer could try to improve the number of people possessing the required skills through an apprenticeship program.

In *Johnson* and *Weber*, the Court was not required to determine the required level of underrepresentation needed to justify a plan because in those cases there were almost no women and minorities in the positions. However, the Court did note that the imbalance need not reach the level of establishing a prima facie case of discrimination.[66] The Court also recognized in *Johnson* that the facts established a conspicuous imbalance in a "traditionally segregated" job category. Traditionally segregated does not mean that the employer adopting the affirmative action plan necessarily engaged in the segregation.

The purpose of the plan must be to remedy the underrepresentation, not to maintain indefinitely a racial or gender "quota." *Johnson* stated that a plan would be valid only insofar as it "was intended to *attain* a balanced work force, not to *maintain* one." In *Johnson*, the Court upheld the plan even though it did not contain an express termination date. The Court assumed that once the expressed goal had been reached the employer would no longer explicitly consider the race or sex of applicants when hiring or promoting workers.

In *Johnson*, the plan used race or sex as one factor among many to consider in making a promotion decision among workers who were qualified for the position based on the employer's listed job qualifications. In *Weber*, the Court approved a 1-1 ratio in accepting workers into an apprenticeship program. Subsequent to *Weber* plaintiffs and the United States Department of Justice made unsuccessful attempts to challenge the use of a fixed ratio. Both on constitutional and statutory grounds, those challenges were rejected by the Court.[67]

More recent cases in the education context have seriously challenged the use of race or sex as an overwhelming plus factor when making decisions, at least when reviewing whether such a plan passes constitutional muster. It is unclear how and whether these cases affect *Weber* and *Johnson* because the school's relied on a diversity rationale to support their admissions programs. They did not rely on past racial imbalance in the student body.

As discussed below, the Court in *Gratz v. Bollinger*[68] held that the University of Michigan's freshman admissions policy was not narrowly tailored to meet the compelling interest in diversity because it allotted one-fifth of the points needed for admission based on race. The Court held that such a system did not require individualized review of applicants. In a subsequent case, the Court held that a school could not have an admissions policy with strict numerical quotas. At the same time, "A university's goals

---

66 *Johnson*, 480 U.S. at 631–34. *See also* Hazelwood School District v. United States, 433 U.S. 299 (1977).

67 Local 98, Int'l Ass'n of Firefighters v. City of Cleveland, 478 U.S. 501 (1986); Local 28 of Sheet Metal Workers' Int'l Ass'n v. E.E.O.C., 478 U.S. 421, 426 (1986).

68 539 U.S. 244, 275 (2003).

cannot be elusory or amorphous—they must be sufficiently measurable to permit judicial scrutiny of the policies adopted to reach them."[69] However, the Court approved a law school admissions plan that allowed race to be considered as one factor among many.[70]

Weber and *Johnson* require that race or sex conscious decisionmaking must not "unnecessarily trammel" the rights of white male employees or "create an absolute bar to their advancement." In *Weber* the Court noted that a plan would not be bona fide if it required the discharge of employees of one class to be replaced by members of another class. However, since whites were not disqualified from admission into the apprenticeship program—indeed 50% of the persons admitted would be white—the plan did not unnecessarily trammel their rights.[71]

In *Johnson*, the Court applied this idea to a single position. In that case, the Court allowed sex to play a role in the decision to promote a specific female candidate over a specific male candidate. The Court held that the male worker did not have a vested interest in the promotion, and the male employee "retained his employment with the Agency, at the same salary and with the same seniority, and remained eligible for other promotions." Because sex was only a factor to consider in making the promotion decision, rather than having the position "reserved" or set aside for a particular race or sex, the Court concluded that the plan did not unnecessarily trammel the rights of the male applicant. In *Johnson*, the promoted worker met the employer's qualifications for holding the position.

An affirmative action plan may not provide for the use of race, national origin, or sex to determine the order of layoff. *Wygant v. Jackson Board of Education*,[72] concluded that a voluntary plan by a public employer that utilized racial ratios to determine the order of layoff violated the Equal Protection Clause of the Fourteenth Amendment. While the Court emphasized that it was not addressing whether a private employer would be permitted by Title VII to use a similar system, the Court's reasoning suggests that a similar result would be reached under Title VII. The plurality opinion noted that racially premised layoffs "impose the entire burden of achieving racial equality on particular individuals, often resulting in serious disruption of their lives."

§ 9.07 Effect of *Ricci*

As of the writing of this book, it is unclear what effect, if any, the Supreme Court's 2009 decision in *Ricci v. DeStefano* has on affirmative action jurisprudence.[73] In *Ricci*, the Court considered whether firefighters could bring a reverse discrimination disparate treatment claim under Title VII. The firefighters contested the city's refusal to certify the results of an exam for captain and lieutenant positions. The city refused to certify the results because it feared that the results created a disparate impact based on race. The Supreme Court held that the firefighters could prevail on a disparate treatment

[69] Fisher v. Univ. of Texas at Austin, 136 S. Ct. 2198, 2211 (2016).

[70] Grutter v. Bollinger, 539 U.S. 306 (2003).

[71] *Firefighters v. City of Cleveland* similarly upheld a consent decree that provided for promotion of set numbers of minority workers. 478 U.S. 501 (1986).

[72] Wygant v. Jackson Bd. of Educ., 476 U.S. 267, 267 (1986).

[73] 557 U.S. 557, 129 S. Ct. 2658, 174 L. Ed. 2d 490 (2009); *see also* Reva B. Siegel, *From Colorblindness to Antibalkanization: An Emerging Ground of Decision in Race Equality Cases*, 120 YALE L.J. 1278 (2011); Roberto L. Corrada, Ricci*'s Dicta: Signaling A New Standard for Affirmative Action Under Title VII?*, 46 WAKE FOREST L. REV. 241, 242 (2011).

claim because the city did not have a strong basis in evidence to believe that the exam created a disparate impact.

The case did not involve an affirmative action plan. On the other hand, affirmative action plans often include a commitment to evaluate the fairness of selection devices. *Ricci* limits an employer's ability to decline to use selection devices after they are administered in certain circumstances.

Title VII also contains a specific provision, 42 U.S.C. § 2000e–2(*l*), that limits an employer's ability to use different cutoff scores based on a protected trait. It provides:

> It shall be an unlawful employment practice for a [covered entity] in connection with the selection or referral of applicants or candidates for employment or promotion to adjust the scores of, use different cutoff scores for, or otherwise alter the results of employment tests on the basis of race, color, religion, sex or national origin.

This provision does not prohibit employers from having different sex-based physical fitness scores, if the fitness scores require the same level of fitness and effort.[74]

In *Ricci*, the Justices clearly stated that Title VII allows space for affirmative efforts by employers prior to the use of the selection device. The Court stated:

> Nor do we question an employer's affirmative efforts to ensure that all groups have a fair opportunity to apply for promotions and to participate in the process by which promotions will be made. But once that process has been established and employers have made clear their selection criteria, they may not then invalidate the test results, thus upsetting an employee's legitimate expectation not to be judged on the basis of race.[75]

The Court continued:

> Title VII does not prohibit an employer from considering, before administering a test or practice, how to design that test or practice in order to provide a fair opportunity for all individuals, regardless of their race. And when, during the test-design stage, an employer invites comments to ensure the test is fair, that process can provide a common ground for open discussions toward that end.[76]

§ 9.08 Affirmative Action and *McDonnell Douglas*

The Supreme Court has specifically addressed the interplay of *McDonnell Douglas v. Green* with affirmative action plans in *Johnson v. Transportation Agency*.[77] In that case, a man alleged that his employer discriminated against him based on his sex by denying him a promotion. The man alleged that the employer promoted a less qualified woman for the position. The employer justified its choice by pointing to an affirmative action plan.

The Supreme Court held that the case should be evaluated under *McDonnell Douglas*. In the first step, the plaintiff proves a prima facie case. In the second step, the

---

[74] Bauer v. Lynch, 812 F.3d 340 (4th Cir. 2016).

[75] Ricci v. DeStefano, 557 U.S. 557, 585 (2009).

[76] *Ricci*, 557 U.S. at 585.

[77] 480 U.S. 616, 626 (1987).

defendant may articulate a legitimate, non-discriminatory reason for acting. The Supreme Court explained:

> The existence of an affirmative action plan provides such a rationale. If such a plan is articulated as the basis for the employer's decision, the burden shifts to the plaintiff to prove that the employer's justification is pretextual and the plan is invalid. As a practical matter, of course, an employer will generally seek to avoid a charge of pretext by presenting evidence in support of its plan. That does not mean, however, as petitioner suggests, that reliance on an affirmative action plan is to be treated as an affirmative defense requiring the employer to carry the burden of proving the validity of the plan. The burden of proving its invalidity remains on the plaintiff.[78]

The courts deem a valid affirmative action plan as a legitimate, non-discriminatory reason for acting. However, an invalid affirmative action plan is not. At the second step, therefore, the employer must produce "evidence which, taken as true, would permit the conclusion that it acted for a 'nondiscriminatory reason,' *i.e.,* pursuant to a valid affirmative action plan."[79] Consistent with *McDonnell Douglas'* general structure, the defendant bears the burden of production only.

The courts have not fully wrestled with the problem of invalid affirmative action plans. If a plan is not valid, it would often represent direct evidence that race, sex, or another protected trait played a role in an outcome. If a plan is not valid and constitutes direct evidence, *McDonnell Douglas* is not the appropriate framework for analysis. Nonetheless, by the time the court determines invalidity, it is already at the pretext step of the *McDonnell Douglas* analysis.

As described above, the plaintiff may establish pretext by demonstrating the affirmative action plan is invalid. A plaintiff also may establish pretext under this analysis by showing that the employer did not follow the terms of its own affirmative action plan in making the contested decision.[80]

At times, the plaintiff in a reverse discrimination case will allege that the employer's decision was impacted by a policy encouraging diversity. These policies are not analyzed in the same ways as more formal affirmative action plans.[81] Courts typically require something more than the existence of such a policy to establish pretext. For example, one court noted that the existence of a diversity policy that focused on generating a wide pool of applicants was not sufficiently tied to the plaintiff's alleged negative outcome to be evidence of discrimination.[82]

In 2009, the Supreme Court decided *Ricci v. DeStefano*.[83] In that case, the Court considered the intersection of disparate treatment and disparate impact jurisprudence.

---

[78] 480 U.S. 616, 626 (1987).

[79] Shea v. Kerry, 796 F.3d 42, 57 (D.C. Cir. 2015). It is unclear why an invalid affirmative action plan is not direct evidence of discrimination. If a plaintiff has direct evidence of discrimination, courts typically do not use *McDonnell Douglas*.

[80] Hill v. Ross, 183 F.3d 586, 590 (7th Cir. 1999).

[81] Stacy Hawkins, *How Diversity Can Redeem the* McDonnell Douglas *Standard: Mounting an Effective Title VII Defense of the Commitment to Diversity in the Legal Profession*, 83 FORDHAM L. REV. 2457, 2471 (2015).

[82] Mlynczak v. Bodman, 442 F.3d 1050, 1058 (7th Cir. 2006); *see also* Coppinger v. Wal-Mart Stores, Inc., No. 3:07CV458/MCR/MD, 2009 WL 3163211, at *6 (N.D. Fla. Sept. 30, 2009).

[83] Ricci v. DeStefano, 557 U.S. 557, 585 (2009).

The Court reviewed the city of New Haven's response to a firefighter promotion exam that resulted in a statistical racial disparity. The city chose not to use the results of the test based on its concern that using the test results would create a disparate impact under Title VII. A group of white and Hispanic firefighters challenged the city's decision, claiming that it constituted reverse race discrimination.

The Supreme Court ruled in the firefighters' favor. It held that the city did not have a strong basis in evidence for believing that it would face disparate impact liability under Title VII.[84] The Court also indicated that unless the employer had such evidence, its decision to nullify the test to avoid disparate impact liability was race-conscious and therefore intentional discrimination under Title VII.[85] The Court did not discuss the intersection of *Ricci* and *McDonnell Douglas*.

As of the writing of this book, the full impact of *Ricci* on *McDonnell Douglas* is unclear.[86] The United States Court of Appeals for the District of Columbia has rejected the idea that *Ricci* impacts how *McDonnell Douglas* works in affirmative action cases.[87] In that case, the court held that *Ricci* did not apply because the employer did not argue that it took an action to avoid disparate impact liability.[88]

The Second Circuit has held that *Ricci* applies to settlement agreements that are not affirmative action plans.[89] The case did not fully explore how *Ricci* would affect the *McDonnell Douglas* inquiry.

§ 9.09 Affirmative Action as a Remedy

Title VII provides that after a finding of liability, a court may "order such affirmative action as may be appropriate."[90]

Title VII also provides that plaintiffs are not entitled to relief simply because the employer's workforce or a union's membership does not mirror the available workforce, in terms of the number or percentage of workers in each protected class.[91] In *Local 28, Sheet Metal Workers v. EEOC*,[92] the Supreme Court held that this provision did not conflict with the availability of affirmative action once the plaintiffs established discrimination. The Court held that affirmative action is an appropriate remedy when there is "persistent or egregious" discrimination or when affirmative action is necessary to dissipate the effects of pervasive discrimination. In *Sheet Metal Workers*, the Court approved a remedial order that required a union to achieve a membership goal of 29% non-white members, based on the percentage of non-white workers in the relevant labor pool in the area. The Court noted that in most cases, such an extreme remedy would not be required because other remedies would make the victims of discrimination whole. It also upheld the remedial order even though it might benefit workers who were not affected by the union's past discriminatory practices.

---

[84] *Ricci*, 557 U.S. at 585.

[85] *Ricci*, 557 U.S. at 585.

[86] For a discussion of *Ricci* generally, see Sachin S. Pandya, *Detecting the Stealth Erosion of Precedent: Affirmative Action After* Ricci, 31 BERKELEY J. EMP. & LAB. L. 285, 286 (2010).

[87] Shea v. Kerry, 796 F.3d 42, 51 (D.C. Cir. 2015).

[88] *Shea*, 796 F.3d at 51.

[89] *See* United States v. Brennan, 650 F.3d 65, 102–04 (2d Cir. 2011).

[90] 42 U.S.C.A. § 2000e–5(g)(1).

[91] 42 U.S.C.A. § 2000e–2(j).

[92] Local 28 of Sheet Metal Workers' Int'l Ass'n v. E.E.O.C., 478 U.S. 421, 426 (1986).

In *United States v. Paradise*[93] the Court held that "pervasive, systematic, and obstinate discriminatory conduct" by the state employer in refusing to hire minority applicants to be state troopers, justified relief in the form of affirmative action. In that case, the Supreme Court approved a trial court order that required the state to promote a certain percentage of black individuals into officer positions until certain numerical goals were met. The order also allowed the employer to develop its own promotion plan that would not result in a disparate impact based on race. In evaluating the relief, the Court considered the necessity of the relief, the efficacy of alternatives, the flexibility and duration of the relief, the relationship of numerical goals to the applicable labor market, and the impact of the relief on the rights of third parties.

It is unclear to what extent subsequent Supreme Court cases related to voluntary affirmative action and affirmative action in the educational context affect the ability of courts to grant affirmative actions as a remedy. However, from both *Sheet Metal Workers* and *Paradise*, it is clear that numerically based affirmative action cannot be ordered in the typical case. Such relief is reserved for systematic or egregious conduct. Later cases suggest that an affirmative action remedy must not "unnecessarily trammel the interests of white employees." A court may not order the discharge of white workers in order to permit the hiring of minority workers or require the layoff of white employees in order to preserve the jobs of similarly situated black employees.[94]

§ 9.10 Constitutional Challenges to Affirmative Action on the Basis of Race

Outside of the remedies context, the federal Constitution also impacts affirmative action plans implemented by state or federal actors, such as public employers. As discussed throughout this chapter, many of the cases addressing affirmative action taken by public actors are in the education context, and it is unclear how these cases translate into the employment context. This section begins by discussing the employment-related cases and then discusses affirmative action cases outside the employment context.

In *Wygant v. Jackson Board of Education*,[95] a plurality of the Justices held unconstitutional a collective bargaining agreement that generally required layoffs by seniority, with an exception for layoffs that would cause the number of minority teachers to fall below the current percentage of employed minority teachers. Thus, the provisions required laying off white teachers who were more senior than minority teachers hired more recently under its affirmative action plan.

Respondents argued that the layoff plan was implemented to remedy past racial discrimination by the school district. However, the plurality stated that the school district did not have a strong basis in evidence for determining that remedial action was required.[96] Even if the school district could make such a showing, the plurality noted that the district could not show that the layoff provision was an appropriate way to accomplish the goal. One problem with the provision was that it unnecessarily

---

93 United States v. Paradise, 480 U.S. 149, 149 (1987).

94 Wygant v. Jackson Bd. of Educ., 476 U.S. 267, 267 (1986).

95 *Wygant*, 476 U.S. at 267.

96 *Wygant*, 476 U.S. at 277.

trammeled the interests of white workers, who were subject to the layoff. The plurality noted that hiring goals do not impose the same hardship.

In *City of Richmond v. J.A. Croson Co.*[97] the Court considered a city plan that required general contractors to subcontract at least 30% of the value of a contract to minority-owned businesses. The plan defined a minority owned business as one "controlled by black, Spanish-speaking, Oriental, Indian, Eskimo, or Aleut citizens." A contractor filed suit after bidding on a contract and not being able to obtain a waiver from the city regarding the minority-owned business requirement.

The Court held that the plan violated the Fourteenth Amendment's Equal Protection Clause. The Court held that there was not sufficient support for the city's finding that it was remedying the present effects of past discrimination. The majority found that the city relied on the following evidence:

> (1) the ordinance declares itself to be remedial; (2) several proponents of the measure stated their views that there had been past discrimination in the construction industry; (3) minority businesses received 0.67% of prime contracts from the city while minorities constituted 50% of the city's population; (4) there were very few minority contractors in local and state contractors' associations; and (5) in 1977, Congress made a determination that the effects of past discrimination had stifled minority participation in the construction industry nationally.[98]

While the majority recognized generalized evidence of past discrimination, it held this generalized evidence was not sufficient to support the "unyielding quota" used by the city. The Court noted that it would not defer to this generalized evidence, and noted that there was little evidence about the number of minority contractors available. The Court also recognized that there was no evidence regarding participation by "Spanish-speaking, Oriental, Indian, Eskimo, or Aleut persons."[99]

The Court also held that the program was not narrowly tailored to remedy prior discrimination. The Court noted the city did not consider race-neutral alternatives and that it relied on a strict race-based quota, rather than a more individualized inquiry. In dissent, Justice Marshall indicated that the majority took a "myopic" view of the facts supporting the city's plan.[100]

In *Adarand Constructors, Inc. v. Pena*,[101] the petitioner challenged federal government contracting rules that provided financial incentives to hire subcontractors from socially or economically disadvantaged groups. The Court held that the Fifth Amendment demanded the rules be governed by strict scrutiny, requiring that they serve a compelling government interest and be narrowly tailored to meet that interest.[102] The Court remanded the case for the lower courts to apply the strict scrutiny standard, leaving many questions unanswered.

---

97 488 U.S. 469, 470 (1989).

98 *Croson*, 488 U.S. at 499.

99 *Croson*, 488 U.S. at 506.

100 *Croson*, 488 U.S. at 530.

101 515 U.S. 200, 204 (1995).

102 *Adarand*, 515 U.S at 235.

In the education context, the Supreme Court has held that a government entity may have a compelling interest in having a diverse student body and may meet that goal with a plan that is narrowly tailored to meet that interest. In *Regents of Univ. of Cal. v. Bakke*[103] the Court considered an affirmative action admissions program for a medical school at UC Davis, which opened in 1968. The first classes admitted into the program had few minority students. The faculty then devised a special admissions program for disadvantaged students.

The special admissions program mostly operated in the same way as the regular admissions program but with a separate admissions committee. Candidates were asked if they wanted to be considered as "economically and/or educationally disadvantaged" applicants and whether they were members of a minority group. If the candidate answered yes to one of these questions, the special admissions committee would review that candidate's application. The process was the same as the regular admission except that the normal GPA cutoff did not apply.[104] The special committee would then present its top choices to the general admissions committee until the number of proscribed special admission seats filled. When the class size was 50, the number of proscribed special admission seats was 8. When the class doubled in size to 100, the special admissions seat doubled to 16. Disadvantaged white applicants applied to the special program, but none of them were admitted. Allan Bakke was a white male who applied to medical school through the general admissions process and was not admitted.[105] He challenged the constitutionality of the special admissions program.

Justice Powell's opinion set forth the judgment of the Court, but was not joined in its entirety by any other Justice. The Court held the special admissions plan was impermissible under the Equal Protection Clause of the Fourteenth Amendment; however, some racially conscious admissions plan could survive constitutional challenge. Justice Powell noted that the present case was different than school desegregation cases and prior cases in the employment context. The desegregation cases involved remedies for clearly determined constitutional violations. The employment discrimination cases were also different because the victims in those cases were discriminated against not only by society at large, but by the defendants in each particular case.[106]

Having determined that strict scrutiny is the correct level of scrutiny and that the school has used a suspect classification, Justice Powell then looked at the admission plan's purpose to determine whether that purpose is substantial enough to support using a suspect classification. He also analyzed whether the use of that classification was necessary to the accomplishment of the stated purpose.[107] The school asserted its program served the interests of: "(i) reducing the historic deficit of traditionally disfavored minorities in medical schools and in the profession; (ii) countering the effects of societal discrimination; (iii) increasing the number of physicians who will practice in communities currently underserved; and (iv) obtaining the educational benefits that flow

[103] 438 U.S. 265, 271 (1978).

[104] *Id.* at 275.

[105] *Id.* at 276.

[106] *Id.* at 301.

[107] *Id.* at 306.

from an ethnically diverse student body."[108] He found the first three purposes to be invalid, but found that the school had a compelling interest in the fourth purpose.[109]

Having found that the school had a compelling interest in attaining a diverse student body, Justice Powell then analyzed whether the special admissions program's racial classification was necessary to promote this interest.[110] He found that reserving a specified number of seats for disadvantaged minority applicants would contribute to the attainment of a diverse student body, but was an improper way to accomplish the goal.[111] Justice Powell observed that interest in a diverse student body is not an interest in simple ethnic diversity, but rather the interest encompasses a broader array of qualifications and characteristics of which race and ethnicity are but a single factor among many. A focus solely on ethnic diversity would hinder the attainment of genuine diversity.

Justice Powell then referenced Harvard's admissions policy. Harvard's policy, which did not set target quotas, focused on race and ethnicity as well as other "plus" factors (such as geographic diversity and life experience) in determining who is admitted and who is not.[112] The weight attributed to each factor varied from year to year. Harvard's policy was flexible enough to consider the pertinent elements of diversity in light of the particular qualifications of each applicant. Further, this policy did not foreclose from consideration any applicants because of race or ethnicity.[113] The Court held that the medical school's interest in diversity could be served by a properly devised admissions policy.[114]

On Bakke's request for an injunction compelling his admission to the school, the Court held that the school conceded that it could not carry its burden proving that, but-for the existence of its special admission program, Bakke would not have been admitted. Hence, the Court found that Bakke was entitled to such an injunction compelling his admission and affirmed the lower court's holding on this point.

Justice Brennan, joined by Justices Marshall, White, Blackmun, concurred and dissented in part. In the opening paragraphs, Justice Brennan pointed out that the four justices on this part of the opinion, along with Justice Powell, made a majority of five standing for the proposition that the continued use of affirmative action was constitutional.[115] He also noted the fractured nature of *Bakke*, with "many opinions, no single one speaking for the Court." However, the four Justices would have held that the school's special admissions program is constitutional and would have reversed the lower court's judgment.[116] Regarding the Equal Protection Clause of the Fourteenth Amendment, Justice Brennan indicated that racial classifications were not *per se* invalid.[117] He then noted that "the [School's] purpose of remedying the effects of past societal discrimination was sufficiently important to justify the use of race-conscious

[108] *Id.* at 305–06.

[109] *Id.* at 306–15.

[110] *Id.* at 314–15.

[111] *Id.* at 315.

[112] *Id.* at 316–17.

[113] *Id.* at 318.

[114] *Id.* at 320.

[115] *Id.* at 325–26.

[116] *Id.*

[117] *Id.* at 356.

admissions programs where there is a sound basis for concluding that minority underrepresentation is substantial and chronic, and that . . . past discrimination is impeding access of minorities to the Medical School."[118]

Justice Brennan concluded that the School's goal of admitting minority students disadvantaged by the effects of past discrimination is sufficiently important to justify the use of race-conscious admission criteria.[119] Justice Brennan then found that the school had a sound basis for believing that the problem of underrepresentation of minorities was substantial and chronic and attributable to past and present racial discrimination. Justice Brennan then noted his (and the three other Justices') disagreement with the lower court's conclusion that the school's special program was unreasonable in light of its objectives. First, he stated that the school had no practical means by which it could achieve its ends without the use of race-conscious measures. Then, he stated that the school's special admissions program did not equate minority status with disadvantage; instead, it considered each applicant's personal history to determine whether he or she has likely been disadvantaged by racial discrimination.[120]

Justice Marshall wrote separately to point out that he agreed with Justice Powell's opinion insofar as it permits a university to consider the race of an applicant in making admission decisions.[121] He did not agree that the school's program violated the Constitution. Justice Marshall explained at length the history of discrimination against African-Americans in the United States.[122] Justice Marshall found it ironic that the Court was unwilling to hold that a class-based remedy for a history of racial discrimination was permissible despite hundreds of years of class-based discrimination against African-Americans.[123]

Justice Blackmun wrote separately to state his belief that the judiciary should rarely step in and determine how applicants are admitted because it is ill-equipped and poorly trained to make those determinations.[124]

Justice Stevens joined by Chief Justice Burger, and Justices Stewart and Rehnquist concurred in part and dissented in part. He would have found that the school, through its special admissions policy, excluded Bakke because of his race.[125] He argued that the plain language of Title VI, that race cannot be the basis of excluding anyone from participation in a federally funded program, required affirmance of the lower court's judgment.[126]

Grutter v. Bollinger[127] is a Supreme Court case that upheld an affirmative action admissions policy of the University of Michigan Law School ("Law School"). The central issue in the case was whether the use of race as a factor in student admissions by the

---

[118] *Id.* at 362. Justice White wrote separately to discuss whether Title VI provided a private right of action.

[119] *Id.* at 369.

[120] *Id.* at 377.

[121] *Id.* at 387.

[122] *Id.* at 388–95.

[123] *Id.* at 400.

[124] *Id.* at 404.

[125] *Id.* at 412.

[126] *Id.* at 418.

[127] 539 U.S. 306 (2003).

school was unlawful.[128] The Court held that it was not. Justice O'Connor wrote the majority's option.[129]

The law school admissions process looked for individuals with substantial promise for success in law school and beyond as well as students who can "contribute in diverse ways to the well-being of others."[130] To implement these goals, the law school sought to implement a policy that complied with the Supreme Court's decision in *Regents of Univ. of Cal. v. Bakke*.[131] The policy focused on an applicant's academic ability coupled with a flexible assessment of talents, experiences, and potential to contribute to the learning of those around them.[132] The policy required admission officers to evaluate each applicant based on all the information available, including a personal statement, letters of recommendation, an essay describing how a student will contribute to the diversity of the school, grade point average, and LSAT score. However, the policy made clear that no score, whether high or low, automatically guaranteed admission or disqualified a student. The policy demanded that admission officers look beyond grades and look into "soft variables" including the enthusiasm of the recommenders, the quality of the application materials, and other similar factors.

The policy's main goal was to achieve a type of diversity that had the potential to enrich everyone's education. The policy did not restrict the types of diversity a student can offer. For instance, a white applicant could be diverse by having grown up in a different country or by facing some type of major life adversity.[133] The policy, however, reaffirmed the law school's commitment to racial and ethnic diversity with special reference to the inclusion of student from groups that have been historically discriminated against.

Petitioner Barbara Grutter was a white Michigan resident who applied to the law school.[134] She had a 3.8 GPA and 161 LSAT score. She made the law school's waiting list but was ultimately rejected. She sued in federal court alleging that the law school and its officers discriminated against her on the basis of race in violation of the Fourteenth Amendment, Title VII, and other statutes.[135]

The district court ultimately held that the school's use of race in its admission policy was unlawful.[136] The Court of Appeals, sitting en banc, reversed. The Court of Appeals held that Justice Powell's opinion in *Bakke* was binding precedent establishing diversity as a compelling state interest. The Court of Appeals also held that the law school's use of race was narrowly tailored because race was a "potential 'plus factor' " and because the admission policy was virtually identical to the admissions policy approved by Justice Powell in his *Bakke* opinion.[137] The Supreme Court then granted certiorari to decide

---

[128] *Id.* at 311.

[129] *Id.*

[130] *Id.* at 313.

[131] 438 U.S. 265 (1978).

[132] 539 U.S. at 315.

[133] *Id.* at 316.

[134] *Id.*

[135] *Id.* at 317.

[136] *Id.* at 321.

[137] *Id.*

whether diversity is a compelling interest that can justify the narrowly tailored use of race in selecting applicants for admission to public universities.[138]

The Supreme Court noted that it last addressed the issue of the use of race in higher public education in 1978 in the *Bakke* case. The Supreme Court, in *Grutter*, held that since the "splintered" *Bakke* decision, Justice Powell's opinion has served as the constitutional touchstone for analysis of race-conscious admissions policies.[139] In Justice Powell's view, when governmental decisions touch on an individual's race or ethnicity, he is entitled to a judicial determination that the burden he is asked to bear is narrowly tailored to serve a compelling governmental interest. Justice Powell, in *Bakke*, approved the university's use of race to further only one interest, the attainment of a diverse student body. However, he also held that "diversity that furthers a compelling state interest encompasses a far broader array of qualifications and characteristics of which racial and ethnic origin is but a single though important element."[140] Thus, a policy that focuses exclusively on race or ethnic background would be unconstitutional.

The Supreme Court stated that strict scrutiny is applied to all racial classifications to "smoke out" illegitimate uses of race by assuring that the government is pursuing a goal important enough to warrant the use a suspect tool.[141] The Court also stated any plans using racial classifications must be narrowly tailored.

With these principles in mind, the Supreme Court held that, while some of its opinions since *Bakke* might suggest that remedying past discrimination is the only permissible justification for race-based governmental discrimination, the law school has a compelling interest in attaining a diverse student body.[142] Further, the Court held that it would defer to the school's educational judgment regarding the essentiality of such diversity.

The Court then engaged in a lengthy discussion regarding the educational benefits diversity is designed to produce, including the breakdown of racial stereotypes and business demand of diverse employees. Further, the Court pointed out that since law schools, in general, serve as one of the main training grounds for the future leaders of America, it follows that it is necessary to have a diverse group of young leaders to help lead an increasingly diverse country.[143]

The Court then held that the school's admission policy was narrowly tailored.[144] To be narrowly tailored, a race-conscious admission program cannot use a quota system. It may, however, consider race or ethnicity only as a "plus" factor within an applicant's file.[145] Further, the Court held that the school's goal of attaining a critical mass of underrepresented minorities is not a quota because the school engaged in highly individualized review of each applicant's file, giving serious consideration to all of its

---

138 *Id.* at 322.

139 *Id.* at 323.

140 *Id.* at 325.

141 *Id.* at 326.

142 *Id.* at 328.

143 *Id.* at 330–32.

144 *Id.* at 333.

145 *Id.*

content. Further, there was no policy of automatic rejection or acceptance based on any single soft variable.[146]

The Court also noted that the school did not define "diversity" solely in terms of race and ethnicity, and that students had the opportunity to highlight their own version of diversity through their personal statements and other application materials.[147] Further, the school frequently accepted nonminority applicants with lower grades and test scores than minority applicants, demonstrating that the school seriously weighed many other "diversity" factors other than race and ethnicity.[148]

The Court disagreed with petitioner's argument that the law school's policy was not narrowly tailored because other neutral means existed to obtain the educational benefits of a diverse student body existed; such as a lottery system. The Court held that narrowly tailoring does not require exhaustion of every conceivable race-neutral alternative. Narrowly tailoring, however, does require serious, good-faith consideration of workable alternatives, which the Court held the school sufficiently considered.

Finally, the Supreme Court held that race-conscious admissions programs must have a logical end point, surmising that in 25 years such policies would no longer be needed.[149] Justice Ginsburg concurred with the majority opinion.[150] She wrote separately to voice her concern with the 25-year timeframe. She stated that, "[f]rom today's vantage point, one may hope, but not know for sure, that over the next generation's span, progress toward nondiscrimination and genuinely equal opportunity will make it safe to sunset affirmative action."[151]

A companion case to *Grutter* was *Gratz v. Bollinger*.[152] In that case, the Court held that the University of Michigan's freshman admissions policy was not narrowly tailored to meet the compelling interest in diversity because it allotted one-fifth of the points needed for admission based on race. The Court held that such a system did not require individualized review of applicants.

In *Parents Involved in Community Schools v. Seattle School District No. 1*[153] the Court rejected the student assignment plans of Seattle Public Schools and Jefferson County Public Schools. The Court held that the plans did not meet the narrowly tailored and compelling interest requirements for a race-based assignment plans because they were used only to achieve racial balance and because public schools may not use race as the sole determining factor for assigning students to schools. However, the Court also held that race-conscious objectives to achieve diverse school environment may be acceptable under certain circumstances.

In the Seattle school district, students could choose the high school they wished to attend. However, because some schools were more popular than others, the school needed a system to rank preferences to avoid school overcrowding. The school district used a series of tiebreakers to avoid overcrowding. One of the tiebreakers depended on

---

146 *Id.* at 337.

147 *Id.* at 338.

148 *Id.* at 339.

149 *Id.* at 341–42.

150 *Id.* at 343.

151 *Id.*

152 539 U.S. 244, 275 (2003).

153 551 U.S. 701 (2007).

the racial composition of the chosen school and the race of the individual student. The overall racial composition of the district is 41 percent white and the remaining 59 percent comprises all other racial groups. For purposes of the tiebreaks all other racial groups are labeled as "nonwhite." If an oversubscribed school was not within 10 percentage points of the district's overall white and nonwhite racial balance, the district labels it "integration positive" and employs a tiebreaker that selects for assignment students whose race "will serve to bring the school into balance."[154] If still needed, the district employs a third tiebreaker, a student's geographical proximity to the school.

Jefferson County Public Schools ("Jefferson County") operates the public-school system in Louisville, Kentucky. In 1973, a federal court found that Jefferson County had maintained a segregated school system, and in 1975 a federal District Court entered a desegregation decree. Jefferson County operated under that decree until 2000, when a federal court dissolved the decree.[155] In 2001, Jefferson County adopted a voluntary student assignment plan. Around 34 percent of the district's students are black and most of the remaining 66 percent are white. The plan required all nonmagnet schools to maintain a minimum black enrollment of 15 percent, and a maximum black enrollment of 50 percent.

The Court indicated it reviewed the school plans under strict scrutiny. The Court stated that in previous cases in the school context, it recognized two compelling interests. The first is remedying the effects of past intentional discrimination. The Supreme Court then pointed out that the Seattle school district had never run a segregated program nor had a desegregation decree. For Jefferson County, the Court noted that while it was subjected to a court-ordered desegregation decree, the decree was removed in the year 2000 after the County had achieved unitary status.[156]

The second compelling interest the Court found was diversity in higher education as evinced by *Grutter*, which dictates that the diversity interest is not in race alone but encompassed all factors that may contribute to student body diversity. The Court then noted that in the present cases, race was not a diversity factor among many, it was determinative standing alone.[157] The school district plans at issue did not provide for a meaningful individualized review and instead relied on racial classifications in a "nonindividualized, mechanical way."

Both school districts asserted additional compelling interests. They argued that educational and broader socialization benefits flow from a racially diverse learning environment, and that because the diversity sought is racial diversity it made sense to promote that interest directly by relying on race alone.[158] A plurality of the Supreme Court disagreed and stated that "[i]n design and operation, the plans are directed only to racial balance, pure and simple, an objective this Court has repeatedly condemned as illegitimate." The plurality further stated that in *Grutter*, "the number of minority students the school sought to admit was an undefined 'meaningful number' necessary to achieve a genuinely diverse student body."[159] The racial balance the school districts sought was a defined range dictated by demographics of the respective school districts.

---

[154] *Id.*

[155] *Id.* at 716.

[156] *Id.* at 721.

[157] *Id.* at 723.

[158] *Id.* at 725–26.

[159] *Id.* at 729.

The plurality stated that this was fatal under existing precedent as outright racial balancing that is patently unconstitutional.[160]

A majority of the Court rejected the idea that the school districts needed to rely on race-conscious policies to achieve their stated goals.

Justice Thomas fully concurred with Chief Justice Roberts' plurality opinion.[161] He wrote separately to discuss that a "benign" reason for using race should be subject to the same constitutional scrutiny as invidious reasons.[162] He stated that Justice Breyer's rhetoric of desegregation is inaccurate and that racial imbalance does not equate to segregation.[163] Justice Thomas stated that both plans lacked a valid interest in remediation and that neither plan could survive strict scrutiny because neither served a genuine compelling state interest.[164] He also disagreed with the dissent's application of "not as strict" strict scrutiny because strict scrutiny applies equally to every racial classification. He continued with a lengthy critique of Justice Breyer's dissent.

Justice Kennedy concurred in part and concurred in the judgment.[165] In Justice Kennedy's view, unlike the plurality's view, "[d]iversity, depending on its meaning and definition, is a compelling educational goal a school district may pursue."[166] He stated that "[i]n the administration of public schools by the state . . . it is permissible to consider the racial makeup of schools and to adopt *general* policies to encourage a diverse student body, one aspect of which is its racial composition."[167] He further noted that this may be done in a "general way and without treating each student in different fashion solely on the basis of a systematic, individual typing by race."[168] These could include strategic site selection of new schools; drawing attendance zones with general recognition of the demographics of neighborhoods; allocating resources for special programs; recruiting students and faculty in a targeted fashion; and tracking enrollments, performance, and other statistics by race.[169]

Justice Stevens dissented.[170] In his short dissent, he wrote that the plurality misapplied Supreme Court precedent. Justice Breyer also dissented.[171] He was joined by Justices Stevens, Souter, and Ginsburg. He noted that the Supreme Court has, in the past, upheld narrowly tailored plans "that are no less race conscious than the plans [at issue here]." Further, he pointed out that the Constitution "permits local communities to adopt desegregation plans even where it does not require them to do so." He also challenged the plurality's characterization of the Court's precedent. He noted that Supreme Court has never held that strict scrutiny means that all racial classification, regardless of whether they include or exclude, must be treated the same.[172] Further, he

---

160 *Id.* at 729–30.

161 *Id.*

162 *Id.*

163 *Id.* at 749.

164 *Id.* at 757.

165 *Id.* at 782.

166 *Id.* at 783.

167 *Id.* at 788.

168 *Id.* at 788–89.

169 *Id.* at 789.

170 *Id.* at 799.

171 *Id.* at 803.

172 *Id.* at 832.

noted that in *Grutter*, the Court said that when reviewing race-based governmental action under the Equal Protection Clause, context matters.[173]

Given this logic, Justice Breyer stated his belief that, in this case, "the law requires application of a standard of review that is not 'strict' in the traditional sense of that word."[174] Under that standard, he would hold that both school district plans are constitutional. In applying his standard, he found three compelling interests. First, he found a historical and remedial interest in setting right the consequences of prior conditions of segregation.[175] Second, he found an educational interest in overcoming the adverse educational effects produced by segregated schools.[176] Third, he found a democratic interest in producing an educational environment that reflects the "pluralistic society in which our children will live."[177] Justice Breyer also described why he believed the school plans were narrowly tailored.[178]

In *Fisher v. Univ. of Texas*,[179] the Supreme Court again considered affirmative action in college admissions.[180] The Supreme Court held that lower appellate court had not applied the standard of strict scrutiny and remanded the case.[181] Justice Kennedy wrote the majority opinion.[182]

Petitioner, Abigail Fisher, was 1 of 29,501 applicants to the University of Texas. From this group, 12,843 were admitted and 6,715 enrolled.[183] Petitioner was denied admission.

In recent years, the University had used three different admission policies. The first policy was used prior to 1997 and it considered two factors, a numerical score, called the Personal Achievement Index, reflecting an applicant's test scores and academic performance in high school, and the applicant's race. However, in *Hopwood v. Texas*, the Fifth Circuit held that this policy was unconstitutional.[184]

As a response to *Hopwood*, the University created its second admissions policy. This policy measured an applicant's leadership and work experience, awards, extracurricular activities, community service, and other special circumstances that give insight into an applicant's background. These included growing up in a single-parent home, speaking a language other than English at home, significant family responsibilities assumed by the applicant, and the general socioeconomic condition of the applicant's family.

The Texas State Legislature also responded to *Hopwood* by enacting a law known as the Top Ten Percent Law.[185] This law granted automatic admission to any public state college, including the University, to all students in the top 10% of their class at high

---

173 *Id.* at 834.

174 *Id.* at 837.

175 *Id.*

176 *Id.* at 839.

177 *Id.* at 840.

178 *Id.* at 846.

179 570 U.S. 297 (2013).

180 *Id.* at 300.

181 *Id.* at 303.

182 *Id.* at 300.

183 *Id.*

184 *Id.*

185 *Id.* at 305.

schools in Texas. According to the majority, the University's second admissions policy, coupled with the operation of the Top Ten Percent Law, resulted in a more racially diverse environment.[186]

After the Supreme Court decided *Grutter*, the University adopted its third admissions policy. Citing a lack of a "critical mass" of minority students, the University included a student's race as a component of the Personal Achievement Index score.[187] Further, the University asked applicants to classify themselves from among five predefined racial categories on the application in which race was not assigned an explicit numerical value but was nonetheless a meaningful factor.[188] Once applications are scored, they are plotted on a grid with the Academic Index on the x-axis and the Personal Achievement Index score on the y-axis. On that grid students are assigned to "cells" based on their individual scores. All students in the cells falling above a certain line are admitted. All students below the line are not.

The Supreme Court first pointed out that there were three previous Supreme Court cases relevant to the issue of considering racial minority status as a positive or favorable factor in a university's admissions process, with the goal of achieving the educational benefits of a more diverse student body.[189] The Court then summarized and characterized three relevant cases of *Bakke*, *Gratz*, and *Grutter*.

The Supreme Court, relying on *Grutter*, held that a university's educational judgment that diversity is essential to its educational mission is one to which the courts defer.[190] A court, however, should ensure that there is a reasoned, principled explanation for the academic decision. The Supreme Court held that the district court properly deferred to the University's "experience and expertise."[191]

However, the Supreme Court also held that once the University has established that its goal of diversity is consistent with strict scrutiny, there must still be a further judicial determination that the admissions process meets strict scrutiny in its implementation. The University must prove that the means it chooses to attain diversity are narrowly tailored to that goal. On this point, the University receives *no* deference. The court must make a determination that the policy in question ensures that each applicant is evaluated as an individual and not in a way in which race or ethnicity is the defining feature.[192]

The Supreme Court stated that strict scrutiny requires a judicial inquiry into whether a university could achieve sufficient diversity without using racial classifications. It noted that strict scrutiny does not require exhaustion of every conceivable race-neutral alternative, however, it does require a court to examine, and not defer to, a university's serious, good faith consideration of workable race-neutral alternatives. Then it held that on this point, the Court of Appeals' conclusion that "the

---

186 *Id.*

187 *Id.* at 306.

188 *Id.*

189 *Id.*

190 *Id.* at 310.

191 *Id.* at 310–11.

192 *Id.* at 312.

narrow-tailoring inquiry—like the compelling-interest inquiry—is undertaken with a degree of deference to the University" was mistaken.[193]

The Supreme Court held that the Court of Appeals' expression of the controlling standard was at odds with *Grutter's* command that "all racial classifications imposed by government 'must be analyzed by a reviewing court under strict scrutiny.' " The Supreme Court then vacated the judgment, so that the admissions process could be considered and judged under the correct analysis.[194]

Justice Scalia concurred.[195] He adhered to the view he expressed in *Grutter*, where he stated, "[t]he Constitution proscribes government discrimination on the basis of race, and state-provided education is no exception." Justice Thomas also concurred. He agreed that the Court of Appeals did not apply strict scrutiny to the University's discrimination in its admissions policy. He wrote separately to explain that he would overrule *Grutter* and hold that a State's use of race in higher education is prohibited by the Equal Protection Clause.[196] Justice Ginsburg dissented.[197] She found that the University sought to achieve student body diversity through an admissions policy that met the guidelines set out by Justice Powell's *Bakke* opinion. She then criticized the majority's understanding that the Top Ten Percent Law and race blind holistic review achieved significant diversity.[198]

In 2016, the Justices again revisited *Fisher v. University of Texas*, this time after the lower courts considered the case on remand.[199] In describing the portion of the admissions process at issue, the Court noted that up to 75 percent of the students were admitted through the Top Ten Percent plan. For some of the remaining admissions decisions, the school used a combination of an academic index and a personal index. The personal index

> evaluates the applicant's potential contributions to the University's student body based on the applicant's leadership experience, extracurricular activities, awards/honors, community service, and other "special circumstances."
>
> "Special circumstances" include the socioeconomic status of the applicant's family, the socioeconomic status of the applicant's school, the applicant's family responsibilities, whether the applicant lives in a single-parent home, the applicant's SAT score in relation to the average SAT score at the applicant's school, the language spoken at the applicant's home, and, finally, the applicant's race.[200]

The individuals who assign the personal index scores undergo training to make sure there is consistency across reviewers, and the university undertook reliability testing to ensure consistency. The University sets a combined academic index and personal index score that an applicant must meet for admission. When the University sets this score, it does not know the races of the applicants who achieved certain scores.

---

[193] *Id.* at 313.

[194] *Id.* at 314.

[195] *Id.* at 315.

[196] *Id.*

[197] *Id.* at 334.

[198] *Id.* at 335.

[199] Fisher v. Univ. of Texas at Austin, 136 S. Ct. 2198 (2016).

[200] *Fisher*, 136 S. Ct. at 2206.

Only seven justices considered *Fisher II*, with Justice Kagan recusing herself from the case. Justice Scalia died in February of 2016. The majority opinion recited three lessons from *Fisher I*. First, that the courts are required to evaluate such plans using strict scrutiny. "Strict scrutiny requires the university to demonstrate with clarity that its purpose or interest is both constitutionally permissible and substantial, and that its use of the classification is necessary . . . to the accomplishment of its purpose."[201] Second, some deference is due to universities that choose to pursue diversity as an educational goal. Finally, no deference is due to the whether the university's plan is narrowly tailored.

The Supreme Court upheld the use of the personal index in this context. The Court held that while a school could not have strict numerical quotas, "A university's goals cannot be elusory or amorphous—they must be sufficiently measurable to permit judicial scrutiny of the policies adopted to reach them."[202] It found that the university had articulated concrete and precise goals about the educational benefits of diversity.

Regarding the narrowness of the plan, the Court noted the personal index was used in only a fraction of the admission decisions at the university and was only one of a number of factors within the personal index. The university also had tried and considered other race-neutral ways to accomplish its diversity goal. The Court also noted that the university must continue to monitor its plan. "Through regular evaluation of data and consideration of student experience, the University must tailor its approach in light of changing circumstances, ensuring that race plays no greater role than is necessary to meet its compelling interest."[203]

The full implications of *Grutter* and *Fisher I* and *II* in the employment context are unclear.

§ 9.11 Constitutional Challenges to Affirmative Action on the Basis of Sex

In *Califano v. Webster*, the Supreme Court held that sex-based classifications designed to remedy past discrimination challenged under the Fifth Amendment should be evaluated under intermediate scrutiny, under which they must "serve important governmental objectives and must be substantially related to achievement of those objectives."[204] Many circuits apply this standard to constitutional analysis of sex-based affirmative action plans.[205] The Sixth Circuit has held that strict scrutiny must be met when sex-based classifications are considered under the Equal Protection Clause.[206]

---

[201] *Fisher*, 136 S. Ct. at 2208 (internal citations omitted).

[202] *Fisher*, 136 S. Ct. at 2211.

[203] *Fisher*, 136 S. Ct. at 2210.

[204] Califano v. Webster, 430 U.S. 313, 316–17 (1977); *see also* Rosalie Berger Levinson, *Gender-Based Affirmative Action and Reverse Gender Bias: Beyond* Gratz, Parents Involved, *and* Ricci, 34 HARV. J. L. & GENDER 1, 12 (2011) (discussing sex-based affirmative action).

[205] Caroline Marschilok, Jessica Moran, Danna Seligman, Aislinn Toohey, *Equal Protection*, 18 GEO. J. GENDER & L. 537, 560 (2017) (summarizing cases).

[206] Brunet v. City of Columbus, 1 F.3d 390, 404 (6th Cir. 1993).

§ 9.12 Age and Disability

In *General Dynamics v. Cline*,[207] the Supreme Court interpreted the ADEA to allow employers to favor older workers over younger workers. The Court held that reducing health care benefits of younger workers (and not older workers) was not age discrimination under the ADEA. The ADEA thus would presumably allow employers to have policies and programs that benefit older workers. Care must be taken in some states, which prohibit age discrimination against both older and younger workers.

Most of the ADA's protections accrue to individuals with a disability.[208] For such provisions, a person without such an impairment does not have a claim under the ADA. The Rehabilitation Act requires certain entities to take "affirmative action to employ and advance in employment qualified individuals with disabilities."[209]

§ 9.13 Executive Orders

Executive Order 11246 imposes on employers with certain federal contracts an obligation to remedy any underutilization of people within certain protected classes by adopting affirmative action plans designed to increase the number and percentage of women and minority employees in underrepresented job categories.[210] Those affirmative action plans may include specific numerical goals and timetables. Courts have held that the executive order is consistent with Title VII.[211]

Executive Order 13,672 added sexual orientation and gender identity to the list of protected traits in Executive Order 11,246.

[207] 540 U.S. 581 (2004).

[208] 42 U.S.C. § 12112(b)(1).

[209] 29 U.S.C. § 793.

[210] A comprehensive review of all executive orders affecting affirmative action in employment is beyond the scope of this book.

[211] Contractors Ass'n of Eastern Penn, v. Secretary of Labor, 442 F.2d 159 (3d Cir. 1971).

Chapter 10

RETALIATION

Analysis

§ 10.01 Retaliation, Generally

Title VII, the ADEA, and the ADA all prohibit discrimination against individuals because they have made a charge, testified, assisted, or *participated* in any manner in an investigation, proceeding, or hearing under the Act, or have "*opposed* any practice made unlawful" by the statutes.[1]

The ADA also contains an additional section that makes it unlawful "to coerce, intimidate, threaten, or interfere with any individual in the exercise or enjoyment of, or on account of his or her having exercised or enjoyed, or on account of his or her having aided or encouraged any other individual in the exercise or enjoyment of, any right granted or protected" by the ADA.[2]

While 42 U.S.C. § 1981 and the ADEA as applied to federal employees have no expressed non-retaliation provisions, both statutes implicitly prohibit retaliation using standards similar to the expressed statutory protection.[3]

To a large extent, the federal discrimination statutes rely on private individuals to enforce them. The retaliation provisions are critical to enforcing the statutes' substantive

---

[1] 42 U.S.C.A. § 2000e–3(a); 29 U.S.C.A. § 623(d); 42 U.S.C.A. § 12203(a); *see also* Deborah L. Brake, *Retaliation*, 90 MINN. L. REV. 18, 77 (2005).

[2] 42 U.S.C.A. § 12203(b).

[3] CBOCS W., Inc. v. Humphries, 553 U.S. 442 (2008); Gomez-Perez v. Potter, 553 U.S. 474 (2008).

goals by providing a remedy for individuals who face retaliation after trying to enforce the statutes' promises. Additionally, the Supreme Court has indicated that the employment discrimination statutes do not just provide a remedy once discrimination has happened. They ideally would prohibit discrimination from occurring in the first place. To that end, the Court encourages employees to complain about workplace discrimination in an effort to stop discrimination from occurring or getting worse. In certain harassment cases, the employee must complain to preserve his or her ability to later recover in court.[4] As the statutes encourage employee complaints, the retaliation provisions ideally should protect employees who do so.

In retaliation cases, there are typically three key issues: (1) whether the worker was subjected to retaliatory conduct as defined by the statute; (2) whether the worker engaged in protected activity; and (3) whether there is a causal connection between the protected activity and the retaliatory conduct.

§ 10.02 Retaliatory Conduct

To succeed on a retaliation claim, the plaintiff must suffer harm. The retaliation provisions of the federal discrimination statutes do not use the same "terms, conditions, or privileges" language as the discrimination provisions. For example, Title VII's retaliation provision makes it illegal for an employer to "discriminate" against an employee for engaging in protected activity, such as complaining about discrimination.[5]

The Supreme Court has interpreted what it means for an employer to "discriminate" in the retaliation context. In *Burlington Northern & Santa Fe Railway Co. v. White*,[6] a worker alleged that after she complained about discrimination, the employer subjected her to negative treatment in the form of different work responsibilities. Although the new responsibilities were within her job description, the employer gave her harder tasks than the ones she performed prior to her complaint. The employer also placed her under surveillance and monitored her activities at work and suspended the plaintiff without pay for alleged insubordination. After pursuing an internal grievance, the employer found that plaintiff was not insubordinate and eventually repaid her.

In the *Burlington Northern* case, the Supreme Court noted that the term "discriminate" "refers to distinctions or differences in treatment that injure protected individuals."[7] The Court determined two issues related to the required level of harm. First, the Supreme Court determined whether the retaliation provision extended beyond negative actions that occurred in the workplace. Second, the Court considered how harmful an act must be to receive a remedy.

The Supreme Court indicated that the retaliation provisions cover harms outside the workplace. The Court compared the text of Title VII's retaliation provision to its discrimination provision and noted that the retaliation provision did not contain the words "terms, conditions or privileges." This omission, the Court reasoned, evinced congressional intent to provide protection.

---

4 Faragher v. City of Boca Raton, 524 U.S. 775 (1998); Burlington Indus., Inc. v. Ellerth, 524 U.S. 742 (1998).

5 42 U.S.C.A. § 2000e–3(a).

6 548 U.S. 53 (2006).

7 Burlington N. & Santa Fe Ry. Co. v. White, 548 U.S. 53, 59 (2006).

The Court noted that limiting the retaliation provision to workplace harms would not accomplish the purpose of the provision, which is unfettered access to the discrimination statutes' remedial provisions. The Court cited several examples of harm outside the workplace that would be retaliation, including filing false criminal charges against an employee. However, it is unclear whether this portion of the opinion is dicta because it was not essential to the ultimate judgment in the case.

The Court continued by addressing the level of harm required to trigger protection. It held that harm must be "materially adverse." An employee presents an actionable claim if the negative consequence would dissuade a reasonable person from complaining about the alleged discrimination. Actionable conduct must rise above "normally petty slights, minor annoyances, and simple lack of good manners."[8]

The Supreme Court stated that the reasonable person standard was an objective one. However, the Supreme Court later provided examples that suggest that the objective standard also includes considering some of the circumstances of the plaintiff. The Court indicated as follows:

> We phrase the standard in general terms because the significance of any given act of retaliation will often depend upon the particular circumstances. Context matters. The real social impact of workplace behavior often depends on a constellation of surrounding circumstances, expectations, and relationships which are not fully captured by a simple recitation of the words used or the physical acts performed. A schedule change in an employee's work schedule may make little difference to many workers, but may matter enormously to a young mother with school-age children. A supervisor's refusal to invite an employee to lunch is normally trivial, a nonactionable petty slight. But to retaliate by excluding an employee from a weekly training lunch that contributes significantly to the employee's professional advancement might well deter a reasonable employee from complaining about discrimination.[9]

The Court held that reassignment of a worker to a job with significantly more onerous duties was materially adverse treatment even though the reassignment resulted in no loss of wages or other tangible benefits. Likewise, the plaintiff could maintain a retaliation claim for her suspension without pay, even though the employer eventually awarded her backpay.

It can be difficult to determine when differences go beyond the "innocuous," and become serious enough to trigger liability. Terminations, demotions, and refusal to grant a promotion are actionable. Work place aesthetics, office locations, allocations of breaks, routine and temporary assignment of job duties within a worker's general job description typically will not be actionable discrimination. By contrast regular assignment of dangerous or unpleasant tasks, such as cleaning toilets or climbing into dangerous places could be "discrimination."[10] If the employer improperly files a lawsuit against the employee, this also is actionable conduct.[11]

---

[8] *Burlington Northern*, 548 U.S. at 68.

[9] *Burlington Northern*, 548 U.S. at 69 (internal citations omitted).

[10] Morales-Vallellanes v. Potter, 605 F.3d 27 (1st Cir. 2010).

[11] Patterson v. N. Cent. Tel. Co-op. Corp., No. 2:11-CV-00115, 2014 WL 5322937, at *10 (M.D. Tenn. Oct. 17, 2014); Gliatta v. Tectum, Inc., 211 F.Supp.2d 992, 1009 (S.D. Ohio 2002); Gill v. Rinker Materials Corporation, 2003 WL 749911 at *5 (E.D. Tenn. Feb. 24, 2003).

Some courts have held that negative evaluations, threats of termination, and shift changes do not rise to the level of actionable retaliation, even if these events happen in response to protected activity. Other courts have held that such conduct is actionable.

Unlawful retaliation can include conduct that occurs after the plaintiff has ceased working for the defendant.[12]

In some instances discrimination against an individual for the protected activity of others is proscribed, even though the plaintiff himself did not file or support a charge of discrimination. In *Thompson v. North American Stainless, LP*,[13] the plaintiff filed a retaliation claim when he was fired after his fiancée filed a sex discrimination charge against their mutual employer. The Court held that the plaintiff stated a claim because his discharge could reasonably dissuade his co-workers, including his fiancée, from filing charges or supporting protected activity. The Court noted: "[F]iring a close family member will almost always meet this standard [of dissuading a reasonable employee from making or supporting a charge], and inflicting a milder reprisal on a mere acquaintance will almost never do so, but beyond that we are reluctant to generalize."

§ 10.03 Protected Activity, Generally

There are two classes of activity protected by the statutes. The first is participation in enforcement proceedings ("participation clause"). The second protects unofficial, more informal, opposition to practices made illegal by the statutes ("opposition clause"). It is important to distinguish between "participation" and "opposition" because "participation" receives more complete, if not absolute, protection, while protection for "opposition" is qualified.

§ 10.04 Participation

Actions classified as "participation" receive complete or nearly complete protection against workplace retaliation.[14]

There is currently a disagreement in the circuits about how complete the protection for participation conduct should be. Some circuits absolutely protect participation conduct.[15] "Protection is not lost if the employee is wrong on the merits of the charge, . . . nor is protection lost if the contents of the charge are malicious or defamatory as well as wrong."[16]

The idea underlying absolute protection for participation conduct is that the statutes rely heavily on workers initiating and participating in the EEOC and court processes. It is often difficult to determine whether an employee is telling the truth when the underlying facts are disputed, especially given that very few employers admit discrimination. For courts granting absolute protection, the focus is on encouraging workers to use the administrative process.

---

12 Patterson v. N. Cent. Tel. Co-op. Corp., No. 2:11-CV-00115, 2014 WL 5322937, at *11 (M.D. Tenn. Oct. 17, 2014).

13 562 U.S. 170 (2011).

14 Pettway v. American Cast Iron Pipe Co., 411 F.2d 998 (5th Cir. 1969).

15 *Pettway*, 411 F.2d at 1007; Booker v. Brown & Williamson Tobacco Co., 879 F.2d 1304, 1312 (6th Cir. 1989); Womack v. Munson, 619 F.2d 1292, 1298 (8th Cir. 1980); *but see* Gilooly v. Missouri Dept. of Health & Senior Services, 421 F.3d 734, 740 (8th Cir. 2005).

16 Johnson v. University of Cincinnati, 215 F.3d 561, 582 (6th Cir. 2000); *see also* Slagle v. Cty. of Clarion, 435 F.3d 262, 268 (3d Cir. 2006).

However, some courts hold that an employee should not be protected if the employee files false charges, lies to an investigator, or defames co-employees.[17]

Participation conduct does not insulate an employee from subsequent negative actions, if those actions are not taken because of the protected activity. As one court noted: "[T]he fact an employee files a complaint or a charge does not create any right on the part of the employee to miss work, fail to perform assigned work, or leave work without notice, unless absence from work is necessitated by proceedings that occur subsequent to the filing of a complaint or charge."[18]

§ 10.05 Examples of Participation

The participation clause protects all aspects of the official proceedings under the federal discrimination statutes. Some examples of participation include filing a Charge of Discrimination, giving information to the EEOC, filing a complaint in court, providing information in pre-trial discovery, and giving trial testimony.[19] Soliciting support of co-workers to join in an EEOC charge or in a private class-action suit is "participation."[20]

Charging parties are not the only ones who can engage in participation conduct. Non-charging parties who participate in official proceedings are also included. Participation conduct includes employees named as voluntary witnesses who never testify and workers who tell their employers they will "tell the truth" if called to testify.[21]

Filing charges and participation in state statutory proceedings is considered "participation."[22]

As of the writing of this book, it is unclear whether internal employer investigations count as participation conduct. Some courts have held that internal investigations that pre-date the formal invocation of EEOC or state processes are not participation conduct.[23] However, it is clear that when employees participate in such investigations, they are engaging in opposition conduct.[24]

Copying of confidential information in advance of possible litigation may not be protected. In *McKennon v. Nashville Banner Pub. Co.*[25] the employer alleged that a worker copied confidential information and took it home and that such conduct was a terminable offense that should cut off the employer's liability for any alleged discrimination. Even though the employee claimed that she took the information home

---

[17] Hatmaker v. Mem'l Med. Ctr., 619 F.3d 741, 745 (7th Cir. 2010).

[18] Booker v. Brown & Williamson Tobacco Co., 879 F.2d 1304, 1312 (6th Cir. 1989) (internal citations omitted).

[19] Hajjar-Nejad v. George Washington Univ., 873 F.Supp.2d 1, 22 (D. D.C. 2012); *see also Booker*, 879 F.2d at 1312; Pettway v. American Cast Iron Pipe Co., 411 F.2d 998 (5th Cir. 1960).

[20] Jute v. Hamilton Sundstrand Corp., 420 F.3d 166, 174 (2d Cir. 2005); Crevier-Gerukos v. Eisai, Inc., No. CV H-11-0434, 2013 WL 12137089, at *6 (S.D. Tex. June 24, 2013); Hutchins v. DirecTV Customer Serv., Inc., No. 1:11-CV-422-REB, 2014 WL 3572045, at *10 (D. Idaho July 21, 2014).

[21] Carpenter v. Mississippi Valley State Univ., 807 F. Supp. 2d 570, 593 (N.D. Miss. 2011).

[22] Klat v. Mitchell Repair Information Co., LLC, 2011 WL 13240301, at *4 (S.D. Cal. April 29, 2011); EEOC v. Kallir, Philips, Ross, Inc., 401 F.Supp. 66 (S.D.N.Y. 1975), supplemented 420 F.Supp. 919 (S.D.N.Y. 1976), affirmed 559 F.2d 1203 (2d Cir. 1977).

[23] Hatmaker v. Mem'l Med. Ctr., 619 F.3d 741, 747 (7th Cir. 2010).

[24] Clark Cty. Sch. Dist. v. Breeden, 532 U.S. 268 (2001); EEOC v. Total Sys. Servs., Inc., 221 F.3d 1171 (11th Cir. 2000).

[25] 513 U.S. 352 (1995).

in anticipation of a future discrimination lawsuit, the Supreme Court held that her conduct could limit her recovery in her discrimination suit.

If an individual threatens to file an EEOC charge, it is unclear whether the threat itself is participation conduct. Some courts have held that such threats are protected "opposition."[26] However, others have held that expressing an intent to file an EEOC charge is participation conduct because it is sufficiently connected to EEOC charge filing.[27]

In some instances, non-participation may be actionable. For example, if an employer as part of an EEOC investigation or related court proceedings asks a worker to sign an affidavit or endorse a report that contains untrue statements, the employee's refusal to do so may be protected participation conduct.[28]

§ 10.06 Opposition, Generally

Federal discrimination statutes make it illegal to discriminate against any individual "because he has opposed any practice made an unlawful employment practice" by the statutes. A person may engage in opposition conduct, even if that person is not affected by the conduct about which he complains. For example, a male employee would be engaging in opposition conduct if he complained about discriminatory hiring criteria being applied to women.

The Supreme Court has defined opposition conduct in the following way:

> "Oppose" goes beyond "active, consistent" behavior in ordinary discourse, where we would naturally use the word to speak of someone who has taken no action at all to advance a position beyond disclosing it. Countless people were known to "oppose" slavery before Emancipation, or are said to "oppose" capital punishment today, without writing public letters, taking to the streets, or resisting the government. And we would call it "opposition" if an employee took a stand against an employer's discriminatory practices not by "instigating" action, but by standing pat, say, by refusing to follow a supervisor's order to fire a junior worker for discriminatory reasons. There is, then, no reason to doubt that a person can "oppose" by responding to someone else's question just as surely as by provoking the discussion[.][29]

Unlike "participation," "opposition" is not absolutely privileged but is analyzed in terms of reasonableness. Reasonableness is judged in three different contexts. First, the opposition conduct itself must be reasonable. For example, if an employee throws a chair at his supervisor to oppose unlawful discrimination, the employee would not be protected because the form of protest is not reasonable. Second, the conduct or speech must reasonably communicate to an employer that the employee is opposing discrimination. Finally, the employee must have a reasonable belief that the conduct she complained about violates the federal discrimination statutes.

---

[26] Keenan v. Shinseki, 2012 WL 6628923, at *4 (E.D. Cal. Dec. 19, 2012); Dreshman v. Henry Clay Villa, 733 F.Supp.2d 597, 618 (W.D. Penn. 2010); Booker v. Brown & Williamson Tobacco Co., 879 F.2d 1304, 1313 n.3 (6th Cir. 1989); EEOC v. Johnson Co., No. 1-75-CIV 317, 1978 WL 197, at *1 (D. Minn. Apr. 27, 1978).

[27] Croushorn v. Bd. of Trustees of Univ. of Tenn., 518 F. Supp. 9 (M.D. Tenn. 1980).

[28] Merkel v. Scovill, Inc., 787 F.2d 174, 179 (6th Cir. 1986).

[29] Crawford v. Metro. Gov't of Nashville & Davidson Cty., Tenn., 555 U.S. 271, 277–78 (2009) (internal citations omitted).

§ 10.07 Opposition, Reasonable Conduct

To be protected, an employee must engage in reasonable opposition conduct. Reasonable opposition conduct includes "utilizing informal grievance procedures as well as staging informal protests and voicing one's opinions in order to bring attention to an employer's discriminatory activities."[30]

The right to oppose is not absolute. In some circumstances, the form of the employee's conduct will not be reasonable and will not be protected. Courts apply a balancing tests that considers "the employer's recognized, legitimate need to maintain an orderly workplace and to protect confidential business and client information, and the equally compelling need of employees to be properly safeguarded against retaliatory actions."[31] For example, a plaintiff did not engage in protected activity when she sent emails from work to her personal email to preserve them when some of the emails did not relate to the underlying claims and also contained private information.[32] However, an employee who discreetly obtained a copy of her job description from a customer was engaged in reasonable conduct.[33] Violent conduct often is not protected.[34]

Spoken or written opposition will not lose protection simply because the accusation is inaccurate. If the statement opposing a practice is made in good faith and based on a reasonable belief that the statute is being violated, the opposition will be protected against retaliation. However, if the employee knowingly makes a false allegation, this will not be protected.[35]

Although strident language is often protected, threats of physical violence typically are not. The line separating strong, but protected, language and unprotected language is not well defined.[36]

§ 10.08 Opposition, Reasonable Communication

The speech or conduct of an employee must reasonably communicate opposition. In other words, a "reasonable employer would have understood [them] to be an expression of opposition *to unlawful discrimination* at work."[37]

For example, in one case, an employee alleged that he engaged in opposition conduct by taking notes. The court held the activity was not protected because the note-taking "had no racial element, and no reasonable employer would have understood it to be an expression of opposition to unlawful discrimination."[38] In another case, the court found against the plaintiff because she complained about another's employee's yelling, but did

---

[30] Cumbie v. Gen. Shale Brick, Inc., 302 F. App'x 192, 194 (4th Cir. 2008) (internal citations omitted).

[31] Armstrong v. Whirlpool Corp., 363 F. App'x 317, 331 (6th Cir. 2010) (internal citations omitted).

[32] Aldrich v. Rural Health Servs. Consortium, Inc., 579 F. App'x 335, 337 (6th Cir. 2014).

[33] EEOC v. Kallir, Philips, Ross, Inc., 401 F.Supp. 66 (S.D.N.Y. 1975).

[34] Green v. McDonnell Douglas Corp., 463 F.2d 337, 341 (8th Cir. 1972), *reversed on other grounds* 411 U.S. 792, 93 S.Ct. 1817 (1973).

[35] Villa v. CavaMezze Grill, LLC, 858 F.3d 896, 901 (4th Cir. 2017); Payne v. WS Servs., LLC, 216 F. Supp. 3d 1304, 1318 (W.D. Okla. 2016).

[36] Argyropoulos v. City of Alton, 539 F.3d 724 (7th Cir. 2008); EEOC v. Total Sys. Servs. Inc., 221 F.3d 1171 (11th Cir. 2000); Hochstadt v. Worchester Found. for Exp. Biology, 545 F.2d 222, 229 (1st Cir. 1976).

[37] Breeding v. U.S. Dep't of Interior, No. CIV.A. 14–948, 2015 WL 1809977, at *8 (E.D. La. Apr. 21, 2015).

[38] Stewart v. RSC Equip. Rental, Inc., 485 F. App'x 649, 652 (5th Cir. 2012).

not make any claim that the yelling was tied to a protected trait.[39] Some courts refuse to recognize as protected activity general complaints that a supervisor or a co-worker is a bully when the complaints are not tied to a protected trait.[40]

However, the plaintiff does not need to specifically invoke the statutes or file a formal complaint to receive protection. There are no "magic words" required.[41] For example, one court found protected activity when a worker made two complaints "even though the first one was made sarcastically, neither complaint included an explicit demand for the employer to correct the problem, and the underlying complained-of activity would have fallen well short of satisfying the standard for a hostile work environment."[42]

Disputes of fact regarding whether the employee's conduct reasonably communicated opposition to unlawful conduct should go to the jury.[43]

§ 10.09 Opposition, Reasonable Belief

The literal statutory language appears to protect opposition only if it is directed toward a practice in fact made unlawful by the particular statutes. Nevertheless, the courts have not applied the literal language of the statute. If the individual engaged in the opposition does so with a reasonable, good faith belief that the employer's action violates the statute, the opposition will not lose its protection simply because the activity does not violate it. In short, opposition to practices that reasonably appear to the protestor to violate the statute is protected opposition.

Whether an individual's belief is "reasonable" should be given a non-legal construction. After all, it is not reasonable to expect a typical worker to understand the intricacies and reach of the federal discrimination statutes. If a reasonable person would have believed the employer committed the acts being opposed and would have perceived the employer's activity to be within the scope of federal discrimination law, then opposition is protected even though an attorney might conclude that the employer's conduct is legal.

The Supreme Court's decision in *Clark Cty. Sch. Dist. v. Breeden*[44] has confused the reasonableness inquiry. In that case, a woman alleged that she was reviewing job applicants with a male co-worker and her male supervisor. One of the candidate's psychological reports disclosed that the applicant had once commented, "I hear making love to you is like making love to the Grand Canyon." The supervisor read the comment aloud and then stated, "I don't know what that means." The other worker replied, "Well, I'll tell you later." Both men chuckled. The woman complained to her supervisor and others and claimed that the employer punished her for these complaints.

The Supreme Court held that the woman could not state a retaliation claim because no reasonable woman would believe that one comment, not made directly about her,

---

[39] Smith v. Int'l Paper Co., 523 F.3d 845, 849 (8th Cir. 2008).

[40] Conary v. Martin Foods, No. 4:12CV582, 2014 WL 261289, at *7 (E.D. Tex. Jan. 23, 2014).

[41] Martin v. Howard Univ., No. 99–1175 TFH, 1999 WL 1295339, at *7 (D.D.C. Dec. 16, 1999), aff'd, 275 F. App'x 2 (D.C. Cir. 2008).

[42] Johnson v. BAE Sys. Land & Armaments, L.P., No. 3:12-CV-1790-D, 2014 WL 1714487, at *22 (N.D. Tex. Apr. 30, 2014).

[43] Martin v. Howard Univ., No. 99–1175 TFH, 1999 WL 1295339, at *7 (D.D.C. Dec. 16, 1999), aff'd, 275 F. App'x 2 (D.C. Cir. 2008).

[44] Clark Cty. Sch. Dist. v. Breeden, 532 U.S. 268, 271 (2001).

would constitute sexual harassment. Recall that the standard for sexual harassment requires the conduct to be "severe or pervasive."

While *Breeden* is best understood as a case with a limited reach because of its strange facts, some lower courts have relied on *Breeden* to limit the reach of retaliation law. It is not appropriate to require workers to show a legal understanding of the reach of harassment law to gain protection for complaints. This is especially true because many employer complaint procedures encourage workers to complain about conduct prior to it reaching the threshold of being "severe or pervasive" as understood in harassment law. Additionally, harassment law encourages employers to create complaint procedures and in some instances penalizes workers for failing to complain.[45] Ideally, workers would complain early because one of the purposes of the complaint is to stop future harassment.

Courts are divided on whether complaints about an employer's discriminatory treatment against *customers* is protected opposition. Some courts have held the treatment of customers has a sufficient connection to an employee's working environment to be considered a protest concerning terms and conditions of employment.[46] This is especially true when workers allege they faced retaliation because they refused to discriminate against non-employees, such as customers or prisoners.[47]

Other courts have held that the discrimination statutes require the opposition to be opposition to an employment practice.[48] The reasoning of these cases goes as follows. As customers are not employees, complaints about their treatment cannot be reasonably perceived to be an unlawful employment practice.

Some courts have given an exceptionally narrow interpretation as to what a reasonable person would consider unlawful. Based on the fallacious assumption that "all persons are presumed to know the law," one court has held that no reasonable person would believe that a practice violates the law if binding precedent within its jurisdiction had held otherwise. Thus, a black employee could be dismissed for raising objections to racial slurs directed at others because the slurs had not yet reached the level that this particular circuit had considered necessary to constitute a hostile environment.[49]

§ 10.10 Examples of Opposition

Protected opposition can take virtually any form: oral complaints to management officials; circulating, signing or presenting written petitions; statements to the media or third parties; and filing complaints with unions or private civil rights organizations. It is opposition when an employee refuses to comply with a discriminatory order by an employer.[50] Requests for religious and disability related accommodations are

[45] Faragher v. City of Boca Raton, 524 U.S. 775 (1998); Burlington Industries, Inc. v. Ellerth, 524 U.S. 742 (1998); *see also* Deborah L. Brake, *Retaliation in an EEO World*, 89 IND. L.J. 115 (2014).

[46] Wrighten v. Metropolitan Hosp. Inc., 726 F.2d 1346, 1356 (9th Cir. 1984). *See also* Womack v. Munson, 619 F.2d 1292, 1297 (8th Cir. 1980).

[47] Moyo v. Gomez, 40 F.3d 982 (9th Cir. 1994).

[48] Klinger v. BIA, Inc., No. 11 C 05346, 2011 WL 4945021, at *1 (N.D. Ill. Oct. 18, 2011); *see also* Bonn v. City of Omaha, 623 F.3d 587 (8th Cir. 2010); Lamb-Bowman v. Delaware State Univ., 39 F. App'x 748, 751 (3d Cir. 2002) (complaints about inequities between men and women's sports programs was protected by Title IX, not Title VII); Artis v. Francis Howell N. Band Booster Ass'n, Inc., 161 F.3d. 1178 (8th Cir. 1998).

[49] Butler v. Alabama Dep't of Transp., 536 F.3d 1209 (11th Cir. 2008); *see also* Kelly v. Shapiro & Assoc., 716 F.3d 10 (2d Cir. 2013).

[50] Foust v. Metro. Sec. Servs., Inc., 829 F. Supp. 2d 614, 629 (E.D. Tenn. 2011); *see also* EEOC v. St. Ann's Hosp., 664 F.2d 128, 133 (7th Cir. 1981).

protected.[51] Accompanying or giving "moral support" to a co-worker who files a complaint with the employer's human resources office is protected "opposition."[52]

As of the writing of this book, there is a circuit split about whether resisting the sexual advances of an individual at work, without a further complaint, is opposition conduct.[53]

These examples are all bound by the reasonableness requirements discussed in the prior sections.

"Opposition" need not concern the treatment of the individual raising the issue, but may address the treatment of other individuals.[54]

§ 10.11 EEO Officers and Opposition

Employees whose job it is to work on matters related to equal employment should be protected against retaliation for opposition conduct.[55] There is no language within the discrimination statutes that excludes these individuals from protection. Additionally, because the statutes rely heavily on internal employer efforts to prohibit discrimination, it would be problematic if the very individuals charged with this important role were not protected when they performed their job functions. Nonetheless, these employees may not be protected if their opposition conduct is not reasonable.

§ 10.12 Causal Link

There must be a causal connection between the protected activity and a subsequent adverse action. The plaintiff must establish that her protected activity was the "but for" cause of the subsequent action.[56]

In *University of Texas Southwestern Medical Ctr. v. Nassar*, the Supreme Court faced the question of the appropriate causal standard for Title VII's retaliation provision. Under Title VII's discrimination provisions, a plaintiff can prevail by establishing that a protected trait was a motivating factor in a negative outcome.[57] The statute specifically provides that a claim by a defendant that it would have made the same decision on legitimate grounds is no defense to liability, but only affects plaintiff's ability to secure the remedies of damages, reinstatement, and back pay. However, in *Gross v. FBL Fin. Serv., Inc.*,[58] the Supreme Court held that the ADEA requires the plaintiff to establish "but for" causation. The question remained as to whether Title VII retaliation claims should follow the model for Title VII discrimination claims or the ADEA model set forth in *Gross*.

---

[51] Prince v. Illinois Dep't of Revenue, 73 F. Supp. 3d 889, 894 (N.D. Ill. 2010).

[52] Collazo v. Bristol-Meyer Squibb Mfg. Co., 617 F.3d 39 (1st Cir. 2010).

[53] *See* Ogden v. Wax Works, Inc., 214 F.3d 999, 1007 (8th Cir. 2000) (holding that such activity is protected); E.E.O.C. v. New Breed Logistics, 783 F.3d 1057, 1067 (6th Cir. 2015) (same); *but see* LeMaire v. Louisiana Dep't of Transp. & Dev., 480 F.3d 383, 389 (5th Cir. 2007).

[54] Novotny v. Great Am. Fed. Savings & Loan Ass'n, 539 F.Supp. 437 (W.D. Pa. 1982).

[55] DeMasters v. Carilion Clinic, 796 F.3d 409, 422 (4th Cir. 2015); *but see* Rice v. Spinx Co., No. 10–1622, 2012 WL 684019, at *5 (D.S.C. Mar. 2, 2012); Hill v. Belk Stores Servs. Inc., No. 06–398, 2007 WL 2997556, at *1 (W.D.N.C. Oct. 12, 2007).

[56] University of Texas, S.W. Medical Ctr. v. Nassar, 570 U.S. 338 (2013); *see also* Chapter 3 (§ 3.29) for in-depth discussion of this case.

[57] 42 U.S.C.A. § 2000e–2(a); 42 U.S.C.A. § 2000e–2(m).

[58] 557 U.S. 167 (2009).

In *Nassar,* the Supreme Court followed the reasoning of *Gross*. The outcome in both of these cases results from a strange understanding of the 1991 amendments to Title VII. In the case of *Price Waterhouse v. Hopkins*, the Supreme Court recognized that a plaintiff could prevail on a Title VII discrimination claim by showing her protected trait was a motivating factor in the company's refusal to promote her.[59] The Court also held that the employer could escape liability by showing that it would have made the same decision even if it had considered the plaintiff's sex.

In 1991, Congress amended Title VII. In doing so, it did two things. First, it affirmed *Price Waterhouse*'s holding that a plaintiff does not need to prove "but for" cause to prevail. Second, it stated that the Supreme Court was too harsh to plaintiffs when it required a verdict for the defendant if the defendant proved the affirmative defense. Instead, Congress believed that workers should still be able to obtain limited remedies in such cases. Congress inserted a provision in Title VII, making it clear that if the employer proved the affirmative defense, the plaintiff could still win the case and obtain declaratory relief, attorneys' fees, and some injunctive relief.

Congress did not specifically amend Title VII's retaliation provisions in 1991. In *Nassar*, the Supreme Court oddly read this congressional inaction as an intent to impose a higher causation burden on plaintiffs in retaliation cases. Other plausible explanations are that Congress forgot to modify other provisions, that it thought its amendments to Title VII would also apply to the retaliation provisions, or that *Price Waterhouse* would govern.

The Court then noted correctly that tort law often requires a plaintiff to establish causation in fact. It then claimed that absent express statutory change, the Supreme Court should assume that the common law standard of "but for" causation should apply. However, this statement assumes two controversial premises. First, that the discrimination statutes are enough like common law torts that the Supreme Court should use tort law. Second, the Supreme Court failed to recognize that tort law allows for a "motivating factor" analysis and also allows for the burden of proving causation to shift to the defendant in certain circumstances.

The Court failed to consider how tort law responded to the special problem of multiple sufficient causes, a problem that most law students encounter in first year torts through the two fires hypothetical. In that hypothetical, two fires are set on opposite sides of a forest and rush together to burn down a house. If we assume two negligent firestarters (Firestarter A and Firestarter B), requiring the plaintiff to prove "but for" cause yields the strange outcome where neither firestarter is liable to the homeowner. Tort law recognizes the problem with the analytical construct of "but for" causation in such instances. Even though some retaliation cases involve multiple sufficient causes, the Supreme Court decision in *Nassar* implies that "but for" cause model should apply, even though this is not the result that would apply in tort law.

The Supreme Court has implied retaliation protections under 42 U.S.C. § 1981 (proscribing race discrimination) and the federal sector ADEA provision.[60] As of the

[59] *See generally* Price Waterhouse v. Hopkins, 490 U.S. 228 (1989).

[60] Gomez-Perez v. Potter, 553 U.S. 474 (2008) (federal employee ADEA retaliation).

writing of this book, it is unclear what standard applies to those claims, although there is a strong argument that the *Price Waterhouse* standard governs.[61]

Courts also have struggled with defining "but for" cause. "But for" cause is not synonymous with sole cause; however, some courts appear to make the plaintiff establish that her protected activity was the only reason for the decision.

Many Title VII cases involve claims of both discrimination and retaliation. Claims of race discrimination that violate 42 U.S.C. § 1981 may be joined in the Title VII suit. In such cases, judges and juries may be required to apply three different standards for liability: the motivating factor standard for the Title VII discrimination claim; *Price Waterhouse* for the § 1981 claim; and "but for" cause for the Title VII retaliation claim.

§ 10.13 Examples of Causal Link

The "causal connection" can be established by many types of evidence including, but not limited to, direct statements linking the negative outcome to a complaint, a pattern of taking negative actions against complaining workers, giving a false reason for negative actions, increased surveillance or scrutiny of the plaintiff's work, or a close time link between the complaint and a negative outcome.

Plaintiffs often use the temporal proximity between their protected activity and a negative action to establish an inference of retaliation.[62] In *Breeden*, the Supreme Court noted that a 20-month period between the filing of an EEOC charge and the adverse action were not close enough in time to create an inference of retaliation.[63] The longer the time period between the protected activity and the adverse action, the weaker the inference that the adverse action was taken in response to the protected activity. When determining whether the time period is short enough, the court should also consider the time period in conjunction with the plaintiff's other evidence. In other words, longer periods of time between the complaint and adverse activity may support an inference of a causal link, when supported by additional evidence.

To establish a causal connection, there must be evidence that the employer was aware of the protected activity at the time it took the negative action.[64] However, this does not mean that an employee must complain to be protected. The Supreme Court has held that an employee's answers to questions during a company-initiated investigation were opposition.[65]

§ 10.14 Retaliation Frameworks

As discussed throughout this chapter, retaliation claims often focus on three issues: (1) whether an individual participated in protected activity; (2) whether the defendant took an adverse action; and (3) whether there is a causal connection between the protected activity and the negative action. These questions can adequately resolve most

---

[61] *See* Welch v. Eli Lilly & Co., No. 1:10-CV-01705-LJM-TA, 2013 WL 4413323, at *19 (S.D. Ind. Aug. 15, 2013) (summarizing arguments); St. Ange v. ASML, Inc., No. 3:10-CV-00079-WWE, 2015 WL 7069649, at *3 (D. Conn. Nov. 13, 2015).

[62] Clark Cty. Sch. Dist. v. Breeden, 532 U.S. 268 (2001).

[63] *Id.* at 273; *see also* Frazier v. Richland Pub. Health, No. 16–3765, 2017 WL 1311684, at *9 (6th Cir. Apr. 7, 2017) (noting that a two to three-month period could create an inference).

[64] *See, e.g.*, Douyon v. N.Y. City Dep't of Educ., 665 F. App'x 54, 58 (2d Cir. 2016).

[65] Crawford v. Metro. Gov't of Nashville & Davidson County, Tenn., 555 U.S. 271 (2009).

retaliation claims. Nonetheless, most federal courts still distinguish between direct and circumstantial retaliation evidence and use different frameworks to consider these cases.

If plaintiff presents direct evidence in the form of oral or written statements that the treatment plaintiff received was because of protected activity, then the burden shifts to the defendant to prove that the plaintiff would have received the same treatment even absent the improper motivation.[66] If plaintiff does not produce direct evidence of discriminatory motivation, the courts often utilize the model of proof developed in *McDonnell Douglas Corp. v. Green*.[67] It is not clear why the courts need the *McDonnell Douglas* framework in retaliation cases; nonetheless, it is commonly used.

A prima facie case requires facts creating an inference of retaliation. Plaintiff must prove first that he engaged in protected activity. Second, the plaintiff must prove that he was subjected to a discriminatory employment action. Third, plaintiff must establish a "causal connection" between the adverse action and the protected activity.[68] Some circuits also require as a separate element of the prima facie case that the plaintiff establish the employer knew about the protected activity.[69]

Establishing the prima facie case creates a rebuttable presumption of retaliation. The burden of production then shifts to the defendant to articulate a legitimate, non-retaliatory reason for its treatment of the plaintiff. The defendant must support its reason with evidence. Mere denial of retaliation will not carry the defendant's burden of articulating a specific reason.

If the defendant articulates a legitimate, non-retaliatory reason, the burden of production shifts[70] back to the plaintiff to establish either that the defendant's reason is pretextual or that there is other evidence showing that her protected conduct was the real reason for the negative treatment. In the third step, such evidence might consist of proof that the articulated reason was not uniformly applied, that it was articulated at a time or in a manner that would raise questions about its credibility, or that the defendant had indicated a retaliatory animus.

The courts have not adequately considered how the *McDonnell Douglas* test intersects with the Supreme Court's holding in *Nassar*. In *Nassar*, the Supreme Court held that a plaintiff proceeding on a retaliation claim must establish "but for" cause to proceed. *Nassar* is inconsistent with *McDonnell Douglas* in at least two respects. Under *McDonnell Douglas* a plaintiff will win her case if she establishes a prima facie case of discrimination, and the employer fails to articulate a legitimate, non-discriminatory reason for its conduct. This is inconsistent with *Nassar* because it would allow the plaintiff to prevail without establishing "but for" cause. Further, the burden-shifting in step two appears inconsistent with *Nassar* in that it shifts a burden of production to the defendant. *Nassar* held that the burdens of production and persuasion remain with the plaintiff at all times. Despite these inconsistencies, courts continue to use the *McDonnell-Douglas* framework after *Nassar*.[71]

---

66 Spengler v. Worthington Cylinders, 615 F.3d 481, 491 (6th Cir. 2010).

67 411 U.S. 792 (1973). For a full discussion of the *McDonnell Douglas* model *see* Chapter 3.

68 Carvalho-Grevious v. Delaware State Univ., 851 F.3d 249, 257 (3d Cir. 2017).

69 Weatherby v. Fed. Exp., 454 F. App'x 480, 491 (6th Cir. 2012).

70 The burden of persuasion remains with the plaintiff at all times.

71 Bender v. Shulkin, No. 3:14-CV-2595-L, 2017 WL 1156327, at *10, n.7 (N.D. Tex. Mar. 23, 2017) (noting a circuit split about how to incorporate "but for" causation into *McDonnell Douglas*).

§ 10.15 People Protected

By protecting "individuals" the statutes implicitly protect former employees from future retaliation. For example, a defined employer may not give bad references to an individual's prospective employers because the individual had participated in EEOC proceedings or had opposed perceived illegal practices of the former employer.[72] Further, it would be improper retaliation for a person's current or prospective employer to take negative action against the individual because he engaged in protected conduct at a former employer.

The statutes also protect some individuals who face negative action after another person engages in protected activity. In *Thompson v. North Am. Stainless, LP*,[73] a worker alleged that he was terminated after his fiancée (who worked for the same employer) filed a charge of discrimination. The Supreme Court held that a reasonable worker might be dissuaded from filing a claim of discrimination if she knew her fiancé would face retaliation. The Court held that the fiancé could file a retaliation claim, even though his wife-to-be engaged in the protected activity. The Supreme Court declined to provide a bright-line rule regarding which relationships would be protected. It noted that "firing a close family member will almost always meet the . . . standard, and inflicting a milder reprisal on a mere acquaintance will almost never do so, but beyond that we are reluctant to generalize."[74] The Court indicated that these cases would depend on their particular circumstances.

§ 10.16 Proper Defendants

To be liable for retaliation, the defendant must be an entity covered by the statutes, such as an employer, labor organization, or employment agency. Since Title VII, the ADEA, and ADA all require employers to have a minimum number of employees to be covered, employers who do not meet these minimum thresholds will not face liability under federal law, even if their conduct might otherwise be retaliatory. Section 1981 and many state laws do not contain these same limits.

Some of the statutes that contain separate protections for federal employees do not contain a separate retaliation provision within those federal sector protections. Nonetheless, the courts have held that the federal sector provisions' prohibition on discrimination naturally encompasses a similar prohibition of retaliation.[75] Likewise, the Supreme Court has recognized a retaliation action under Section 1981.[76]

§ 10.17 Concerted Activity

Workers also may be protected against retaliatory conduct by the National Labor Relations Act (NLRA), 29 U.S.C. § 157 and 158, or the Railway Labor Act, 45 U.S.C. § 151 (covering rail and airline employees). Although these statutes are not the focus of this book, they often intersect with retaliation claims brought under the federal discrimination statutes. The NLRA prohibits discrimination against employees for

---

72 Robinson v. Shell Oil Co., 519 U.S. 337 (1997).

73 562 U.S. 170, 175 (2011).

74 *Id.*

75 Gomez-Perez v. Potter, 553 U.S. 474, 479 (2008).

76 CBOCS W., Inc. v. Humphries, 553 U.S. 442 (2008).

engaging in any "concerted activity" for their "mutual aid and protection."[77] Concerted activity means activity joined by more than one employee or by one employee acting on behalf of other persons.

Employees are not required to be members of unions or be engaged in trying to form a union to be protected for engaging in concerted activity. Workers presenting job-related grievances to their employer are engaged in concerted activity for mutual aid and protection. Courts construe these protections broadly and apply them to many concerted efforts to improve the terms and conditions of work. Workers have this protection even if their complaints would not be protected under federal discrimination law.[78]

---

[77] 29 U.S.C.A. § 158(a)(3).

[78] Boese Hilburn Electric Serv. Co., 313 N.L.R.B. 372 (1993).

Chapter 11

DEFENSES

Analysis

§ 11.01 Generally

The federal discrimination statutes include several defenses. Many of these defenses allow conduct to occur that might otherwise be characterized as discriminatory.

This chapter supplements the chapter on Scope and Coverage (Chapter 1), which discusses exemptions from coverage. For example, Title VII exempts Native American tribes and bona fide private membership clubs from coverage. Additionally, some defenses are discussed in the context of the proof structure in which they are used. For example, in an ADEA disparate impact claim the defendant might argue that it does not face liability because its policy is a reasonable factor than age (RFOA). In the Title VII context, the defendant might assert that disparate impact liability is inappropriate because its policy is job-related and consistent with business necessity.

This chapter covers bona fide occupational qualifications (BFOQ), seniority systems, the Bennett Amendment, and the national security exemption. The direct threat defense under the ADA is covered in Chapter 8. The *Faragher/Ellerth* affirmative defense is discussed in Chapter 5.

§ 11.02 Bona Fide Occupational Qualification ("BFOQ") Generally

Title VII and the ADEA both allow an employer to explicitly discriminate based on a protected trait, if it "is a bona fide occupational qualification reasonably necessary to the normal operation of that particular business or enterprise."[1] Bona fide occupational qualification is typically abbreviated to "BFOQ."

BFOQ recognizes that in a very limited set of circumstances it is appropriate for a protected trait to play a role in employment decisions. For example, if an employer is hiring for a towel attendant in a gym locker room, the employer may hire a woman to

[1] 42 U.S.C.A. § 2000e–2(e) (Title VII), 29 U.S.C.A. § 623(f)(1) (ADEA).

work in the women's locker room and may exclude male applicants from the position. Nonetheless, the types of situations where such discrimination is appropriate are rare. The courts narrowly construe the BFOQ defense.

Title VII specifically limits the BFOQ defense to sex, religion, and national origin. The statutory provision explicitly excludes race and color from the defense. The idea is that while there may be limited circumstances where sex, religion, or national origin might play a legitimate role in an employment decision, there are few, if any, circumstances where race or color should do so.

While the ADA does not contain a BFOQ defense, other ideas within the statute perform a similar function. The ADA allows employers to exclude an employee whose disability is a direct threat to himself or others.[2] The ADA also only requires an employer to employ individuals who can perform the essential functions of a job with or without reasonable accommodation. These concepts are discussed in Chapter 8.

§ 11.03 BFOQ Elements

The BFOQ defense has three key elements.[3] First, the employer must have a business purpose for the exclusion. Second, the exclusion must be reasonably necessary to effectuate the business purpose. Third, either all or substantially all of the members of the class must be unable to meet the business purpose. In cases involving safety risks, the employer might be able to show that it is impossible or highly impractical to deal with members of the excluded class on an individualized basis. Additionally, the courts have repeatedly reiterated that the BFOQ defense is narrow and will only be allowed in special circumstances.

BFOQ is an affirmative defense, meaning the defendant has the burden of both pleading and proving it. The defendant must present evidence to support its rationale and cannot simply rely on generalized threats or fears.[4] The good faith of the defendant cannot be used to justify a BFOQ.

In cases alleging disparate treatment, it is not appropriate for the defendant to argue that its policy is job related and consistent with business necessity. This is an affirmative defense available to defendants in disparate impact cases. This standard is more employer-friendly and less demanding than the BFOQ standard.

§ 11.04 BFOQ and Business Purpose

To establish a BFOQ, the employer must show that the class-based exclusion serves a legitimate business purpose. Commonly litigated business purposes include safety, privacy, and authenticity.

In *UAW v. Johnson Controls*, the employer had a policy that prohibited fertile women (but not fertile men) from taking jobs with exposure to lead.[5] The company argued that its policy would protect the unborn children of employees from such exposure and from potential birth defects. The Supreme Court considered whether sex could

---

[2] 42 U.S.C.A. § 12113(b); Chevron U.S.A., Inc. v. Echazabal, 536 U.S. 73 (2002).

[3] UAW v. Johnson Controls, Inc., 499 U.S. 187 (1991); Western Air Lines v. Criswell, 472 U.S. 400 (1985).

[4] Teamsters Local Union No. 117 v. Washington Dep't of Corr., 789 F.3d 979, 987 (9th Cir. 2015). *Cf.* Torres v. Wisconsin Dep't of Health & Soc. Servs., 859 F.2d 1523, 1531 (7th Cir. 1988).

[5] 499 U.S. 187 (1991).

constitute a BFOQ. It held that the purpose of an employer's restriction must relate to the worker's ability to do the job.

In *Johnson Controls*, the Court stated that protecting fetuses did not relate to a business purpose. Women should be able to decide whether to work in certain jobs and to make decisions about the impact of exposure to them and their future children, just as the men working at Johnson Controls were allowed to do. The company also argued that it feared potential tort liability from women or their children who experienced birth defects from lead exposure. The Court rejected the company's claim that fear of lawsuits was a legitimate business purpose. The Court indicated that if the company was complying with federal standards for lead exposure, the chance of birth defects and lawsuits was minimal. Additionally, the employer did not present evidence that it had faced such costs.

Courts have recognized safety as a proper business purpose in limited circumstances. For example, there is a long line of cases approving airline policies that require women to transfer to on-the-ground jobs at stages in their pregnancy when the safety of passengers might be affected.[6]

In *Dothard v. Rawlinson*,[7] the Court also recognized a safety purpose to justify a state's exclusion from women in certain positions in all-male prisons. Given the especially hostile conditions of the state's prisons, the Court found that it was a BFOQ for the state to exclude women from certain positions because of a risk to the safety of the prisoners and other guards. Importantly, the safety of the woman herself would not be a BFOQ as Title VII permits women (like men) to make decisions about whether to accept the risks of a dangerous job. However, it should be noted that *Dothard* has unique facts that limit its applicability to other cases. In *Dothard*, the state prisons were inadequately staffed, violated Constitutional norms for a prison environment, and were not structured in ways to promote safety.

Courts have rejected sex-based safety rationales in most other instances. For example, an employer typically cannot use BFOQ to justify a policy prohibiting women from a job because it requires her to work alone, at night, or in a high-crime area.[8] An all-woman prison cannot refuse to hire men in contact positions with prisoners based on a general fear that male personnel will sexually abuse female prisoners.[9]

In *Western Air Lines v. Criswell*, the Court rejected a safety rationale for an airline's policy requiring flight engineers to retire at age 60.[10] The Federal Aviation Administration had rules requiring retirement or transfer for pilots and co-pilots, but those regulations did not cover flight engineers. A flight engineer is a third person in the plane cockpit who would only take over flight operations in the most extreme of emergencies. The Court recognized that safely transporting passengers was a legitimate reason to support a BFOQ. However, the Court found that the employer had not presented evidence that its policy met the final two prongs of the BFOQ affirmative defense.

---

[6] 499 U.S. at 202 (citing cases).

[7] 433 U.S. 321 (1977).

[8] Weeks v. Southern Bell Tel. & Tel., 408 F.2d 228 (5th Cir. 1969).

[9] Breiner v. Nev. Dep't of Corrections, 610 F.3d 1202 (9th Cir. 2010); *but see* Everson v. Michigan Dep't of Corr., 391 F.3d 737, 753 (6th Cir. 2004).

[10] 472 U.S. 400 (1985).

Customer or co-worker preferences are not valid reasons to justify a BFOQ.[11] For example, an airline cannot exclude men from flight attendant positions by arguing that its largely male clientele prefers to be served by female flight attendants.[12] A woman cannot be excluded from an international position because men in other cultures prefer doing business with other men.[13] Cost is typically not accepted as a BFOQ. For example, an employer could not refuse to hire women because it would need to provide bathroom facilities for them.[14]

In limited circumstances, some courts have recognized the privacy of patients or customers as a BFOQ allowing sex-based distinctions in hiring or assignments.[15] These typically involve situations where a position involves intimate contact with a patient, customer, or a prisoner, such as positions that require intimate care or strip searches. However, patient privacy arguments are unlikely to be upheld when other protected traits are at issue.[16]

In limited circumstances, authenticity can be a BFOQ. The legislative history of Title VII recognizes authenticity as a BFOQ for certain acting roles, for fashion models and to enhance a restaurant theme.[17]

§ 11.05 BFOQ and Reasonably Necessary

To constitute a BFOQ, the defendant's policy must be reasonably necessary to the normal operation of that particular business. Courts often consider whether the business reason goes to the essence of the business. This element often involves distinguishing interests that are a core or a central part of the business from those interests that are peripheral.

For example, courts have held that maintaining prison security, protecting prisoners, and protecting prisoner privacy are central to running a prison.[18] However, *Johnson Controls* recognized that protecting employee's unborn children from birth defects caused by lead exposure was not central to the employer's business of making batteries.[19]

In looking at whether a policy is reasonably necessary, courts also consider whether there are other alternatives to meet the asserted interest that are less discriminatory.[20] For example, if a prison that houses women has a blanket rule that no men can work at the facility in any position, this rule would not survive the second element of the BFOQ inquiry because there are less restrictive policies that would meet the prison's interests.[21] For example, the prison could distinguish those positions that require

---

[11] Olsen v. Marriott Int'l, Inc., 75 F. Supp. 2d 1052, 1071 (D. Ariz. 1999).

[12] Diaz v. Pan American Airways, Inc., 442 F.2d 385 (5th Cir. 1971).

[13] Fernandez v. Wynn Oil Co., 653 F.2d 1273 (9th Cir. 1981).

[14] Henry v. Milwaukee County, 539 F.3d 573 (7th Cir. 2008).

[15] *See* Chaney v. Plainfield Healthcare Ctr., 612 F.3d 908, 913 (7th Cir. 2010) (citing cases).*Cf.* Olsen v. Marriott Int'l, Inc., 75 F. Supp. 2d 1052, 1071 (D. Ariz. 1999); *see also* Emily Gold Waldman, *The Preferred Preferences in Employment Discrimination Law*, 97 N.C. L. REV. 91 (2018).

[16] Chaney v. Plainfield Healthcare Ctr., 612 F.3d 908, 913 (7th Cir. 2010).

[17] 110 Cong. Rec. 7232.

[18] Everson v. Michigan Dep't of Corr., 391 F.3d 737, 753 (6th Cir. 2004).

[19] UAW v. Johnson Controls, Inc., 499 U.S. 187 (1991).

[20] Everson v. Michigan Dep't of Corr., 391 F.3d 737, 749 (6th Cir. 2004).

[21] Ambat v. City & Cty. of San Francisco, 757 F.3d 1017, 1030 (9th Cir. 2014).

intimate contact with prisoners and those that do not. An employer could not prohibit women from serving in prison positions requiring occasional strip searches of male candidates if that occasional job function could easily be assigned to others.[22] At times, courts appear to weigh the costs of these alternatives, refusing to recognize a BFOQ when the less discriminatory alternatives do not impose substantial costs.[23]

§ 11.06 BFOQ's Third Element

In most BFOQ cases, the employer must be able to establish that all or substantially all of the members of the protected class would not be able to perform the duties from which they are excluded.[24] In some instances, this is easy to do. For example, if an employer was hiring someone to be a wet nurse, the person would be required to be able to lactate to perform that function.

However, the employer cannot use stereotypes or generalizations to support a BFOQ. For example, if a job legitimately requires a person to be six feet tall to perform it, an employer could not exclude all women from the position. Although most women are not six feet all, some are, and those women should be allowed to apply for and obtain the position. An employer cannot exclude pregnant women from positions because some pregnant women may be limited in performing those functions. To do so would allow the employer to make an inappropriate generalization about pregnant women.

For safety risks, the employer can prevail on a BFOQ by showing that (1) *some* members of the excluded class possess a trait that precludes safe job performance, (2) an inability to perform creates a substantial risk to third parties, and (3) the inability to safely perform cannot be ascertained by means other than knowledge of the applicant's membership in the class, in that it is impossible or highly impractical to deal with members of the excluded class on an individualized basis so as to reduce the safety risk to acceptable levels.[25]

In *Criswell*, the employer had a policy requiring flight engineers to retire at age 60 based on a belief that people at this age are at increased risk for disabling physical issues that might occur during a flight. The airline asserted that there was no way to distinguish between those individuals likely to have such an incident and those that were not, thus justifying the blanket age-based exclusion. The airline's BFOQ defense failed because it did not provide sufficient evidence showing the substantiality of the risk or that there were not other avenues to reduce the risk to an acceptable level (i.e., doing individualized physical assessments).

§ 11.07 Seniority Systems

Title VII and the ADEA specifically allow the employer to take action based on bona fide seniority systems as long as those actions are not taken with the intent to

---

22 Hardin v. Stynchcomb, 691 F.2d 1364 (11th Cir. 1982).

23 White v. Dep't of Corr. Servs., 814 F. Supp. 2d 374, 386 (S.D.N.Y. 2011).

24 Western Air Lines v. Criswell, 472 U.S. 400, 414 (1985).

25 *Id.*

discriminate.[26] The Supreme Court has also upheld the use of seniority systems under the ADA.[27]

The seniority system safe harbor allows an employer to avoid liability for disparate impact based on actions taken pursuant to a bona fide seniority system. For example, assume than an employer implemented a seniority system with no intent to discriminate. Under that system, during a reduction in force, those with the least seniority are fired first. The employer follows this seniority system during a reduction in force with the result that substantially more women are fired than men. The employer will not face disparate impact liability in such a case because of the seniority system safe harbor.

The statutes do not otherwise define what is required to create a bona fide seniority system. The Supreme Court has noted, "Unlike other methods of allocating employment benefits and opportunities, such as subjective evaluations or educational requirements, the principal feature of any and every 'seniority system' is that preferential treatment is dispensed on the basis of some measure of time served in employment."[28] The Supreme Court has indicated "[a] 'seniority system' is a scheme that, alone or in tandem with non-'seniority' criteria, allots to employees ever improving employment rights and benefits as their relative lengths of pertinent employment increase."[29]

In *Teamsters*, the Supreme Court held a seniority system was bona fide under the following circumstances:

> The seniority system in this litigation is entirely bona fide. It applies equally to all races and ethnic groups. To the extent that it "locks" employees into non-line-driver jobs, it does so for all. The city drivers and servicemen who are discouraged from transferring to line-driver jobs are not all Negroes or Spanish-surnamed Americans; to the contrary, the overwhelming majority are white. The placing of line drivers in a separate bargaining unit from other employees is rational in accord with the industry practice, and consistent with National Labor Relations Board precedents. It is conceded that the seniority system did not have its genesis in racial discrimination, and that it was negotiated and has been maintained free from any illegal purpose.[30]

A seniority system can be bona fide even if it perpetuates discrimination that pre-dated the particular federal statute's enactment.[31]

§ 11.08 Bennett Amendment

While Title VII was being debated in the House of Representatives, an amendment was offered to make "sex" a classification protected by the statute. The proposal was accepted without significant comment, and the House adopted the amended bill with no apparent consideration of its relationship to the Equal Pay Act. The Senate began debate of the House version without reference to committee. During the floor debate some

---

[26] 42 U.S.C.A. § 2000e–2(h); 29 U.S.C.A. § 623(f)(2)(A). The Title VII provision also protects employers that make location-based differentials.

[27] U.S. Airways v. Barnett, 535 U.S. 391 (2002).

[28] California Brewers Ass'n v. Bryant, 444 U.S. 598, 606 (1980).

[29] AT & T Corp. v. Hulteen, 556 U.S. 701, 708 (2009) (quoting California Brewers Assn. v. Bryant, 444 U.S. 598, 605–606 (1980)).

[30] Int'l Bhd. of Teamsters v. United States, 431 U.S. 324, 355–56 (1977).

[31] *Teamsters*, 431 U.S. at 353.

senators recognized a potential conflict between the broad prohibitions of Title VII and the relatively precise formulation of the Equal Pay Act. The concern seemed to be that Title VII might be interpreted to restrict or nullify the recently enacted Equal Pay Act.[32] To this end Senator Bennett offered a "technical" floor amendment. That "amendment," named after its sponsor, was accepted without objection and was incorporated into Title VII. It reads:

> It shall not be an unlawful employment practice under this title for any employer to differentiate upon the basis of sex in determining the amount of the wages or compensation paid or to be paid to employees of such employer if such differentiation is authorized by the provisions of Section 6(d) of the Fair Labor Standards Act of 1938 as amended [Equal Pay Act].[33]

The Supreme Court has interpreted the Bennett Amendment to mean that if a pay distinction is subject to one of the Equal Pay Act defenses it will be legal under Title VII notwithstanding the adverse effect of the factor and the inability of the employer to establish the necessity of the factor.[34] Under 29 U.S.C.A. § 206(d)(1), an employer is protected from Title VII liability if compensation decisions are based on a bona fide (1) a seniority system; (2) a merit system; (3) a system which measures earnings by quantity or quality of production; (4) or a differential based on any other factor other than sex.

The Supreme Court has held that a woman proceeding on a Title VII disparate treatment claim for sex-based compensation discrimination does not have to show that she performed equal work as a similarly situated male comparator as required under the Equal Pay Act.[35]

§ 11.09 Title VII and National Security

Some jobs require that a person have a security clearance from the federal government. This requirement may impact workers based on race or national origin. For example, security clearance rules may prohibit granting a security clearance to people who have close relatives living in countries that are hostile to the United States.[36] Nonetheless, Title VII specifically permits employers to refuse employment if the position or access to the premises requires the individual to have a federal security clearance, and the individual is unable to obtain the necessary clearance.[37] The provision allows an employer to refuse to hire or terminate an individual if the person does not meet a requirement imposed by a statute or an executive order in the interest of national security.

However, some courts recognize a Title VII claim if an employer knowingly submits false information about an employee based on a person's protected trait and that false information results in the denial of a security clearance.[38]

---

[32] County of Washington v. Gunther, 452 U.S. 161 (1981).

[33] 42 U.S.C.A. § 2000e–2(h).

[34] County of Washington v. Gunther, 452 U.S. 161 (1981).

[35] *Id.*

[36] *See* Molerio v. Federal Bureau of Investigation, 749 F.2d 815 (D.C. Cir. 1984).

[37] 42 U.S.C.A. § 2000e–2(g).

[38] Rattigan v. Holder, 689 F.3d 764, 771 (D.C. Cir. 2012).

Chapter 12

REMEDIES

Analysis

§ 12.01 Introduction

This Chapter considers the remedies available under Title VII, the ADA, the ADEA and 42 U.S.C.A. Section 1981. It begins by focusing on Title VII remedies. Title VII provides the best template for discussing the remedies available in the other statutory regimes. Remedies available under the ADA are essentially the same as those found within Title VII.

The ADEA and Section 1981 have very different remedy regimes. The ADEA has a more restrictive set of remedies than Title VII, and the Section 1981 regime is less restrictive. ADEA and Section 1981 remedies are easiest to understand by contrasting them with the remedies available under Title VII. Additionally, the remedies available to people who prevail against a government employer may be different than those available against a private employer. This chapter first provides an overview of remedies available under Title VII against a private employer and then describes how remedies under other regimes or against government employers differ.

Title VII provides for numerous, potential remedies after proof of a statutory violation: (1) back pay; (2) retroactive seniority; (3) reinstatement, (4) front pay; (5) injunctive relief; (6) declaratory relief; (7) certain kinds of compensatory damages; and (8) punitive damages.

Prevailing plaintiffs are generally allowed attorneys' fees under fee-shifting provisions discussed in detail later in the chapter. Prevailing defendants may be granted attorneys' fees in limited instances under Title VII, the ADA, and Section 1981. The ADEA only provides for attorneys' fees for prevailing plaintiffs; however, some courts have allowed prevailing defendants to obtain attorneys' fees in limited circumstances under other fee-shifting statutes.[1]

Pre-judgment and post-judgment interest may also be awarded.

The purpose of the federal discrimination statutes and their remedies provisions is to encourage employers to "self-examine and to self-evaluate their employment practices and to endeavor to eliminate, so far as possible, the last vestiges" of discrimination.[2] The Supreme Court has further noted: "Deterrence is one object of these statutes. Compensation for injuries caused by the prohibited discrimination is another."[3]

One of the purposes of relief under Title VII is to make the plaintiff whole. As the Supreme Court has stated:

> [The] scope of relief under that section of the Act is intended to make the victims of unlawful discrimination whole, and that the attainment of this objective rests not only upon the elimination of the particular unlawful employment practice complained of, but also requires that persons aggrieved by the consequences and effects of the unlawful employment practice be, so far as possible, restored to a position where they would have been were it not for the unlawful discrimination.[4]

Originally, Title VII only provided certain kinds of relief, which the courts defined as equitable relief. Section 706(g)(1) of Title VII, as originally enacted in 1964, provided:

> If the court finds that the respondent has intentionally engaged in or is intentionally engaging in an unlawful employment practice charged in the complaint, the court may enjoin the respondent from engaging in such unlawful employment practice, and order such affirmative action as may be appropriate, which may include reinstatement or hiring of employees, with or without back pay (payable by the employer, employment agency, or labor organization, as the case may be, responsible for the unlawful employment practice).

This language provides that a respondent is liable for "intentionally" engaging in unlawful employment practices. This language does not mean that a person must act with specific intent or a particular kind of animus to create liability. Instead

---

1 29 U.S.C.A. § 216; E.E.O.C. v. Memphis Health Ctr., Inc., 526 F. App'x 607, 612 (6th Cir. 2013).

2 Albemarle Paper Co. v. Moody, 422 U.S. 405, 417–418 (1975) (internal quotation marks and citation omitted); *see also* Franks v. Bowman Transp. Co., 424 U.S. 747, 763 (1976).

3 McKennon v. Nashville Banner Pub. Co., 513 U.S. 352, 358 (1995).

4 Albemarle Paper Co. v. Moody, 422 U.S. 405, 421 (1975) (internal citations omitted).

"intentional" means that the employee faced a particular consequence that resulted from volitional, rather than accidental, conduct.[5]

This provision also uses the word "may," which implies that courts have broad discretion in whether to award relief. However, the Supreme Court has significantly limited the courts' ability to deny relief, repeatedly finding that backpay and similar relief generally should be awarded if the plaintiff establishes liability.

In *Albemarle Paper Co. v. Moody*,[6] the Supreme Court addressed when courts should grant backpay. In that case, the trial court found that the defendant engaged in race discrimination, but did not order backpay because it found no bad faith. The Supreme Court held that generally courts should award backpay. Although backpay is not a mandatory remedy under Title VII, this does not mean that the trial court has unfettered discretion to grant or deny it. The Court looked to the purposes of Title VII, including achieving equality in employment opportunities, removing unnecessary barriers, providing incentives for employers to review and revise their employment practices, and making victims of employment discrimination whole. If the trial court is to limit or deny remedies of hiring, reinstatement, back wages, interest on back wages, and seniority, it must carefully articulate its reasons for doing so, and the denial will be "permissible only for reasons which, applied generally, would not frustrate the central purposes of eradicating discrimination throughout the economy and making persons whole for the injuries suffered through past discrimination."[7]

Title VII also allows the courts to grant "any other equitable relief the court deems appropriate."[8]

§ 12.02 Backpay

Backpay is the amount of lost wages and other benefits from the time of the discriminatory act until the date judgment is entered.[9] In *Albemarle Paper Co. v. Moody*[10] held that generally a court should grant backpay when the plaintiff establishes a violation of Title VII.[11] If the trial court denies backpay, the trial court is required to provide the reason for doing so. Additionally, denial will be "permissible only for reasons which, applied generally, would not frustrate the central purposes of eradicating discrimination throughout the economy and making persons whole for the injuries suffered through past discrimination."[12]

However, the Supreme Court also has given guidance about the limited circumstances where denying backpay would be warranted.[13] In *Los Angeles Dept. of Water & Power v. Manhart,* the Supreme Court held that retroactive monetary relief was not appropriate.[14] In that case, an employer required female employees to pay more into

---

5 *Albemarle*, 422 U.S. at 422.

6 422 U.S. 405 (1975).

7 *Id.* at 421.

8 118 Cong. Rec. 7168 (1972).

9 Pollard v. E.I. du Pont de Nemours & Co., 532 U.S. 843, 850 (2001) (indicating that in some instances backpay may extend past the date of judgment).

10 422 U.S. 405 (1975).

11 Los Angeles, Dept. of Water & Power v. Manhart, 435 U.S. 702 (1978).

12 *Albemarle*, 422 U.S. at 421.

13 Arizona Governing Committee v. Norris, 463 U.S. 1073 (1983).

14 City of Los Angeles, Dep't of Water & Power v. Manhart, 435 U.S. 702, 719 (1978).

their pension funds given that women statistically outlive men. The Supreme Court held that these unequal payments violated Title VII as the women were being required to pay more because of their sex. Many of the women would not outlive their male counterparts, and the Court held that it was not permissible to treat all women collectively as if they would live longer. Although the Court noted that monetary relief is typically appropriate, it held such relief was not appropriate in this particular case. The legal issue presented in the case was complex, and there was not a legal consensus on the correct outcome. Importantly, retroactive liability would be financially disastrous for many pension plans.[15]

Backpay may be awarded even if the plaintiff cannot prove it with exact, mathematic precision and uncertainties may be resolved against the defendant.[16] However, a plaintiff may be denied relief if she fails to offer reasonable proof of lost pay or benefits.[17]

Backpay awards in pattern or practice cases work a little differently. In a pattern or practice case, the plaintiff proves that an employer had a pattern or practice of discriminating against workers in a particular group and usually in a subset of particular jobs. A person who is within the identified group during the applicable period is presumptively entitled to backpay.[18] For example, if the case establishes that the company would not hire women as truck drivers, a woman who applied for a truck driver job during the period would be presumptively entitled to backpay. Even if a plaintiff did not apply for the job, she may also be entitled to backpay if she can show that she was deterred from seeking the position because of the defendant's discriminatory practices.[19]

In pattern or practice cases, the defendant may be able to avoid providing backpay if it shows that it would have made the same employment decision absent the discriminatory policy.[20] For example, if a woman applies to be a truck driver but does not have the required license, the employer may be able to avoid paying backpay by showing that it never hired truck drivers without the required license. In this hypothetical lawsuit, women generally may have been affected by the discriminatory policy, but this particular woman was not because she could not meet the minimum requirements of the job that were universally applied.

Backpay is calculated by determining the value of all wages and benefits the plaintiff would have received absent discrimination. Backpay is broad and includes the value of all benefits (such as insurance premiums, bonuses, retirement plan contribitions), including any increases the plaintiff would have received. This amount is determined from the time the plaintiff suffered discrimination until the time the judge enters the judgment on behalf of the plaintiff. Courts have included wage increases, bonuses and promotions where there is a reasonable probability that the plaintiff would have received them in the ordinary course of events. As discussed throughout this chapter, a defendant is not always required to pay the full amount of backpay from the

---

[15] *Manhart*, 435 U.S. at 723.

[16] Hance v. New York Southern Ry. Co., 571 F.3d 511, 520 (6th Cir. 2009).

[17] Szeinbach v. Ohio State Univ., 820 F.3d 814, 821 (6th Cir. 2016).

[18] Int'l Bhd. of Teamsters v. United States, 431 U.S. 324, 367 (1977) (internal citations omitted).

[19] *Teamsters*, 431 U.S. at 367 (internal citations omitted).

[20] *Teamsters*, 431 U.S. at 362.

date of the discriminatory act to the judgment because the statutes recognize several offsets to backpay.

§ 12.03 Offsets to Backpay

Title VII provides: "Interim earnings or amounts earnable with reasonable diligence shall operate to reduce the back pay otherwise allowable."[21] This provision explicitly requires the plaintiff to reasonably mitigate damages. If a plaintiff obtains another position, the amounts earned during the applicable period will be deducted from the plaintiff's backpay award. For example, if a person obtains a job with the exact same pay and benefits the day after being discriminatorily terminated, the plaintiff will not receive any backpay for the Title VII violation. A plaintiff can recover for expenses incurred in mitigating damages.[22]

Amounts received from collateral sources generally are not deducted from backpay. There are exceptions to this general rule. For example, if the employer makes a payment to the plaintiff that it would not have made absent its unlawful action, this payment may be able to be deducted from backpay.[23] There is a split of authority regarding whether unemployment compensation is collateral source income and whether courts have the discretion to set off unemployment compensation against defendant's back wage obligations.[24]

Backpay is awarded to place the plaintiff in the same position she would have been in absent the discrimination. Backpay is not intended to place the plaintiff in a better position than she would have been absent the discrimination. In some circumstances, backpay may not be awarded or may be reduced for periods of time in which the plaintiff was unable to work due to illness, disability, or injury.[25] If the employee would have been laid off or subject to a reduction in force even absent the discrimination, she would not be entitled to backpay for those time periods. Likewise, if the employer goes out of business and would have terminated the plaintiff's employment without pay, the employee would not receive backpay for the period of time when the employer was not in business. To do so would place the plaintiff in a better position than she would have been absent the discrimination.

Title VII requires that "amounts earnable with reasonable diligence shall operate to reduce the back pay otherwise allowable."[26] This means that the plaintiff must mitigate damages by seeking substantially equivalent employment. If the plaintiff fails to do this, the court will not award backpay for the period that the plaintiff failed to mitigate damages.

---

[21] 42 U.S.C.A. § 2000e–5(g)(1).

[22] U.S. Equal Employment Opportunity Comm'n v. United Bible Fellowship Ministries, Inc., No. 4:13-CV-2871, 2015 WL 13649825, at *4 (S.D. Tex. May 19, 2015).

[23] Ramey v. Dist. 141, Int'l Ass'n of Machinists & Aerospace Workers, 362 F. App'x 212, 217 (2d Cir. 2010) (noting trial court has discretion whether to set off); Naton v. Bank of California, 649 F.2d 691 (9th Cir. 1981); Rangel v. El Paso Nat. Gas Co., 996 F. Supp. 1093, 1099 (D.N.M. 1998).

[24] *See, e.g.*, McLean v. Runyon, 222 F.3d 1150, 1156 n.7 (9th Cir. 2000) (collecting cases); Thurman v. Yellow Freight Sys., Inc., 90 F.3d 1160, 1171 (6th Cir. 1996) (holding unemployment should not be used to reduce backpay); Leidel v. Ameripride Servs., Inc., 276 F. Supp. 2d 1138, 1144 (D. Kan. 2003).

[25] Saulpaugh v. Monroe Cmty. Hosp., 4 F.3d 134, 145 (2d Cir. 1993); *see also* Kelmendi v. Detroit Bd. of Educ., No. 12–14949, 2017 WL 1502626, at *14 (E.D. Mich. Apr. 27, 2017) (noting that some pay or benefits might continue during disability period).

[26] 42 U.S.C.A. § 2000e–5(g)(1).

The obligation to use "reasonable diligence" does not require plaintiff to seek or to accept jobs that are not the substantial equivalent to the one unlawfully denied the plaintiff.[27] "Substantially equivalent employment is that employment which affords similar promotional opportunities, compensation, job responsibilities, working conditions, and status as the position from which the Title VII claimant has been discriminatorily [denied]."[28]

To prevent the plaintiff from obtaining backpay when substantially equivalent employment is available, the defendant must demonstrate substantially equivalent jobs were available and that the efforts by plaintiff to secure those jobs were not reasonable.[29] If the defendant establishes this, the plaintiff should not be awarded backpay for the time that she would have been employed in a substantially equivalent job.

Backpay amounts are offset or reduced during periods where the plaintiff is employed, but they may be offset even further if the plaintiff is fired or quits her job in certain circumstances. For example, backpay amounts may also be offset if the plaintiff mitigates her damages by obtaining a new job, but then quits that position without good cause or is fired from the position due to her own misconduct.[30] Backpay would not be offset if the plaintiff lost her job due to economic circumstances.

A defendant may also limit its backpay liability by offering the plaintiff an unconditional offer of reinstatement.[31] If the defendant makes such an offer, its backpay liability stops during the time plaintiff would have held the reinstated position. This is true even if the defendant does not offer the plaintiff other relief she seeks in the lawsuit. The defendant would still be liable for this additional relief, should plaintiff continue the suit and prevail.

§ 12.04 Remedial Seniority

In some discrimination cases, a plaintiff would have accumulated seniority if she obtained or continued in a position. Length of service often affects the benefits to which an individual would be entitled. For example, an employee's number of vacation days or the amount placed in a retirement account may change with seniority. In some workplaces, seniority affects the ability to bid for jobs or the order of layoffs. A prevailing plaintiff will typically be awarded remedial seniority and all of the benefits that would flow from that seniority. Awarding such relief serves the make whole purpose of Title VII because it puts the plaintiff in the same position he would have been in absent the discriminatory conduct.

Title VII explicitly provides that it is not an unlawful employment practice for an employer to apply a bona fide seniority system.[32] In *Franks v. Bowman Transportation* Co.[33] the Supreme Court considered how the remedial provision allowing retroactive seniority intersected with the seniority system provision. The Supreme Court held that the plaintiffs were not seeking to dismantle or alter the terms of the seniority system.

---

27 Pittington v. Great Smoky Mountain Lumberjack Feud, LLC, 880 F.3d 791, 800 (6th Cir. 2018).

28 Overman v. City of E. Baton Rouge, 656 F. App'x 664, 670 (5th Cir. 2016) (internal citation omitted).

29 Pittington v. Great Smoky Mountain Lumberjack Feud, LLC, 880 F.3d 791, 800 (6th Cir. 2018).

30 Johnson v. Spencer Press of Maine, Inc., 364 F.3d 368, 379, 382 (1st Cir. 2004) (noting that trial court has discretion to re-activate backpay).

31 Ford Motor Co. v. EEOC, 458 U.S. 219 (1982).

32 42 U.S.C. § 2000e–2(h).

33 424 U.S. 747 (1976).

Rather, they were seeking remedial seniority they would have obtained under the plan had the company not engaged in unlawful discrimination. The Court held that Title VII's seniority provision did not conflict with the remedies provision.

The Court also held that in most cases when a plaintiff proves a violation of Title VII, the court should award retroactive seniority. Doing so supports the make whole purpose of Title VII's remedies structure. The Court noted that in *Bowman*, competitive seniority determined many aspects of the plaintiffs' terms and conditions of employment, including the order of layoff and recall, the ability to bid for jobs (which affected salary), the length of vacation, and the amount of pension benefits. The Court cited *Albemarle* and noted:

> No less than the denial of the remedy of back pay, the denial of seniority relief to victims of illegal discrimination in hiring is permissible "only for reasons which, if applied generally, would not frustrate the central purpose of eradicating discrimination throughout the economy and making persons whole for injuries suffered through past discrimination."

The Court recognized that retroactive seniority might affect white employees whose seniority would be diluted; however, the majority reasoned that white employees were not entitled to any particular seniority rights and that the public policy interests underlying Title VII justified remedial seniority for the plaintiffs. The Court noted that there may be circumstances in individual cases that would allow a court to modify or deny retroactive seniority. In such cases, the court would need to ensure that the individual circumstances would not thwart the purposes of Title VII, if applied generally.

§ 12.05 Reinstatement and/or Front Pay

A plaintiff illegally denied a position or discharged from her current position presumptively is entitled to the job illegally denied along with any step increases or promotions that would have occurred as a matter of course. In theory, courts have stated that reinstatement is a preferred remedy over front pay. Front pay is an award of damages from the time of judgment going forward for a reasonable period, typically in lieu of reinstatement. In some cases, a court may order both reinstatement and front pay. For example, if a plaintiff can be reinstated in six months, the court may order six months of front pay and reinstatement.[34]

If reinstatement is not feasible, then front pay should be awarded, if doing so is required to make the plaintiff whole.[35] If a court decides to award front pay in lieu of reinstatement, it should articulate the reasons that reinstatement is not feasible.[36]

The First Circuit has noted some reasons why reinstatement might not be feasible.

> Where reinstatement is not immediately available as a remedy, either due to the plaintiff's condition, or due to conditions at the employer that preclude the plaintiff's return (such as hostility of other employees, or the need for an innocent employee to be "bumped" in order to reinstate the plaintiff), front pay is available as an alternative to compensate the plaintiff from the conclusion of

---

[34] Selgas v. Am. Airlines, Inc., 104 F.3d 9, 12 (1st Cir. 1997).

[35] Pollard v. E.I. du Pont de Nemours & Co., 532 U.S. 843, 850 (2001).

[36] Palasota v. Haggar Clothing Co., 499 F.3d 474, 489 (5th Cir. 2007), order clarified (Sept. 27, 2007).

trial through the point at which the plaintiff can either return to the employer or obtain comparable employment elsewhere.[37]

The Tenth Circuit has held that front pay may be awarded in lieu of reinstatement, "when the employer has exhibited such extreme hostility that, as a practical matter, a productive and amicable working relationship would be impossible."[38]

A front pay order may require the defendant to make periodic payments to the plaintiff until she is able to obtain comparable employment. Some front pay orders require the defendant to pay the plaintiff a lump sum amount, representing front pay for a particular period. The period of front pay awarded should represent "a reasonable future period required for the victim to reestablish her rightful place in the job market."[39] The Third Circuit has noted that such calculations necessarily are imprecise and require some educated speculation about the plaintiff's future salary and market conditions.[40]

Title VII provides: "[N]o order of the court shall require the admission or reinstatement of an individual . . . or the payment to him of any back pay . . . if such individual was refused admission, suspended, or expelled or refused employment or advancement or was suspended or discharged for any reason other than discrimination on account of race, color, religion, sex, or national origin, or in violation of section 2000e–3(a)."[41] It was unclear whether courts could order reinstatement or backpay in cases where the defendant engaged in discrimination but the plaintiff also engaged in misconduct. The Supreme Court held that once a plaintiff established discrimination, a court should generally grant reinstatement and front pay, even if the plaintiff engaged in misconduct.[42] Only if the plaintiff would have been discharged wholly apart from the illegal considerations may the court deny reinstatement. [43]

Title VII does not require the court to order the discharge of an incumbent who was awarded the job over the plaintiff, and except in extraordinary circumstances, courts will not do so.[44] However, if there is no immediate vacancy the court should order that plaintiff be offered the first substantially equivalent vacancy that becomes available, and should provide, in addition to back wages, prospective compensation or front pay until the defendant offers substantially equivalent employment.[45]

Although undocumented workers may obtain some remedies under federal discrimination law, a plaintiff may not be reinstated if he is not legally allowed to work within the United States.[46]

§ 12.06 Injunctive and Declaratory Relief

Title VII specifically allows courts to do the following:

---

37 Selgas v. Am. Airlines, Inc., 104 F.3d 9, 12 (1st Cir. 1997).

38 McInnis v. Fairfield Communities, Inc., 458 F.3d 1129, 1145 (10th Cir. 2006).

39 Donlin v. Philips Lighting N. Am. Corp., 581 F.3d 73, 87 (3d Cir. 2009).

40 *Id.*

41 42 U.S.C.A. § 2000e–5(g)(2)(A).

42 McDonald v. Santa Fe Trail Transp. Co., 427 U.S. 273 (1976).

43 *See* Serrano v. Cintas Corp., 699 F.3d 884, 893 (6th Cir. 2012) (discussing pattern or practice remedies).

44 *See* Walters v. Atlanta, 803 F.2d 1135 (11th Cir. 1986) (describing extraordinary circumstances).

45 International Br'hd of Teamsters v. United States, 431 U.S. 324, 367–371 (1977).

46 Hoffman Plastics Compounds, Inc. v. NLRB, 535 U.S. 137 (2002).

> enjoin the respondent from engaging in such unlawful employment practice, and order such affirmative action as may be appropriate, which may include, but is not limited to, reinstatement or hiring of employees, with or without back pay (payable by the employer, employment agency, or labor organization, as the case may be, responsible for the unlawful employment practice), or any other equitable relief as the court deems appropriate.[47]

This section specifically mentions two kinds of injunctive relief: enjoining the defendant from engaging in an unlawful employment action and reinstatement or hiring of employees. In addition, this provision broadly allows the court to "order such affirmative action as may be appropriate" and to issue "any other equitable relief as the court deems appropriate." Title VII specifically grants broad injunctive power to courts, in addition to the inherent equitable power already possessed by the federal courts and most state courts.

Examples of other kinds of injunctive relief include orders requiring defendant's employees to receive anti-discrimination training, requiring the defendant to remove negative items from the plaintiff's personnel file, requiring the defendant to post notices relating to Title VII or the lawsuit, requiring the defendant to monitor and report certain employment decisions, or preventing the defendant from providing negative references about the plaintiff to prospective employers.

If a plaintiff establishes that her protected trait was a motivating factor in an employment outcome, Title VII specifically authorizes the court to issue declaratory relief.[48] In addition, other sources of law provide courts the ability to grant declaratory relief. For example, federal courts may issue declaratory relief pursuant to the Declaratory Judgment Act.[49]

The EEOC "may bring an action for appropriate temporary or preliminary relief" pending final disposition of a Charge of Discrimination.[50]

Title VII does not otherwise address temporary restraining orders and preliminary injunctions because these are granted prior to a finding of liability. Courts retain their general powers to issue such relief. However, as a practical matter, courts are reluctant in many cases to grant such preliminary relief in most cases, especially when the harm suffered by the plaintiff can be at least partially ameliorated through an award of remedies after a finding of liability.

§ 12.07 Compensatory and Punitive Damages

In 1991, Congress amended Title VII to allow compensatory and punitive damages.[51] Prior to 1991, Title VII did not provide for such relief. A plaintiff who prevails on a disparate impact claim may not receive compensatory or punitive damages.[52]

The statute defines compensatory damages in a way that is different than common law definitions of compensatory damages. Under Title VII, compensatory damages do

---

[47] 42 U.S.C.A. § 2000e–5(g)(1).

[48] 42 U.S.C.A. § 2000e–5(g)(2)(B)(i).

[49] 28 U.S.C.A. § 2201.

[50] 42 U.S.C.A. § 2000e–5(f)(2).

[51] 42 U.S.C.A. § 1981a(a)(1).

[52] 42 U.S.C.A. § 1981a(a)(1).

not include backpay, interest on backpay, or any relief allowed under section 706(g).[53] These exclusions are important because Title VII caps combined punitive and certain compensatory damages. As discussed below, the relief excluded from the definition of compensatory damages is not subject to the cap on damages.

Additionally, within the language defining the damages falling within the statutory cap, the statute provides a list of examples of compensatory damages. These include "future pecuniary losses, emotional pain, suffering, inconvenience, mental anguish, loss of enjoyment of life, and other nonpecuniary losses."[54] Compensatory damages also include past pecuniary losses (out of pocket expenses), which are not subject to the cap.[55]

The EEOC has issued policy guidance related to compensatory and punitive damages.[56] The following are examples of pecuniary losses, "moving expenses, job search expenses, medical expenses, psychiatric expenses, physical therapy expenses, and other quantifiable out-of-pocket expenses that are incurred as a result of the discriminatory conduct."[57] The following are examples of non-pecuniary losses:

> intangible injuries of emotional harm such as emotional pain, suffering, inconvenience, mental anguish, and loss of enjoyment of life. Other nonpecuniary losses could include injury to professional standing, injury to character and reputation, injury to credit standing, loss of health, and any other nonpecuniary losses that are incurred as a result of the discriminatory conduct.[58]

Like in other contexts, the plaintiff must establish she is entitled to such damages by presenting evidence. Expert testimony is not required to establish compensatory damages, but is often used.

The purpose of punitive damages is to punish the defendant and to deter future discriminatory behavior by both this defendant and by others. A plaintiff may only recover punitive damages if she establishes that the defendant engaged in unlawful practices with "malice or reckless indifference" to the federally protected rights.[59]

In *Kolstad v. Am. Dental Ass'n*,[60] the Supreme Court determined the circumstances under which a jury could consider a plaintiff's request for punitive damages. In the case, a woman sued for sex discrimination after being denied a promotion. The Court noted that the structure of 42 U.S.C.A. § 1981a, suggested that punitive damages should only be awarded in a subset of intentional (non-disparate impact) cases. The Court held that a plaintiff is not required to show outrageous or egregious behavior to obtain punitive damages. The Court indicated that the terms "malice" and "reckless indifference" pertain to the "employer's knowledge that it may be acting in violation of federal law, not its awareness that it is engaging in discrimination."[61] The Court clarified that "an employer

[53] 42 U.S.C.A. § 1981a(b)(2).

[54] 42 U.S.C.A. § 1981a(b)(3).

[55] EEOC Policy Guidance No. 915.002 § II.A.1 (July 14, 1992).

[56] EEOC Policy Guidance No. 915.002 (July 14, 1992).

[57] EEOC Policy Guidance No. 915.002 § II.A.1 (July 14, 1992).

[58] EEOC Policy Guidance No. 915.002 § II.A.2 (July 14, 1992).

[59] 42 U.S.C.A. § 1981a(b)(1).

[60] 527 U.S. 526, 529 (1999).

[61] Kolstad v. Am. Dental Ass'n, 527 U.S. 526, 535 (1999).

must at least discriminate in the face of a perceived risk that its actions will violate federal law to be liable in punitive damages."[62]

The Court also noted circumstances under which it would not be appropriate to grant punitive damages.

> In some instances, the employer may simply be unaware of the relevant federal prohibition. There will be cases, moreover, in which the employer discriminates with the distinct belief that its discrimination is lawful. The underlying theory of discrimination may be novel or otherwise poorly recognized, or an employer may reasonably believe that its discrimination satisfies a bona fide occupational qualification defense or other statutory exception to liability.[63]

The Supreme Court also noted that an employer's liability for punitive damages would be limited by agency principles. Agency principles are typically modified in employment discrimination statutes to be a hybrid of common law agency with court-created changes specific to the federal employment discrimination context. Although the Court did not completely describe how agency principles would limit punitive damages, it did hold "an employer may not be vicariously liable for the discriminatory employment decisions of managerial agents where these decisions are contrary to the employer's good-faith efforts to comply with Title VII."[64] Thus, many punitive damages cases require a court to determine whether the employer can be held liable for punitive damages for the acts of its agents under modified agency principles and then, if so, whether the agent's acts are contrary to the employer's good faith efforts.

In considering whether punitive damages are appropriate, the EEOC recommends considering a non-exhaustive list of factors, including the nature of the defendant's conduct and its egregiousness; the nature, severity, and extent of the harm to the plaintiff; the duration of the harm; past instances of discriminatory conduct; whether the defendant planned or concealed the conduct; the defendant's actions after it was notified that the conduct might be discriminatory; and proof of threats or retaliatory action.[65]

Punitive damages may also be limited by constitutional concerns.[66] However, given the explicit statutory caps within Title VII, constitutional limits are rarely imposed in Title VII cases.[67]

ADA remedies are similar to Title VII remedies. In 1991, Congress also approved compensatory and punitive damages under Title I of the ADA and for certain provisions of the Rehabilitation Act.[68] The compensatory and punitive damages regime under the ADA is similar to that provided for Title VII. As of the writing of this book, it is unclear whether compensatory and punitive damages are available for retaliation claims under the ADA.[69]

---

[62] *Kolstad*, 527 U.S. at 536.

[63] *Kolstad*, 527 U.S. at 536–37.

[64] *Kolstad*, 527 U.S. at 545 (internal citation omitted).

[65] EEOC Policy Guidance No. 915.002 § II.B.1 (July 14, 1992).

[66] *See, e.g.*, BMW of N. Am. v. Gore, 517 U.S. 559 (1996).

[67] White v. Burlington Northern & Santa Fe R.R. Co., 364 F.3d 789, 806 (6th Cir. 2004).

[68] 42 U.S.C.A. § 1981a(a)(1).

[69] *See* Kovelesky v. First Data Corp., 534 F. App'x 811, 816 (11th Cir. 2013) (summarizing cases).

The ADA specifically includes an affirmative defense to compensatory and punitive damages in certain failure to accommodate cases. Compensatory and punitive damages may not be awarded when the defendant does the following:

> demonstrates good faith efforts, in consultation with the person with the disability who has informed the covered entity that accommodation is needed, to identify and make a reasonable accommodation that would provide such individual with an equally effective opportunity and would not cause an undue hardship on the operation of the business.[70]

Plaintiffs may not recover punitive damages against the government, government agencies, or political subdivisions.[71]

§ 12.08 Right to Jury Trial and Damages

Prior to the 1991 amendments to Title VII, the statute did not provide a right to jury trial. Due to the original wording of Title VII, the courts have deemed relief available prior to the 1991 amendments to be equitable in nature.[72] Even in modern cases, backpay, reinstatement, retroactive seniority, injunctive relief, and front pay are all considered to be equitable remedies under Title VII, and thus, are awarded by judges, even when a jury is hearing the case. The jury is responsible for determining the amount of compensatory and punitive damages.[73] However, as discussed in the following section, some of these damages are subject to damages caps, which are applied by the judge after the verdict.

A similar analysis applies under the ADA. Under the ADA, if a jury is hearing a claim, the jury determines compensatory damages or punitive damages as defined by the statute.[74] Juries have determined backpay in some Title VII and ADA cases where the plaintiff requested both legal and equitable remedies and the defendant did not object to the trial of backpay to the jury.

In ADEA cases, a "person shall be entitled to a trial by jury of any issue of fact in any such action for recovery of amounts owing as a result of a violation of this chapter, regardless of whether equitable relief is sought by any party in such action."[75] Backpay and liquidated damages are legal remedies under the ADEA.[76]

§ 12.09 Statutory Caps

When Congress added compensatory and punitive damages to Title VII and to certain provisions of the ADA and Rehabilitation Act, it also included a cap on some of those damages. The statutory caps are different than caps found in other regimes

---

[70] 42 U.S.C.A. § 1981a(a)(3).

[71] 42 U.S.C.A. § 1981a(b)(1).

[72] Albemarle Paper Co. v. Moody, 422 U.S. 405, 415–16 (1975); *see* Jarod S. Gonzalez, *SOX, Statutory Interpretation, and the Seventh Amendment: Sarbanes-Oxley Act Whistleblower Claims and Jury Trials*, 9 U. PA. J. LAB. & EMP. L. 25, 62–63 (2006) (arguing that backpay is best viewed as a legal remedy).

[73] 42 U.S.C.A. § 1981a(c).

[74] 42 U.S.C.A. § 1981a(b)(2).

[75] 29 U.S.C.A. § 626(c)(2).

[76] Lorillard v. Pons, 434 U.S. 575, 583 (1978); Sailor v. Hubbell, Inc., 4 F.3d 323, 325 (4th Cir. 1993).

because they apply to both punitive damages and certain compensatory damages. The statutory caps also vary depending on the size of the employer.[77]

The statutory caps do not apply to relief that was previously available under the statutes.[78] Backpay and front pay, are thus, not covered by the statutory cap. Front pay must be distinguished from future pecuniary losses. Front pay is not subject to the cap, but future pecuniary losses are included.[79] Compensatory damages also include past out of pocket costs, which are not subject to the cap.[80]

Judges may not inform juries of the statutory cap.[81] Instead, judges will reduce jury awards to comply with the statutory caps after the jury returns its verdict and when the judge enters the final judgment in the case.

The statutory caps do not apply to claims under Section 1981, the ADEA, or the Equal Pay Act.

Many states have uncapped liability for discrimination claims or cap liability higher than federal statutes. In such cases, the plaintiff may obtain relief higher than the federal statutory caps, if the plaintiff prevails on the underlying state claim.

§ 12.10 Affirmative Defense to Some Damages in Same Decision Cases

In 1991, Congress amended Title VII in a way that affected remedies in certain cases. If a plaintiff establishes that the defendant violated Title VII's discrimination provisions by showing that a protected trait was a motivating factor in the outcome, the plaintiff is entitled to damages. However, if the defendant can establish that it "would have taken the same action in the absence of the impermissible motivating factor, the court shall not award damages or issue an order requiring admission, reinstatement, hiring, promotion, or [payment of back wages]."[82]

In such cases, the plaintiff is still the prevailing party, but the defendant has an affirmative defense that prohibits the plaintiff from receiving the enumerated damages. The plaintiff may still obtain declaratory relief, other injunctive relief, and attorney's fees.

If the plaintiff establishes that a protected trait was a motivating factor under Title VII and the defendant does not prove the affirmative defense, the plaintiff is entitled to normal remedies under Title VII.

This provision does not apply to the ADEA or to Section 1981.

Application of this provision in ADA cases is more complex. The ADA incorporates by reference the Title VII remedies provision, including its reference to 42 U.S.C.A. § 2000e–5(g). However, Congress did not amend the ADA to include the motivating factor language that it added to Title VII. The issue is further complicated by the fact

---

77 42 U.S.C.A. § 1981a(b)(3).

78 42 U.S.C.A. § 1981a(b)(2), (3).

79 42 U.S.C.A. § 1981a(b)(2).

80 42 U.S.C.A. § 1981a(b)(2); EEOC Policy Guidance No. 915.002 § 2 (July 14, 1992).

81 42 U.S.C.A. § 1981a(c).

82 42 U.S.C.A. § 2000e–5(g)(2)(B)(ii).

that the ADA does not use the same operative language as Title VII. For example, Title VII and the ADA use different causal language.[83]

§ 12.11 "Affirmative Action"

Title VII provides that after a finding of liability, a court may "order such affirmative action as may be appropriate."[84]

Title VII also provides that plaintiffs are not entitled to relief simply because the employer's workforce or a union's membership does not mirror the available workforce, in terms of the number or percentage of workers in each protected class.[85] In *Local 28, Sheet Metal Workers v. EEOC,*[86] the Supreme Court held that this provision did not conflict with the availability of affirmative action once the plaintiffs established discrimination. The Court held that affirmative action is an appropriate remedy when there is "persistent or egregious" discrimination or when affirmative action is necessary to dissipate the effects of pervasive discrimination. In *Sheet Metal Workers,* the Court approved a remedial order that required a union to achieve a membership goal of 29% non-white members, based on the percentage of non-white workers in the relevant labor pool in the area. The Court noted that in most cases, such an extreme remedy would not be required because other remedies would make the victims of discrimination whole. It also upheld the remedial order even though it might benefit workers who were not affected by the union's past discriminatory practices.

In *United States v. Paradise*[87] the Court held that "pervasive, systematic, and obstinate discriminatory conduct" by the state employer in refusing to hire minority applicants to be state troopers, justified relief in the form of affirmative action. In that case, the Supreme Court approved a trial court order that required the state to promote a certain percentage of black individuals into officer positions until certain numerical goals were met. The order also allowed the employer to develop its own promotion plan that would not result in a disparate impact based on race. In evaluating the relief, the Court considered the necessity of the relief, the efficacy of alternatives, the flexibility and duration of the relief, the relationship of numerical goals to the applicable labor market, and the impact of the relief on the rights of third parties.

It is unclear to what extent subsequent Supreme Court cases related to voluntary affirmative action and affirmative action in the educational context affect the ability of courts to grant affirmative actions as a remedy. However, from both *Sheet Metal Workers* and *Paradise,* it is clear that numerically based affirmative action cannot be ordered in the typical case. Such relief is reserved for systematic or egregious conduct. Later cases suggest that an affirmative action remedy must not "unnecessarily trammel the interests of white employees." A court may not order the discharge of white workers in order to permit the hiring of minority workers or require the layoff of white employees in order to preserve the jobs of similarly situated black employees.[88]

---

[83] *See, e.g.,* Gentry v. E. W. Partners Club Mgmt. Co. Inc., 816 F.3d 228, 235 (4th Cir. 2016); Lewis v. Humboldt Acquisition Corp., 681 F.3d 312, 320 (6th Cir. 2012).

[84] 42 U.S.C.A. § 2000e–5(g)(1).

[85] 42 U.S.C.A. § 2000e–2(j).

[86] Local 28 of Sheet Metal Workers' Int'l Ass'n v. E.E.O.C., 478 U.S. 421, 426 (1986).

[87] United States v. Paradise, 480 U.S. 149, 149 (1987).

[88] Wygant v. Jackson Bd. of Educ., 476 U.S. 267, 267 (1986).

§ 12.12 Prevailing Plaintiff Attorneys' Fees and Costs

The American rule on attorneys' fees provides that each side in litigation is responsible for its own attorneys' fees. However, fee-shifting statutes often alter this default rule in the context of civil rights litigation.[89] A prevailing plaintiff may recover her attorney's fees under Title VII, the ADA, the ADEA, and section 1981.

The Supreme Court has noted that fee-shifting plays an important role in enforcing federal civil rights, which rely on individual actors to serve as private attorneys general, vindicating both private and public interests.[90]

Title VII provides as follows:

> In any action or proceeding under this subchapter the court, in its discretion, may allow the prevailing party, other than the Commission or the United States, a reasonable attorney's fee (including expert fees) as part of the costs, and the Commission and the United States shall be liable for costs the same as a private person.[91]

The ADA incorporates Title VII's fee-shifting provision.[92] The ADEA also allows a prevailing plaintiff to recover attorney's fees.[93] Although this section focuses on attorney's fees under Title VII, the ADA, and ADEA, 42 U.S.C.A. § 1988 allows an award of attorney's fees for plaintiffs who prevail under other civil rights statutes, including 42 U.S.C.A. § 1981 and § 1983.

The Title VII and ADA attorney's fees provisions uses words like "may" and "in its discretion" that suggest that a court has broad discretion in whether to grant or deny attorneys' fees to a prevailing plaintiff. *Newman v. Piggie Park Enterprises, Inc.*,[94] examined a provision for attorney's fees under Title II of the Civil Rights Act of 1964. The Court held that attorney's fees should "ordinarily" be awarded to successful plaintiffs in all but "special circumstances." *Albemarle Paper Co. v. Moody*[95] in dicta, assumed that the *Piggie Park* standard would apply under Title VII. In *Christiansburg Garment Co. v. EEOC*[96] the Court held: "[U]nder § 706(k) of Title VII a prevailing *plaintiff* ordinarily is to be awarded attorney's fees in all but special circumstances."

A plaintiff acting *pro se* cannot claim a fee as an "attorney."[97] If a civil rights or similar organization represents the plaintiff, the organization can obtain attorneys' fees if the plaintiff is the prevailing party. The plaintiff may also obtain attorneys' fees under the statute if she agreed to pay her attorney based on a contingency fee.

The EEOC may not collect attorney's fees as a prevailing plaintiff. However, the EEOC may be required to pay attorneys' fees to a successful defendant, in limited circumstances. The standard will be the same as applied to private plaintiffs.

---

89 Alyeska Pipeline Service Co. v. Wilderness Society, 421 U.S. 240 (1975).

90 Newman v. Piggie Park Enterprises, Inc., 390 U.S. 400, 402 (1968).

91 42 U.S.C.A. § 2000e–5(k).

92 42 U.S.C.A. § 12117(a).

93 29 U.S.C.A. § 216(b).

94 390 U.S. 400 (1968).

95 422 U.S. 405 (1975).

96 434 U.S. 412 (1978).

97 Kay v. Ehrler, 499 U.S. 432 (1991); Zucker v. Westinghouse Elec., 374 F.3d 221, 228 (3d Cir. 2004).

A party is not required to obtain a final judgment or a ruling on the merits to be a prevailing party.[98] The Supreme Court explained that the "touchstone" for a prevailing party is whether there is a "material alteration of the legal relationship of the parties . . . marked by "judicial imprimatur."[99] Examples of when a plaintiff meets these requirements include when the plaintiff secures a judgment on the merits or a court-approved or court-ordered consent decree or settlement.[100] A settlement that is not court-approved may qualify if the court retains jurisdiction to enforce the settlement agreement.[101]

In *Buckhannon Bd. and Care Home, Inc. v. West Virginia Dept. of Health and Human Resources*,[102] the Supreme Court held that a plaintiff could not base prevailing party status on a catalyst theory. Under a catalyst theory, the plaintiff argued that it was a prevailing party because its lawsuit caused the defendant to voluntarily change its behavior. The Court held that such a result "although perhaps accomplishing what the plaintiff sought to achieve by the lawsuit, lacks the necessary judicial *imprimatur* on the change."[103]

A plaintiff may be a prevailing party by obtaining other kinds of relief. The test for determining whether the relief qualifies varies by circuit. For example, some courts will consider whether the "other court action [is] equivalent to a judgment on the merits or a court-ordered consent decree."[104] The Ninth Circuit asks whether there is a material alteration of the parties' relationship and whether such a change has a judicial imprimatur.[105]

Title VII also has the following provision:

> On a claim in which an individual proves a violation under section 2000e–2(m) of this title and a respondent demonstrates that the respondent would have taken the same action in the absence of the impermissible motivating factor, the court . . . may grant . . . attorney's fees and costs demonstrated to be directly attributable only to the pursuit of a claim under section 2000e–2(m) of this title.[106]

Several circuits have held that a plaintiff need not be a prevailing party to obtain attorneys' fees under this section.[107] It may be more accurate to state that if a party meets the requirements of this provision, that it has prevailed in a sense, because the plaintiff proved that the employer took a protected trait into account when making its decision.

---

98 CRST Van Expedited, Inc. v. E.E.O.C., 136 S. Ct. 1642, 1646, 194 L. Ed. 2d 707 (2016).

99 *CRST*, 136 S. Ct. at 1646 (internal citations omitted) (emphasis in original).

100 *CRST*, 136 S. Ct. at 1646.

101 Corren v. Condos, 898 F.3d 209, 231 (2d Cir. 2018).

102 532 U.S. 598 (2001).

103 Buckhannon Bd. & Care Home, Inc. v. W. Virginia Dep't of Health & Human Res., 532 U.S. 598, 605 (2001).

104 Universal Fid. LP v. United States, 70 Fed. Cl. 310, 314 (2006); *see also* Sole v. Wyner, 551 U.S. 74, 83 (2007).

105 Higher Taste, Inc. v. City of Tacoma, 717 F.3d 712, 716 (9th Cir. 2013); *see also* Doe v. Nixon, 716 F.3d 1041, 1048 (8th Cir. 2013) (using a different articulation to determine whether a preliminary injunction qualifies).

106 42 U.S.C.A. § 2000e–5(g)(2)(B).

107 Peterson v. Bell Helicopter Textron, Inc., 807 F.3d 650, 651 (5th Cir. 2015) (citing cases).

Fed.R.Civ.P. 54(d) grants costs as a matter of course to prevailing party. Costs are paid by the non-prevailing party. Costs may be awarded to prevailing plaintiffs or prevailing defendants. Costs are a statutorily defined set of expenses, such as filing and service fees and deposition costs against the non-prevailing party. Absent unusual circumstances, a prevailing defendant normally will recover these costs, even when plaintiff's action was reasonably based. The *Christiansburg Garment*[108] standard for awarding attorney's fees to defendants is inapplicable to the award of such costs.

Fed.R.Civ.P. 68 provides that if a defendant makes a formal, valid offer of judgment that is rejected by the plaintiff, and "if the judgment finally obtained by the offeree is not more favorable than the offer," the plaintiff "must pay the costs incurred after the making of the offer." In *Marek v. Chesny,*[109] the Supreme Court considered how offers of judgment intersected with the prevailing plaintiff's ability to obtain attorney's fees for statutes like Title VII, ADA, and section 1981 that define attorney's fees as part of costs. The Court held, "Civil rights plaintiffs—along with other plaintiffs—who reject an offer more favorable than what is thereafter recovered at trial will not recover attorney's fees for services performed after the offer is rejected." The Court did not reach the issue of whether plaintiff would have to pay for defendant's attorney's fees, if the plaintiff was the prevailing party, but obtained a judgment less than the offer of judgment.[110] By its terms, Rule 68 only applies when the party who is offered the judgment prevails in the case. Thus, the rule does not apply when the defendant prevails.

Since attorneys' fees under the ADEA are awarded independently of "costs," this difference in statutory language of the ADEA could produce a different result.[111]

§ 12.13 Prevailing Defendant Attorneys' Fees

As discussed in the prior section, Title VII and the ADA use the words "prevailing party" to describe who should be awarded attorneys' fees. In contrast, the ADEA on its face only allows the court to award attorneys' fees to the prevailing plaintiff.[112] However, some courts have allowed fee-shifting to the defendant in ADEA cases in limited circumstances using other applicable statutes.[113]

Because Title VII and the ADA use "prevailing party" language without distinguishing between plaintiff and defendant, it was argued that a successful defendant should be granted attorney's fees under the same terms as they are granted to a successful plaintiff.[114] *Christiansburg Garment Co. v. EEOC*[115] rejected this interpretation. The Court found that there are reasons to grant attorneys' fees to prevailing plaintiff that do not apply to prevailing defendants. When a plaintiff prevails, the defendant has been found to have violated federal law. Plaintiff, however, has violated no federal law or policy by adjudicating, even unsuccessfully, protections created by Title VII. Furthermore, an award of attorney's fees to plaintiffs allows them to secure

---

108 434 U.S. 412 (1978).

109 473 U.S. 1 (1985).

110 Several courts have held the defendant is not entitled to recovery of attorney's fees in such a case. Boisson v. Banian Ltd., 221 F.R.D. 378, 381 (E.D.N.Y. 2004) (citing cases).

111 Dalal v. Alliant Techsystems, Inc., 927 F. Supp. 1374, 1379 (D. Colo. 1996), aff'd, 182 F.3d 757 (10th Cir. 1999).

112 29 U.S.C.A. § 216.

113 E.E.O.C. v. Memphis Health Ctr., Inc., 526 F. App'x 607, 612 (6th Cir. 2013).

114 42 U.S.C.A. § 1988, which governs attorney's fees in section 1981 cases, also uses this language.

115 434 U.S. 412 (1978).

the legal counsel necessary to protect the individual's rights and to implement the public policy advanced by the statutes. Finally, the concept of "make whole" relief supports awarding attorneys' fees to the prevailing plaintiff.

The Court held: "[A] plaintiff should not be assessed his opponent's attorney's fees unless a court finds that his claim was frivolous, unreasonable, or groundless, or that plaintiff continued to litigate the claim after it clearly became so." This standard does not require that the plaintiff initiate the suit in bad faith. As a practical matter, courts rarely award attorneys' fees to prevailing defendants.

While the EEOC may not collect attorney's fees as a prevailing plaintiff, the EEOC may be required to pay attorneys' fees to prevailing defendants in limited circumstances. The standard will be the same as applied to private plaintiffs.

Prevailing federal employees may obtain attorney's fees under Title VII.[116] Federal employees proceeding on an ADEA claim under 29 U.S.C.A. § 633a may recover attorney's fees under the Equal Access to Justice Act.[117]

In *CRST Van Expedited, Inc. v. E.E.O.C.*,[118] the Supreme Court held that a defendant could be a prevailing party, even if the plaintiff's case was not dismissed on the merits. In other words, a ruling on the merits is not a predicate to finding a defendant is a prevailing party. In *CRST*, the Court held that a defendant was a prevailing party when a court dismissed several claims based on the EEOC's failure to investigate and conciliate the claims prior to filing suit.

Fed.R.Civ.P. 54(d) grants costs as a matter of course to prevailing party. Costs are paid by the non-prevailing party. Costs may be awarded to prevailing plaintiffs or prevailing defendants. Costs are a statutorily defined set of expenses, such as filing and service fees and deposition costs against the non-prevailing party. Absent unusual circumstances, a prevailing defendant normally will recover these costs, even when plaintiff's action was reasonably based. The *Christiansburg Garment*[119] standard for awarding attorney's fees to defendants is inapplicable to the award of such costs.

§ 12.14 Calculating Attorneys' Fees

The statutes provide little guidance regarding the amount of attorneys' fees courts should award, other than that the amount awarded be "reasonable." Typically, the trial court determines the amount by first considering the reasonable hourly rate for an attorney of similar expertise in the area. This hourly rate is multiplied by the number of hours that were reasonably expended by the attorneys for the prevailing party. This produces a "lodestar" amount that serves as the starting point for making the appropriate calculation.[120] Generally, the court may refuse to count excessive, unnecessary, or redundant hours.

In calculating the lodestar, some courts use a twelve-factor test that considers the following:

---

[116] Burke v. Mattis, 315 F. Supp. 3d 907, 912 (E.D. Va. 2018); Chris v. Tenet, 57 F. Supp. 2d 330, 334 n.12 (E.D. Va. 1999), aff'd, 221 F.3d 648 (4th Cir. 2000).

[117] Hamilton v. McDonald, 247 F. Supp. 3d 812, 823 (E.D. Ky. 2017).

[118] 136 S. Ct. 1642, 1646, 194 L. Ed. 2d 707 (2016).

[119] 434 U.S. 412 (1978).

[120] *See, e.g.*, Maner v. Linkan LLC, 602 F. App'x 489, 491 (11th Cir. 2015).

> (1) the time and labor expended; (2) the novelty and difficulty of the questions raised; (3) the skill required to properly perform the legal services rendered; (4) the attorney's opportunity costs in pressing the instant litigation; (5) the customary fee for like work; (6) the attorney's expectations at the outset of the litigation; (7) the time limitations imposed by the client or circumstances; (8) the amount in controversy and the results obtained; (9) the experience, reputation and ability of the attorney; (10) the undesirability of the case within the legal community in which the suit arose; (11) the nature and length of the professional relationship between attorney and client; and (12) attorneys' fees awards in similar cases.[121]

In *Hensley v. Eckerhart,*[122] the Supreme Court considered whether a prevailing party could be awarded attorneys' fees for claims on which the party did not prevail. The Court held that if the unsuccessful claim is unrelated to the other claims, the prevailing party should not be awarded attorneys' fees for the unsuccessful claim. However, the Court recognized that the unsuccessful claim may overlap with successful claims in that they rely on the same set of facts or are based on related legal theories. In these instances, the Court stated that it may not be appropriate to separate the attorneys' fee request into separate claims. Rather, the court should view the success of the lawsuit as a whole and award a reasonable attorneys' fee When excellent results are obtained, a full attorneys' fee should be awarded. However, the Court noted that a full award might be excessive in cases where the prevailing party obtained limited or partial relief. In such instances, the trial court may reduce the amount of attorneys' fee awarded. The Court held that there is no precise rule for making these determinations.[123]

Total time expended on issues, including time spent during state and federal administrative proceedings, discovery, trial, post-trial motions, hearings on attorney's fees, appeals and opposition to certiorari may be included.[124]

The court must also determine a reasonable rate for the attorneys' services. Typically, the judge applies the prevailing hourly rate for attorneys in the geographical area who have the background and experience similar to that of the prevailing party's attorneys.[125] This rate is not determined by the rate the client agreed to pay the attorney.[126] For example, a client who agreed to pay the attorney a contingent fee is not limited by the contingent fee in seeking an attorneys' fee award.

Some courts will adjust the lodestar amount by applying additional factors.[127] Some courts have noted that while upward adjustments are possible, they should be rare.[128]

---

[121] Basil v. Maryland Transp. Auth., No. CIV.A. RDB-12-0556, 2015 WL 505951, at *3 (D. Md. Feb. 5, 2015).

[122] 461 U.S. 424 (1983).

[123] *See also* City of Riverside v. Rivera, 477 U.S. 561 (1986) (emphasizing discretion of trial court).

[124] New York Gaslight Club, Inc. v. Carey, 447 U.S. 54, 71 (1980); *but see* Chris v. Tenet, 221 F.3d 648, 653 (4th Cir. 2000) (holding that a plaintiff who does not file suit may not later sue for attorney's fees incurred for administrative action).

[125] Blum v. Stenson, 465 U.S. 886 (1984).

[126] *See, e.g.*, Barrios v. Diamond Contract Servs., Inc., 461 F. App'x 571, 573 (9th Cir. 2011); Sullivan v. Crown Paper Board Co., Inc., 719 F.2d 667 (3d Cir. 1983); Wheatley v. Ford, 679 F.2d 1037 (2d Cir. 1982).

[127] Perry v. Autozone Stores, Inc., 624 Fed. Appx. 370, 372 (6th Cir. 2015).

[128] Pennsylvania v. Delaware Valley Citizens' Council for Clean Air, 483 U.S. 711, 711 (1987) (indicating adjustments for risk are not permitted).

The amount of attorneys' fees awarded may exceed the monetary recovery otherwise obtained by the plaintiff.

A court may also allow additional expenses to be added as attorneys' fees. There is no clear authority as to precisely what items are included in the attorney's hourly rate, and what expense items may be added to that rate. Usual "overhead" items that are not traditionally billed separately to clients, such as salaries for clerical work, utilities, postage, and local travel are most likely to be included in the hourly rate, and may not be added to the "lodestar." However, expenses for which clients are separately charged can be added to the hourly rate. Such additional expenses may include the charge for time expended by law clerks and paralegals for non-clerical work.[129] Title VII and the ADA specifically include reasonable expert fees as recoverable as part of costs to the prevailing party awarded under the statute.[130] 42 U.S.C.A. § 1988(c) specifically allows recovery of reasonable expert fees for the prevailing party, other than the United States, for § 1981 claims.

Costs allowed under each statutory regime are analyzed separately from generally allowable costs. To avoid confusing the two, it is easiest to first analyze available costs under the specific statute and then determine whether additional costs are allowable under generally applicable rules and statutes. Fed.R.Civ.P. 54(d) provides that costs should generally be allowed to the prevailing party unless a statute, the Federal Rules of Civil Procedure, or a court order disallows them. 28 U.S.C.A. § 1920 defines "costs" to include: (1) fees of the clerk and marshal, (2) fees for certain printed or electronically recorded transcripts, (3) fees for printing and witnesses, (4) fees for copies of necessary papers, (5) docket fees, and (6) compensation for court appointed experts and interpreters. The witness fee in (3) above is set by 28 U.S.C.A. § 1821.

§ 12.15 Pre-Judgment and Post-Judgment Interest

Pre-judgment interest is interest on damages that arose from the date of the injury until the judgment. Outside the context of federal discrimination law, the Supreme Court has held that pre-judgment interest is not a separate remedy, but rather is part of make-whole relief.[131]

While courts have discretion on whether to grant pre-judgment interest, generally, courts should award pre-judgment interest on backpay and lost wages awards.[132] The Ninth Circuit has held that in most cases where the court awards backpay, "complete justice" requires an award of pre-judgment interest on that backpay.[133] "The basic

[129] *See, e.g.,* Mid-Continent Cas. Co. v. Chevron Pipe Line Co., 205 F.3d 222, 234 (5th Cir. 2000) (describing non-clerical paralegal work as compensable); Wilson v. Oupac, Inc., 995 F.2d 223 (5th Cir. 1993) (noting that copying and long-distance call charges should be included in lodestar as part of overhead and not separately compensable); *see generally* Gisbrecht v. Barnhart, 535 U.S. 789, 800 (2002) (discussing how lodestar is designed to include overhead and to allow for an appropriate amount of profit).

[130] 42 U.S.C.A. § 2000e–5(k).

[131] State of Kan. v. State of Colo., No. 105, ORIGINAL, 2000 WL 34508307, at *40 (U.S. Aug. 31, 2000).

[132] Pittington v. Great Smoky Mountain Lumberjack Feud, LLC, 880 F.3d 791, 795 (6th Cir. 2018) (Title VII). *See also* Gerstenbluth v. Credit Suisse Sec. (USA) LLC, 728 F.3d 139, 146 (2d Cir. 2013) (noting pre-judgment interest on lost wages under the ADEA should typically be awarded); Williamson v. Handy Button Mach. Co., 817 F. 2d 1290, 1297 (7th Cir. 1987) (same for section 1981).

[133] Clemens v. Centurylink Inc., 874 F.3d 1113, 1116 (9th Cir. 2017).

purpose of prejudgment interest is to put a party in the position it would have been in had it been paid immediately."[134]

The Fifth Circuit has held that pre-judgment interest is not available under the ADEA if the court awards the plaintiff liquidated damages.[135] Courts have awarded pre-judgment interest on lost wages under the ADEA in cases where the court also awarded liquidated damages, arguing that the two forms of damages have separate purposes.[136]

Courts have also awarded pre-judgment interest on compensatory damage awards, which are available under Title VII, the ADA, and section 1981.[137] Some courts have refused to provide pre-judgment interest on compensatory damage awards for non-pecuniary losses.[138]

Courts have allowed pre-judgment interest on attorney's fees, at least in cases where the court used an attorney's past (rather than present) hourly rate in determining fees.[139] Pre-judgment interest is not available on punitive damages.[140]

The rate of pre-judgment interest is not specified in the discrimination statutes. Court have used various methods for determining the rate, sometimes using the post-judgment rate provided in 28 U.S.C.A. § 1961 to pre-judgment interest.[141] However, the Sixth Circuit has held that applying the post-judgment interest rate can be an abuse of discretion when the rate is not adequate to make the plaintiff whole.[142]

Post-judgment interest is allowed under 28 U.S.C.A. § 1961(a).[143] Post-judgment interest generally runs from the date of judgment until the judgment is paid.[144]

---

[134] Pickett v. Sheridan Health Care Ctr., 813 F.3d 640, 647 (7th Cir. 2016) (internal citation omitted).

[135] Miller v. Raytheon Co., 716 F.3d 138, 148 (5th Cir. 2013). It is unclear whether this holding only applies in cases where the court also awards liquidated damages.

[136] Marcus v. PQ Corp., 458 F. App'x 207, 214 (3d Cir. 2012).

[137] Thomas v. Texas Dep't of Criminal Justice, 297 F.3d 361 (5th Cir. 2002); *see also* Idom v. Natchez-Adams Sch. Dist., No. 5:14-CV-38(DCB)(MTP), 2016 WL 320954, at *7 (S.D. Miss. Jan. 25, 2016); *but see* Rodriguez v. Express World Wide, LLC, No. 12 CV 4572 RJD RML, 2014 WL 1347369, at *7 (E.D.N.Y. Jan. 16, 2014), report and recommendation adopted, No. 12 CV 4572 RJD RML, 2014 WL 1350350 (E.D.N.Y. Mar. 31, 2014) (not awarding pre-judgment interest when compensatory damages made plaintiff whole); E.E.O.C. v. Everdry Mktg. & Mgmt., Inc., 556 F. Supp. 2d 213, 223 (W.D.N.Y. 2008), aff'd, 348 F. App'x 677 (2d Cir. 2009).

[138] McKenna v. City of Philadelphia, No. CV 98–5835, 2009 WL 10687501, at *2 (E.D. Pa. July 27, 2009) (citing cases).

[139] Pickett v. Sheridan Health Care Ctr., 813 F.3d 640, 647 (7th Cir. 2016); *see also* Shott v. Rush-Presbyterian-St. Luke's Med. Ctr., 338 F.3d 736, 746 (7th Cir. 2003) (allowing pre-judgment interest on attorney's fees).

[140] Thorncreek Apartments I, LLC v. Vill. of Park Forest, No. 08 C 1225, 2015 WL 2444498, at *9 (N.D. Ill. May 20, 2015), aff'd sub nom. Thorncreek Apartments III, LLC v. Mick, 886 F.3d 626 (7th Cir. 2018).

[141] Norville v. Staten Island Univ. Hosp., 112 F. App'x 92, 95 (2d Cir. 2004); *see also* Hylind v. Xerox Corp., 481 F. App'x 819, 822 (4th Cir. 2012) (allowing use of state interest rate to federal claim); Woods v. Von Maur, Inc., No. 09 C 7800, 2011 WL 6945763, at *2 (N.D. Ill. Dec. 12, 2011) (noting that "back pay interest should be calculated by compounding monthly the prime rate set by the Federal Reserve during the month in which interest is sought").

[142] Pittington v. Great Smoky Mountain Lumberjack Feud, LLC, 880 F.3d 791, 807 (6th Cir. 2018).

[143] Eaves v. Cty. of Cape May, 239 F.3d 527, 530 (3d Cir. 2001).

[144] *But see* Eaves v. Cty. of Cape May, 239 F.3d 527, 530 (3d Cir. 2001) (finding that post-judgment interest on attorney's fee award did not begin to run until amount quantified by court; also citing majority of circuits hold that interest runs from the date attorney's fees awarded, not quantified).

Federal employees may not be able to recover interest in some circumstances.[145]

§ 12.16 ADEA Damages

The ADEA's remedy provisions are modeled from the Fair Labor Standards Act, rather than Title VII. The ADEA allows the following as remedies: (1) back pay; (2) retroactive seniority; (3) reinstatement, (4) front pay; (5) injunctive relief; (6) declaratory relief; and (7) liquidated damages.[146] Generally, backpay, seniority, reinstatement, front pay, injunctive relief and declaratory relief are governed by the same principles that apply in Title VII and ADA cases. However, under the ADEA, backpay is not considered to be equitable in nature. For additional discussion of these topics, see earlier sections in this chapter.

The main sources of monetary relief under the ADEA are backpay and liquidated damages.[147] Compensatory damages as defined under Title VII are not available under the ADEA. Nor are punitive damages. However, a minority of courts (now supported by EEOC Guidance) have allowed a plaintiff to seek compensatory and punitive damages in ADEA retaliation cases.[148]

If the prevailing plaintiff can establish a "willful" violation of the ADEA, the plaintiff is entitled to an award of liquidated damages equal to the amount of back pay awarded.[149]

As discussed in the prior section, pre-judgment and post-judgment interest may also be awarded. As discussed earlier in this chapter, prevailing plaintiffs are entitled to attorneys' fees under the ADEA.

The Equal Pay Act has a similar (although not identical) remedies regime to the ADEA.[150]

§ 12.17 Liquidated Damages Under the ADEA

Unlike Title VII, the ADEA provides for liquidated damages. Successful plaintiffs may obtain liquidated damages in an amount equal to the back pay liability. The ADEA provides that "liquidated damages shall be payable only in cases of willful violations."[151]

However, the courts could not agree on a definition of willful. *Trans World Airlines, Inc. v. Thurston,*[152] resolved this issue. The Court held: "[A] violation of the Act was 'willful' if the employer knew or showed reckless disregard for the matter of whether its conduct was prohibited by the ADEA."[153] The Court rejected the plaintiff's argument that liquidated damages should be available if the defendant is cognizant of an appreciable possibility of an ADEA violation. The Court held that liquidated damages

---

[145] *See* 42 U.S.C.A. § 2000e–16(d); Loeffler v. Frank, 486 U.S. 549, 564 (1988) (discussing pre-judgment interest in context of Title VII); Wagner v. Geren, No. 8:08CV208, 2009 WL 837728, at *2 (D. Neb. Mar. 26, 2009) (same in context of ADEA). Complete coverage of this issue is beyond the scope of this book.

[146] McKennon v. Nashville Banner Pub. Co., 513 U.S. 352, 357 (1995).

[147] 29 U.S.C.A. §§ 216(b), 626(b).

[148] Vaughan v. Anderson Reg'l Med. Ctr., 849 F.3d 588, 591 (5th Cir. 2017) (refusing to allow, but discussing split in detail); Forster v. Deere & Co., 925 F. Supp. 2d 1056, 1060 (N.D. Iowa 2013) (same).

[149] 29 U.S.C.A. §§ 216(b), 626(b).

[150] 29 U.S.C.A. § 216(b).

[151] 29 U.S.C.A. § 626(b).

[152] 469 U.S. 111 (1985).

[153] *Id.* at 126.

could not be awarded in the case because the employer acted reasonably and in good faith to determine whether its policy would violate the ADEA. The Court also noted that liquidated damages are punitive in nature and should not be awarded in every case.

Those federal employees protected from age discrimination under 29 U.S.C.A. § 633a have different available remedies. That section provides that these federal employees are entitled to "legal and equitable relief as will effectuate the purposes of this chapter."[154] Courts have held that federal employees protected under § 633a may not recover liquidated damages.[155]

§ 12.18 Injunctive Relief Under the ADEA

The main provisions of the ADEA allow a court to grant equitable relief as required to effectuate the purposes of the statute.[156] For those federal employees protected from age discrimination under 29 U.S.C.A. § 633a, the statute explicitly states that they may obtain "legal and equitable relief as will effectuate the purposes of this chapter."[157]

§ 12.19 Section 1981 Damages

Section 1981 does not explicitly mention damages. However, the Supreme Court has held that courts may award full equitable and legal relief under section 1981.[158] Section 1981 is not limited by the damages cap on compensatory and punitive damages that applies to Title VII and the ADA.

Section 1981 claims may not be maintained against the federal government.[159]

§ 12.20 Damages Against Government Employers

Title VII provides a separate substantive provision that governs suits by certain federal employees.[160] Federal employees governed by this provision also use a different procedural path to effectuate claims.

Under the federal sector provision of Title VII, the EEOC may enforce the statute "through appropriate remedies, including reinstatement or hiring of employees with or without back pay, as will effectuate the policies of the federal sector provision."[161] The Supreme Court has held the EEOC may grant compensatory damages under the federal sector provision.[162]

Federal sector employees covered by 42 U.S.C. § 2000e–16 that file suit in court may obtain all of the remedies available under Title VII in suits against private employers,

---

[154] 29 U.S.C.A. § 633a(c).

[155] Miller v. Kerry, 924 F. Supp. 2d 133, 138 (D.D.C. 2013) (citing cases).

[156] 29 U.S.C.A. § 626(b); McKennon v. Nashville Banner Pub. Co., 513 U.S. 352, 357 (1995).

[157] 29 U.S.C.A. § 633a(c).

[158] Johnson v. Railway Express Agency, Inc., 421 U.S. 454 (1975).

[159] *See, e.g.*, Matthews v. Shulkin, 698 F. App'x 550, 551 (9th Cir. 2017); Marcus v. Geithner, 813 F. Supp. 2d 11, 19 (D.D.C. 2011).

[160] 42 U.S.C.A. § 2000e–16.

[161] 42 U.S.C.A. § 2000e–16(b). Although generally beyond the scope of this treatise, a similar analysis applies for discrimination claims against federal employers under the Rehabilitation Act. 29 U.S.C.A. § 794a(a)(1).

[162] West v. Gibson, 527 U.S. 212, 217 (1999).

except for punitive damages.[163] Federal employees may not be able to recover interest in some circumstances.[164]

The ADEA also has separate provisions for federal sector employees.[165] Those federal employees protected from age discrimination under 29 U.S.C.A. § 633a have different available remedies. That section provides that these federal employees are entitled to "legal and equitable relief as will effectuate the purposes of this chapter."[166] Courts have held that federal employees protected under § 633a may not recover liquidated damages.[167]

The federal government is not a proper defendant for claims under Section 1981.[168]

The Eleventh Amendment also limits damages against states under the ADEA and ADA. These limits do not apply to Title VII and section 1981. These limits do not limit the recovery that the EEOC can obtain for victims.

When originally enacted, the ADEA only applied to private employers. However, Congress later amended the ADEA to include state employers.[169] In *Kimel v. Florida Board of Regents*,[170] the Supreme Court considered whether Congress abrogated states' Eleventh Amendment immunity when it amended the ADEA. The Court held that the states retained Eleventh Amendment immunity because when Congress enacted the ADEA it did so under its Commerce Clause powers and not under the powers given to it under the Fourteenth Amendment.[171] The Court had previously held that Congress does not have the power to abrogate state Eleventh Amendment immunity through the use of the Commerce Clause.

In a subsequent suit, the Supreme Court held that Congress did not abrogate states' Eleventh Amendment immunity under Title I of the ADA.[172]

The Eleventh Amendment immunity applies to states, their subsidiary units, and individual employees sued in an official capacity.[173] However, the Eleventh Amendment does allow suits for prospective injunctive relief against state officials.[174] A state may also waive its Eleventh Amendment immunity. State discrimination statutes often provide a mechanism for victims of age discrimination to obtain relief from a state employer.

---

[163] 42 U.S.C.A. § 1981a(a)(1), (b)(1).

[164] *See* 42 U.S.C.A. § 2000e–16(d); Loeffler v. Frank, 486 U.S. 549, 564 (1988) (discussing pre-judgment interest in context of Title VII); Wagner v. Geren, No. 8:08CV208, 2009 WL 837728, at *2 (D. Neb. Mar. 26, 2009) (same in context of ADEA). Complete coverage of this issue is beyond the scope of this book.

[165] 29 U.S.C.A. § 633a(b).

[166] 29 U.S.C.A. § 633a(c).

[167] Miller v. Kerry, 924 F. Supp. 2d 133, 138 (D.D.C. 2013) (citing cases).

[168] Khaksari v. Chairman, Broad. Bd. of Governors, 451 F. App'x 1, 4 (D.C. Cir. 2011).

[169] Kimel v. Fla. Bd. of Regents, 528 U.S. 62, 68 (2000).

[170] *Id.*

[171] *Id.* at 80.

[172] Bd. of Trustees of Univ. of Alabama v. Garrett, 531 U.S. 356, 360 (2001).

[173] Smith v. Sec'y of Dep't of Envtl. Prot. of Pennsylvania, 540 F. App'x 80, 82 (3d Cir. 2013) (internal citation omitted).

[174] *Smith*, 540 F.App'x at 82.

Title VII does not allow a party to obtain punitive damages against a government, government agency, or political subdivision.[175]

§ 12.21 EEOC Remedies

Under Title VII, the ADEA, and the ADA (Title I), the EEOC has the ability to file suit for violations of the law on its own or on behalf of aggrieved individuals.[176] The EEOC also has the ability to gather evidence and witness testimony related to Charges of Discrimination and to issue subpoenas related thereto.[177] The Ninth Circuit has noted:

> The EEOC's right of action is independent of the employee's private action rights. The EEOC "is not merely a proxy for the victims of discrimination," but "acts also to vindicate the public interest in preventing employment discrimination." Its interests in determining the legality of specific conduct and in deterring future violations are distinct from the employee's interest in a personal remedy.[178]

If the EEOC prevails under Title VII or the ADA, it is not entitled to attorney's fees; however, it may be liable for attorney's fees to prevailing defendants in limited circumstances.[179]

§ 12.22 After-Acquired Evidence

After a discriminatory act, the defendant may discover evidence that would have resulted in the discharge of the plaintiff. Such evidence is called "after-acquired" evidence. For example, in *McKennon v. Nashville Banner Pub. Co.*,[180] the plaintiff filed a claim alleging the employer terminated her because of her age in violation of the ADEA. During discovery in that suit, the employer learned that the plaintiff had taken confidential documents and copied them. It argued that such conduct nullified any relief to which the plaintiff might be entitled.

The Supreme Court disagreed. Upholding the employer's position would not effectuate the ADEA's goals of deterring age discrimination and compensating victims.[181] The Court held that after-acquired evidence does not prevent a plaintiff from establishing liability under the statute. However, the Court stated that the employee's misconduct could affect the remedies available to the plaintiff.

The Court reached this conclusion, by noting that the federal discrimination statutes do not broadly regulate the workplace. Rather, they contain specific limits on employer actions taken because of protected classes. Outside of such conduct, the employer still retains broad power to terminate or discipline employees. For example, in the *McKinnon* case particularly, the employer retained the ability to terminate the employee for taking confidential documents.

---

[175] 42 U.S.C.A. § 1981a(b)(1).

[176] 42 U.S.C.A. § 2000e–5(f)(1) (Title VII); 42 U.S.C.A. § 12117(a) (ADA); 29 U.S.C.A. § 626(b).

[177] 42 U.S.C.A. § 2000e–8(a); 42 U.S.C.A. § 2000e–9.

[178] E.E.O.C. v. Goodyear Aerospace Corp., 813 F.2d 1539, 1542 (9th Cir. 1987) (internal citations omitted).

[179] 42 U.S.C. § 2000e–5(k).

[180] 513 U.S. 352 (1985).

[181] *McKinnon*, 513 U.S. at 358.

To balance the interests of the plaintiff in obtaining a remedy for discrimination and the interests of the employer to take non-discriminatory actions, the Court created an affirmative defense to certain damages. The Court refused to completely describe the details of this doctrine, as it noted that how the doctrine works would be determined by the particulars of cases.[182]

The affirmative defense requires the employer to prove that the employee engaged in conduct for which it would have terminated the plaintiff had the employer known about the conduct.[183] "[A]s a general rule in cases of this type, neither reinstatement nor front pay is an appropriate remedy. It would be both inequitable and pointless to order the reinstatement of someone the employer would have terminated, and will terminate, in any event and upon lawful grounds."[184]

In some cases, limits on backpay will also be appropriate. The Court held:

> The beginning point in the trial court's formulation of a remedy should be calculation of backpay from the date of the unlawful discharge to the date the new information was discovered. In determining the appropriate order for relief, the court can consider taking into further account extraordinary equitable circumstances that affect the legitimate interests of either party. An absolute rule barring any recovery of backpay, however, would undermine the ADEA's objective of forcing employers to consider and examine their motivations, and of penalizing them for employment decisions that spring from age discrimination.[185]

The Court also recognized that its holding might encourage discovery abuses by the employer. The Court stated that such abuses could be handled through judicial authority to grant attorneys' fees and by sanctioning authority under the Federal Rules of Civil Procedure.

The Court also distinguished after-acquired evidence from so-called mixed-motive cases. In a true mixed-motive case, the factfinder is asked to determine what motivated the employment action. If the factfinder concludes that both discriminatory and non-discriminatory reasons motivated the action, then the case is labeled as a mixed-motive case. In contrast, the after-acquired evidence issue exists in cases where liability is established or assumed (given the procedural posture of the case). After a discriminatory action is taken, the employer argues that some remedies are limited because of the actions taken by the employee.

§ 12.23 Intervention by Third Parties Affected by Consent Decrees or Judgments

At times, a consent decree issued by a court may affect the interest of employees who are not formally parties to the litigation. For example, the consent decree might order affirmative action based on race or sex. The Supreme Court held in *Martin v.*

---

[182] *McKinnon*, 513 U.S. at 361.

[183] *McKinnon*, 513 U.S. at 362–63; *see also* Holland v. Gee, 677 F.3d 1047, 1065 (11th Cir. 2012).

[184] *McKinnon*, 513 U.S. at 361–62.

[185] *McKinnon*, 513 U.S. at 362.

Wilks[186] that these employees were not bound by res judicata and could challenge the consent decree.

In 1991, Congress added a provision that limits the ability of people to challenge court judgments and consent decrees in discrimination cases under federal law or the Constitution. The statute now provides that a person who prior to the entry of such a judgment or decree had notice of the judgment and that it might adversely affect his legal rights, cannot later challenge it if there was an opportunity to provide objections.[187]

[186] Martin v. Wilks, 490 U.S. 755 (1989).

[187] 42 U.S.C.A. § 2000e–2(n).

Chapter 13

PROCEDURE

Analysis

§ 13.01 Introduction to Procedure

Private litigants seeking relief under Title VII, the ADEA, and the ADA must navigate a complicated, multi-step administrative process prior to seeking relief in court. The statutes impose very tight time deadlines. Failure to follow the process within the required time limits often means that the aggrieved individual will not be entitled to relief, even if the person otherwise has a valid discrimination claim.

The process for Title VII and the ADA involves the following steps: (1) filing a charge of discrimination with the Equal Employment Opportunity Commission (EEOC), (2) EEOC gives notice of the charge; (3) EEOC investigates the charge; (4) the EEOC makes a determination on the charge; (5) the EEOC issues a right to sue letter, and (6) the plaintiff files suit in state or federal court. While ADEA claims generally follow the same requirements, there are important differences that will be discussed. This chapter will use Title VII as the model for describing procedure and note any important differences between Title VII and the ADEA.

A different set of procedures and time deadlines apply to federal employees.

Section 1981 does not require the same pre-court processes. An person filing suit under Section 1981 can go to court and file a complaint, without notifying the EEOC or a comparable state agency.

§ 13.02 The Charge: Its Nature

Title VII, the ADEA, and the ADA each require that a person seeking relief under those statutes first file a charge of discrimination. The charge sets in motion the investigation and conciliation efforts of the EEOC, and it establishes the scope of any claims that can later be filed in court. If a charge is not timely filed, a court may dismiss the plaintiff's claims for failure to do so.

Typically, the charge is filed by the aggrieved individual or an attorney representing that individual. However, a charge may also be filed on behalf of an aggrieved individual by others. For example, a union might file a charge on behalf of its members. EEOC commissioners may also file charges.

Title VII provides that "[c]harges shall be in writing under oath or affirmation and shall contain such information as the Commission requires."[1] The EEOC has a form document (called the EEOC Form 5), that a person can complete and sign under oath. Properly completing this document will constitute a charge. As of the writing of this book, the EEOC is in the process of allowing some documents to be filed electronically.

However, questions arose about what constituted a charge. In *Federal Express Corp. v. Holowecki*,[2] the Supreme Court considered what a person needed to do to comply with the ADEA's charge requirement. In that case, the plaintiff had filed an Intake Questionnaire along with additional supporting information. An Intake Questionnaire is a document the EEOC uses to help people articulate their claims. The EEOC often uses this questionnaire when assisting individuals in drafting a charge.

The EEOC had issued regulations indicating that a charge should contain an allegation of discrimination and the name of the charged entity.[3] However, a question remained about whether this alone was sufficient to constitute a charge. The EEOC expressed concern that such a reading of the statute would not allow it to fully carry out its statutory mandate. Some people who come to the EEOC do so to request information about their rights and do not intend to invoke the EEOC's formal processes. For example, some workers come to the EEOC to determine whether their employers' actions are illegal, and they are not yet ready to charge their employer with discrimination. The EEOC advocated for a charge standard that required the information listed above plus a statement that could reasonably be construed as a request for the EEOC to act. The Court adopted this standard, finding it was a reasonable interpretation of the statute that allows the EEOC to perform its dual functions.

---

1 42 U.S.C.A. § 2000e–5(b). A charge is not required to be sworn under the ADEA. 29 C.F.R. §§ 1626.6, 1626.8.

2 552 U.S. 389 (2008).

3 29 C.F.R. § 1626.8(b).

The Court recognized that this broad definition of what constitutes a charge would allow many types of documents to counts as charges. The Court indicated this was consistent with the goals of federal discrimination law, especially considering that at the charge-filing stage many individuals are acting without the assistance of counsel.

The charge is supposed to comprehensively describe the aggrieved individual's claims, so that, in theory, the EEOC or state agency may investigate them and possibly mediate the dispute with the employer. If the charge is not comprehensive, then the agency does not have a full opportunity to investigate and conciliate. In practice, the EEOC and state agencies often lack the resources to fully investigate every charge filed with them. Despite this reality, Title VII, the ADEA, and the ADA impose a significant penalty for failure to describe issues in the charge. In later court proceedings, an aggrieved individual may only raise issues that are "like or related to" issues raised in the charge or issues that were or could reasonably have been discovered during the EEOC's investigation of the facts charged.[4] The charging party must inform the EEOC of all claimed discrimination and retaliation or risk later being unable to raise those claims in court.

Typically, the charge must identify the entity or person responsible for discrimination or retaliation and only that person or entity could properly be named as a defendant in a later suit filed in court. However, in limited circumstances, a person not named in the charge may later be made a party in the subsequent suit if: (1) the unnamed person had actual notice of the EEOC charge, and (2) if there is an identity of interest between the unnamed and named people or entities so that the EEOC investigation and conciliation reasonably would have included the unnamed person or entity.[5]

§ 13.03 When and Where to File the Charge

Title VII, the ADA, and the ADEA have two separate time periods for the timely filing of a charge of discrimination: 180 or 300 days from the date of the discriminatory act.[6] Most states have a state agency that enforces state anti-discrimination laws. In such states, the charge must be filed with the EEOC no later than 300 days from the discriminatory act.[7] In states without such an agency, the charge must be filed within 180 days of the discriminatory act.

The language of Title VII imagines that in states with state agencies that a worker will first file with the state agency to give it an opportunity to investigate the worker's claims before federal action begins. In such states, a charging party has additional time to file a charge with the EEOC under the assumption that the state process will take time. These states are often called referral states or deferral states.

In practice, given work agreements between state agencies and the EEOC, workers often file their charge simultaneously with the EEOC and the state agency. In these

[4] McClain v. Lufkin Indus., 519 F.3d 264, 276 (5th Cir. 2008); Jorge v. Rumsfeld, 404 F.3d 556, 564–65 (1st Cir. 2005).

[5] Zeller v. Canadian Nat'l Ry. Co., 666 F. App'x 517, 524 (6th Cir. 2016).

[6] 42 U.S.C.A. § 2000e–5(e)(1); 29 U.S.C.A. § 626(d).

[7] Oscar Mayer & Co. v. Evans, 441 U.S. 760 (1979) (noting that ADEA requires filing with state agency, but this filing is not required to be timely under state law). If a charging party first files an ADEA claim with a state agency, the EEOC charge must be filed within 300 days of the discriminatory act or 30 days after receipt of notice that the state agency process is concluded, whichever is earlier.

circumstances, if the injured party files a charge initially with the EEOC, the practice of the EEOC is to refer that charge to the state agency. That referral by the EEOC is considered as filing the charge with the state agency even though the charging party never personally presented a petition to the state agency.

Title VII and the ADA envision that the state agencies will have exclusive jurisdiction for 60 days.[8] The ADEA does not require that state agencies have exclusive jurisdiction for 60 days.[9] Most states have waived their 60-day exclusive jurisdiction.[10] In such instances, the plaintiff meets Title VII and ADA requirements by filing the charge within 300 days of the discriminatory act.[11]

However, some states have not waived their exclusive jurisdiction. In such a state, the EEOC charge is not considered to be filed with the federal agency until the 60 day exclusive jurisdiction window passes, unless the state agency terminates its jurisdiction earlier. This means that a charge submitted to the EEOC later in the 300-day window may not be timely filed because sufficient time is not allotted for the 60 day exclusive jurisdiction of the state agency.

The Supreme Court addressed this scenario in *Mohasco v. Silver*.[12] The plaintiff in that case submitted a charge to the EEOC 291 days after his termination. The EEOC referred the charge to the state agency, which had exclusive jurisdiction for 60 days. The defendant argued that the EEOC charge was filed late because the proper filing date was after the 60 days period of exclusive state jurisdiction lapsed. The Supreme Court agreed and held the plaintiff did not timely file the charge. Even though the charge was submitted to the EEOC within the proper window, the Court viewed "filing" with the EEOC as only occurring after the state completed its proceedings or the end of the state's exclusive jurisdiction. In such situations, a plaintiff must submit her charge to the EEOC within 240 days of the discriminatory act to meet the statutory deadline.

Thus, in a deferral jurisdiction, if the state has waived its exclusive jurisdiction, the charging party timely files her EEOC charge if it is done within 300 days of the discriminatory act.

In deferral states that have not waived exclusive jurisdiction, a charge may be filed with the EEOC at any time prior to the lapse of 300 days following the discriminatory act. That charge will be deferred for up to 60 days to allow state agency action. If the state agency relinquishes jurisdiction or the 60 days pass prior to the lapse of 300 days from the discriminatory act, there will be a timely filing of the charge. Therefore, if the charge is initially filed with the EEOC before the end of 240 days from the discriminatory act, the charge will be timely. If the initial charge is filed with the EEOC *after* 240 days but less than 300 days from the discriminatory act, the charge will be timely *only* if the state agency relinquishes its jurisdiction prior to the lapse of 300 days from the discriminatory act.

---

8 42 U.S.C. § 2000e–5(c); 29 U.S.C. § 633(b).

9 29 C.F.R. § 1626.7.

10 EEOC v. Commercial Office Prods., Co., 486 U.S. 107 (1988).

11 29 C.F.R. § 1601.13.

12 447 U.S. 807 (1980); *see also* Koch v. CGM Grp., Inc., No. THOO-0216-C-M/H, 2001 WL 392523, at *4 (S.D. Ind. Apr. 3, 2001).

§ 13.04 The Discriminatory Act

Title VII, the ADEA, and the ADA all require timely filing of a charge. The consequence for failure to do so is severe. The EEOC will not investigate untimely charges. If a plaintiff later files a claim in court based on an untimely charge, the court can dismiss that claim (in most instances). This occurs even if the plaintiff otherwise has a credible claim of discrimination.

In many cases, there is a clear, discrete discriminatory act that triggers the charge-filing period.[13] This occurs in many cases involving failure to hire, failure to promote, or termination. For example, in discharge cases, the act of discrimination occurs when the charging party is unequivocally informed of a final decision to terminate the relationship.

In many instances, the worker is informed about the negative outcome at the same time it becomes effective, but this is not always the case. Consider the facts of *Delaware State College v. Ricks*.[14] In that case, a college had a procedure that notified professors about negative tenure decisions, but allowed the professor to continue teaching for an additional year after being denied tenure. The professor argued that his employment ended at the end of the academic year, and this date should determine the start of the charge filing period. The Supreme Court held the professor did not file his charge on time because he was required to file it when he received notice of the adverse tenure decision, the alleged discriminatory act. The Court held this even though the plaintiff was allowed to challenge the decision through an internal grievance procedure. The presence and use of such a procedure does not toll the charge-filing period as long as the original decision is not tentative.

In *Ricks*, the notice requirement hurt the worker; however, in some cases it extends the period that the worker would have to file a charge. This would occur, for example, where an employer suggests that a worker is going to be fired, but does not convey the final decision until a later date. The charge filing period begins to run on the later date.[15]

In some discrimination cases, there is not a single, discrete act that triggers the charge filing deadlines. For example, harassment cases often allege conduct that occurs over a period of time. The Supreme Court had held that as long as one act contributing to the harassment claim takes place within the charging period, the charge is timely filed.[16]

In the past, compensation decisions presented challenges. Imagine that a company starts paying Tom and Susan different wages, even though they do the same job. Imagine that the pay differential is because Susan is a woman. The pay discrimination occurs for years because Susan does not know how much Tom is paid. When she finds out, she files a charge of discrimination. A question arises regarding whether Susan can only sue for the pay discrimination that occurred within the past 180/300 days or whether she can sue for the combined pattern of pay discrimination. In *Ledbetter v. Goodyear Tire & Rubber Co., Inc.*,[17] the Supreme Court held that pay discrimination is a discrete

---

[13] National R.R. Corp. v. Morgan, 536 U.S. 101, 110 (2002).

[14] 449 U.S. 250 (1980).

[15] Wright v. AmSouth Bancorporation, 320 F.3d 1198, 1203 (11th Cir. 2003).

[16] National R.R. Corp. v. Morgan, 536 U.S. 101, 110 (2002).

[17] 550 U.S. 618 (2007).

discriminatory act and that the plaintiff must file within the 180/300 day period when the discriminatory pay decision was made.

Congress soon passed and President Obama signed the Lilly Ledbetter Fair Pay Act of 2009. The Act amends Title VII, the ADEA, the ADA and the Rehabilitation Act. The Act defines when discrimination occurs in compensation. It does so "when an individual becomes subject to a discriminatory compensation decision or other practice, or when an individual is affected by application of a discriminatory compensation decision or other practice."[18] This includes "each time wages, benefits, or other compensation is paid, resulting in whole or in part from such a decision or practice." If a plaintiff faces the same situation as Lilly Ledbetter, she will now be able to recover for compensation discrimination. There is also a two-year look-back period from the time of the filing of the charge. The plaintiff will not be able to recover for discriminatory pay outside of this look-back window.

Disparate impact cases also present questions about when the discriminatory act occurs. For example, an employer might decide to implement a pen and paper test for certain jobs and then give that test to job applicants over a period of years. A question arises about whether the discrete, discriminatory act occurs when the employer adopted the test or when it applied it to the particular plaintiff. In *Lewis v. City of Chicago*,[19] the Supreme Court held that the discrete act of discrimination occurs each time the employer uses or applies the test or policy that creates the disparate impact.

§ 13.05 Extending Charge Filing

In *Zipes v. Trans World Airlines*[20] the Supreme Court held that timely filing of a charge was not a jurisdictional prerequisite to a later suit, "but a requirement that, like a statute of limitations, is subject to waiver, estoppel or equitable tolling." Although it is technically possible for a court to extend the charge filing period, it is not advisable to rely on such an extension, because the courts rarely use waiver, estoppel or equitable tolling to excuse the failure to timely file the charge.

One question that arises is what date triggers the charge filing period when a plaintiff is notified of an adverse action on one date, but only later discovers facts suggesting that the adverse action might be discriminatory. Some circuits have held that the charge-filing period starts on the date that the discriminatory act occurs, but that courts may use equitable tolling to extend the time period if the plaintiff only later learns of facts showing that the action was discriminatory.[21]

In extraordinarily rare cases, the courts may apply equitable doctrines such as waiver, equitable estoppel, and equitable tolling.[22] The plaintiff's ignorance of the law or of the time filing requirements is generally not sufficient to extend the charge filing period. In limited situations, an employer's misrepresentations or attempts to prevent the worker from asserting her rights in a timely manner will result in the court applying

[18] 42 U.S.C.A. § 2000e–5(e)(3)(A); 29 U.S.C.A. § 626(d)(3); 42 U.S.C.A. § 12117(a); 29 U.S.C.A. § 791(g).

[19] 560 U.S. 205 (2010).

[20] 455 U.S. 385, 393 (1982).

[21] Amini v. Oberlin Coll., 259 F.3d 493, 500 (6th Cir. 2001).

[22] National R.R. Corp. v. Morgan, 536 U.S. 101, 109 (2002).

an equitable doctrine and allowing the worker to continue the suit even if she did not technically file her charge or her claim within the required time windows.[23]

Some individuals are protected by both a collective bargaining agreement and federal discrimination law. Such an individual is entitled to seek both contractual remedies under the collective bargaining agreement and statutory remedies. Pursuit of the contractual remedy will not toll the running of statutory time limits.[24] Similarly, the filing of a suit under the Equal Pay Act, 42 U.S.C.A. § 1981 or 42 U.S.C.A. § 1983 will not toll the running of the time for filing a Title VII, ADEA, or ADA charge.[25]

The failure to file a charge will not preclude the grant of final relief to individual class members who did not file charges.[26]

§ 13.06 The Response of the EEOC to the Charge

After the charge is filed with the EEOC, the EEOC notifies the respondent of the charge. The EEOC is directed to investigate the charge for the initial purpose of determining whether there is "reasonable cause" to believe that the charge is true.

The EEOC has issued regulations describing its investigatory process. After notifying the respondent of the charge, the EEOC might ask the respondent for a position statement.[27] A position statement is an opportunity for the respondent to reply to the allegations made by the charging party. For example, in a position statement an employer might provide facts showing why it did not discriminate against the charging party. The EEOC may ask both parties for additional information and has the power to issue subpoenas to get additional information. The regulations also state that the EEOC may have a fact-finding conference with the parties.

Due to financial constraints, the EEOC is not able to robustly investigate every charge filed. Indeed, many charges proceed through the EEOC with little investigation. As discussed below, in some cases the charging party files a charge and then quickly requests a right to sue letter from the EEOC.

§ 13.07 EEOC Determination

After its investigation, the EEOC may make a determination on the charge.

If the Commission finds no "reasonable cause to believe the charge is true," it will dismiss the charge, inform the parties, and notify the charging party of the right to bring a private suit. If the agency finds no "reasonable cause," this does not prevent the charging party from later filing suit in court.

If reasonable cause exists, the Commission is directed to "endeavor to eliminate any such practice by informal methods of conference, conciliation, and persuasion."[28] After a reasonable cause finding, the EEOC often will encourage the parties to settle the dispute. Such settlements typically occur because reasonable cause findings by the EEOC are not

---

[23] Jenkins v. Widall, 211 F.3d 1269 (6th Cir. 2000). The plaintiff may also be able to obtain relief if the EEOC or a court misleads the plaintiff.

[24] International Union of Electrical Workers v. Robbins & Myers, Inc., 429 U.S. 229, 236–39 (1976).

[25] Johnson v. Railway Express Agency, Inc., 421 U.S. 454, 454 (1975).

[26] Albemarle Paper Co. v. Moody, 422 U.S. 405, 414 n. 8 (1975).

[27] 29 C.F.R. § 1601.15(a).

[28] The EEOC may encourage conciliation and perhaps reach a formal settlement prior to a formal finding of reasonable cause. 29 C.F.R. § 1601.20.

common. This is because the EEOC does not have the resources to fully investigate most of the charges presented to it. If the parties settle the suit, the dispute is resolved. If they do not settle it, the EEOC may decide to prosecute a suit in court on behalf of the charging party. Or, the EEOC may decline to file such a suit and provide the charging party with a right to sue letter, so that the charging party may begin a private suit. In some cases, the EEOC allows the charging party to start a private lawsuit, and the EEOC intervenes in that case.

There are some instances where the EEOC may choose not to investigate a charge. For example, if a charging party files a charge against a private employer with 10 employees, the EEOC can dismiss the charge without an investigation because such an employer is not large enough to fall within Title VII, the ADEA, or the ADA. Or, if the charging party does not file a timely charge, the EEOC may dismiss the charge and end its administrative process. As discussed throughout this chapter, the EEOC often lacks the financial capacity to investigate all charges. In many instances, a charging party files a charge and then requests a right to sue letter from the EEOC, even though the agency has not thoroughly investigated the charge.

§ 13.08 Notice of Right to Sue

Under Title VII and the ADA, an individual who has filed a timely charge with the EEOC is not free to proceed with a private suit until the government agency has relinquished jurisdiction and provided the charging party with a "notice of right to sue." In most cases if a plaintiff files a claim in federal court without having received a notice of right to sue, the claim will be dismissed for failure to exhaust administrative remedies.

Once the EEOC determines that no "reasonable cause" exists to believe that the law has been violated, the EEOC must relinquish jurisdiction and authorize private suit. If "reasonable cause" has been found, the EEOC will relinquish its jurisdiction in charges against private entities once it determines that a satisfactory conciliation agreement cannot be reached and concludes that it will not file a public suit.

Title VII provides that the agencies "*shall* so notify the person aggrieved," if, after 180 days of jurisdiction, no suit has been filed or conciliation agreement reached, and provide the charging party with a notice that a private civil action may be brought. This requires the EEOC to relinquish jurisdiction over pending charges upon the request of the charging party at any time after the lapse of 180 days from the date of the charge. If the party does not request a right to sue letter, the EEOC may retain jurisdiction over the charge until its concludes its process. This may take months or even years. The charging party is not required to request a right to sue letter within a certain time.

In most cases where the charging party is represented by counsel, the counsel will request a notice of right to sue letter. EEOC regulations allow a charging party to request a right to sue letter prior to the end of the 180-day period.[29] The EEOC has recognized that in many instances it will not have the resources to conduct and conclude its investigation within that time frame. Several circuits have approved of these early requests for the right to sue letter.[30]

---

[29] 29 C.F.R. § 1601.28(a)(2).

[30] *See, e.g.*, Walker v. United Parcel Serv., Inc., 240 F.3d 1268, 1277 (10th Cir. 2001); Sims v. MacMillan, 22 F.3d 1059, 1061–63 (11th Cir. 1994); *but see* Martini v. Fed. Nat. Morg. Ass'n, 178 F.3d 1336, 1347 (D.C. Cir. 1999) (holding that regulation was invalid and disallowing practice of early requests).

The ADEA has a slightly different process. The charging party may obtain a right-to-sue letter but is not required to do so.[31] Instead, a plaintiff under the ADEA may file a claim in court 60 days after submitting the charge. If the ADEA plaintiff does obtain a right to sue letter, the 90-day filing period discussed in the next section applies.

§ 13.09 Filing Period

The charging party has 90 days to file a civil complaint in court after receiving the right to sue letter. The 90 days runs from the date the notice was *received* by the charging party or by his designated attorney.[32] When there is no evidence of when the plaintiff receives the right to sue letter, courts consider the date of issuance on the notice to be the mailing date and then apply a presumption (that varies by circuit) about the number of days that would typically occur between mailing and receipt.[33]

The 90-day statutory period to file suit following receipt of the notice of right to sue is not "jurisdictional," but is in the nature of a statute of limitations and is subject to doctrines such as equitable tolling, estoppel, and waiver.

If the EEOC dismisses the charge because it finds that no reasonable cause exists, plaintiff still is free to file a complaint. The Supreme Court stated, "The Act does not restrict a complainant's right to sue to those charges as to which the Commission has made findings of reasonable cause, and we will not engraft on the statute a requirement which may inhibit the review of claims of employment discrimination in the federal courts."[34]

§ 13.10 Section 1981 Statute of Limitations

Section 1981 does not require a claimant to exhaust an administrative process. Section 1981 claims must be filed within the appropriate statute of limitations. The statute of limitations varies depending on whether the section 1981 claim asserts pre-employment conduct or post-employment. For pre-employment conduct, the forum state's statute of limitations for personal injury tort claims governs.[35] For post-employment conduct, a four-year statute of limitations applies.[36]

§ 13.11 Government Suits

The EEOC is authorized to initiate litigation against a defendant in certain instances described in the federal discrimination statutes. This section begins by describing the EEOC's authority in Title VII cases.

Before the EEOC may file a suit against a defendant, the statute requires it to first wait 30 days and also find reasonable cause that there is a violation of the statute. The EEOC also must "endeavor to eliminate [the] alleged unlawful employment practice by informal methods of conference, conciliation, and persuasion."[37] After conciliation fails,

[31] 29 U.S.C.A. § 626(d).

[32] 42 U.S.C.A. § 2000e–5(f)(1); Sumitomo Shoji Am., Inc. v. Avagliano, 457 U.S. 176, 178 (1982).

[33] *See, e.g.*, Garcia v. Penske Logistics, L.L.C., 631 F. App'x 204, 208 (5th Cir. 2015); Sherlock v. Montefiore Med. Cts., 84 F.3d 522, 525–26 (2d Cir. 1996).

[34] McDonnell Douglas Corp. v. Green, 411 U.S. 792, 798–99 (1973).

[35] Mitchell v. Crescent River Port Pilots Assoc., 2008 WL 410414 (5th Cir. Feb. 14, 2008).

[36] Jones v. R.R. Donnelly & Sons, 541 U.S. 369 (2004).

[37] 42 U.S.C.A. § 2000e–5(b).

the EEOC may file suit.[38] However, "[n]othing said or done during" conciliation may be "used as evidence in a subsequent proceeding without written consent of the persons concerned."[39]

To meet the statutory requirement of conciliation, the EEOC "must tell the employer about the claim—essentially, what practice has harmed which person or class—and must provide the employer with an opportunity to discuss the matter in an effort to achieve voluntary compliance."[40] The Supreme Court has noted that the EEOC has wide latitude in determining when it has endeavored conciliation. It noted that the EEOC is not required to "devote a set amount of time or resources" to conciliation.[41]

> Further, the attempt need not involve any specific steps or measures; rather, the Commission may use in each case whatever "informal" means of "conference, conciliation, and persuasion" it deems appropriate. . . . And the EEOC alone decides whether in the end to make an agreement or resort to litigation: The Commission may sue whenever "unable to secure" terms "acceptable *to the Commission*." . . . Congress left to the EEOC such strategic decisions as whether to make a bare-minimum offer, to lay all its cards on the table, or to respond to each of an employer's counter-offers, however far afield. So too Congress granted the EEOC discretion over the pace and duration of conciliation efforts, the plasticity or firmness of its negotiating positions, and the content of its demands for relief.[42]

In most cases, the EEOC can prove that it met its obligation through a sworn affidavit.[43]

There is no statutory time limitation on the government's right to bring suit. In *Occidental Life Ins. Co. of California v. EEOC,*[44] the Supreme Court confirmed this and noted that the equitable doctrine of laches limited the right of the government to sue.

Title VII contains two different provisions authorizing the government to file suit. Section 707 of Title VII authorizes the EEOC to prosecute actions where defendant has engaged in a "pattern or practice" of illegal discrimination. Section 706(f)(1) provides a power to bring suit on behalf of individuals.[45] The government may proceed either under § 707 or § 706(f)(1) without satisfying the class action requirements of Fed.R.Civ.P. 23. The Attorney General has the exclusive power to sue state and local governments.[46]

If the EEOC enters into a binding conciliation agreement with the charged party, or if the EEOC files a suit, this will preclude suit by a private party. A charging party may intervene in the EEOC suit.[47]

The government is not required to file suit once the EEOC has determined "reasonable cause" exists, even in cases where the EEOC cannot reach a conciliation agreement with the respondent. If the agency determines that no suit will be filed, the

[38] 42 U.S.C.A. § 2000e–5(f)(1).

[39] 42 U.S.C.A. § 2000e–5(b).

[40] Mach Mining, LLC v. E.E.O.C., 135 S. Ct. 1645, 1652 (2015).

[41] 42 U.S.C.A. § 2000e–5(b); *Mach Mining,* 135 S. Ct. at 1654–55.

[42] *Mach Mining,* 135 S. Ct. at 1654–55 (internal citations omitted).

[43] *Mach Mining,* 135 S. Ct. at 1656.

[44] 432 U.S. 355 (1977).

[45] General Telephone Co. of Northwest v. EEOC, 446 U.S. 318. 326 (1980).

[46] 42 U.S.C. § 2000e–5(f)(1).

[47] 42 U.S.C. § 2000e–5(f)(1).

agency should inform the charging party and notify the charging party of the right to bring a private suit. Once a private suit is filed the government may intervene in the private action.[48]

The ADA incorporates by reference the same enforcement powers and remedies as provided in Title VII.[49] The EEOC can also bring suits to enforce the ADEA.[50] The EEOC does not have authority to file claims under Section 1981.

§ 13.12 Federal Employee Administrative Enforcement Procedures

In-depth coverage of the process covering federal employee administrative enforcement is beyond the scope of this book. Many federal employees are required to follow a different procedure to obtain relief under Title VII and the ADEA than the process described throughout this chapter.[51] Disability discrimination claims for many federal employees are covered by the Rehabilitation Act, not the ADA, but follow a similar process.

The first step in the process is for the worker to contact an Equal Employment Opportunity (EEO) counselor at the agency that is engaging in discrimination. At this pre-complaint step, the employee may resolve the dispute through counseling or an alternative dispute resolution program. If the dispute is not resolved at this point, a more formal process is available, where the employee files a discrimination complaint with the agency within a short time period.

The agency may reject the complaint for procedural or other reasons or may investigate it.[52] At the end of the investigation period, the employee may either request a hearing before an EEOC administrative judge or request the agency itself to issue a determination about whether discrimination happened. If the employee requests an agency determination and disagrees with the result of that determination, the employee can appeal the decision to the EEOC or pursue review in court. There are additional points in the process where the federal employee can go to court. For example, if the employee waits the required period and does not receive a response from the agency, the employee may go to court.[53]

The ADEA does not require federal employees to exhaust administrative remedies prior to filing suit.[54] Under the ADEA, federal employees may invoke the agency administrative processes and then file suit in federal district court if unsatisfied by the resolution. Or, the federal employee may go to federal court without invoking an administrative process.[55]

---

[48] 42 U.S.C. § 2000e–5(f)(1).

[49] 42 U.S.C.A. § 12117(a).

[50] 29 U.S.C.A. § 626(b).

[51] It should be noted that some federal employees are not covered by Title VII. 42 U.S.C. § 2000e–16. Not all federal employees must follow the process described in this section. 29 C.F.R. § 1614.103.

[52] 29 C.F.R.§ 1614.107.

[53] 29 C.F.R. § 1614.407.

[54] *See* 29 U.S.C.A. § 633a; 29 C.F.R. § 1614.201.

[55] 29 U.S.C.A. § 633a(c); *see also* Stores v. Brennan, No. 7:16CV00088, 2016 WL 4939362, at *4 (W.D. Va. Sept. 14, 2016).

Some state employees may also be required to follow different enforcement procedures under the Government Employee Rights Act.[56] The Government Employee Rights Act prohibits discrimination against certain appointed and policy-making officials of a state.

§ 13.13 The Suit

Once a discrimination claim reaches a court, it follows the same rules and procedures followed within that court system. Most claims can be filed in either federal or state court, although most federal employee claims must be filed in a federal court.[57] The remainder of this chapter will focus on employment discrimination specific issues that arise in litigation and arbitration.

Some of the statutes have their own venue provisions. For example, Title VII has a venue provision, allowing suits to be brought "in any judicial district in the State in which the unlawful employment practice is alleged to have been committed, in the judicial district in which the employment records relevant to such practice are maintained and administered, or in the judicial district in which the aggrieved person would have worked but for the alleged unlawful employment practice . . . ."[58]

Employment discrimination complaints must follow the same rules provided by the applicable court system. In *Swierkiewicz v. Sorema N. A.*,[59] the Supreme Court considered whether a plaintiff's discrimination complaint in federal court needed to provide facts to support each portion of the *McDonnell Douglas* test. The Court held that a plaintiff does not need to plead the individual factors of the test. This holding recognizes that the *McDonnell Douglas* test is not the only way for a plaintiff to prove discrimination. Additionally, the *McDonnell Douglas* test does not spell out the "elements" of a Title VII claim. Rather, the test is an evidentiary framework that the courts use to evaluate discrimination claims. Additionally, because the prongs of the *McDonnell Douglas* may change depending on the specific facts of the plaintiff's claim, the plaintiff may not be able to advocate a particular version of the test until after discovery.

For claims that require administrative exhaustion, the scope of the complaint is limited by the content of the charge originally filed with the EEOC. The complaint may only raise issues that are "like or related to" those contained in the charge, or which reasonably could have been uncovered in the EEOC administrative investigation of the charge. For example, if a plaintiff informs the EEOC of facts related to sex discrimination, but does not inform the EEOC of facts related to disability discrimination, the plaintiff may not raise the disability discrimination claim in court, even if the plaintiff otherwise could prevail on a disability discrimination claim.

If discrimination or retaliation occurs after the original charge, the plaintiff should either amend the original charge or file a second charge asserting the new conduct. This is the safest course, as it avoids any later challenges regarding administrative exhaustion. However, if activity subsequent to the charge is part of the same course of conduct as that alleged in a charge, the complaint may be able to include that subsequent

[56] 42 U.S.C.A. § 2000e–16(d).

[57] As discussed in the prior section suits by federal employees have different rules. *See, e.g.*, 29 U.S.C.A. § 633a (requiring suits by federal employees under the ADEA to be filed in federal district court).

[58] 42 U.S.C.A. § 2000e–5(f)(3).

[59] 534 U.S. 506, 508 (2002).

activity without amending the charge or filing a new one. Continuing patterns may be "reasonably related" to the charge.[60] Retaliation based on the filing of the EEOC charge or the judicial complaint may be "ancillary" to the original charge and may not require further EEOC action.[61] If the plaintiff fails to file a charge regarding certain events, the plaintiff may still use these events as background evidence to support a timely charge.

Typically, the charge must identify the entity or person responsible for discrimination or retaliation and only that person or entity could properly be named as a defendant in a later suit filed in court. However, in limited circumstances, a person not named in the charge may later be made a party in the subsequent suit if: (1) the unnamed person had actual notice of the EEOC charge, and (2) if there is an identity of interest between the unnamed and named people or entities so that the EEOC investigation and conciliation reasonably would have included the unnamed person or entity.[62]

In suits against governments, particularly federal agencies, the individual who heads the agency, rather than the agency itself, is the party to be named in the complaint. However, in the event that proper individuals are not named, the trial court should allow a retroactive amendment to name the proper party.[63]

In most cases, an individual must file a charge to later participate in a suit. However, if one person files a charge other individuals who did not file a charge may file suit in certain circumstances that vary by circuit. For example, some circuits allow a second person to piggyback on the first claim if the allegations are similar and relate to the same time period. Other circuits require more stringent standards.[64]

§ 13.14 Class Actions (a Summary)

Class actions are a procedural joinder device that allow courts to adjudicate the claims of numerous individuals within one suit. Claims are brought by named plaintiffs who then represent the interests of the unnamed individuals who are part of the class. The judgment entered then binds the class members, precluding them from raising the same claim in a later suit.[65]

Title VII and ADA class actions brought in federal court by private litigants are governed by Fed.R.Civ.P. 23. The EEOC has the power to bring suits on behalf of classes without meeting the requirements of Rule 23.[66] As discussed in the next section, Rule 23 does not govern ADEA class actions.

Class actions allow named parties to represent the interests of an entire class. They are contrary to normal civil procedure joinder devices, which usually do not allow joinder of so many plaintiffs. The Rules provide for class actions because class actions allow large

---

[60] Wallace v. Beech Aircraft Corp., 87 F.Supp.2d 1138, 1146 n.6 (D. Kan. 2000)

[61] *See, e.g.*, Mercer v. Alabama Dep't of Transportation, No. 2:16-CV-01204-RDP, 2018 WL 4489504, at *12 (N.D. Ala. Sept. 18, 2018) (discussing cases); *see also* Jones v. Calvert Grp., Ltd., 551 F.3d 297, 302 (4th Cir. 2009).

[62] Zeller v. Canadian Nat'l Ry. Co., 666 F. App'x 517, 524 (6th Cir. 2016).

[63] Fed.R.Civ.P. 15; Robert v. Michaels, 219 F.3d 775, 778 (8th Cir. 2000).

[64] Peeples v. City of Detroit, 891 F.3d 622, 632 (6th Cir. 2018) (discussing standards).

[65] Cooper v. Fed. Reserve Bank of Richmond, 467 U.S. 867, 876 (1984) (claims of individual discrimination can proceed even if class claims of pattern or practice fail).

[66] General Tel. Co. of the Nw., Inc. v. EEOC, 446 U.S. 318, 320 & 324 (1980); Equal Employment Opportunity Comm'n v. Bass Pro Outdoor World, L.L.C., 826 F.3d 791, 797 (5th Cir. 2016).

groups of people to band together to vindicate common claims in a more efficient manner than if all of the individuals sued separately. The class action mechanism also makes it easier for plaintiffs to sue on claims that it would be difficult or inefficient to raise in individual cases. The typical example of this is the so-called negative value suit, where each individual has a claim for a small amount of money that only makes sense to litigate in the aggregate.

A plaintiff seeking class certification typically identifies the proposed class and requests the court to certify the class. In federal court to certify a class, a class representative must meet two separate requirements. First, the class representative must establish all of the requirements of Rule 23(a): numerosity, commonality, typicality, and adequacy of representation.

After meeting all the requirements of 23(a), the class must also be certified under at least one of the three options provided by Rule 23(b). There are three important aspects of Rule 23(b). First, Rule 23(b)(1) & (2) classes do not allow class members to opt out of the lawsuit in most circumstances. Thus, if the class is certified under one of these two mechanisms, individuals with strong individual cases would be covered by the class resolution, in most circumstances. Second, Rule 23(b)(1) & (2) classes do not require notice to potential class members (unless the court orders it), but certification under Rule 23(b)(3) does require such notice. This notice can be very expensive, especially because many courts require individual, written notice (usually via mail) to the last known address of all potential class members. Finally, the basis for certification under 23(b)(1) & (2) are considered to be less controversial than (b)(3) certifications. It is worth noting that 23(b)(2) has traditionally been viewed as an important mechanism for vindicating civil rights, at least where the relief sought is primarily injunctive or declaratory relief.

Under Rule 23(a), "numerosity" requires that the number of persons in the defined class be so numerous that joinder of all class members would be impracticable. "Practicality of joinder depends on many factors, including, for example, the size of the class, ease of identifying its members, and determining their addresses, facility of making service on them if joined, and their geographic dispersion."[67] There is no precise number that meets the numerosity requirement. As a "rule of thumb," certification of classes with fewer than 40 members is unusual.

"Commonality" requires that there be questions of law and fact common to the class. The Supreme Court addressed the commonality requirement in employment discrimination class actions in *Wal-Mart Stores, Inc. v. Dukes*.[68] In that case, the plaintiffs alleged that the company gave individual supervisors discretion in making pay and promotion decisions. The plaintiffs claimed that this discretion resulted in a disparate impact to women, who were paid less and promoted less often than men. The plaintiffs also claimed that because the company was aware of the effect of this discretion and did not cabin it, that the company was liable for intentional discrimination.

Two issues predominated the majority's discussion of the class certification issue. First, the Court considered whether the women's claims evidenced commonality under Rule 23(a). The fact that the majority opinion characterized the argument under Rule 23(a) is important, because the holding on commonality would affect all class actions, no

---

[67] Kilgo v. Bowman Transportation Co., 789 F.2d 859, 878 (11th Cir. 1986).

[68] Wal-Mart Stores, Inc. v. Dukes, 564 U.S. 338, 344 (2011).

matter which Rule 23(b) certification is sought. The second issue was whether the claims could be certified under Rule 23(b)(2), which requires that "the party opposing the class has acted or refused to act on grounds that apply generally to the class, so that final injunctive relief or corresponding declaratory relief is appropriate respecting the class as a whole."

The district court and the Ninth Circuit Court of Appeals sitting en banc certified the class. The Supreme Court reversed the Ninth Circuit holding that the class cannot be certified because the named plaintiffs could not establish commonality and because class certification failed under 23(b)(2).

The plaintiffs all alleged injury under the same federal statute. They all alleged sex discrimination for pay and promotion on the same theories. Despite these similarities, the majority held that plaintiffs did not establish commonality. The Court noted "[t]hat common contention, moreover, must be of such a nature that it is capable of classwide resolution—which means that determination of its truth or falsity will resolve an issue that is central to the validity of each one of the claims in one stroke."

The majority then suggested ways that plaintiffs might be able to establish commonality. They could allege a common testing or other evaluative method that created a disparate impact or was a result of intentional discrimination. They also could allege a general policy of discrimination. However, because the managers each exercised their discretion in a different way, this discretion could not be the basis of a common answer.

After holding that the plaintiffs did not establish commonality, the Court also indicated that the case could not be certified under Rule 23(b)(2) because the request for money damages was more than incidental to the requests for declaratory and injunctive relief.

Justice Ginsburg, with whom Justice Breyer, Justice Sotomayor, and Justice Kagan joined, concurred in part and dissented in part. These Justices agreed that certification under Rule 23(b)(2) was improper; however, these Justices would not have precluded certification under Rule 23(b)(3). Justice Ginsburg argued that Wal-Mart's tap on the shoulder promotion process and the discretion given to supervisors to make pay and promotion decisions demonstrated enough factual commonality to bind together the class.

The context of *Wal-Mart* is important. If certified, the class would have consisted of a million and a half people, and any verdict likely would have been very large. Further, if the named plaintiffs pursued their claims separately there are two practical considerations that would make their individual claims weaker. First, given the amount of research, effort, and expense required to prove the allegations in this suit, it is unlikely to make economic sense for a private plaintiff's lawyer to pursue the individual case with individual damages. Second, even if the named plaintiffs were allowed to band together to sue without class certification, a court may not allow them to make nationwide allegations against Wal-Mart. Instead, a court might determine that nationwide evidence is not relevant (or more prejudicial than probative) and limit the plaintiffs' evidence to the store or the region in which they worked. Thus, the fact that this case is fashioned as a class action has overwhelming practical importance

"Typicality" requires that the claims of the named plaintiffs be similar to those of the class. For example, a plaintiff alleging disability discrimination would likely not meet the typicality requirement if she sought to represent a class of individuals subjected to sex discrimination. The named plaintiff's claim is not similar enough to the claims of the other class members. The Supreme Court has noted that the analysis on commonality and typicality often blend together.

"Adequacy of representation" requires the court to determine whether the named plaintiffs, those who will be controlling the litigation, will fairly and adequately represent the class.[69] Rule 23(g) also specifically delineates inquiries the court should make in determining whether a person may serve as class counsel. These inquiries are designed to ensure that the named representative is capable of representing the class and that the interests of the named representative do not conflict with the class. They also try to ensure that the attorney representing the class has the resources, expertise, and knowledge to prosecute the class action.

The Supreme Court held in *East Texas Motor Freight System v. Rodriguez*[70] that individuals who lacked the qualifications to be hired at a company could not represent a class of applicants and employees. The Court also indicated that the proposed named plaintiffs had a conflict with class members because the named plaintiffs sought a remedy (the merging of two seniority lists) that many of the class members rejected.

§ 13.15 Class Actions Under the ADEA

The ADEA's procedural mechanisms are largely drawn from the Fair Labor Standards Act (FLSA), rather than Title VII. The ADEA therefore follows FLSA standards for class actions. Fed.R.Civ.P. 23 does not govern class actions under the ADEA. Instead, courts first determine whether a named class member is "similarly situated" to people in the proposed class.[71] After the district court judge makes an initial determination that a class is appropriate, potential members of the class receive notice of the proposed class. To be within the class, individuals must opt in to the class.[72] The "opt-in" class action mechanism for ADEA suits is very different than Rule 23 class actions, which do not typically require plaintiffs to affirmatively opt in to fall within the class.

§ 13.16 Preliminary Relief

Under Title VII and the ADA, when a timely charge is filed and if, "on the basis of a preliminary investigation," it appears "that prompt judicial action is necessary to carry out the purposes of [the Act]," the EEOC is authorized to seek and secure preliminary injunctive relief pending final disposition of the charge.[73] The EEOC may immediately issue a notice of right to sue for the purpose of allowing the charging party to seek injunctive relief. The courts also possess inherent equity powers to grant privately sought equitable relief.

Fed.R.Civ.P. 65 provides the standard for obtaining preliminary relief in federal court. The person or entity seeking a preliminary injunction must show a likelihood of success on the merits, irreparable injury caused by the opposing party's action, the threatened injury to the proponent outweighs the harm to the opposing party, and the

---

[69] Fed.R.Civ.P. 23(a)(4).

[70] 431 U.S. 395, 403 (1977).

[71] 29 U.S.C.A. § 216(b).

[72] 29 U.S.C.A. § 216(b).

[73] 42 U.S.C.A. § 2000e–5(f)(2).

injunction would not be contrary to the public interest. It may be difficult to establish irreparable injury in discrimination cases, if the plaintiff would be entitled to receive money damages at the end of the suit. However, injunctive relief may be available if the plaintiff suffers harms that cannot be later remedied through money damages, and some courts have expressed a policy of presuming such harm in discrimination cases.[74]

§ 13.17 Appointment of Counsel

Title VII and the ADA specifically allow a court to appoint counsel for plaintiffs and authorize the court to allow cases to proceed without the payment of fees, court costs, or security.[75] Courts can appoint lawyers to represent plaintiffs who were not able to retain counsel on their own. The ADEA does not contain a separate appointment of counsel provision; however counsel may be appointed under 28 U.S.C. § 1915(e)(1).

§ 13.18 Trial

Trials under Title VII, the ADEA, and ADA are *de novo* on all the issues of fact and law presented in the pleadings.[76] Neither party is bound by the findings of state administrative proceedings or the findings by the EEOC.

Discriminations suits often raise difficult issues of intent, motivation, or causation, often involving questions of witness credibility. Where motive, intent, or causation is at issue, summary judgment should rarely be granted for the employer.[77] Where appropriate, the jury (or trial court judge, if the case is bench tried) should hear all of the evidence and make appropriate findings of fact based thereon. Nonetheless, trial courts frequently grant summary judgment in discrimination cases.

In many cases, the plaintiff is entitled to a jury trial on her discrimination claims. Under the Federal Rules of Civil Procedure, the plaintiff must properly request a jury trial. The plaintiff typically does this by requesting a jury trial in her complaint. Failure to timely request a jury trial may result in a waiver of the right to a jury trial.

Prior to the 1991 amendments to Title VII, courts had interpreted Title VII as not providing a jury trial. Cases decided prior to that time were bench tried. In 1991, Congress amended Title VII to provide for jury trials in cases seeking compensatory or punitive damages.[78] Under Title VII, backpay is not defined as compensatory damages.[79] Therefore, a suit that seeks backpay, but not punitive damages or other compensatory damages, does not qualify for a jury trial under Title VII. Compensatory and punitive damages are not available for disparate impact claims under Title VII; therefore, jury trials are not available for disparate impact claims.[80]

The ADA also allows for jury trials in cases seeking compensatory or punitive damages.[81] Although many courts allow jury trials in ADA retaliation cases, some courts

---

[74] Baker v. Buckeye Cellulose Corp., 856 F.2d 167, 169 (11th Cir. 1998).

[75] 42 U.S.C.A. § 2000e–5(f)(1).

[76] McDonnell Douglas Corp. v. Green, 411 U.S. 792, 799 (1973).

[77] Gallagher v. Delaney, 139 F.3d 338, 342-43 (2d Cir. 1998).

[78] 42 U.S.C.A. § 1981a(c).

[79] 42 U.S.C.A. § 2000e–5(g)(1); Gryder v. Mineta, No. 1:00-CV-2437-ECS, 2010 WL 11468980, at *6 (N.D. Ga. Sept. 15, 2010), aff'd sub nom. Gryder v. Dennin, 427 F. App'x 844 (11th Cir. 2011).

[80] Allison v. Citgo Petroleum Corp., 151 F.3d 402, 423 (5th Cir. 1998).

[81] 42 U.S.C.A. § 1981a(c)(2).

have held that plaintiffs are not entitled to jury trials for such claims.[82] A jury trial is available in Section 1981 cases in which legal relief is sought.[83]

A jury trial is available under the ADEA in cases seeking damages under the statute.[84] A jury trial is not available in cases brought by federal employees under the ADEA.[85]

§ 13.19 Admissibility of EEOC Determinations

Trials in some discrimination cases occur after the EEOC or a comparable state agency has issued a determination, either finding discrimination or finding no discrimination. Most courts have held than whether to admit an EEOC or state agency determination of discrimination is within the sound discretion of the trial court.[86] Courts may find that admitting EEOC or state agency determinations is more prejudicial than probative and exclude such evidence under Fed.R.Evid. 403 (or comparable state court rules of evidence). A judge may be concerned that a jury will unduly rely on the EEOC or state determination and give it too much weight. Further, concerns arise because the factual and legal theories of a case may be much more developed after full discovery than they were at the administrative stage.

§ 13.20 Appellate Review

In the federal system, appeal of the district court's decision is to the appropriate United States Court of Appeals.

After a trial, a question arises in some discrimination cases about the continuing use of *McDonnell Douglas* on appeal. During a trial on the merits, the employer almost always offers a legitimate, non-discriminatory reason for its actions. Therefore, in these cases, it is inappropriate on appeal or during post-trial motions for a court to dismiss a case against a plaintiff based on problems with the plaintiff's prima facie case. The purpose of the prima facie case is to create a rebuttable presumption of discrimination, triggering the defendant to try to rebut that presumption. Once the defendant articulates a legitimate, non-discriminatory reason for its actions, it is no longer appropriate to revisit whether the plaintiff met the elements of the prima facie case.[87]

§ 13.21 Arbitration

Many employees waive their right to file a discrimination claim in court, as it is common for employers to require employees to sign arbitration agreements. These arbitration agreements require employees to adjudicate their employment discrimination claims through arbitration, rather than through a public, court process.

Arbitration agreements in this context are controversial, given the disproportionate bargaining position of the parties and the fact that the employer often refuses to bargain with the employee about arbitration. The employee typically must either sign the arbitration agreement or forego employment with the particular employer. Additionally,

---

[82] Alvarado v. Cajun Operating Co., 588 F.3d 1261, 1268 (9th Cir. 2009).

[83] Johnson v. Ry. Exp. Agency, Inc., 421 U.S. 454, 460 (1975).

[84] Lorillard v. Pons, 434 U.S. 575, 580 (1978); 29 U.S.C.A. § 626(c).

[85] 29 U.S.C.A. § 626(c).

[86] *See, e.g.*, Patten v. Wal-Mart Stores East, Inc., 300 F.3d 21, 26–27 (1st Cir. 2002); Paolitto v. Brown E & C, Inc., 151 F.3d 60, 65 (2d Cir. 1998).

[87] U.S. Postal Serv. Board of Governors v. Aikens, 460 U.S. 711, 713–14 (1983).

arbitration often does not provide the same access to discovery and procedural safeguards offered in traditional litigation. There is also a concern about the lack of public transparency in arbitration and concern about whether arbitrators favor employers who tend to be repeat players in arbitration. There is also a concern that if too many claims are taken to arbitration, the courts will not be able to sufficiently develop the law in particular areas, especially where statutory ambiguity exists. Nonetheless, the Supreme Court has upheld arbitration agreements that waive an employee's ability to file suit in court.[88]

In *14 Penn Plaza LLC v. Pyett*, the Supreme Court held that a "provision in a collective-bargaining agreement that clearly and unmistakably requires union members to arbitrate ADEA claims is enforceable as a matter of federal law."[89] Thus, even if an individual worker does not enter into an arbitration agreement with the employer, the employee may still be bound by arbitration if the collective bargaining agreement clearly and unmistakably requires arbitration of employment discrimination claims.

The Supreme Court has upheld arbitration agreements that require employees to waive their ability to proceed as a class through arbitration.[90]

The Federal Arbitration Act permits courts to invalidate arbitration agreements based on general contract doctrines, such as unconscionability, fraud, and duress.[91]

Arbitration agreements do not affect the EEOC's ability to file claims on behalf of employees.[92]

§ 13.22 Waivers and Releases

Agreements to arbitrate are just one kind of agreement an employer may request an employee to sign. As discussed in the prior section, arbitration agreements are governed by the Federal Arbitration Act, which limits courts' ability to strike down arbitration agreements. However, other types of agreements (such as jury trial waivers) are not subject to the Federal Arbitration Act, and courts have more power to review and nullify such agreements.

A prospective release of employment discrimination claims violates public policy and, as such, is unenforceable. However, a knowing and voluntary release of existing claims in return for valid consideration will be upheld.[93] Different rules apply to ADEA claims and are discussed later in this section.

Courts have reasoned that allowing prospective waivers of employment discrimination claims would upset the statutory scheme created by Congress, which vindicates important public and private functions through private actions. Additionally, employers will not be deterred from discriminating, if they know that their employees have already prospectively waived any discrimination claim.

---

[88] Circuit City Stores v. Adams, 532 U.S. 105 (2001); Gilmer v. Interstate/Johnson Lane Corp., 500 U.S. 20, 27 (1991).

[89] 556 U.S. 247 (2009).

[90] American Express Co. v. Italian Colors Restaurant, 133 S.Ct. 2304, 2309 (2013); AT&T Mobility v. Conception, 563 U.S. 333, 344 (2011); *see also* Epic Sys. Corp. v. Lewis, 138 S. Ct. 1612, 200 L. Ed. 2d 889 (2018).

[91] AT&T Mobility v. Conception, 563 U.S. 333, 339 (2011).

[92] EEOC v. Waffle House, 534 U.S. 279 (2002).

[93] Richardson v. Sugg, 448 F.3d 1046, 1054 (8th Cir. 2006).

When a worker waives or settles employment discrimination claims, this does not affect the EEOC's ability to file a claim.[94]

In most cases, the validity of settlement and waiver agreements in the employment discrimination context is governed by the same law that governs these agreements in other contexts. However, the Older Worker Benefits Protection Act (OWBPA) places special rules on settlements and waivers of ADEA claims. Like with the other employment discrimination statutes, workers may not prospectively waive claims under the ADEA.[95]

The OWBPA requires that all other waivers of ADEA claims must be knowing and voluntary.[96] The statute then defines what knowing and voluntary means. To be enforceable, a waiver under the ADEA must, at a minimum meet the following requirements: (1) be calculated to be understood by an average person; (2) must specifically mention that the worker is waiving ADEA claims; (3) the employer must provide new consideration; (4) the worker is advised in writing to consult an attorney prior to signing the agreement; (5) the individual is given 21 days to consider the agreement; and (6) the employee may revoke the agreement for seven days following its execution.[97] If the agreement is part of a group incentive program, the employer must make additional disclosures.[98] Slightly different rules affect settlements of charges with the EEOC.[99]

§ 13.23 Preclusion: Individual Suits Following Class Actions

Preclusion doctrines, such as res judicata and collateral estoppel, apply in discrimination cases. In *Cooper v. Federal Reserve Bank of Richmond*[100] the Supreme Court held that individual plaintiffs were not precluded from bringing a suit alleging individual discrimination even though they were part of a prior class action alleging a pattern or practice of discrimination. A finding that an employer did not systematically discriminate against a group of people does not preclude a later suit against the employer alleging individual discrimination.

§ 13.24 Individual Suits Following EEOC Actions

An aggrieved person may file suit in court after an EEOC determination and receive a *de novo* review of the underlying claim. An EEOC finding that there is no "reasonable cause" to believe discrimination occurred does not preclude subsequent filing of a claim in court.[101] Generally, if the EEOC files suit on behalf of an individual, the individual is bound by the resolution of that suit.[102]

---

[94] EEOC v. Waffle House, 534 U.S. 279 (2002); 29 U.S.C.A. § 626(f)(4).

[95] 29 U.S.C.A. § 626(f).

[96] 29 U.S.C.A. § 626(f)(1).

[97] *Id.*

[98] 29 U.S.C.A. § 626(f)(1)(H).

[99] 29 U.S.C.A. § 626(f)(2).

[100] 467 U.S. 867, 874 (1984).

[101] McDonnell Douglas Corp. v. Green, 411 U.S. 792, 799 (1973).

[102] Vines v. Univ. of La., 398 F.3d 700, 706 (5th Cir. 2005) (also noting this is not universally true).

Under Title VII and the ADA, an aggrieved individual has a right to intervene in a suit filed by the EEOC on her behalf.[103] The ADEA does not contain a provision allowing intervention of right.[104]

§ 13.25 Prior State Fair Employment Determinations

Under 28 U.S.C.A. § 1738, federal courts must give the same full faith and credit to state court judgments as the judgments would have in their own state's courts. Questions arose about what effect a state agency's finding would have on a later discrimination claim in federal court.

When a state agency makes an administrative finding related to a charge of discrimination and that finding is not reviewed by a state court, a plaintiff is not barred from filing suit related to that charge.[105]

However, in *Kremer v. Chemical Construction Corp.*[106] the Supreme Court held that a state's finding that a charge lacked merit could preclude a later suit in some instances when a state court enters a judgment after the agency determination. In *Kremer*, state procedure provided for a full investigation and allowed the charging party to present and contest evidence. Additionally, it provided for court review of the administrative proceeding, and the plaintiff sought such court review. The Supreme Court also noted that the claim of discrimination submitted to the state agency was similar to the one that would have been available under federal law.

---

[103] 42 U.S.C.A. § 2000e–5(f)(1); *see also* 42 U.S.C.A. § 2000e–2(n).

[104] 29 U.S.C.A. § 626(c)(1); EEOC v. Woodman of World Life Ins., 479 F.3d 561, 579 (8th Cir. 2007).

[105] Astoria Fed. Sav. & Loan Ass'n v. Solimino, 501 U.S. 104 (1991); University of Tennessee v. Elliott, 478 U.S. 788, 794 (1986).

[106] 456 U.S. 461, 466–67 (1982).

Chapter 14

OTHER SOURCES OF DISCRIMINATION LAW

Analysis

§ 14.01 Introduction

Although this book focuses on Title VII, the ADEA, the ADA, and section 1981, there are other sources of anti-discrimination law. At the federal level, these include the Equal Pay Act (EPA), the Genetic Information Non-Disclosure Act, the Rehabilitation Act, and executive orders. This chapter provides a basic overview of these sources of anti-discrimination law. The Immigration Reform and Control Act of 1986 (IRCA) is discussed in Chapter 2 (§ 2.07).[1] The Family Medical Leave Act (FMLA) was created in part to provide equal opportunity in the workplace. While not technically a non-discrimination statute, an overview of the FMLA is included because of its close ties to discrimination law.

This chapter provides a broad overview of these additional sources of law. Comprehensive coverage of these topics is provided in Mark Rothstein, et al., EMPLOYMENT LAW (West).

States, counties, and cities often have anti-discrimination statutes or ordinances. At times, state law differs from federal law in substantive coverage, procedural requirements, and the remedies provided. Some sources of state law have substantive provisions that mirror the federal statutes and in these cases, federal courts' interpretation of federal law often provides the baseline for evaluating the state law.[2]

---

[1] The Uniformed Services Employment and Reemployment Rights Act (USERRA) is beyond the scope of this book. USERRA is a federal statute that prohibits discrimination based on military service, such as service in the Army Reserve. Public employees may also bring discrimination claims under 42 U.S.C.A. § 1983. This treatise does not cover section 1983.

[2] It is likely that states will begin to differentiate their state jurisprudence from federal jurisprudence. Most states have one omnibus statute that prohibits discrimination in a single statute, rather than separating claims between statutes modeled after Title VII and the ADEA. To the extent that the Supreme Court has started to differentiate ADEA claims from Title VII claims by imposing different causal standards and by providing different disparate impact frameworks, it is difficult for states with omnibus statutes to interpret their statutes to be consistent with both Title VII and the ADEA. *See also* Alex B. Long, *"If the Train Should Jump the Track . . .": Divergent Interpretations of State and Federal Employment Discrimination Statutes*, 40 GA. L. REV. 469 (2006).

§ 14.02 Equal Pay Act

Title VII prohibits compensation discrimination because of sex. The Equal Pay Act is a separate statute that prohibits compensation discrimination because of sex. Congress enacted the EPA in 1963, one year before it passed Title VII.

Part of the Fair Labor Standards Act, the EPA provides:

> No employer having employees subject to any provisions of this section shall discriminate, within any establishment in which such employees are employed, between employees on the basis of sex by paying wages to employees in such establishment at a rate less than the rate at which he pays wages to employees of the opposite sex in such establishment for equal work on jobs the performance of which requires equal skill, effort, and responsibility, and which are performed under similar working conditions, except where such payment is made pursuant to (i) a seniority system; (ii) a merit system; (iii) a system which measures earnings by quantity or quality of production; or (iv) a differential based on any other factor other than sex: *Provided*, That an employer who is paying a wage rate differential in violation of this subsection shall not, in order to comply with the provisions of this subsection, reduce the wage rate of any employee.[3]

There are noticeable differences between Title VII and the EPA regarding sex discrimination in compensation. The EPA has a different statute of limitations: two years (three for willful violations).[4] The EPA's remedies regime is centered on unpaid wages and liquidated damages, versus the broader remedies provided under Title VII. The EPA does not require a person to exhaust administrative remedies prior to filing suit in court.

The Equal Pay Act of 1963[5] requires that men and women who perform "equal" work be paid at a rate not less than the rate paid the opposite sex. Equal work is defined by the statute to be work requiring equal skill, effort, and responsibility, which is performed under similar working conditions. The Act permits pay differences for "equal work," "where such difference is made pursuant to (i) a seniority system, (ii) a merit system, (iii) a system that measures earnings by quantity or quality of production, or (iv) a differential based on any other factor other than sex."

The plaintiff carries the initial burden of proving unequal rates of pay between the sexes and the fact that the jobs are substantially equal.[6] The Equal Pay Act standard provides that jobs are "equal" if they involve "substantially equal" skill, effort, and responsibility, and are performed under similar working conditions.[7] The employer's motive for the salary difference is not an element.

Unequal pay for "equal" work shifts the burden to the employer to justify the unequal pay for the equal work by proving one of the four statutory defenses. The jobs

---

[3] 29 U.S.C.A. § 206(d)(1).

[4] 29 U.S.C.A. § 255(a).

[5] 29 U.S.C.A. § 206(d).

[6] Corning Glass Works v. Brennan, 417 U.S. 188, 195 (1974); Gordon v. United States, 903 F.3d 1248, 1252 (Fed. Cir. 2018).

[7] *See, e.g.*, Gordon v. United States, 903 F.3d 1248, 1252 (Fed. Cir. 2018).

need not be simultaneously occupied. Differences in pay to sequential occupants of the same job can state a claim.

The defendant must prove that the wage disparity was justified by one of four permissible reasons: (1) a seniority system; (2) a merit system; (3) a pay system based on quantity or quality of output; or (4) a disparity based on any factor other than sex.[8]

A note on comparable worth. Employers traditionally set wage rates within certain occupational groups. As a result, a firm's accountants may be paid more than its nurses. A city's attorneys may make more than its teachers. Such differences are justified as being products of economic market forces. It has been asserted, however, that when compensation is based upon such general market forces, there is an unjustified adverse impact on women and minorities who were traditionally segregated into certain jobs and excluded or discouraged by social forces from entering the more lucrative trades and professions. If the jobs are of "comparable worth" to the employer but salaries are based upon what a trade or profession can command on the market, this will have the unjustified effect of perpetuating the previous discriminatory patterns.

Generally, courts have rejected comparable worth as a theory of pay discrimination.[9] Because of the "Bennett Amendment," defendant can prevail by showing that the market is a bona fide "factor other than sex."[10]

For coverage of the Bennett Amendment, see Chapter 11 (§ 11.08).

§ 14.03 Genetic Information Non-Discrimination Act (GINA)

Title II of the Genetic Information Non-Discrimination Act of 2008 (GINA)[11] limits employers' ability to request and use genetic information (as defined by the statute). GINA prohibits an employer from discriminating or taking adverse actions against an employee "because of genetic information with respect to the employee."[12] The Act also makes it unlawful "for an employer to request, require, or purchase genetic information with respect to an employee or a family member of the employee," with some exceptions.[13] It also prohibits retaliation. The statute requires employers who already have access to genetic information to limit its distribution.

"Genetic information" is specifically defined by the statute and means "genetic tests" of an individual or her family members, and information about "the manifestation of a disease or disorder in family members of such individual."[14] "Genetic test" means "an analysis of human DNA, RNA, chromosomes, proteins, or metabolites, that detects genotypes, mutations, or chromosomal changes."[15]

---

[8] 29 U.S.C.A. § 206(d)(1); Gordon v. United States, 903 F.3d 1248, 1252 (Fed. Cir. 2018).

[9] Washington Cty. v. Gunther, 452 U.S. 161 (1981); *see also* Sims-Fingers v. City of Indianapolis, 493 F.3d 768, 771 (7th Cir. 2007).

[10] *Id.*

[11] 42 U.S.C.A. § 2000ff *et seq.* For an overview of GINA, see Stephen E. Trimboli, Marissa Becker Ruggiero, *Navigating the Genetic Information Nondiscrimination Act of 2008*, FED. LAW., November/December 2011, at 24, 25; Jessica L. Roberts, *Preempting Discrimination: Lessons from the Genetic Information Nondiscrimination Act*, 3 VAND. L. REV. 439, 445 (2010).

[12] 42 U.S.C. § 2000ff–1(a)(1), (2).

[13] *Id.* § 2000ff–1(b); Ortiz v. City of San Antonio Fire Dep't, 806 F.3d 822, 826 (5th Cir. 2015).

[14] 42 U.S.C.A. § 2000ff(4)(A); *see also* 29 C.F.R. § 1635.3(c).

[15] 42 U.S.C.A. § 2000ff(7)(A).

For employees covered by Title VII, GINA incorporates the enforcement and remedies procedures of Title VII.[16]

§ 14.04 Rehabilitation Act

The Rehabilitation Act of 1973 is a precursor to the ADA. An express purpose of the Act is to "promote and expand employment opportunities in the public and private sectors for handicapped individuals." The provisions of the Act regarding the employment rights of people with disabilities are contained in three separate statutory sections: § 501 (29 U.S.C.A. § 791) applies to federal employment, § 503 (29 U.S.C.A. § 793) regulates the practices of employers which have service, supply, or construction contracts with the federal government, and § 504 (29 U.S.C.A. § 794) applies to the practices of entities who receive federal financial grants or who operate federal programs.

The Rehabilitation Act protects individuals with disabilities from discrimination in a wide range of employment decisions. Other than differences in the covered entities, the ADA and Rehabilitation Act are "otherwise similar in substance" and "cases interpreting either are applicable and interchangeable."[17] The main difference between the two is that the Rehabilitation Act "imposes a requirement that a person's disability serve as the *sole* impetus for a defendant's adverse action against the plaintiff."[18]

§ 14.05 Executive Orders

Several executive orders state that it is federal policy to provide equal opportunity in federal employment and to prohibit discrimination based on race, color, religion, sex, national origin, handicap, age, sexual orientation, or status as a parent.[19]

The executive orders also impose on employers with certain federal contracts an obligation to remedy any underutilization of people based on these protected traits by adopting affirmative action plans designed to increase the number and percentage of employees in those protected classes.[20] Those affirmative action plans may include specific numerical goals and timetables.

§ 14.06 Family and Medical Leave Act (FMLA)

Title VII does not require an employer to grant parental leave. As originally enacted, the Family and Medical Leave Act (FMLA) entitles covered employees to up to 12 weeks unpaid leave for four different reasons: (1) the birth and care of a newborn child; (2) the placement of a child for adoption or foster care; (3) the care of a child, spouse, or parent with a serious health condition; or (4) the employee's own serious health condition.[21]

---

[16] *See* 42 U.S.C.A. § 2000ff–6(a)(1). This section describes the enforcement and remedies for other employees other than those protected by Title VII's main provision.

[17] Wojewski v. Rapid City Reg'l Hosp., Inc., 450 F.3d 338, 344 (8th Cir. 2006) (internal citations omitted); Crochran through Shields v. Columbus City Sch., No. 17–4110, 2018 WL 4922973, at *4 (6th Cir. Oct. 10, 2018).

[18] *Wojewski*, 450 F.3d at 344 (internal citations omitted).

[19] Executive Orders 11,246, 11,478, 13,087, 13,672.

[20] A comprehensive review of all executive orders affecting affirmative action in employment is beyond the scope of this book.

[21] 29 U.S.C.A. § 2612(a)(1).

When Congress enacted the FMLA in 1993, it expressly found that existing employment policies did not adequately respond to an increase in "single-parent households and two-parent households in which . . . both parents work."[22] Congress also recognized that the primary responsibility for caretaking falls upon women, with resulting negative effects on the employment opportunities of women.[23] The express purposes of the statute were "to minimize . . . employment discrimination on the basis of sex and . . . to promote the goal of equal employment opportunity for women and men."[24]

In two subsequent amendments, Congress provided additional FMLA leave entitlements. An employee who is the spouse, son, daughter, parent, or next of kin of a covered service member may take up to 26 work weeks of leave to care for a member of the Armed Forces undergoing medical treatment for certain reasons.[25] Additionally, the Act provides for "qualifying exigency leave," which entitles a spouse, son, daughter, or parent of certain members of the Armed Forces up to 12 weeks of leave to take care of "qualifying exigencies" that arise because the member of the Armed Forces is on active duty or called to active duty.[26]

The FMLA limits coverage to specific employees and employers. To be eligible for leave, an employee must:

(1) have worked for the employer for a total of 12 months;

(2) have worked at least 1,250 hours over the previous 12 months; and

(3) work for a covered employer.

Covered employers include private sector employers that employ 50 or more employees, *as well as* state, local and federal employers.

All leave does not need to be taken at the same time. In certain circumstances, an employee may request that leave be taken intermittently (in separate blocks of time) or that it be granted through a reduced work schedule. During the leave period, employers are required to keep paying any portion of an employee's health benefits that the employer previously paid; however, under certain circumstances, the employer may recover the premiums paid if the employee fails to return to work after FMLA leave.

Notice that the leave provided under the FMLA is unpaid. Some states require paid leave.

Upon the conclusion of the leave, employees who are well enough to return to work generally are entitled to be restored to the position held prior to leave or an equivalent position.

In 2010, Congress added new protections for nursing mothers. The Patient Protection and Affordable Care Act ("PPACA") of 2010 amended Section 7 of the Fair Labor Standards Act to require certain employers to provide breaks for nursing mothers to express breast milk for the first year of the child's life. Employers must provide a private location for this purpose other than a bathroom. The employer is not required to provide compensated break time and is not required to provide breaks for individuals

---

[22] 29 U.S.C.A. § 2601(a)(1).

[23] 29 U.S.C.A. § 2601(a)(5).

[24] 29 U.S.C.A. § 2601(b).

[25] 29 U.S.C.A. § 2612(a)(3).

[26] 29 U.S.C.A. § 2612(a)(1)(E).

who are exempt from the overtime pay requirements of the FLSA. The protections provided in the FLSA do not preempt state law that provides greater protection for mothers.[27]

[27] Fact Sheet #73, Break Time for Nursing Mothers Under the FLSA, http://www.dol.gov/whd/regs/compliance/whdfs73.htm (last visited December 7, 2018).

Table of Cases

Table of Statutes

Table of Regulations

Table of Rules

Index

References are to Sections